Islay

Biography of an island

Margaret Storrie

The  Press

First Edition 1981
Second revised Edition 1997
Third revised and enlarged Edition 2011

ISBN 978-0-907651-04-8

Printed by Henry Ling Ltd

The Oa Press
Isle of Islay
PA42 7AL

Islay

Biography of an island

List of illustrations and tables

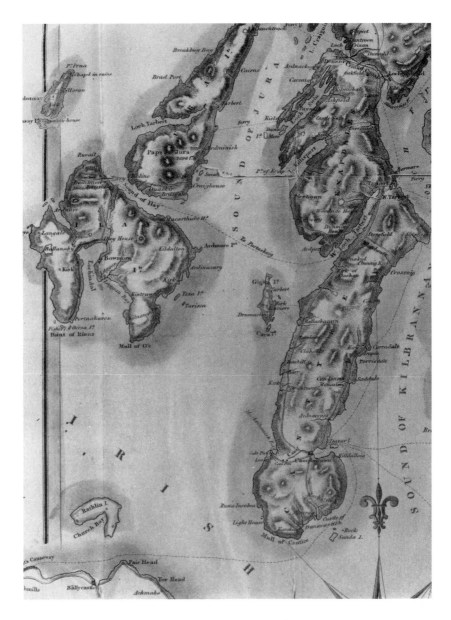

'Leaving West Loch-Tarbert, a most extensive prospect of the Atlantic Ocean opens up to view, in which is seen a multitude of islands . . . and the extensive peninsula of Cantyre, stretching many a rugged point far into the sea . . . and behind the lofty Goatfell in Arran . . . through Islay the roads are excellent, and the natives are proverbial for their hospitality' (Lumsden, *Steam-Boat Companion*).

CHAPTER 1

Perspective

Almost the first requirement of a prospective visitor to Islay is some help in pronouncing its name. Probably the most definite thing that can be said is that it is not pronounced the way it is spelled. In Gaelic it is *Ìle*, pronounced *eel-eh*, while English speakers say *eye-la* as in island, with a pause between syllables and an upward lilt at the end. Others may say *eye-lay*, but it should never be pronounced as in 'mislay'. Since Adomnàn recorded it as Ilea at the end of the seventh century AD the written name has had various forms, but to begin with these were usually phonetically faithful to the Gaelic Ìle.[1] The anglicised spelling appeared by the seventeenth century and still seems almost perversely different; in addition, the meanings offered for the name are almost as diverse as the spellings.[2] Its origins are unknown, several thousand years old, pre-Celtic and perhaps even pre-Indo-European. While the pre-Celtic *Il*, 'island', was a common Basque name, other attributions include *I-leithe*, 'the divided island', *Yla or Eila,* after a Danish princess, and a Gaulish man's name, Ilio, 'flank or buttock'.[3]

Anomalous and varied Hebridean isle

Someone sailing or flying to Islay finds an island less Highland in its physical grandeur than neighbouring Jura, or Mull which can be seen to the north. It is not typically Hebridean either, in the sense of the crofting and grazing islands of Skye or the Outer Hebrides. Presenting rapid contrasts and constantly changing scenes on both large and small scales, it boasts an Atlantic-washed wildscape on the west; farmscapes along the tidy coasts of Loch Indaal and in the central valleys; natural woodlands and plantations of hardwoods and conifers; rugged eastern hills and cliffs on the Oa promontory; peat bogs over much of the lowland; a ridged and skerried south-east coast; Georgian planned villages and industrial distillery villages; large Georgian houses and traditional cottages, all amid a kaleidoscope of magnificent beaches, moors and lochs. From the extensive sand dunes on several of the coasts, across the peat moors to the settled areas of the foothills and valleys, there are many details to catch

On one of the earliest printed maps of Scotland in 1573, Abraham Ortelius described Islay as 'the greatest and the most renowned' of the Hebrides, 'fertile in grain and rich in minerals'. North is to the right, and the orientation of the two main sea lochs is good, but neighbouring Jura is mis-identified as Iona.

Raised beach deposits between Lochs Indaal and Gruinart link the two parts of Islay together. Former shorelines stand out near Blackrock (foreground) and Uisgeantsuidhe.

the inquisitive eye. The splendid tradition of whitewashing enhances the attractiveness of the villages and the scattered rural buildings. Based originally on locally-quarried Dalradian limestone, the rapid weathering of the local product required a fresh coat of whitewash as an annual part of Islay's life in late spring and early summer; then the whole appearance of the island appeared at its best. Nowadays, less regular treatment with weather-resistant finishes adds further diversity to the scene.

As the southernmost of the Inner Hebrides, south even of the latitude of Glasgow, it is not surprising that the island shows characteristics of both Highland and Lowland Scotland. The geographical situation of Islay has affected the development of its economy, landscape and society from archaeological to present times. Relative accessibility to, as well as isolation from, political and cultural centres elsewhere in Highland, Hebridean or Lowland Scotland and beyond, have affected the ways in which people have influenced and left their imprint on Islay. For example, during the late-medieval lordship of the Isles, Islay was a focus of political power and cultural influence along and beyond the western seaboard of Highland Scotland; in the eighteenth century, innovations in agriculture, industry and village planning, adapted from the Lowlands, were amongst the earliest attempted in the Highlands and Hebrides. Until then, most of the population lived in amorphous clusters of buildings similar to those to be found at the time over much of Scotland. These clusters of turf or stone buildings housed up to a score of families and their beasts. Their stony remains can still be seen in the remoter parts of the island.

Islay's distinctiveness was recognised early; the island was for long known to the Hebrideans as *Banrigh Innse Gall*, 'Queen of the Isles', as a 'green island', and so on. In 1573 Abraham Ortelius had eulogised on the reverse of his map of Scotland 'Maxima omnium & nominatissima Ila est, frumenti ferax, & metalli dives', ('Of all [the Hebrides] the greatest and most renowned is Ila, fertile for grain, and rich in minerals').[4] But at the beginning of the eighteenth century, the island's resources were still relatively undeveloped. Scotland herself was on the threshold of change, following parliamentary union with England in 1707. In Islay, as over the rest of Scotland, however, the eighteenth century had some way to go before economic, landscape and social changes were achieved. They were part of the more general Scottish period of enlightenment that eventually flowered half a century after the Union. The creation of the village of Bowmore in Islay and of Edinburgh New Town in the late 1760s were simultaneous events, albeit different in scale.

One of the most notable and characteristic features of the Islay landscape comprises the villages around the shores of Loch Indaal and elsewhere on the island. The number, size and importance of the Islay villages are features inherited from the changes of the late-eighteenth century and after. Here Islay differs from most other areas in the Highlands and Islands of Scotland, which possess few such settlements. Bowmore was one of several early villages deliberately planned to absorb population in Highland and Lowland Scotland, like the weavers' village of Eaglesham in Renfrewshire, founded by the tenth earl of Eglinton, also in 1768. Others in Islay such as Port Wemyss were established later, in the 1830s, as fishermen's settlements. However, in a closer view of many of the island's villages, distinctive features comprised a tall chimney and pagoda-like malt-drying kilns typical of a whisky distillery, most dating from the early-nineteenth century. It is the presence of all these different villages in the island that provides the most obvious contrast between Islay and all other Highland and Hebridean areas.

Evidence of Change

Since Islay's distinctiveness rests to a large extent in its somewhat unusual historical evolution, it is fortunate that a wide variety of evidence has survived. For example, the island is rich in sites and examples of archaeological interest, with relics of Mesolithic, Neolithic, Bronze and Iron Ages; and from Early Christian, Norse and medieval times. Apart from such visible evidence on the island's surface, whether archaeological, historical or modern, there are other facets that illuminate the interaction between the island and its peoples, such as place names. Published sources of information for a Hebridean island are inevitably incomplete; but Islay is generally well documented. Early topographers, agriculturalists and fisheries' advocates left worthwhile accounts of changing times on Islay from the eighteenth century: they include Martin Martin, Thomas Pennant, James Anderson, John Walker and James Macdonald.[5] Proto-social scientists such as Alexander Webster, Sir John Sinclair and their successors also provided invaluable accounts for our use today.[6]

The most detailed published sources relating to Islay's earlier history, however, appeared after the middle of the nineteenth century. In the *Book of The Thanes of Cawdor*, published by the Spalding Club of Aberdeen in 1859, the noted antiquarian, Cosmo Innes, included many documents relating to the Cawdor Campbells in seventeenth-century Islay; this remains the most readily accessible source for this period.[7] Three important volumes appeared in the 1890s. Two were sponsored by Lucy Ramsay, wife of one of the then island landowners. Each tome was printed privately in editions limited to 250 copies. In her preface to *The Stent Book*, Mrs Ramsay explained that the passing of the Local Government (Scotland)

Act of 1889 had prompted her to publish the minutes taken at meetings of what she claimed was 'The Local Parliament' in Islay, from 1718 until 1843 when the 'annual meeting came to an abrupt termination'.[8] *The Stent Book* contains much information on the type of business now dealt with by local government, including fiscal and other responsibilities for roads, education, housing and public utilities. Rather different to it is *The Book of Islay*, which Gregory Smith subsequently edited for Mrs Ramsay.[9] This is a collection of items from different sources that refer to the island mainly since Norse times; it concludes with a considerable amount of material on the early decades of the eighteenth century, selected from archives in Cawdor, Islay, Edinburgh and elsewhere. Also in 1895 the antiquarian, R. C. Graham, then laird of Skipness in Kintyre, compiled *The Carved Stones of Islay*.[10] Twentieth-century landmarks were the publication in 1984 of the *Argyll Inventory* of the monuments of Islay, Jura, Colonsay and Oronsay, produced by the Royal Commission on the Ancient and Historic Monuments of Scotland and *The Acts of the Lords of the Isles* collated and edited by J. and R. W. Munro in 1986.[11]

Much of the material incorporated in the present book comes from original sources themselves, in the archives of the earl of Cawdor, lord Margadale of Islay and of the Ramsay family, formerly of the Kildalton Estate.[12] In addition, documents in many Scottish, British and overseas archives, governmental and other agencies have been scrutinised. Many islanders have also contributed to the author's knowledge and enjoyment of the island. While much of its heritage and present life still remains unpublished, a focus and repository for the island's social heritage was established in 1977 with the opening in Port Charlotte of the Museum of Islay Life. The Finlaggan Trust and National Museums Scotland have also unearthed and displayed artefacts, commemorative stones and interpretative material from the islands in Loch Finlaggan which were at the centre of the medieval lordship of the Isles.[13] Genealogical interests are served by the Islay Family History Trust in Islay House Square at Bridgend. In a converted whisky warehouse in Port Charlotte, the Islay Natural History Trust displays its collections, while the Royal Society for the Protection of Birds has developed ornithological fieldwork, research and displays in and around their reserves at Loch Gruinart and on the Oa. In the 1990s, Scottish Natural Heritage extended its activities to the island. A short-lived Islay Land Use Forum was set up to promote the development of an integrated approach to the use of land in Islay in order to sustain the outstanding quality of the island's natural resources. This century an Islay Energy Trust was established to develop renewable energy projects for community benefit. Other organisations have periodically organised conferences covering themes from the more academic to those of more topical or practical interest.

Islay Gaelic and Lore

Islay Gaelic today includes elements from the Irish Gaelic-speaking colonisation of the island, possibly superimposed on Pictish-speaking tongues, through the period of Scandinavian influences, to the later Scots Gaelic and English-speaking times. Just as the decline of Gaelic usage and the concomitant rise of English can be seen in the island's place and personal names, a similar change can be traced in the spoken language, in the published volumes of the *Census of Scotland*. The first census in which questions on Gaelic usage were asked was that of 1891, when over seventy per cent of Ilich were recorded as speaking Gaelic and English, while sixteen per cent spoke only Gaelic.[14] By 1961, almost two-thirds of the islanders were still recorded as speaking Gaelic, a high proportion for an island which was the most southerly of the Hebrides and which had some of the earliest connections with the mainland.[15] But the percentage had fallen to just over one-third by 1991, with only eleven per cent able to speak, read and write Gaelic.[16] In the next decades it reduced further to under one-quarter Gaelic speaking.

As in much of Gaeldom today, the balance between vitality and decline in Islay's language and culture is precarious. Strenuous efforts are being made to encourage many and varied Gaelic activities, focused on the attractive setting and building of Ionad Chaluim Chille Ìle, also known as the Columba Centre, just outside Bowmore, and there has been a Gaelic immersion unit in the primary school since 1989. There is an annual festival or feis and both *An Commun Gaidhealach* (The Gaelic Association) and *Comunn na Gaidhlig* (The Gaelic Language Society) as well as other organisations such as the Islay, Jura and Colonsay Gaelic Partnership are involved in running events and workshops throughout the year. Individuals and adult and junior choirs have for long had major successes in musical competitons at local, provincial, national and overseas Gaelic Mods. Highland dancing and piping have revived, with dancers and the Islay Pipe Band participating at Highland Games and piping competitions. Ceilidhs are organised in village halls and hotels with traditional and more modern music performed by islanders and visitors. Satellite television reached Islay, but did not eradicate local oral individuality and traditions, many of which now feature in television documentaries, films and radio broadcasts. The annual Islay Gathering of the Glasgow Islay Association begun in 1862 is one of the largest meetings of Hebridean exiles on the Scottish mainland, celebrating its sesquicentenary in 2012.

Over a century ago some of the differences between Islay and other Gaelic speakers were noted: 'peasants come from Connaught to Islay, and in a very short time converse freely, though their accent betrays them; an Islay man is detected in Mull, and a native of one parish in Islay is detected when he speaks in another'.[17] Today Islay Gaelic is still regarded by some as idiosyncratic or even 'coarse' and 'differing to a greater degree than the surrounding dialects from 'the Gaelic mainstream'.[18] Moving from Jura to Islay, a first impression is that Islay Gaelic is more staccato and rather slower in sound and delivery. The most striking illustration of this difference in dialect is the insertion of the glottal pause before certain consonants in the middle of words, or a hiatus instead of an aspirated consonant. Particularly in the Rinns, words beginning with a broad *l* in Gaelic, sound as if they were a *d* in some of the older words, though not in recent borrowings from English. So *doch* is said for loch, but lamp remains *lamp*. Archaic forms of words and vocal peculiarities also exist. Older people in particular pronounce common words like *uisge* (water) differently, with greater emphasis on the *sh* sound.

Some words common in Islay usage are rare or unique. In the middle of the nineteenth century a noteworthy Ileach, Neil MacAlpine, compiled one of the few Scots Gaelic dictionaries, in which he included many of these Islay words such as *caile* (girl), *gealbhan* (domestic hearth), *gearraidh* (hare), *fail-moine* (peat spade) and *sgeir-moine* (peat bank), measured by the *peirsa* (perch).[19] As well as these differences, there are also some idiosyncratic grammatical habits, as well as Islay sayings and proverbs.[20] But with the decline in the use of the language, there has also been a decline in the standard of grammar and wealth of vocabulary. Noun and adjective declensions are obsolescent today; nevertheless there are stronger traditional or idiosyncratic forms of spoken Gaelic than one might expect in an area with many external contacts over the past two centuries. Tales and anecdotes can still be heard on the island but, as informants pass away, fewer remain.[21]

Just outside Bridgend, on a prominent hillock at the head of Loch Indaal, stands an obelisk erected in 1887 by the Glasgow Islay Association with a fulsome inscription in Gaelic and English to John Francis Campbell or Iain Og Ìle. One of the island's most celebrated figures, he has been described as the 'world-famous father of Celtic Folklore Studies'.[22] Born in 1822 as heir to the Islay estate, barrister, secretary to various government commissions, a courtier of Queen Victoria's, a world-wide traveller, fluent speaker of several Nordic and other languages, and an inventor, he nevertheless found time to organise the collection of folklore of the Scottish west and it is for this work that he is perhaps most remembered.

John Francis Campbell of Islay was a man of many parts; here in a public house in Paisley, as folklorist, he listens to an Ileach shoemaker, Lachlan MacNeill. Schoolmaster, Hector MacLean of Ballygrant, writes down part of the week-long tale of 'Kane's leg', which filled 260 pages of foolscap, despite Campbell's remark that both of his companions were 'rather screwed, Hector the worse' (Trustees of the National Library of Scotland).

The inscription on the obelisk at Bridgend, erected in 1887 by the Glasgow Islay Association, commemorates one of the most famous of Ilich.

His still-unpublished manuscripts, diaries and travel sketches are in the National Library of Scotland and National Galleries of Scotland in Edinburgh.

With the Gaelic he had acquired in his youth from his island piping tutor, John Francis Campbell did some fieldwork when he visited Islay in 1857, his family by then no longer owning Islay House. Collection continued for several years and his network of story-tellers and collectors grew. In his introduction to the first volume of these tales, published in 1860,[23] he outlined his working method in considerable detail, including his return to the sources of the stories, proofs in hand, to check the accuracy of transcriptions and translations. With the help of several assistants, two further volumes of tales and a final volume of various Celtic matters including the Ossian controversy, were subsequently published in English, with some Gaelic examples. A second edition was run in 1890, five years after John Francis's death in Cannes. A century later the Scottish composer, Judith Weir, used three of the tales in her opera, *The Vanishing Bridegroom*; each story remains distinct in the libretto, but some characters are shared in the general theme of loss and deliverance.[24]

One name less well known outside the Gaelic-speaking world than that of John Francis Campbell is that of William Livingston or 'Uilleam Ileach', 'William the Islayman'. Meek has acclaimed him as 'the most distinguished of all the Gaelic poets of the nineteenth century', although some deem this arguable.[25] Livingston, along with John Francis Campbell, Hector MacLean and Islay émigrés including John Murdoch, Nigel McNeill, Thomas Pattison and Archibald Sinclair, created the Gaelic literary world 'that we know today', Meek averring that Islay had provided its intellectual power-house during the nineteenth century.[26] Writing in both English (mainly prose) and Gaelic (mainly poetry) Livingston esteemed Gaelic above English. Regarding himself as both a *bard* (of poetry and song) and a *filidh* (poet or seer), Livingston's overall concern was to harness the dualistic (nature versus invader) dynamism of the Gaelic world in such a way as to give meaning to Gaelic history and the Gaels' predicament in his own day. Self taught and conversant with Greek, Hebrew, French, Welsh and Irish, his best known epic poems on battles, real and imaginary,[27] incorporated deliberate anachronisms to further his need to defend Gaelic culture from attrition. His verse is remarkably different from his prose, avoiding 'explosions of wild indignation' and 'seething anger'. But his poems also encompass the critical events of population displacement in Islay, especially after mid-century. Innovative and brimming with fluid and vivid descriptions of land and sea battles and heroic Gaels, the first edition of his poems was published in 1858.[28] Over half was devoted to epic poems from the Roman Mons Graupius, medieval battles of Dalry, Bannockburn, the Norse in Islay and Kintyre men's defeat of the Norse, to the Battle of Traigh Gruinart in 1598. As part of the vibrant Glasgow Gaelic world the rest of his output concerned poesy itself, songs, elegies and commentaries both passionate and comic.

Other Islay bards were also concerned with socio-economic changes in Islay. John McCormick emoted 'a conversation between Dùn Nosebridge and a Visitor returning to the Glen emptying of people . . . since the island's landlord went bankrupt, Islay is spewing out its natives', as he imagined the dun telling him, with Trustee Brown, Factor Webster and Clerk Robert Cross all being singled out for making 'many farmers in the Glen . . . go across the Atlantic'.[29] On the other hand, emigré Hugh McCorkindale, looking back in old age from Ontario in January 1877 in his 'Song by an Old Islayman', euologised Canada as 'a place doubly better for me . . . my way has not been hindered . . . what a wonderful day for many Gaels when they sailed across to this part'. While praising the onetime laird, Walter Frederick Campbell, and graphically describing the hardships of pioneering in the harsh Canadian winter climate, he was nevertheless content about his fellow Gaels:

Tha iad saor bho mhaor no bàirlinn,	They're free from ground-officer and removal notice,
'S bho àrdan an uachdarain;	and from the pomp of landlord,
Bho gach factor *agus bàillidh*	from every factor and baillie,
B'àbhaist bhith gan gualadh,	who used to be their torment;
'So thoirt a-nuas an còmhdaich chinn.	free too from having to doff bonnets.[30]

An occasional poem even stood up for the factors, albeit from the pen of a biased wife such as Flora MacNeill. She was an Islay tacksman's daughter married to John Campbell of Ardmore in Islay, who became factor/chamberlain for the duke of Argyll in Mull and Tiree:

Tha thu foghainteach mar Bhàillidh	You are mighty as a Factor,
Buidhinn cliù o Earra-Ghàidheal;	gaining commendation from Argyll;
Cà bheil aon a lìonadh d'àite,	where is one who could fill your place,
Led innleachd, pàirt neo-chearbach?	with your way of dealing honestly?[31]

His death was, however, bitterly and sardonically celebrated in the four verses of Eugene Ross's 'Lament for the Great Factor'.[32]

Nigel McNeill was another exile, minister of the Free Church congregation in London and *Oban Times* correspondent for that city, who composed a paean, 'The Desire of the Islay Folk', to John Iain Og Ìle when the latter chaired the Glasgow Islay Gathering in 1878:

Tha thu de theaghlach flathail, àrd;   You are of a noble family of high rank;
'S gach ceàrn gheibh Caimbeul Ìle fàilt'; Campbell of Islay is welcome in each part;
Do bhaintighearnan na h-Il' biodh slàint, may Islay's ladies enjoy good health,
'S am bòich's gach àit' air aideachadh. their beauty is mentioned everywhere.[33]

Apart from this reference to John Francis Campbell's beautiful grandmother, Lady Charlotte Campbell and many of her relations, McNeill empathised with his having had to go into exile far from the island 'whose heart is yours . . . she has many natives of great worth, who, . . . in their hearts, will cherish you'.[34]

Notes and References

[1] These include, in chronological order, Epidion, Ilea, Ìl, Ila, Ìle, Ìlar, Isle Insula, Ysle, Yle, Yle, Ilay, Ylay, Yley, Ile, Illaye, Yla, Illa, Isla, Islay and Isla. See Margaret Storrie, 'Settlement and Naming in the southern Hebridean Isle of Islay', in J. Derrick McClure, John M. Kirk and Margaret Storrie (eds.), *A Land that Lies Westward. Language and Culture in Islay and Argyll*, (Edinburgh, 2009), Appendix 1, pp. 38–9. For discussion of spelling evolution see K. H. Steer and J. W. M. Bannerman, *Late Medieval Sculpture in West Highland Scotland*, (Edinburgh, 1977), pp. 126–7.

[2] For meaning of name, see Alexander B. Taylor, 'Skio and Il Pridiji Vikingafundur', Third Viking Congress, Reykjavik 1956, *Arbók hins islenzka Fornleifafélags Fylgirit*, 1957, pp. 52–60.

[3] W. F. Skene, quoted in J. G. MacNeill, *The New Guide to Islay*, (Glasgow, 1900), p.1; C. F. Gordon Cumming, *In the Hebrides*, (London, 1883), p. 36; W. F. H. Nicolaisen, 'Arran Place-names: A Fresh Look', *Northern Studies* 28 (1991), p. 2.

[4] A. Ortelius, *Scotiae Tabula in Theatrum Orbis Terrarum*, (Antwerp, 1573).

[5] Martin Martin, *A Description of the Western Islands of Scotland*, 2 vols., (London, 1703); T. Pennant, *A Tour in Scotland and Voyage to the Hebrides, 1772*, (Chester, 1774); J. Anderson, *An Account of the Present State of the Hebrides and Western Coasts of Scotland . . . being the Substance of a Report to the Lords of the Treasury . . . together with the evidence before the Committee of Fisheries*, (Edinburgh, 1785); J. Walker, *An Economical History of the Hebrides and Highlands of Scotland*, 2 vols., (Edinburgh, 1808) and J. Macdonald, *General View of the Agriculture of the Hebrides or Western Isles of Scotland; with Observations on the Means of their Improvement together with a Separate Account of the Principal Islands*, (Edinburgh, 1811).

[6] J. G. Kyd, *Scottish Population Statistics*, (Edinburgh, 1952), p. 33; Sir John Sinclair (ed.), *The Statistical Account of Scotland*, 21 vols., (Edinburgh, 1791–99); 11, (1794), pp. 298–302. Hereafter, Sinclair, *OSA*.

[7] C. Innes, *The Book of the Thanes of Cawdor*, (Edinburgh, 1859).

[8] L. Ramsay (ed.), *The Stent Book and Acts of the Balliary of Islay* 1718–1843, (Kildalton, 1890). Hereafter, *Stent Book*. The 'gentlemen' of Islay met annually to arrange or stent the cess or tax required of each holder of land to pay for surgeon, schoolmaster, pacquet master and to consider problems such as evasion of excise duty, shortages of grain, provision for widows and so on. They were self selected, comprising a committee rather than a parliament.

[9] G. G. Smith (ed.), *The Book of Islay*, (Edinburgh, 1895). Reprinted in soft cover by House of Lochar (Colonsay, 2010).

[10] R. C. Graham, *The Carved Stones of Islay*, (Glasgow, 1895); see also A. Graham, *Skipness: Memories of a Highland Estate*, (Edinburgh, 1993).

[11] Royal Commission on the Ancient and Historical Monuments of Scotland [RCAHMS], *Argyll: An Inventory of the Monuments, 5*; (Edinburgh, 1984). J. and R. W. Munro, *Acts of the Lords of the Isles 1336–1493*, (Edinburgh, 1986).

[12] The Cawdor Papers in Cawdor Castle, Nairn, are listed in the National Register of Archives (Scotland) Survey [NRAS] 1400.
The Islay Estate Papers in the Islay Estate Office, Bridgend, Isle of Islay, are listed in NRAS 0123. Some of the Papers are deposited on loan in the City of Glasgow Archives. Photocopies of Islay Estate Plans are held in the National Records of Scotland, Edinburgh. The Kildalton Papers are deposited on loan in the City of Glasgow Archives, listed under TD1284. See F. Ramsay, *John Ramsay of Kildalton* (Toronto, 1970) and *The Day Book of Daniel Campbell of Shawfield 1767*, (Aberdeen, 1991).

[13] The site at Finlaggan can be explored on foot, and displays viewed at its expanded visitor centre. It also comprises one of the island's licensed marriage sites. See also D. H. Caldwell, *Islay. The Land of the Lordship* (Edinburgh, 2008).

[14] *Census of Scotland, 1891*, Table I.

[15] *Census 1961, Supplementary Leaflet 27: Gaelic*, 1966.

[16] *Census 1991, Small Area Statistics; Census 2001, Standard Area Statistics*, DVD.

[17] J. F. Campbell, *Popular Tales of the West Highlands*, 4 vols., (Edinburgh, 1860–2), 1, cxxi.

[18] G. Jones, 'The Gaelic of South Argyll', in McClure, Kirk and Storrie (eds.), *A Land that Lies Westward*, pp. 1–16.

[19] N. MacAlpine, *The Argyleshire Pronouncing Gaelic Dictionary*, (Edinburgh, 1832) and *A Pronouncing Gaelic Dictionary*, (Edinburgh, 1847). He gave his occupation to the 1851 census taker as 'student and author' (Census of Scotland, 1851, 543).

[20] See Alexander Nicolson, (ed.), *A Collection of Gaelic Proverbs and Familiar Phrases*, (Edinburgh, 2006).

[21] E. Edwards, (ed.), *Seanchas Ìle*, (Glendaruel, 2007), also CD.

[22] K. H. Jackson, *Campbell of Islay*, Celtica Catalogue 6, National Library of Scotland (Edinburgh, 1967), p. 32; R. M. Dorson, *The British Folklorists; A History*, (London, 1968), chapter 11. A. Mackechnie, *Carragh-chuimhne: Two Islay Monuments and Two Islay People. Hector MacLean and John Francis Campbell*, (Bowmore, Isle of Islay, 2004)

[23] J. F. Campbell, *Popular Tales of the West Highlands*, 4 vols., (Edinburgh, 1860–2); J. G. Mackay (ed.), *More West Highland Tales* 1, (Edinburgh, 1940), 2, (Edinburgh, 1960); J. Mackechnie, (ed.), *The Dewar Manuscripts* I, (Glasgow, 1964); J. H. Delargy, 'Three Men of Islay', *Scottish Studies* 4 (1960), pp. 126–33; A. Duncan, 'Hector MacLean of Islay, 1818–1893', *An Gaidheal*, 1964, January, pp. 9–11; and National Library of Scotland, *Lamplighter and Story-teller, John Francis Campbell of Islay, 1821–1885*, (Edinburgh, 1985); J. F. Campbell in 1853 designed a 'self-registering sundial', which, modified, has become the Campbell-Stokes sunshine recorder still in use today, although ironically, no sustained sunshine data are presently recorded on the island. See W. E. K. Middleton, *Invention of the Meteorological Instruments*, (Baltimore, 1969), pp. 238–43.

[24] *New Grove Dictionary of Opera*, (London, 1992), 4, p. 1131.

[25] D. E. Meek, 'The World of William Livingston', in McClure, Kirk and Storrie (eds.), *A Land that Lies Westward*, pp. 149–72.

[26] John Francis Campbell (1822–85), William Livingston(1808–70), Hector MacLean (1818–93), Nigel McNeill (1853–1910), John Murdoch (1818–1903), Thomas Pattison (1828–65) and Archibald Sinclair (1813–70).

27 D. E. Meek, 'Making History: William Livingston and the Creation of "Blàr Shunàdail"', McClure, Kirk and Storrie (eds.), *A Land that Lies Westward*, pp. 197–218; Uilleam MacDhunlèibhe, 'Blàr Thràigh Ghruinneard', in D. E. Meek, (ed.), *Caran an t-Saoghail. The Wiles of the World*, (Edinburgh, 2003), pp. 318–37.

28 Meek, 'The World of William Livingston', p. 156.

29 Meek, *Caran an-t Soghail*, p. 41.

30 *Ibid.*, pp. 82–5.

31 *Ibid.*, pp. 194–5.

32 *Ibid.*, pp.170–1.

33 *Ibid.*, pp. 196–7.

34 *Report of the proceedings at the annual meeting of the Islay Association . . . 30 October, 1878*, (Glasgow, 1878).

The shores along the Sound of Islay, as depicted by marine watercolourist Schetky in the mid-nineteenth century, apparently contradict Sir Walter Scott's allusion in 'The Lord of the Isles' to 'green Islay's fertile shore'. Yet signs of former homes and cultivation even in these glens and along the shores can still be seen from the ferry. Such remote glens and caves were also useful for illegal distilling or smuggling.

CHAPTER 2

Island frame

The physical landscape on which the human history has taken place is rather atypical of the Hebridean islands and of the West Highlands. Apart from the east coast above the Sound of Islay the island's relief is not on so grand a scale as Harris, Skye, Mull, Jura or Arran. Islay is almost divided into two by the indentations of Lochs Indaal and Gruinart; although it is approximately 40 kilometres from Rubha a'Mhail in the north-east to the Mull of Oa in the south and about 25 kilometres from Coul Point in the west to McArthur's Head on the Sound of Islay, the total area is only just over 600 square kilometres.

Sailing to Islay on a fine day, one is impressed by neighbouring Jura's glistening Paps or Beinns, which reach almost 800 metres. From many viewpoints on Islay these conical mountains notably enhance the scenery. On Islay similar quartzitic rocks do not have quite the same visual impact; instead of distinct peaks they form two dissected upland areas, one in the in the south-east, culminating in Beinn Bheigir (491m) and the other reaching 364m in Sgarbh Breac. The dissected upland in the south-east forms the largest area of high ground in Islay and includes several summits between 450 and 500m. On the east coast of the island a steep face is presented to the Sound of Islay, broken only by a few hanging glens such as Glen Logan. At McArthur's Head the lighthouse is perched somewhat precariously on cliffs that rise over a hundred metres above the Sound. Other quartzitic outcrops also form high ground along the north-western coast of the Oa promontory and between Bowmore and Beinn Bhàn. These rocks have been quarried for building, especially for decorative purposes, as in the lodge entrances of the former Kildalton estate in the south-east. The north-eastern upland is lower and is bounded by magnificently-developed Quaternary cliffs, marine platforms and a 'classic' series of interglacial and postglacial raised beaches that impress the layman as much as they do the geomorphologist.[1] To the west of this upland, kilometres of sand dunes and raised beaches border Loch Gruinart, south of which an extensive area of bog developed.

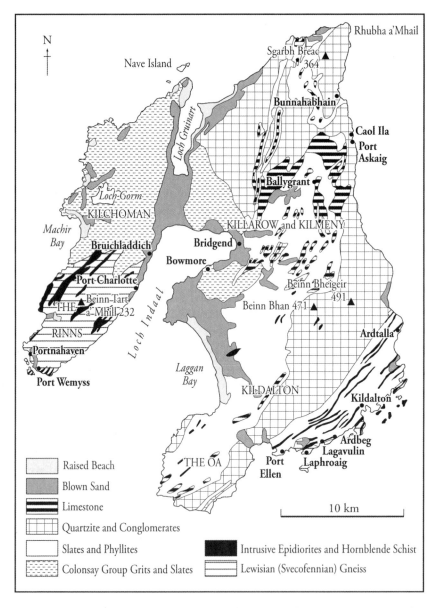

Islay's lithology and superficial deposits have produced a varied environment and scene for man's use and enjoyment. Most important have been the limestone, minerals, peat, and beach, river and other deposits (Based on Geological Survey of Scotland, *Quarter Inch Geology*, sheet 13 and *One Inch Solid and Drift* sheets 19 and 27).

Between these two quartzitic uplands, the central lowlands are underlain by strongly-metamorphosed Precambrian slates and phyllites, with some calcareous quartzose schists, and igneous intrusions. These give rise to a more varied topography quite different in character from the relatively bare areas of the hills. The topography of the central belt, from the Mull of Oa in the south through to Bunnahabhain in the north-east, is generally of lower altitude, although relative relief is sometimes considerable. In the northern part of the Oa promontory, outcrops of black slates and grey phyllites form spectacular cliffs, especially along the southern edge of Laggan Bay and near the Mull of Oa. From Dùn Mòr Ghil to Port nan Gallon east of the Mull, the cliffs fall almost sheer to the sea. They are 200 metres high near the monument which commemorates the loss of the troopships *Otranto* and *Tuscania*, in 1918.

Further north, in other Precambrian areas of the central belt, these rocks have been more eroded and underlie 'The Glen' (the upper drainage basin of the Laggan) and much of the Sorn basin. They include the Esknish slates, similar to the more renowned Easdale slates and formerly quarried in Islay at Emeraconart between Bridgend and Ballygrant. More remarkable is the extensive occurrence of fairly pure and little-metamorphosed Dalradian limestone. Islay has an unusual amount of limestone, whereas neighbouring Jura has scarcely any. Its outcrop in Islay is easily visible, as in the very green area around Tallant farm and in many parts of the Sorn valley. The limestone has been used as a building material, as decorative whitewash and as road metal, but it was most valuable agriculturally, being almost pure calcium carbonate. Five major quarries have been worked in the Islay limestone; these are visible today, as are some of the kilns, where the limestone was burned to form quicklime, then dissolved in water and applied to the ground. The older quarries can be seen at Lower Cragabus, Leorin, Persabus and Bridgend; the fifth, opened in the late 1940s at Ballygrant, is the only one still in use, producing road metal. Veins of minerals intruded into the limestone have also been worked at various times, the most important being lead, copper and silver; evidence of these former workings is still visible near Ballygrant at Mulreesh, Robolls and elsewhere. Subsequently, there has only been spasmodic interest in these minerals. The early 1990s saw the possibility of a superquarry being opened up to produce aggregate at Baleachdrach on the Sound of Islay, but the controversial project did not then go ahead.

South-east of the main Beinn Bheigir upland is another, narrower, zone of more highly-metamorphosed and contorted slates and phyllites extending from Port Ellen to Ardtalla, but there is no limestone outcrop. There are additional quartzitic and calcareous schists outcropping along

Dalradian limestone was burned in peat-fired kilns, dissolved in water and then used to counteract soil acidity.

the coast from Laphroaig to Kildalton and north from Claggain to Carraig Mhòr. Texa, one of the larger of Islay's many offshore islands, is also built of these rocks. In this south-eastern area of Kildalton the slates and phyllites have been much more extensively intruded by igneous sills of epidioritic material than in the central belt. In an area almost free of superficial deposits, differential erosion of the harder intrusive rocks and the relatively softer country rocks has created a sequence of minor ridges and valleys. Trending south-west to north-east, the ridges continue seawards in the form of many small islets and skerries. The scenery is further complicated here, as in the central belt, by the intrusion of many Tertiary doleritic dykes traversing all rocks in a north-west to south-east direction. The distinctive hill of Cnoc Rhaonastil and its extension jutting out into Ardelistry Bay, is the largest of these doleritic intrusions. The igneous and metamorphic rocks have all been used as building materials, mainly in the south-east of the island; easily identifiable are the chlorite schists of the medieval crosses, dolerite from a quarry near Kildalton House used for houses and farm buildings and roofing slates from a large quarry near Port Ellen lighthouse, now disused.

The two main upland masses and the areas adjacent to them, show considerable evidence of the movement of ice sheets from east-south-east to west-north-west during the Quaternary period. Examples of striae notched deeply into the quartzite can been seen for instance on Glas Beinn (471m) to the north of Loch Allallaidh and in many other areas that require less energetic searching such as at Kilchiaran. In the glens much glacial drift has accumulated, on which some of the largest peat bogs in Islay have developed. These also cover parts of the raised beaches and are bordered by the windblown sands along Laggan Bay in Loch Indaal. Much of Islay's glacial drift is of reddish colour and can be seen capping the cliffs at McArthur's Head or flanking the sides of Glen Ghaireasdail and Glen

Logan along the Sound of Islay. The drift is also well developed in other glens of the south-eastern hills and along the valleys of the Laggan and its tributaries, where river action has exposed depths of over 13 metres of drift. The tiny valley glaciers which remained towards the end of the Ice Age have also left their own moraines, as can be noticed east of the 'high' or eastern road between Port Ellen and Bridgend: the farmhouse of Leorin stands on one of these. Sands and gravels in the form of kames and eskers can be seen near Torra Farm and some of the large rivers have fluvoglacial and deltaic deposits of considerable extent, such as the mouth of the Laggan river.

Raised beaches around the head of Loch Indaal join the eastern part of Islay to the western portion comprising the Rinns of Islay. Except for numerous intrusive igneous dykes, the western peninsula is entirely made up of rocks of Precambrian age. The northern and larger portion of the Rinns consists of Torridonian (Colonsay Group) grits, slates and conglomerates, while the acid and basic gneisses of the Lewisian (Svecofennian) complex occupy the area south of Kilchiaran Bay and Bruichladdich. The rolling landscape of much of the northern Rinns is covered with glacial drift on which extensive peat bogs, marshes and the largest inland loch in Islay, Loch Gorm, have developed. Where the rocks are exposed there is some fine coastal and cliff scenery. The highly individual appearance of the Sanaig cliffs, developed on Torridonian grits, the numerous basalt dykes intruded into the slates and phyllites further east and the many caves, offer fascinating explorations, as does Nave Island. The eastern shores of the northern Rinns along Loch Gruinart and of the southern Rinns along Loch Indaal have well-developed raised beaches and windblown sands, providing yet further contrasts.

Almost all of the western coastline, from Ardnave Point south to Portnahaven, shows fairly spectacular cliff development, interrupted occasionally by stretches of sands and dunes, as in Machir Bay and Saligo Bay. Intrusive dykes and differential erosion along the coasts of the Rinns south of Port Charlotte have given rise to a highly-accidented topography. Orsay Island, on which the earliest Islay lighthouse was constructed, is separated from the rest of the Rinns by a narrow strait through which strong tidal currents flow. The highest point in the Rinns, Beinn Tart a'Mhill (232m) is in fact not composed of Precambrian rocks, but owes its characteristic bulky shape to intrusive epidiorite.

The geological and lithological base of Islay is thus complex and gives rise to very varied scenery, even if the grandeur of scale found in certain of the more 'Highland' Hebrides is lacking. Islay, however, has been particularly fortunate in superficial deposits. Much of the area from

Port Askaig to Bridgend and Bowmore is overlain by glacial, postglacial, fluvoglacial and fluvial materials. Especially where these have been derived from underlying limestone, they provide a soil and land with a reasonable agricultural quality and capability rarely encountered in the Highland zone of Britain and clearly visible in satellite images. For centuries it has been because of its farming that Islay has been regarded as favoured and even exceptional in the Hebrides, prized by its earliest settlers, then the Norse, and the focus for the lordship of the Isles in the fourteenth and fifteenth centuries. The different soils facilitated the agricultural changes of the eighteenth and nineteenth centuries, when the island's owners and farmers were extolled by many agriculturalists and other observers. As subsequent chapters show, the island's population increased to a maximum in the 1830s of almost 15,000, the limits of cultivation being extended by reclaiming hill and peat lands. Today there are many signs of these times visible in the central and northern Rinns, the Glen and the Oa. The island's other land-based resources of minerals and peat and its many beaches, have likewise contributed to the island's varied economy.

The vagaries of island weather
Islay's varied landscapes are further enhanced by constant changes in weather and colours on the island, on the large indentations of Lochs Indaal and Gruinart and on the many lochs and streams. The weather may make its first and most memorable impact while the visitor is en route to the island. The early-nineteenth century lack of lighthouses, the small vessels and the chances of being wrecked, as four craft were in a single night in September 1870, and four more in November 1881, have all changed.[2] But winds of gale or storm force can still disrupt communications by sea, while the ability to enjoy scenery, as well as the number of days when aircraft can connect with the mainland, are controlled by the height of the cloud base.

Weather observations for different parts of the island are now relatively few. In the relatively sheltered garden at Eallabus at the head of Loch Indaal, daily precipitation has been recorded almost continuously since 1866.[3] Temperature and precipitation records were also kept for varying lengths of time at some of the lighthouses: at Port Charlotte and Rhuvaal from 1900 and at McArthur's Head from 1900. But with lighthouse automation these ceased. Rainfall records were also kept for brief periods during the Second World War at the airfield at Glenegedale, near Port Ellen, and at the seaplane base at Bowmore. Apart from sunshine, hourly recordings at Islay airport are automatic and transferred electronically to the Meteorological Office. These comprise pressure, wind velocity and direction, precipitation and maximum and minimum temperatures.

As in the other Hebridean islands, the most noticeable weather features are expressed better as frequencies than as absolutes or averages. Devotees of the BBC shipping forecasts must listen for Malin area, Malin Head and Machrihanish Automatic. The average number of days with winds of gale force on nearby Tiree is 35 per year and Islay's experience is likely to be similar.[4] Fog occurs, on average, less than five times a year on Islay, but the number of days with low cloud base is much higher. The amount of precipitation in the Islay lowlands averages over 130cm (50 ins) per year; very little of this normally falls as snow. Rainfall is distributed unevenly throughout the year, with more in the winter half of the year from October to March, while between one-half and two-thirds of the days are likely to have some rain.[5] Cloud cover and the related number of sunshine hours are also highly variable. There is usually more sunshine than in mountainous Jura, but less than in flatter Tiree. The average duration of sunshine is four hours per day, varying from an hour or so on average in winter to over six in summer. Temperatures are rarely excessively high or low and frosts are likewise rare. The growing season has been suggested as 216 days, fairly long in British terms, but salty winds can often deter growth.[6]

There are, of course, exceptional periods. Grim winters, with blocking high pressure over much of Britain, can, in Islay, be ones with relatively little cloud cover and precipitation and a high total of sunshine hours. Similarly, wet and grey early summers over much of eastern Britain may contrast with the near-drought conditions in Islay, causing concern to farmers, fishermen and whisky distillers, but providing weeks of continuous sunshine for the other islanders and visitors. Then, even the sphagnum moss crackles underfoot on the moors and fire is a constant island hazard, especially if heather-burning gets out of control on the moors. The weather often varies from one part of the island to another. In particular, it is almost always possible to find some beach or favoured spot, sheltered from the day's prevailing wind.

Islay's peaty habitat

The island provides a considerable range of habitat and even although the highest hill, Beinn Bheigir, rising only to just under 500m, excludes subalpine plants, a 'rich native flora' has been claimed; almost 800 taxa have been recorded, including introduced species.[7] One of Islay's Hebridean anomalies is the amount of woodland and plantations of hard and soft woods, including exotics. Extensive sand dunes, salt marshes, limestone and slate outcrops and the many lochs each have their own distinctive flora and fauna.

Peat-banks are an important feature of the Islay scene. They are cut annually for domestic and, particularly, distillery needs.

The Atlantic breaks over the Big Strand beside the links golf course at Machrie, opened in 1891 (Eric Thorburn).

But it is perhaps in the wide expanses of peat bogs that the combined effects of topography, soils, climate and flora have had the most noticeable impact on Islay's economy and landscape. Vegetation on the bogs consists mainly of heather and purple moor grass, with lesser proportions of cotton grass, cross-leaved heather and sphagnum moss. The bulk of the peat itself has been formed through the centuries from the remains of sphagnum species, the resistant leaf sheaths of cotton grass, small twigs of heather and in the lower layers, reeds and some sedges; a few pieces of birch were found in the two bogs sampled by the Scottish Peat Survey of the 1950s and 1960s.[8] Peat has traditionally been cut by foot for domestic fuel from rented pieces or banks of moor. At the cost of a few pounds' rent, some hard work and a mass of midge bites, the fuel supply for heating some island homes can be assured. Peat has also long been used in the distilleries as an integral part of the whisky-making process and formerly also as a fuel. Extensive new cuttings were opened up in 1980 for cutting by machine and a new access road was subsequently constructed east of the 'High Road' between Port Ellen and Bridgend up to Castlehill.

Islay's main peat bogs cover around ten per cent of the surface. There are others that are smaller in extent, shallower in depth or higher in altitude. Since much of the peat overlies raised beach and river-borne materials, reclamation for other uses is not difficult. In the 1960s the Forestry Commission began to plant conifers, predominantly Sitka spruce, on peatlands in the valley of the Laggan and some of its tributaries, on land purchased from the Dunlossit estate and subsequently from the Laggan estate. Felling began in the middle of the 1990s, with timber being exported by barge and ship. The cleared land was left as open ground, allowed to regenerate naturally into woodland, or planted with indigenous species. In 1980 the Commission drained part of the Rinns near Ballimony prior to planting and for much of the 1980s fiscal forestry resulted in further plantings in north-east Islay and in the Oa.

Tourists, naturalists and sportsmen

By the nineteenth century, writings about Islay by topographers and early agricultural scientists and by survey-conscious ministers, were being supplemented by early guidebooks for visitors to the island. The renowned *Steam-Boat Companion* of James Lumsden, in its various editions of the 1820s and later, and various topographical dictionaries made the island better-known to the public.[9] The Victorian expansion of leisure activities for the upper classes encouraged this new interest in Islay. A later guidebook explained that the variety of Islay's shootings was due to the 'remarkable diversity of natural features, to the combination of moor and pasture, of rich cornfields and desolate hillside . . . the bag includes red fallow and roe deer, grouse, partridges, pheasants, blackgame, snipe, rock pigeons, wild duck, golden plover, teal, wild geese, hares and rabbits'.[10] Today, shootings still form part of the island's seasonal activities and economy on several of the estates, with woodcock especially prized. Another sport attracted attention to Islay from the late-nineteenth century. Salmon and trout fishing often warranted praise in the appropriate journals and guides. When in spate, the major salmon rivers are the Sorn, Laggan and Duich and trout lochs are numerous. Surveys, stocking and poaching have been a main concern of the lairds and their agents. Sea-angling is also popular with islanders and visitors alike. Crabs, clams or scallops and lobsters are fished commercially for export to the Iberian peninsula and elsewhere.

Even before the Forestry Commission plantings began in the later 1960s, the map of Islay showed much more evidence of natural woodlands and plantations than has been characteristic of most of the other Hebrides since the eighteenth century. The woodlands are a sheltered haven in winter and early spring, with their succession of snowdrops, wild daffodils and bluebells. The hedgerows too were planted mostly during the agrarian reforms of the late-eighteenth and early-nineteenth centuries; fewer stone dykes were necessary in the less stony, lower parts of the island. The hedges provide shelter for a profusion of wildflowers in spring and early summer, when the island is ablaze with gorse and they also provide sanctuary for birds and game.

The extremely varied habitat of Islay with its varied flora and fauna on land and in water has led to various designations including several Sites of Special Scientific Interest, RAMSAR sites, and the Argyll Islands Environmentally Sensitive Area. It is particularly for its bird life, however, that the island is renowned. Many ornithologists have testified to the large range of birds inhabiting or visiting the island on migration. Due to an amazing variety of habitat, woodland, moor, hill, seacliff, machair and sand dunes, agricultural land, hedgerows, rivers, marshes, freshwater lochs and shallow sea lochs, over 250 bird species have been recorded, almost half of which breed on Islay.[11] In a week's visit it is often possible to see over a hundred different birds, including fairly uncommon ones such as the barn owl, chough, corncrake and golden eagle. In winter and early spring, Islay is host to tens of thousands of barnacle geese and several thousand Greenland white-fronted geese, grazing the fields near the tidal flats and lochs, or wheeling overhead at dusk in their great V-shaped chevrons. Smaller numbers of other visitors include Brent and Canada geese and there are many rafts of wigeon and scaup.

As well as providing for visitors interested in shooting, fishing and watching whales, dolphins, seals, otters and birds, the island attracted golfers after 1891 when Mrs Lucy Ramsay opened the Machrie course beside the Big Strand of Laggan Bay. By the end of the decade the Rev J. G. MacNeill was claiming in his guidebook that 'this splendid course of eighteen holes is second to none in Scotland . . . many of our foremost statesmen, titled and untitled, are here frequently seen on the golfing links'.[12] Competitions were instituted, the main one being the Kildalton Cross Championship, still held annually in the first week of August. Shorter courses at Gartmain and Uisgeantsuidhe were also played earlier in the twentieth century and 'an excellent nine-hole golf course' has even been claimed for Port Askaig.[13] The nine-hole pitch-and-putt course behind the White Hart Hotel was superseded by the one at the Port Ellen Playing Fields, established in 1953.

The sands of Islay have not all been laid down to golf links; the sandy beaches include the sometimes wild and dangerous ones of the western Rinns at Lossit, Kilchiaran, Machir, Saligo and around Sanaig. There are extensive beaches on both sides of Loch Gruinart and around Loch Indaal, while there are many smaller, sometimes sheltered ones along the south-eastern coasts of Kildalton and the Oa. Only the eastern shore of the island along the Sound of Islay is without accessible beaches.[14]

An island of considerable character and contrasts, one of the few Hebridean islands with woodlands, one with a wild and bare west, a tidy central heartland and a fragmented south-east, Islay's distinctiveness is in part a reflection of its physical setting and structure. To a much greater extent it is the result of a history very different from that of the remainder of the Hebrides and the Highlands. More particularly it reflects the perception and initiative of relatively few individuals during a century or more after about 1750. To appreciate their vision, it is necessary to go back in time to see what Islay was like before the early-eighteenth century.

Notes and references
[1]   Ordnance Survey, *1:50,000 Second Series*, 60, 1987; *1: 25,000*; *Pathfinder Series*, 1987–8; *1: 10,000. Second Edition*, 1899, revised 1981.
      Geological Survey of Scotland *Quarter Inch Geology, Sheet 13*, 1921; *One Inch Solid and Drift, Sheet 98*, 1918 and *Sheet 27*, 1900; British Geological Survey *1:50,000 South Islay Sheet 19 (Scotland) Solid and Drift Geology Provisional Series 1996*; and *North Islay Sheet 27*, 1995; and S. B. Wilkinson, *The Geology of Islay, including Oronsay and portions of Colonsay and Jura*, (Glasgow, 1907).
      A. G. Dawson, 'Lateglacial sea-level changes and ice-limits in Islay, Jura and Scarba, Scottish Inner Hebrides', *Scottish Journal of Geology* 18 (1982) pp. 253–65; J. M. Gray, 'Glacio-isostatic shoreline development in Scotland: an overview', *Queen Mary College*

Occasional Papers, 24, (London, 1985), S. B. McCann 'The Raised Beaches of North-East Islay and Western Jura', *Transactions of the Institue of British Geographers* 35 (1964), pp. 1–15; and F. M. Synge and N. Stephens, 'Late and Post-glacial Shorelines and Ice Limits in Argyll and North-East Ulster', *ibid.* 39 (1966), pp. 101–25. A special issue of *Scottish Geographical Magazine* 122 (2006) was devoted to the Loch Lomond Readvance.

2   Register of Examinations . . . concerning Wrecks and Casualties, NRS, CE60/4/24.

3   Meteorological Office communication, 1972. Gales are winds of 34 knots or over (8 on Beaufort scale) blowing for at least ten minutes.

4   Meteorological Office communication, 1981.

5   *The Monthly Weather Report*, 1976, Table 3. M. Storrie, 'Weather Records', *Ileach* 29, 4 May 2002, pp. 8–9.

6   M. L. Anderson and W. A. Fairbairn, 'Division of Scotland into Climatic Sub-regions as an Aid to Silviculture', *Bulletin of the Forestry Department, University of Edinburgh* 1, (1955), p. 8.

7   J. K. Morton, 'The Flora of Islay and Jura (V.C. 102)', *Proceedings of the Botanical Society of the British Isles, Supplement*, 1958–60, part 3, pp. 1–59.

8   Department of Agriculture and Fisheries for Scotland, *Scottish Peat Surveys: Western Highlands and Islands*, (Edinburgh, 1966), 5 vols. Islay is in vol. 2.

9   J. Lumsden and Son, *The Steam-Boat Companion and Stranger's Guide to the Western Islands and Highlands of Scotland*, (Glasgow, 1825); S. Lewis, *A Topographical Dictionary of Scotland*, (London, 1846), 2 vols. and Atlas.

10 L. MacNeill Weir, *Guide to Islay*, (1924 edition, revised, Glasgow, 1936), pp. 48–51.

11 C. G. Booth, *Birds in Islay*, (Islay, 1981), p. 11; R. E. Elliott, *Birds of Islay*, (London, 1989); M. A. Ogilvie, Wild Geese, (Islay, 1978) and 'Wildfowl of Islay', *Proceedings of the Royal Society of Edinburgh* 83B (1983), pp. 473–89.

12 J. G. MacNeill, *The New Guide to Islay*, (Glasgow, 1900), p. 23. See also J. Cubbage, *The Chronicle of Islay Golf Club and Machrie Links*, (Glasgow, 1996).

13 J. W. Robertson, *Islay Official Guide*, 2nd edition, (n.d), p. 27.

14 W. G. Ritchie and R. Crofts, *The Beaches of Islay, Jura and Colonsay*, (Aberdeen, 1974).

CHAPTER 3

Earlier islanders

In what has been termed the Atlantic Ends of Europe, from the mouth of the Douro in Portugal to the Lofoten Islands beyond the Arctic Circle, the seas around the Highlands and Islands have always been important for transport and as a source of food.[1] The south-west to north-east geological trend of Islay provides a long coastline with shelter around the compass. It was probably from south-western Europe in Mesolithic times that the first visitors voyaged to an island still uninhabited after the retreat of the last ice sheet around 10,000 years ago. Islay abounds in visible and invisible remains of many different settlers and cultures from then onwards.

The *Statistical Account* authors of the late-eighteenth century and subsequent topographers noted some of Islay's antiquities, although the estate maps of the early-nineteenth century, made for innovative purposes, did not show many. It was not until the first edition of the Six-Inch Ordnance Survey maps of the later-nineteenth century and in several publications around that time, that the rich archaeological heritage of the island was hinted at. Various archaeologists, including Childe in the 1930s and Piggott in the 1940s, were followed in the later 1950s by Lacaille who was the instigator of a branch of the Thames Basin Archaeological Observers' Group being formed, called the Islay Archaeological Survey Group.[2] It attempted to produce an exhaustive survey of all the antiquities of Islay. *The Preliminary Handbook of the Archaeology of Islay*, published in 1960, recorded much archaeological and historical material, but the IASG became defunct in 1971. At about the same time as it had begun its work, a local Natural History and Antiquarian Society of Islay had been formed and with the activities of this, of the Museum of Islay Life, the Finlaggan Trust and, above all, of the Royal Commission on the Ancient and Historical Monuments of Scotland and National Museums Scotland, more of Islay's archaeological and later story has been unravelled.

Prehistoric islanders
People have been using and modifying this island environment for over nine thousand years.[3] Maps of geology, lithology and superficial deposits,

The Neolithic chambered cairn at Cragabus is a reminder that this settlement has probably been occupied for several thousand years.

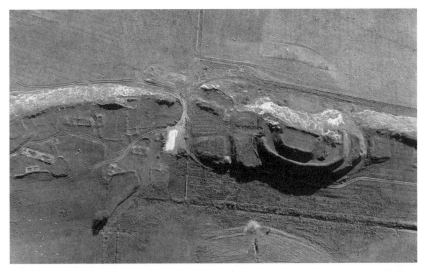

The compact, multivallate fort or dun at Nosebridge defended the upper Laggan valley during the Iron Age or later. It contrasts with the scattered buildings to the left (east), occupied when Islay's population reached its maximum around 1830 (John D. H. Radford).

and satellite images all illustrate that, even in these 'Atlantic Ends of Europe', this southern Hebridean island is relatively well-endowed topographically and edaphically, with a good fuel source in peat, and at times, wood. Sheltered anchorages, raised beaches, inland valleys with southern-facing, well-drained alluvial and loamy soils, minerals including Dalradian limestone and veins of lead and silver, all combined to ensure that Islay was a favoured and desirable place in which to live and settle, particularly at times when climate co-operated. The island was also strategically placed on the sea routes between southern and northern Europe via Ireland and Man.

When the Mesolithic hunters and fishers approached Islay from the adjacent mainland about 7,000 BC, sea-level was higher than it is today, with less land, for instance, between Lochs Indaal and Gruinart.[4] The climate was milder than at present, with warmer summers and consequently Islay may have been more wooded. Shell middens such as that found at Ardnave resulted from the use of limpet hammers and bone fish hooks belonging to the Mesolithic fisher folk. Deer supplied meat, bones for implements and skins for shelter and clothing. Other flint implements and weapons have been found on the valleyside near Bolsay in the Rinns.

As the search for food evolved to one of permanent settlement based on farming, the evidence for Neolithic times in Islay from about 3,500 BC to about 2,500 BC shows that woods were cleared with stone axes for pasture, while pottery was used for the first time. Immigrant farmers and their progeny were buried in multi-chambered tombs with cairns, such as at Cragabus or Port Charlotte. Sea-level then fell to around its present limits. To the later-Neolithic and earlier-Bronze Age times the many standing stones and the Cultoon stone circle belong. Islay is well endowed with standing stones, single, or aligned in pairs or trios. At Cultoon only three stones stand upright, with a dozen prone. While the sockets were excavated in an oval arrangement, Cultoon was probably never completed, despite its astronomical and perhaps navigational potential. Bronze Age cultivation and settlement to about 600 BC have been confirmed by the beakers, food vessels and tools uncovered in the sandhills at Ardnave and Kilellan. Burial in chambered tombs was replaced by the use of round cairns as at Carnduncan and in individual cists. Hut-circle settlements in isolated, dispersed or nucleated groups and their associated field systems on the low-lying moorlands also belong to this time. Some comprised isolated houses, others were in dispersed groups and still others in nucleated settlements. The field systems provided plots for paddocks or fields for cattle and grain, as at An Sithean, near Carnduncan, where grains of pollen have been recovered.

Following this somewhat benign period, there was gradual climatic deterioration, resulting in moorland and more peaty lands during the wetter period that continued through the Iron Age to around 400 AD. In Islay this seems to have been a time of conflict, with around eighty fortified sites of varied sizes. There were small stone hill forts like Dùn Chroisprig overlooking Machir Bay and the Atlantic, with many others in the hills, ridges, promonotories and offshore islets. The peoples of the early Iron Age have bequeathed timber-framed hill forts and Trudernish vitrified hill fort. The only drystone defended settlement or broch on Islay is that of Dùn Bhoraraic above Lossit in Kilmeny, characteristically circular and galleried. Towards the end of the Iron Age or later, two large forts were constructed that are unique in the west of Scotland: the two multivallate, earthwork fortifications of Dùn Nosebridge, near Neriby, on a commanding site in the upper Laggan valley, and Dùn Guaidhre, near Kilmeny, in the upper Sorn valley. Neither of these has been excavated and little about them is agreed among archaeologists, but both command strategic positions overlooking fertile valleys and were probably subsequently reoccupied. Crannogs were constructed on stilts or artificial islands in lochs such as Ardnave, Finlaggan, Gorm and Lossit.

Milder conditions began to characterise the Christian era, and the Norse settlement period following the late-eighth century Viking raids was followed by a warmer phase from the mid-twelfth century; this coincided with the rise of the kingdom and lordship of the isles. Winters were mild and wet and summers warm and dry, which sounds quite Mediterranean. This was succeeded by colder, drier winters and cool, damp summers with occasional better spells after about 1400, but towards the end of the seventeenth century a sharp decline in summer temperatures occurred. This 'Little Ice Age' lasted into Victorian times, with a southward shift of Atlantic depressions[5] and was characterised by very severe cold winters, cool summers and storminess. The two last decades of the seventeenth century proved especially difficult, vulcanism in Iceland and Indonesia in 1693 and 1694 blotting out the sun and its warmth. After some respite, the second half of the eighteenth century again had colder winters. Variability became pronounced with a relatively warmer climate interspersed with cold spells in the 1820s, 40s and 90s. Then warmth peaked about mid-twentieth century, followed by cooler and now again warmer temperatures. Climatic variability indeed.

Island naming
In comparison to the previous 7.5 millennia there is evidence from only 1.5 millennia for place names in Islay, the majority of the several thousand

topographic and habitative names only being precisely recorded in the last quarter of the nineteenth century during the compilation of the first edition of the Ordnance Survey maps and plans. While there has been debate about the relative and absolute chronology of settlement, on one topic most writers through time have agreed that the origins of the island name itself are unknown, although certainly several thousand years old, pre-Celtic and perhaps even pre-Indo-European.

Place names indicate language and speakers of a language, but can usually suggest only relative settlement sequence. The names are not dictionary words, but onomastic ones. They are, however, only one result of the sequence and interplay of differing languages and cultures. More clearly seen in the landscape of Islay are, for instance, the Neolithic cairns, the later Iron Age duns and forts, medieval chapels or the more recently deserted and now ruinous settlements. As in Scotland as a whole, place names have passed from one language to another and perhaps even into a third by contact or adaptation. Names can be bestowed at any time and hundreds of years may elapse between settling and naming before eventual recording. On the modern Ordnance Survey maps of Islay, names have Gaelic, Norse and English origins. These maps and names reflect the situation in the island when the surveyors were mapping in the third quarter of the nineteenth century; Gaelic was then the predominant language, names often being moulded to fit its phonetics. At all scales, whether settlement, topographic or field and other minor names, Gaelic names predominate, although often, as with Norse names, in an anglicised form. Not all names are of equal significance, however, in trying to establish settlement history, but those of major topographic features and of religious sites and settlements are likely to be of longer standing than the many minor ones. Some names are simplex, but most are compound, often having two parts, and sometimes involving tautological elements from more than one language. The two parts comprise a generic element, usually a noun; and a descriptive element, often an adjective or a genitive noun. In Gaelic the descriptive part generally follows, as in Ardbeg, while in Norse and English it generally precedes, as in Margadale. How far back does one have to go to imagine the first namers and their motives? Were places or names stored as locations in the minds of seafarers and landlubbers of the Dalradian or later Norse and medieval 'kingdoms'? A major naming motive seems to have been to establish the locality on the 'mental map of the user' whether occupier or immigrant.

Early Christians
Islay had probably been occupied by peoples from both western and eastern

The Celtic High Ring Cross in Kildalton churchyard is the only one surviving intact in Scotland. It was carved from local stone about 800AD, probably by a sculptor from Iona. Pictish, Irish, Northumbrian and Celtic motifs include the virgin and the child, David and the Lion on the front, and animals and carved bosses on the back (Eric Thorburn).

directions before Gaelic-speaking 'Scots' of Ireland built coracles towards the end of the fifth century AD, to cross what is now known as the North Channel, establishing the Dalriada kingdom in Earra-ghaidheal or Argyll on the western seaboard. It is only after classical reference to the Aebudae (Hebrides) and Epidion (Islay) that the earliest written references to Islay appear from the Irish chroniclers of the fifth century and subsequently of Columba's biographer, Adomnàn.[6] In the early-sixth century, Angus MacErc claimed Islay where his descendants formed Clan Donald and later became the lords of the Isles. The Ulster writings of the seventh century, *Senchus fer nAlban*, published five centuries later,[7] reveal the first list of names within the island; they comprise community or district names, with numbers of 'houses', each of which would support two boats and 28 oarsmen.[8] Possible locations of these areas are suggested:

Odeich	20 houses	Kildalton including Texa
Aitha Cassil	30	The Oa
Freag	100	Kilarrow
Ardbes	30	Kilmeny
Cladrois	60	South Rinns
Loch Rois	30	North Rinns

It has been claimed that the Gaelic topographic *sliabh* name is the only pre-Norse Scottish place name.[9] Coinciding with the few centuries of early Dalriadic settlement of Irish-Scots Gaelic speakers from the mid-fifth to seventh centuries, it is mainly concentrated in the Rinns of Galloway and Islay.[10] In Islay *sliabh* is more usually applied to natural features of moorland or rounded hills, since mountains are few; several of the dozen names were subsequently reflected in settlement names, such as Sleivemore and Sleidmeall.

Also representing Gaelic-speaking settlers with strong Irish connections, may be some of the almost forty *cill-* [anglicised as *kil*] names denoting foci for Christian worship and burial. At first these Columban missionaries probably lived as hermit monks in cells or as priests in tiny buildings, which developed into monastic settlements both secular and religious, these churches and burial grounds ministering to islanders and answering to an abbot. The chapel at Kilslevan has a doorway at the west end that might indicate an early dating and the almost circular enclosure there may also be early-Celtic. At other places the shape is more rectangular and greater Norse influences seem to have appeared later on. These tiny churches probably continued in use with Norse colonists subsequently adopting the Christian religion, each district building its own small chapel

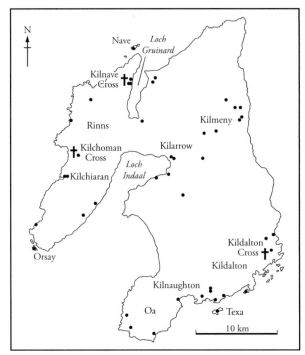

While some of the *Cill-* or Kil- names were bestowed to commemorate early Celtic clerics and saints up to the ninth century, most probably date to the twelfth century when the parochial system was developed.

The twelfth-century parish boundaries followed an earlier tripartite division of Islay. With the increased population of the nineteenth century, each was further divided into *quoad sacra* parishes of Portnahaven, Kilmeny and the Oa.

and burial ground.[11] Clergy later canonised included not only Columba who founded Iona monastery, but others whose names live on in the parish and place names of Islay. Some names may have been given by sizeable Gaelic-speaking Christian communities in posthumous commemoration of a particular saint, or of followers of such a saint, perhaps with up to two hundred years for names to have been bestowed. Many of the identifiable saints' names are Irish: Brendan (*c.* 484–*c.* 577), Brigid or Bride (452–525), Ciaran (d. 549), Collum or Columba (*c.* 628–704), and Maol Rubha (640–722), and have given rise to names such as Kilbride, Kilchiaran, Kilcollumkill or Kiells and Killarow. Other *cill*-names were later to be bestowed during a Norse archbishopric and a Manx bishopric, and during the twelfth-century establishments of parishes and of smaller places of worship or burial grounds for an expanding population. The *Argyll Inventory* referred to 'the quite exceptional' number of physical remains at many of these places, mostly from this later time.[12]

It gradually became the practice to set up commemorative crosses in the burial grounds to dedicate places and people to the Lord. The Islay carved stones were first illustrated by Graham in 1895, then by Lamont, Steer and Bannerman and the Royal Commission on the Ancient and Historical Monuments of Scotland.[13] There are many types and ages of carved stones on Islay, some hewn from local rocks, others sculpted locally from imported stones and others brought in already carved. Many are still to be seen in the island, though some are now in National Museums Scotland in Edinburgh. Most of the earliest upright stones were simple incised-outline cross slabs, then, about the eighth century, carving in relief began. At first this was also simple, but later the carving became more elaborate in the Celtic Ring Crosses, erected to the glory of God. Visually the most outstanding are the High Crosses at Kilnave and Kildalton which Lamont described as being 'in astonishing contrast' to the simple cross slabs. He suggested that the 2.5m-high Kilnave Cross dated from around 759, and could be ascribed to Irish and Iona traditions. On a thin slab of local flagstone, only one face is carved. The remarkably preserved spiral motif of the top arm recalls the illustrations in the *Book of Kells*. The 2.7m-high Kildalton Ringed Cross, remaining intact in Scotland, may be from even earlier in the century; both of its faces are carved with the artistic sophistication of the Iona tradition, with Pictish, Irish, Northumbrian and Celtic motifs. The grey-green epidiorite, with numerous granules of felspar, was quarried over a kilometre away at Port na Cille. Lamont's assessment of these crosses is that 'artistically as well as physically the crosses of Kilnave and Kildalton tower above everything else in the ancient sculpture of Islay'.

The Norse and Naming

The Viking or Norse longships or galleys which plied the seas off western Europe from about the eighth century AD, pulled from fifty to eighty oars. They carried a mast which was always lowered aft when using oars. A single square sail was hoisted on a yard for working to windward and for running. With neither deck nor keel, these proved fairly unstable vessels with little protection for their crews; they experienced difficulty operating in rougher winter seas, even in the climatic optimum of the time, yet still managed some remarkable voyages. From around 800 the Scandinavians raided, traded and settled in Islay as well as in many parts of the Atlantic fringe of Europe. They spread from the Nordreys or Northern Isles southwards into what became the Sudreys, or Inner Hebrides, and beyond as far south as the Isle of Man and Ireland. Their active association with these areas lasted for over four centuries. There is, however, no documentary evidence for Islay between a reference in the *Annals of Ulster* to an earthquake in the island in 740[14] and a papal reference of 1203.[15] Archaeology, linguistics and onomastics have to be gleaned for evidence of the island's land and people.

Small pointed out in 1968 that 'problems are created in the analysis of the Norse settlement of the western seaboard by the lack of extensive archaeological sites',[16] and this largely remains the case. Only one possible Norse settlement has yet been physically identified in Islay, although graves of both Norse men and women of some substance in the ninth and tenth centuries, and stone markers have so far come to light, some distance from habitations, and not in Christian burial places. From those at Cruach Mhor and Ballinaby, equal numbers of men's and women's graves, yielding brooches, give some indication of permanent settlers. The Norse had arrived as pagans, but subsequent intermarriage with the local Celts produced the Gael-Gall or Gaelic foreigners, and most were probably converted to Christianity. While many funerary slabs continued in the older Celtic tradition, the Dòid Mhàiri slab, now in Edinburgh, was completely different from any other stone found on the island. With both Celtic and Norse symbols, it probably marked the grave of an important Gael-Gall chief.[17]

Although no Norse settlement site has yet been authenticated, many place names survive that are associated with the Norse peoples. The *Argyll Inventory* recorded that place names of Norse origin were to be found in all the islands, but 'only in Islay are a considerable number of them applied to farms and settlements, as well as to natural landscape features'.[18] In 1950 Macdonald had opined that the 'Argyll islands were never at any time completely "Norsised", being essentially Gaelic islands in which Gaels lived, in contrast to the Outer Hebrides which were termed 'Innse Gall' or islands of the strangers or foreigners.[19] By 1997, however, it was being argued from linguistics and onomastics that 'the volume of place names of Norse origin . . . suggests a thorough renaming by the Norse settlers and traders . . . Given the converse influence of Gaelic over the intervening centuries . . . the survival of [Norse] place names containing habitative elements argued for a well established pattern of Norse landholding in Islay, Coll and Tiree'.[20] Two university theses in the early 1980s[21] and Macniven's 2006 doctoral thesis on Norse settlement history[22] continued and contributed to the controversy of the impact of the Norse on Islay. While Nieke considered that the Norse had infilled among pre-Norse settlements, Macniven claimed in 2006 that the fairly even distribution of Old Norse topographic and farm names over the island as a whole, suggested an early and fairly complete settlement process.[23] It is unsurprising that in 2007 Abrams could still aver that 'The Hebrides have proved to be fertile ground for speculation and disagreement about the activities and impact of Scandinavians in the Irish Sea and North Atlantic . . . [even] the date at which Scandinavians became a permanent presence in the Hebrides is difficult to pin down'.[24] Assessing the extent, distribution and density of Norse settlement that followed Viking raids in the late-eighth century is thus not straightforward. Brown in 1997 could find no evidence of how the Norse took possession of land in the Hebrides, 'beyond that of later landholding and fiscal organisation'.[25] Did the Norse take over existing settlements and rename them; or, as perhaps suggested by the few *baile* names and lack of *achadh* evidence, did they instead expand the area of settlement, outwards and upwards? The ultimate controlling factor was the availability of cultivable land: flat land was not desirable; slope gave drainage, and aspect, warmth.

Norse names would first have been bestowed when approaching from the sea, such as Loch Gruinart (Old Norse *Grunn-fjörðr*, the shallow firth), Loch Indaal (*Loch na Dala*, the loch of the division), or Beinn Tart a'Mhill (from *Hartafjall,* stag mountain). Many of the smaller islands' names (Nave, Orsay or Texa) are also attributable to the Norse, as also are many inland waters (Lochs Kinnabus, Lossit or Uigeadail). Old Norse words, often for topographic features, were subsequently attached to settlements including *dalr*, valley, of which there are over a score in Islay, as in Tormsdale and Margadale; *vik*, bay, with over a dozen instances, as in Port Askaig, Proaig and Laphroaig; and *ness*, headland, as in Trudernish and Stremnish; and a score of other Norse names as in Avinlussa and Bolsay. Such Norse names are spread fairly evenly across all Islay land types, inland and coastal, valley and hill, machair and limestone.

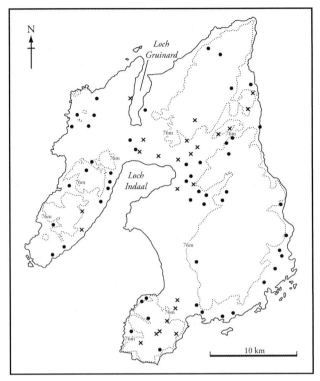

Norse generics from the ninth to eleventh centuries are widespread in Islay place names. They include *borgr, byr, dalr, land, ƿing, nes, staðir,* and, *vik.* The most common is *bólstaðr* (marked with x), on some of the best lands and most strategic locations in the island. (Based on OS Name Books).

There are probably almost a dozen instances of high-status individual settlement names in Islay derived from *staðir,* dwelling place, particularly in the southern Rinns, as in Olistadh and the Ellisters, or Ardelistry in Kildalton, although the latter has also been suggested as deriving from Old Norse *still,* an enclosure.[26] The *byr* generic (perhaps from east Norway) also indicates high status holdings. Brown pointed to Conisby (*Konnungsbaer,* king's village) and thought it raised 'the question of the political and administrative organisation of the King of the Sudreys'.[27] Other examples are Neriby and Ballinaby. The generic *borgr,* fortress, as in Dùn Nosebridge or the broch, Dùn Bhoraraic, also indicated high status. There are several *land* names suggesting prestigious and early Norse settlements, such as Sunderland, Foreland and Tallant. For Sunderland, an alternative to the personal Gaelic name *Sionnarlainn,* which underlies some of the islanders' pronunciation of the name, has been posited as Old Norse *Sjóverland,* the farm by the lake. *ƿing,* implying an assembly, may be contained in the district name around Sunderland as Old Norse *Sjovarping* or *Sjonarping*.[28] This area includes the fertile lands of Kilchoman and fortified sites on Loch Gorm. For such a name implying a Norse administrative network to have survived, but without remaining an important administrative centre, implies that the subsequent Gaelic Somerled dynasty, or the MacSorleys, removed their administration away from the Norse one to their new focus at Finlaggan.

One of the stimuli to the Norse expansion overseas appears to have been land shortage,[29] and Nicolaisen argued that 'the main early period of Norwegian emigration . . . appears to have been a two-generation span . . . up to 850 . . . with a fairly accurate idea of those parts of Norway from which most of the emigrants came . . . the coastal district between Fjordane-Möre and Tröndelag',[30] almost half of the Islay Old Norse names having exact cognates in the latter area. The Norwegian word commonly given to a farm, *bólstaðr,* has, notably, received much more onomastic attention abroad than in its homeland.[31] With a range of meanings from farm to settled land, *bólstaðr* was extensively used in the Norse colonies whenever permanent settlements were formed by the Scandinavians and probably showed Norse settlement and power at its most extensive.[32] A number of conditions had to be present in order for it to be applied as a place name element, the most important being predominantly Norse culture, suitable topography and prolonged settlement during the late-ninth and tenth centuries. It is not only the commonest Old Norse generic in Islay but it occurs more there than anywhere else in the Inner or Outer Hebrides. There are at least two dozen settlement names in Islay based on the generic *bólstaðr,* with the form today of -bus, although historically it was often written and pronounced as -bolls.[33] Examples are Eallabus (eel farm) and Robolls (parson's holding). Clusters may reflect division of large holdings into smaller units, perhaps within a short period of time. Landholdings with *bólstaðr* names have continued to dominate the Oa, the northern half of the Rinns, the adjoining part of Kilarrow, north-eastern Kilmeny, south-eastern Kilarrow, the valley of the river Sorn and upper Laggan. Few of the nearby islands such as Jura, Colonsay or Gigha feature this generic, in the first instance understandably perhaps due to the paucity of good land, in the others, perhaps because they were so small.

In asserting that 'For so many Norse farm names to have survived into modern times . . . points more clearly to disjuncture than continuity – certainly in language and probably also population',[34] Macniven's view has tended to contradict that of many earlier writers, apart from MacNeill who viewed 'the place names in the Hebrides' as proving 'how complete the Norwegian occupation of the isles has been'.[35] Others, such as Cant, thought that despite considerable Norse infiltration, Celtic culture had persisted,[36] while Brown had also speculated 'whether Old Norse ever completely replaced an earlier Celtic tongue in any of the southern Hebrides'.[37] But she continued 'the volume of place-names of Norse origin . . . suggests a thorough renaming by the Norse settlers and traders'. Macniven viewed the arrival of the Norse in Islay as being followed by 'sweeping changes to the island's nomenclature',[38] with the survival of nature names *in situ* in almost every part of the island suggesting that 'the island-wide lingua franca was at the time Old Norse . . . Although the Norse impact was of shorter duration on Islay than elsewhere, it was not necessarily less intense or destructive with regards to pre-existing ethno-linguistic identity . . . The island was a fully integrated part of the Norse world . . . into the 11th century or beyond . . . no substantial part of Islay escaped Norse settlement names . . . the island as a whole was at one point dominated by speakers of Norse'. Only two district names, however, have survived, Na Herra (Kilmeny) and Lanndaidh (Kildalton).

It has been suggested that in Orkney, land units and boundaries already existed when the Norse arrived to settle and that the Norse kept and developed the system of land administration, with continuity of settlement sites.[39] Although not used administratively in Norway, the adoption of a unit of taxation to raise an ounce of silver payment from a community and its land, was introduced by the Norse in the northern isles, and subsequently into the Hebrides. Land was described for fiscal and rental purposes by 'extent', which was not areal but expressed the ability to produce crops and carry stock, and hence produce revenue as tax or rent. There is little reason why this unit, the 'ounceland', should not have been adopted as a fundamental settlement unit for Islay. Following earlier Norwegian work, Johnston, in her ingenious published study relating to the islands of Coll and Tiree, employed such extents in analysing settlement development and subsequent divisions.[40] For Islay, a similar approach was essayed for the Rinns, using the MacDougall 1749–51 pre-agrarian revolution map of landholdings, together with legal documents such as sasines, retours, fiscal lists, rentals and so on, some archival, others published.[41] Although the map and the extents in estate rentals were complied seven or eight centuries after the Norse were settling in Islay, it seems at least possible that boundaries of holdings were relatively unchanging. Such an analysis was subsequently extended for the whole island by Macniven, who posited that the Norse, in taking over existing boundaries and units, (though neither their terminology nor nomenclature) grouped them into ouncelands each worth five Marks. Each ounceland contained at least one main high-status Norse settlement name as well as others, and he concluded that the settlements and their naming had been accomplished not only swiftly (perhaps following a mass plantation of Norse speakers on the island), but ubiquitously (assuming that some holdings had subsequently been renamed in Gaelic).

The Gael-Gall and Clan Donald

When Kenneth MacAlpine united Picts and Scots north of the Forth as king of Alba in 843, the Highlands and Islands were virtually left in Norse hands and these areas subsequently developed differently from the rest of Scotland. The Sudreys and Man formed almost an independent kingdom, acknowledging Norwegian sovereignty. A renowned 'King' of Man and the Isles in the last quarter of the eleventh century was Godred Crovan who ruled with a Council which included many local lords from Man and the other isles. He is reputed to have died in Islay in 1095. Three years later, King Magnus Barefoot became the last Norwegian king to venture to the Hebrides for over a century. He sailed to claim sovereignty and in the resulting Treaty of Tarbert in 1098 between Magnus and Edgar, king of the Scots, gave up all claim to the mainland but was confirmed in his control of the islands. Allegiances in Man and the islands continued in both directions, to the Norse and Scottish kings, with very little interference from either, on the whole. In the twelfth century Godred Crovan's son Olaf endowed the bishopric of the Isles under the See of the Sudreys (Sodor) and parishes were established,[42] an older tripartite division of Islay being perpetuated.[43] Southward became Kildalton and Oa, Midward Killarow and Kilmeny, and the Rinns, Kilchoman. The eastern ends of the churches at Kilnaughton and Kilchiaran may belong to this period. Kilbride, Kilchoman and Kilnave can probably be dated to the end of the twelfth century, Kildalton parish church to the early-thirteenth century and Killarow parish church to the late-thirteenth century. Macniven extended earlier work of Ní Ghabhláin in Ireland[44] and posited that the secular ounceland units appeared to correspond to six 'parishes' and their tripartite subdivisions, territorial extents replacing the earlier monastic spheres, and producing the proliferation and fairly even distribution of *cill*-names.

With the Norse embrace of Christianity, intermarriage and integration of Norse and Gaelic people and culture proceeded.[45] Somerled, of mixed Gael-Gall heritage, married Olaf's daughter, Raghnild, but Olaf's unpopular son, Godfred, was deposed by some of the island chiefs, led by his brother-in-law, Somerled, after a sea battle off Islay in 1156. In his fleet of small and manoeuvrable galleys or birlinns, equipped with the newly-introduced rudder (as opposed to the Viking steering oar), Somerled

defeated the Godfred forces and forced a division of the Norse Kingdom
of Man and the Isles, which stretched from the Isle of Man to Lewis.
Early Celtic society was kin-based, ruled by a rì or king; tanistry decided
succession. Somerled became Rì Innse Gall – king or ruler of the Isles of
the Strangers[46] as well as Rì Airir Goìdel,[47] and ruled over a wide-ranging
lordship of islands and the mountainous western seaboard. Norse settling,
naming and influence were then truncated in the southern islands and the
influence of Gaelic language and culture increased. Somerled thus emerged
as the key political figure of the Hebrides around mid-century.[48]

The relationship between David I and Somerled was based on the
Celtic system of 'a rì rendering tribute to a rì ruirech, not on any kind of
feudal system . . . the importance of Somerled's title needs to be stressed
in this context'.[49] David being much preoccupied with English affairs,
Somerled became a kind of regional governor for the Scots king, overseeing
a seaboard province, using his birlinns. Somerled's alliances suggest a
very real and very close-knit community within and beyond the western
isles, an Atlantic sea-faring community encompassing Man, Ireland, the
Hebrides, Orkney, Zetland and Norway. The site at Dunyvaig probably
invited occupation and fortification from at least the Early Historic
period.[50] A stronghold could be created on the coastal promontory on the
east side of Lagavulin Bay, guarding the entrance to the anchorage there
and commanding a prospect of the coasts of Kintyre and Antrim.

While Somerled ruled his lands in semi-independence in David I's
reign, the young Malcolm IV, acting under the influence of the Anglo-
French barons, was determined to extend his power westward. Somerled
was not alone in being concerned that the expansionist policies of the
Crown were threatening to encroach on his traditional territory and
undermine his powers. His relations with the kings of Scots reached a
low ebb over the feudal, primogeniture succession of David's grandson,
Malcolm, as king, instead of a Gaelic collateral choice among several
branches of the ruling house. Fluid clan organisation was at odds with the
formal, universal feudalism imposed by the Crown. Land grants were given
by the Crown to 'foreign' magnates, bringing them into closer proximity
to Somerled's territory and to the Atlantic community in general. Tensions
in twelfth-century Scotland often ran high between natives and incomers
and the feudalisation of Scotland was anything but peaceful.[51] In 1164,
Somerled invaded the mainland and sailed up the Clyde with 160 galleys,
but met his end at Renfrew.

After his death Somerled's lands were divided amongst three surviving
sons, Ranald or Reginald, Angus and Dougall. His disputatious son, Ranald
acquired Islay, probably Jura and Colonsay, lands on the Argyll mainland,

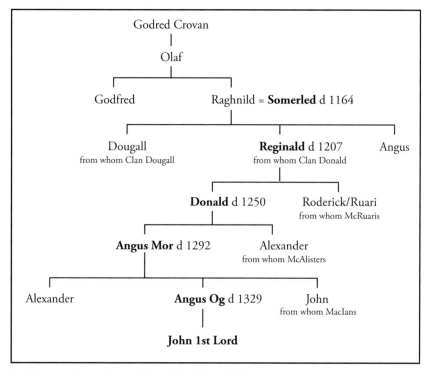

Godred Crovan
|
Olaf
|
┌─────────────────┴─────────────────┐
Godfred   Raghnild = **Somerled** d 1164
┌──────────────┼──────────────────┐
Dougall   **Reginald** d 1207   Angus
from whom Clan Dougall   from whom Clan Donald
┌──────────┴──────────┐
Donald d 1250   Roderick/Ruari
from whom McRuaris
┌──────────┴──────────┐
Angus Mor d 1292   Alexander
from whom McAlisters
┌──────────────┼──────────────────┐
Alexander   **Angus Og** d 1329   John
from whom MacIans
|
John 1st Lord

Outline genealogy of Somerled and Clan Donald (Various sources).

and subsequently others. He adopted the title, *dominus insularum*, king of the isles and *dominus de Argil*, lord of Argyll.[52] Angus' lands subsequently came to Donald, the son of Ranald and to Dougall, Somerled thus being the progenitor of both Clan Donald and Clan Dougall. By the mid-thirteenth century the three lines of Somerled held the islands from the king of Norway and the mainland from the king of Scots.[53]

Politically the region remained largely unaffected by the policies of the Scottish kings until early in the thirteenth century when the Scottish king, Alexander II, mounted expeditions to Argyll in the 1220s. Alexander II died in 1249 and was succeeded by his son, a minor. Later, wanting to consolidate his kingdom, Alexander III moved against the Norse and the rulers of the islands. The thirteenth-century rivalries and feuds among the descendants of Somerled helped to ensure that while the MacDougalls co-operated with the Scots Crown in the 1260s, the MacDonalds did not. They seemed closer to their Norwegian overlords, even joining King Haakon's 1263 expedition against Scotland, although speedily changing sides after the latter's defeat at Largs. Whilst retaining the northern isles in the Treaty of Perth in 1266, the Norse finally ceded the Sudreys

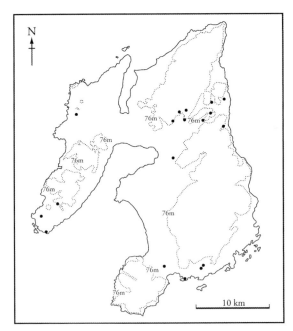

Some of the *baile* (farmstead) names may be later re-namings of *bólstaðr* ones by the resurgent Gaelic dynasty of Somerled from the mid-twelfth century. (Based on OS Name Books).

Shielings (black dots) in Islay tended to be close to settlements, since Islay was hilly rather than mountainous. Many of these *airigh* and *setr* names were not recorded on paper until the early-eighteeenth century, while others became permanent settlements. The *bealach* or pass names (clear dots) are appropriately in the most rugged terrain in the island. (Based on OS Name Books).

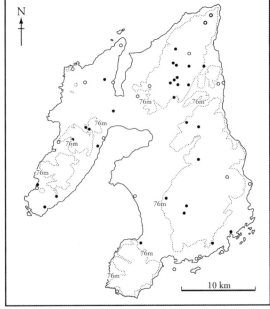

and Man to Scotland and Alexander III formally added the isles to his Scottish dominion. The diocese of the Isles was also transferred to the king of Scots in 1266. The former vassals of the king of Norway were left in possession of their islands; the MacDougalls were at first favoured, but the Macdonalds, in return for fighting for (if not always siding with) the Scottish kings, were termed Rì Innse Gall or Lords of the Isles by the middle of the fourteenth century. In this thalassocratic lordship there was a remarkable flourishing of Gaelic culture based on their leadership and patronage from the centre of the lordship at Finlaggan, with outposts on the island at Kilchoman, Mulindry and Dunyvaig. Somerled's grandson, Angus Mòr (d. *c.* 1293–6), was the first of the family to designate himself specifically 'de Île'.

The Norse language and its use had been declining with little further immigration from Norway by the eleventh century, and with the rise of the Gael-Gall, names of settlements and features were likely to have been Gaelicised by Somerled and his followers. *Baile*, farmstead, was the generic bestowed towards the end of the Norse period,[54] although there are comparatively fewer than one might perhaps expect, particularly in the Rinns and the Oa, (there are also very few *baile* names in the Isle of Lewis). Some of the *baile* names may have been tacked on to Norse words such as Bail' Ola, (Olaf's farm, now Balole), or perhaps even renamed as in Bail' Uileamh (Ullfur's farm, now Balulive) and Baile Gillán (Gillan's farm, now Ballighillin) all in one small area of Kilmeny parish. *Achadh* (field), has only a few instances of use in western islands' place names except in Arran and Mull.[55] It may represent an element later than the *baile*, and perhaps never replaced the Old Norse term *gardr*, an enclosure, which continues in Gaelic as *gearraidh*; examples in Islay include Gearach and Garreallabus. *Gart*, a field or garden, is another generic used in Islay names (Gartloist, Gartachossan, Gartness), as well as *gort,* an enclosure (Gortan, Gortanilvorrie and Gortantoid).

Such Gaelic names form the stratum which directly underlies English place nomenclature. Sometimes the name in English is a translation or part translation of the Gaelic or Gaelicised Norse. There are many Gaelic words such as *cnoc* or *knock*, usefully describing much of the landscape of Islay: Martin Martin, while riding from Port Askaig to Kilarrow (Bridgend) at the end of the seventeenth century described 'one thousand little Hills'.[56] Cnoc na Daal, Knockdon, and Knocklearoch are some of the habitative names. Most of the Gaelic names on the Ordnance Survey maps past and present similarly reflect the use of other Gaelic words describing small topographic features such as *beinn, carn, creag, druim, maol, meall* and *torr*. Many of the smaller coastal features protruding from the land and seen from the near seas were described as *geodha, rubha,* and so on, eclosing a bay or *port.* But many Gaelic names are neither particularly rich in significance nor association, often just describing a given feature, such as a grey ridge or a grassy knoll. It becomes more interesting when a castle or shieling is ascribed to someone such as the Caìsteal Mhic Dhòmhnaill (Macdonald's Castle).

There are a few *setr* (temporary, then permanent dwelling) or *saeter* (shieling) names such as the Staoinshas and Erasaid, indicating (temporary) pastoral dwellings and herding activities. The Gaelic *airge* or *airigh* might have been borrowed by the Norse as *áergi* or *erg*,[57] but such names and locations were unrecorded in rentals or on maps until the early-eighteenth century. As Islay is not mountainous, the shielings tended to be fairly close to the settlements and not far from the stone head dyke around the outfield; they therefore may not have required separate legal existence. If the Jura summer dwellings at the shielings drawn by Moses Griffith for Thomas Pennant[58] were similar to those on Islay, the most iconic, typifying the idea of somewhat distant location of summer grazing, were probably at Margadale in the north-east. Others have personal names attached (Airigh Ghitharandh – Godfred's shieling), while some became permanent settlement names – Ariquary, Arivolchallum and Aryhalloch. Given the hilly rather than mountainous nature of Islay, it is perhaps surprising to find the element *bealach*, pass, in over two dozen locations. But cattle have always been the main agricultural money earner for Islay, so the paths later known as drove roads would be prime candidates for such naming, as at Bealachroy above the Sound of Islay.

Notes and references

[1]   E. E. Evans, 'The Atlantic Ends of Europe', *Advancement of Science* 15 (1958–9), pp. 54–64.

[2]   V. G. Childe, 'Notes on some duns in Islay', *Proceedings of the Society of Antiquaries of Scotland* 69 (1934–5), pp. 81–4; S. and C. M. Piggott, 'Field work in Colonsay and Islay 1944–45', *ibid.* 80 (1945–6), pp. 83–103; Islay Archaeological Survey Group, *The Preliminary Handbook to the Archaeology of Islay*, (Keele, 1960); and G. Ritchie (ed.), *The Archaeology of Argyll*, (Edinburgh, 1997). A. Ritchie, (ed.), *Kilellan Farm, Ardnave, Islay: excavations*, (Edinburgh, 2005).

[3]   RCAHMS, *Argyll Inventory* 5; S. Mithen, *Hunter-gatherer landscape and archaeology. The Southern Hebridean Mesolithic Project 1988–2008*, (Cambridge, 2000); S. Mithen, *To the Islands. An archaeologist's relentless quest to find the prehistoric hunter-gatherers of the Hebrides*, (Lewis, 2010).

[4]   I. Morrison, 'Climatic Changes and Human Geography: Scotland in a North Atlantic Context', *Northern Studies* 27 (1990), p. 2.

[5]   R. A. Dodgshon, 'The Little Ice Age in the Scottish Highlands and Islands: Documenting the human impact', *Scottish Geographical Magazine* 121 (1995), pp. 321–37. I. D.

Whyte, 'Climatic Change and the North Atlantic Seaways during the Norse expansion', *Northern Studies* 21 (1984), pp. 22–3.

[6] W. F. Skene (ed.), *Adomnàn: Vitae S. Columbae*, (Edinburgh, 1874).

[7] J. W. M. Bannerman, *Studies in the History of Dalriada*, (Edinburgh, 1974).

[8] W. D. Lamont, *The Early History of Islay*, (Glasgow, 1966), pp. 7–8, and M. M. Brown, 'The Norse in Argyll', in Ritchie, *Archaeology of Argyll*, p. 206.

[9] W. F. H. Nicolaisen, 'Arran Place Names. A fresh Look', *Northern Studies* 28 (1991), p.5.

[10] W. F. H. Nicolaisen, *Scottish Place Names. Their Study and Significance*, (London, 1976), p. 44.

[11] W. D. Lamont, *Ancient and Mediaeval Sculptured Stones of Islay*, (Edinburgh, 1972), p. 4.

[12] RCAHMS, *Argyll Inventory* 5, p. 27.

[13] R. C. Graham, *The Carved Stones of Islay*, (Glasgow, 1895). Graham is reputed to have made plaster casts of the majority of Islay stones from papier mâché moulds, which he dried on the spot in a tent, and transported back to base on stretchers and in crates specially designed for the purpose. These accurate replicas were then photographed in the studio under special lighting designed to emphasise the ornamentation. (K. H. Steer and J. W. M. Bannerman, *Late Medieval Sculpture in the West Highlands*, (Edinburgh, 1977), p. 9.

[14] Sean MacAirt and Gearóid MacNiocaill, (eds.), *Annals of Ulster to A. D. 1131*, (Dublin, 1983), 740.3.

[15] G. Gregory Smith, *The Book of Islay*, (Edinburgh, 1895), pp. 5–8.

[16] A. Small, 'The Historical Geography of the Norse Viking Colonization of the Scottish Highlands', *Norsk Geografiske Tidskrift* 22 (1968), pp. 1–16.

[17] Lamont, *Sculptured Stones*, p. 22.

[18] RCAHMS, *Argyll Inventory* 5, p.32.

[19] C. M. Macdonald, *The History of Argyll, Up to the Beginning of the Sixteenth Century*, (Glasgow. 1950), p. 52.

[20] Marilyn M. Brown, 'The Norse in Argyll', in Graham Ritchie (ed.), *The Archaeology of Argyll*, (Edinburgh, 1997), p. 232.

[21] M. Nieke's unpublished doctoral thesis, University of Glasgow (1984), 'Settlement patterns in the Atlantic Province of Scotland in the first millennium AD: a study of Argyll' included a case study on Islay. See also Nieke, 'Settlement patterns in the first millennium AD: a case study of the island of Islay', in (eds.), J. C. Chapman and H. C. Mytum, *Settlement in North Britain 1000BC – 1000AD* (Oxford, 1983), pp. 229–326. David Olson, 'Norse Settlement in the Hebrides', unpublished history graduate thesis, University of Oslo, (1983). Olson examined two areas of Islay as case studies, the southern Rinns and the south-western Oa, some of his results being subsequently referred to in Gammeltoft's writings.

[22] Alan Macniven, 'The Norse in Islay: a settlement historical case-study for Medieval Scandinavian activity in Western Maritime Scotland', unpublished doctoral thesis, University of Edinburgh (2006).

[23] Nieke, 'Case Study', p. 313; Macniven, 'The Norse in Islay', p.198.

[24] Lesley Abrams, 'Conversion and the Church in the Hebrides in the Viking Age: "a very difficult thing indeed"', in (eds.), Beverley Ballin Smith *et al*, *West Over Sea* (Leiden and Boston, 2007), p. 171.

[25] Brown, 'The Norse in Argyll', p. 231.

[26] Leslie and Elizabeth Alcock , 'Scandinavian Settlement in the Inner Hebrides: recent research on place-names and in the Field', *Scottish Archaeological Forum* 10 (1980), p. 64.

[27] Brown, 'The Norse in Argyll', p. 232.

[28] Macniven, 'The Norse in Islay', p.196.

[29] Alan Small, 'The Historical Geography of the Norse Viking Colonization of the Scottish Highlands', *Norsk Geografisk Tidsskrift* 22 (1968), p. 3.

[30] W. F. H. Nicolaisen, 'Early Scandinavian Naming in the Isles', *Northern Scotland* 3 (1979–80), p. 108.

[31] Peder Gammeltoft, *The Place-Name Element bólstaðr in the North Atlantic Area* (Copenhagen, 2001), p. 13.

[32] W. F. H. Nicolaisen, 'Norse settlement in the Northern and Western Isles', *Scottish Historical Review* 48 (1969), p. 14. This view has again been modified.

[33] 'That the l has survived in Islay seemingly at the expense of t is somewhat puzzling – ls all featured until recently', Gammeltoft observed, *Bólstaðr*, p. 92.

[34] Macniven, 'The Norse in Argyll', p. 140.

[35] J. G. MacNeill, *The New Guide to Islay*, (Glasgow, 1900), p. 6.

[36] Ronald G. Cant , 'Norse Influences in the organization of the medieval church in the Western Isles', *Northern Studies* 21 (1984), p. 8.

[37] Brown, 'The Norse in Argyll', p. 232.

[38] Macniven, 'The Norse in Argyll', p. 209.

[39] Jessica Bäcklund, 'War or Peace? The relations between the Picts and the Norse in Orkney', *Northern Studies* 36 (2001), p. 35.

[40] Anne Johnston, 'Norse Settlement in Coll and Tiree', in B. E. Crawford, *Scandinavian Settlement in Northern Britain. Thirteen Studies of Place-Names in their Historical Context*, (London, 1995), pp. 108–25.

[41] Margaret Storrie, 'Islay Place Names' paper delivered at the Eighth International Conference on the Languages of Scotland and Ulster held in Islay, July 1996.

[42] J. Trevorrow, *Celtic Foundations*, (Islay, 1985); *Norse Invasion*, (Islay, 1987) and *Parish Churches*, (Islay, 1988).

[43] Macniven, 'The Norse in Islay', chapter 8.

[44] S. Nì Ghabhlàin, 'The Origin of Medieval parishes in Gaelic Ireland: the Evidence from Kilferna', *Journal of the Royal Society of Antiquities of Ireland* 126 (1996), pp. 37–61.

[45] R. A. McDonald, *The Kingdom of the Isles. Scotland's Western Seaboard c. 1100 – c. 1336* (East Linton, 1997), pp. 29–30.

[46] Munro, *Acts of the Lords*, p. xx.

[47] A. Grant, 'Scotland's "Celtic Fringe" in the late Middle Ages: the MacDonald Lords of the Isles and the kingdom of Scotland', in R. R. Davies (ed.), *The British Isles 1100– 1500: comparisons, contrasts and connections*, (Edinburgh, 1988), p. 122.

[48] R. A. McDonald and S. A. McLean, 'Somerled of Argyll: A New Look at Old Problems', *Scottish Historical Review* 71 (1992), p. 7.

[49] *Ibid.*, p. 10.

[50] RCAHMS, *Argyll Inventory* 5, p. 274.

[51] A. Grant, 'To the Medieval Foundations', *Scottish Historical Review* 73 (1994), p. 8.

52 A. Grant, 'Scotland's "Celtic Fringe"', p. 133.

53 *Acts of the Lords*, p. xx.

54 Nicolaisen, *Scottish Place Names*, pp. 136–7.

55 Nicolaisen, 'Arran Place Names', p. 6 and *Scottish Place Names*, p. 140.

56 Martin Martin, *A Description of the Western Islands of Scotland* (London, 1703), p. 239. See M. Storrie, 'Martin Martin: "Green Islay" and the "Green Isle"', in (ed.), The Islands Book Trust, *Martin Martin – 300 Years on*, (Isle of Lewis, 2004), pp. 25–32.

57 Gillian Fellows- Jensen, Common Gaelic *àirge*, Old Scandinavian *aerge* or *erg*? *Nomina* 4 (1980), pp. 67–74 and R. A. V. Cox (1988–9) suggested that the Gaelic *àirge* or *airigh* might have been borrowed by the Norse as *áergi* or *erg*.

58 Thomas Pennant, *A Tour in Scotland and Voyage to the Hebrides, 1772*, (Chester, 1774).

Ruined gables and walls of Finlaggan chapel and hall on Eilean Mor.

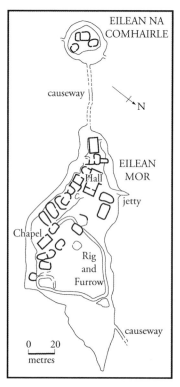

Eilean Mòr (the big island) and Eilean na Comhairle (the Council Island) in Loch Finlaggan, were the focus for the many activities of the lords of the Isles in the fourteenth and fifteenth centuries (After D. H. Caldwell).

CHAPTER 4

Lordship of the Isles and aftermath

The relationship between the centre and localities always depended essentially upon the Crown's relations with the local magnates. The ideal was to have loyal, responsible magnates controlling outlying areas on behalf of the king; that was the foundation of the Crown's success in the twelfth and thirteenth centuries.[1] In the forty years between the final winning of the west in 1266 and the outbreak of civil war caused by Robert Bruce's seizure of the throne in 1306, the MacDougall lords of Lorn acted as the main royal agents in the task of governing the west. By the last decade of the century the MacDonalds of Islay were serving Edward I of England, whilst the MacDougalls were upholding the Scottish cause. But in 1306, when the MacDougalls sided with the English in opposing Bruce, Angus Og chose to help the Scots king. Unfortunately for the MacDougalls, they took what turned out to be the losing side in the civil war. The Clan Donald, by supporting Bruce, had their position strengthened at the expense of the pro-Balliol Clan Dougall. Robert I destroyed the MacDougalls and granted much of their territory to the MacDonalds, though much of the western seaboard was still under the hegemony of the Bruce family. After Angus Og (the Younger) died, and following infighting amongst the kindred, his son John emerged in the 1330s as chief of the Clan Donald (see p. 43). At Perth in 1336 he signed letters of indenture with Edward Balliol which conferred title to all the lands inherited from his father, as well as Kintyre, Knapdale, Lewis and Skye.

Alexander III's Scotland, instead of being split between Celt and Norman, or Gael and Gall, was a hybrid country, with hybrid kingship, hybrid institutions, hybrid law, a hybrid church and an increasingly hybrid landowning class.[2] While Alexander had introduced the feudal system and created four great baronies in the Scottish Highland area, Highland society continued to be based on kinship, modified by feudalism.[3] The application of the latter to Islay initiated a changed basis on which the local chiefs held their land. Charters in Gaelic and Latin included that given by the king to Donald's son, Angus Mor, for Islay and elsewhere, acknowledging him as feudal Baron of Islay. But he and his successors continued to view their attachment to territory and kin by older Celtic laws and customs and paid uneasy homage to the kings of the Scots. When creating the baronies,

Alexander III had had a general assessment made for Scottish taxation purposes. In Islay this list of all lay lands became known as the 'Old Extent', traces of its use still existing in the estate documents and place-names of the eighteenth and early-nineteenth centuries.[4]

The late-thirteenth century Campbells had also been feuding with the MacDougalls and also supported Bruce. After the 1307 turning point in Highland history, a new balance resulted from the Bruce-Balliol civil war. Campbells, MacDonalds and others became prominent instead of Lowland lords. Over the following centuries the Campbells would become the most feudal of Celtic kindreds, basing their expansion on royal patronage, judicious marriage, feudal charters, the newly-created Sherrifdom of Argyll and aggressively adopting Lowland ways. The MacDonalds, by contrast, while becoming the greatest magnate house of the medieval Scottish west, fostered a self-conscious, pan-Celtic Gaeldom.

The lordship of the Isles has long engaged the attentions of historians: it encompassed a highly aristocratic and civilised society in a semi-independent kingdom, eventually covering almost the entire seaboard of west Highland Scotland and Antrim and stretching as far as Dingwall on the Moray Firth. The hegemony and power of the lordship was based on control of the sea. The West Highland galleys (or birlinns or nyvaigs) were the most advanced of their kind in Scotland, having replaced the Viking steering oar with a rudder. Perhaps nowhere is the importance of the galley in the organisation of the lordship more clearly indicated than as a motif on legal seals and on funerary monuments of the area. As well as a potent image for a lordship, the fast, flexible ships gave the Hebridean lords mastery of their sea kingdom.

The descendants of Somerled's grandson Donald, the Clan Donald or the MacDonalds, remained the focus of military and political power in the west and Islay continued to be the main seat of power in the west. The relations between the lords of the Isles and the Scottish Crown varied greatly during the fourteenth and fifteenth centuries, depending on the relative strength of the parties. The lords of the Isles frequently appear in English records, related to the changing state of English relations with the Scottish Crown. The Isle of Man came under English control after 1346 and Ireland was also under English dominance. The distance from Antrim to Islay was short, so direct communication by sea among the lords of the Isles was relatively easy. The lordship thus presented a challenge to the Scottish kings, often acknowledging only token allegiance to the Crown and frequently acting independently in relations with England.

It was Finlaggan, on shore and island sites of the eponymous inland loch surrounded by good land, that became the focus for the activities of the sea realm of the lords of the Isles for over a century and a half. The court at Finlaggan became a centre where there was a significant concentration of population with council meetings, inaugurations, fairs and markets.[5] A stone and timber causeway led to Eilean Mòr where the lord had his hall, with a timber-sprung floor, a large open fire and serving area for food. Claret was brought from France while pilgrim and other badges from the continental mainland suggest wide-ranging connections. The hall, chapel and other living quarters were linked by paved roads. Another causeway was constructed to a nearby artifical island, eponymously the Eilean na Comhairle, where some of the peripatetic Council meetings were held, and to which chiefs of cadet branches travelled.

Conciliar government
The administration within the lordship was conducted by the Council of the Isles, a body which advised the incumbent lord of the Isles. The exercise of MacDonald lordship was peculiarly effective and cohesive, applying male primogeniture, giving charters and, especially, through the Council of the Isles. The heads of major kindreds were associated with all matters of rule to do with succession, inauguration, acquisition of territory, marriage, relations with the Scots Crown and with England, finance, justice and patronage. Through the Council, the dependent chiefs were closely tied into the lordship. After the middle of the fourteenth century the MacDonalds were exercising something approaching sovereignty, implied in the word 'dominus', 'a notoriously difficult word to translate'.[6] The lords of the Isles arranged 'inaugurations' on the main island of Eilean Mòr with much ceremony.[7] The bishop of Argyll, the bishop of the Isles and priests were present, along with the chieftains of all the principal families. There was a square stone, seven or eight feet long, and the 'trace of a man's foot thereon, upon which [the lord] stood . . . clothed in a white habit', with a white rod and his sword. The ceremony being over, mass was said.

Throughout Scotland law and order was still largely a local concern. The supreme court of appeal in the lordship of the Isles was the Council through its judges. The law administered within the lordship almost certainly had Celtic features. In 1357 a new system of taxation was introduced, based on a revaluation of agricultural yields.[8] While it is not known how much of the land the lords granted to their followers, military service usually consisted of the provision of galleys and crews rather than men for the king's army.

The lordship brought relative stability to the Western Isles and over the century and a half of its existence created the context for a veritable golden age of Gaelic culture. The lordship was almost a state within a state, an independent kingdom and an overtly Gaelic institution with a distinctive culture.[9] No other region of Scotland can be so clearly distinguished by its culture as the lordship of the Isles: in many ways it was a unique and distinct phenomenon.[10] Much has been written about the cultural and social influence of the lordship of the Isles. The lords were the chief patrons of a renaissance of Gaelic culture and art, preserving traditional links with Ireland, yet developing a distinct identity. Poets held pride of place as the intellectual leaders of medieval Gaelic society. The MacMhuirich or Currie family were the hereditary seanachies (genealogists), poets and bards to the lords of the Isles.[11] Most of the early poetry was conventional praise poetry, which sang the virtues of chiefs and warriors. Poetry was recited to a harp or clarsach accompaniment and harpists were sometimes poets and singers in their own right. Hereditary harpists to the lords of the Isles were the MacSenach family and harp pins have been uncovered at Finlaggan. Other professionals attached to the courts included the chief judge and lawyers of the Clan Morrison, the medical MacBeths or Beatons who had come from Derry about 1300 and had settled at Ballinaby.[12]

The association of church and state in the lordship of the Isles was a close one. The lords became builders of the abbeys and chapels, turning their backs on the Columban church and introducing great medieval orders to their lands, such as the Augustinians in Oronsay Priory and the Benedictines in Iona Abbey. Benedictines were also given abbey lands and churches in Islay, such as at Ballinaby. The second lord, Donald, and his grandson may even have adopted the monastic life. Priors and canons were supplied to Islay from Iona and Oronsay. Society was reasonably well served by its church in the century and a half before the Reformation, but it is difficult to establish who said mass when and where and many chapels supplemented parish churches. These places of worship were especially thickly spread in well-populated Islay, a few at least being endowed with specific lands, as at Finlaggan, Texa and Orsay.[13] There were three independent parishes in fifteenth-century Islay with secular clergy. Macniven has postulated further tripartite subdivisions of parishes to serve local populations.[14] Communities were well supplied with clergy in fifteenth and early-sixteenth centuries and links with the Vatican were strong in a kin-based society where marriage was closely monitored. Islay became notionally Protestant in the inaugural year of Reformation. In general the first two centuries of reformed worship saw the old parish churches still in use, with the possible exceptions of the buildings at Ellister and Kilbride.[15]

The Aberdeen chronicler, John of Fordun, recorded in 1380 that John, first of the lords, had two places of residence or 'mansiones' in Islay.[16]

One of these is traditionally said to have been at Kilchoman, the other on the island in Loch Finlaggan.[17] Two centuries later Dean Monroe was to confirm 'the town of Kilchomain in which the Lords of the Ules dwelt offtymes'.[18] The architecture of medieval secular lordship in this group of islands exhibits a character that is different from much of the rest of Argyll. Dunyvaig and Finlaggan apart, there is a notable absence of recognised fortified houses. The first specific reference to a castle of Dunyvaig, 'castrum Dounowak', was also that of John of Fordun. About then, possession of the stronghold passed from the lords of the Isles to a cadet branch of the family, the MacDonalds of Dunyvaig and the Glens of Antrim, who held the castle until after rebellion and forfeiture in 1493.

The importance of the patronage exercised by the MacDonald lords of the Isles is particularly illustrated in monumental sculpture.[19] Craftsmen were highly skilled workers in stone, metal and wood. Of their work in metal and wood very little remains, but from the hereditary stonemasons there remain many examples of their artistically sophisticated and unique style of decoration. Some were carved in low relief with no human figures, but with a sword and scroll. Others, up to the middle of the sixteenth century, depicted effigies of warriors or churchmen. The commissioned crosses and graveyard slabs also commemorated heads of kindreds, their families and members of professions and crafts. The typical character of the sculptural renaissance in Argyll and the isles produced late-medieval stones that had no ancestry in the ancient Scots-Irish tradition but were, rather, a unique West Highland and Hebridean product, whose initial inspiration came mainly from monumental sculpture in northern England. Tall, freestanding crosses reappeared after nearly four centuries and Islay today is still unusually rich in them. There were at least a dozen, of two types: those devoid of human figures and, better known, the disc-headed crosses displaying the Crucifixion. Especially notable is the unbroken Kilchoman cross, now standing over 2.5m high. It is one of the finest of the group of medieval crosses in the western Highlands and Islands that are dated about 1500, many of the others having been subsequently broken during the Reformation.

Lords and Kings
The four lords of the Isles between 1336 and 1493 were John, Donald, Alexander and another John, each the son of his predecessor. Rì Innse Gall came to be reflected in the Latin designation 'dominus Insularum', though it did not always apply to all of the Hebrides. The title was not the result of a royal creation, but was adopted by the first lord, whose great-grandfather was Donald, the eponymous founder of the Clan

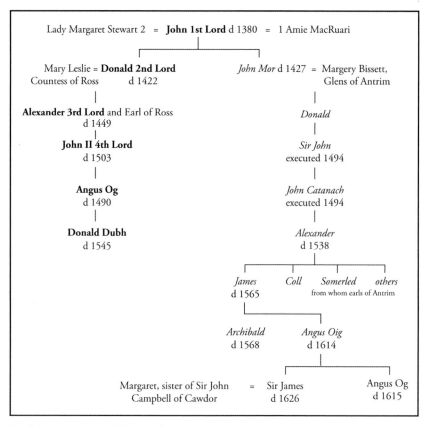

To left: the MacDonald lords of the Isles, their successors; to right: the MacDonalds of Dunyvaig and the Glens of Antrim (Munro and Munro, *Acts of the Lords*).

Donald.[20] In the fourteenth and fifteenth centuries the designations 'de Ile' and 'de Insulis' came into use. The designation 'de Ile' or 'de Yle' was normally reserved for use by the lords of the Isles, their sons who did not succeeed to the lordship and for their daughters. The chief families of the various branches of the Clan Donald designated themselves 'de Insulis' (a form sometimes used by the lords themselves) or else used a name derived from the forenames of their progenitors. The name MacDonald or MacDhomnuill rarely appeared in official documents before about the middle of the sixteenth century, the most notable exception being a Gaelic charter of 1408. Though self-styled lords of the Isles, they were not in fact officially recognised as such until 1476.[21]

The first of the lords of the Isles succeeded near the end of the reign of King Robert I, during which Clan Donald and Clan Ruari had supported Bruce and so prospered, while Clan Dougall, by taking the Balliol side, had lost much of its power in the Hebrides. John was at first hostile to Robert I's west-coast policy but later made agreements with Edward Balliol and David II over MacDougall lands.[22] Relations were often strained but several family marriages indicate that in the middle of the fourteenth century John was establishing links with his former rivals. This first John, a benefactor of the church, referred to by his contemporaries as 'Good John of Isla', made two ambitious and auspicious marriages. His first wife was the sister of the MacRuari chief and when her childless brother died in 1346, John took over his lands.[23] By 1350 he was sailing to the Clyde with three score longships, each of some twenty or more oars, to marry Lady Margaret Stewart. She was daughter of Robert the Steward who became king as Robert II in 1371. The children of this second, royal, marriage displaced those of the first and after Robert II's succession to the throne the lands of the lordship of the Isles and those of Kintyre were made into a jointure for John and his wife.

John's death in the 1380s, however, was the signal for an acrimonious dispute between his widow and his sons over the jointure of Kintyre, a jointure being alien to Gaelic society. The result was a dispute between the lordship and the Crown which lasted for two generations, the Stewart kings intermittently trying to tackle their problems in the north and west. John's first son of his second marriage, Donald, followed him. Harking back to older customs, it was the second son who was Donald's deputy or tanist, John Mòr, progenitor of the section of Clan Donald which became known as the MacDonalds of Dunyvaig and the Glens of Antrim.[24] The MacDonalds' dealings with the Crown included a sequence of confrontations and crises, several pitched battles and, eventually, the long drawn-out forfeiture. Donald is notable for having been granted the only extant Gaelic charter, written on goatskin and now preserved in Edinburgh, and for his efforts in trying to secure the earldom of Ross.[25] In 1411 he fought to uphold his wife's claim to the earldom in the inconclusive battle at Harlaw. James I launched an assault on the Highland problem between 1428 and 1431, but retreated and came to an accommodation with MacDonald power.

It was Donald's heir, Alexander, who was eventually confirmed as earl of Ross in 1437 and while he was often at loggerheads with central authority, he lived to become a mainland magnate as well as island prince. Alexander's acquisition of Ross brought the MacDonald possessions right across Scotland to the Moray Firth. They were now by far the most dominant power in the whole of the Highlands and in terms of area, the greatest landowners in the kingdom.[26] In the minority of James II Alexander held public office as Chief Justice north of the Forth. He and his son John, with their followers,

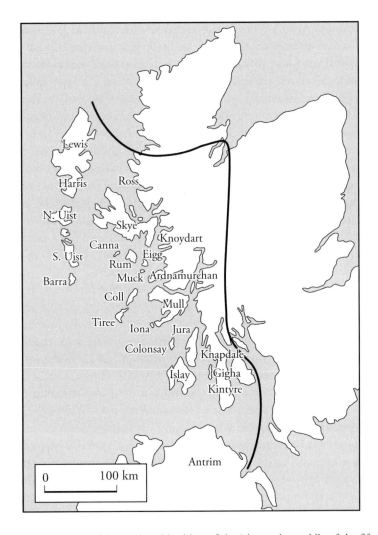

The maximum extent of the sea-based lordship of the Isles in the middle of the fifteenth century, when it included the earldom of Ross (McNeill and Nicholson, *Historical Atlas of Scotland*).

spent more and more time in Ross. With hindsight, the acquisition of the earldom of Ross was perhaps over-ambitious. MacDonald power was over-extended and the preoccupation of the lords of the Isles with establishing authority over this earldom probably contributed to their gradual loss of political influence over Argyll and to deteriorating relations with the Crown during the fifteenth century with the growing power of the Campbells.

The fourth and last lord, John II, was involved in several confrontations with the Crown, going as far as signing the secret Treaty of Westminster-Ardtornish in 1462 with Edward IV of England, agreeing the division of Scotland in the event of a successful English invasion.[27] In 1475 James III condemned John for treason and the earldom of Ross, Kintyre and Knapdale were forfeited, though not the lordship of the Isles. Created a Parliamentary Peer of Scotland in 1476 with the formal title of Lord of the Isles, John II was confirmed in his rule of the lordship, Kintyre being added again to his lands subsequently. But disagreements arose with his illegitimate son Angus over the management of the lordship and the latter's attempts to regain the earlship. A sequence of raids seems finally to have provoked the Crown. In 1493 James IV directly attacked the lordship of the Isles and imposed forfeiture on the lord.[28] John II was deposed as Rì Innse Gall and lost all of his considerable influence and possessions, dying as a Crown pensioner ten years later.[29] In his published collection of Gaelic oral literature collected in the first half of the sixteenth century, the Dean of Lismore summed up the accomplishments of the lords:

Nì h-eibhnas gan Chlainn Domnhaill,	It is no joy without Clan Donald,
nì comhnairt bheith 'ne n-éagmhais;	it is no strength without them;
an chlann dob 'fhearr san gcruinne:	the best race in the round world:
gur dhiobh gach duine céatach.	to them belongs every goodly man.[30]

Aftermath in the long sixteenth century

For most of the fourteenth and fifteenth centuries the MacDonald lordship of the Isles had been relatively a force for peace rather than a destabilising influence, compared to the century which followed. When the lordship collapsed, a long period of turmoil ensued which endured through the sixteenth century into the early-seventeenth century. The forfeit has been considered to have been 'a political mistake for Scotland' because the MacDonald supremacy was not replaced by an equivalent one for many generations.[31] After the final forfeiture in 1493 the next fifty years witnessed many serious rebellions against the Crown and its agents by west coast chiefs, aimed at restoring John's heirs. Finlaggan was abandoned about 1494 and Dunyvaig and Castle Gorm were increasingly used.[32]

Royal minorities in the sixteenth century added to Scotland's internal strife and in Islay from the time of the forfeiture 'there was a bewildering spate of charters, leases, cancellations and regrants of land'.[33] James IV and James V made strenuous efforts to control affairs in the north and west and did not hesitate to play off clan against clan. He journeyed to confront the islesmen in person at least five times after 1493. Of the half

This monumental slab in the Kildalton churchyard dates from the first half of the sixteenth century. Two men in armour wear high pointed bascinets, aventails and knee-length aketons. One carries a sword, symbol of land power at his waist while the other bears one on his right shoulder. Below is a galley or birlinn, with spread sail, symbol of sea power (Royal Commission on the Ancient and Historical Monuments of Scotland).

The MacDonald fortress of Dunyvaig in Lagavulin Bay, from which the seas between the mainland and Ireland could be scanned or crossed.

dozen major risings in the Isles between 1494 and 1545, the fact that the most serious was the last one emphasised the failure, even of James V, to 'daunt' the Isles.

In 1493, King James IV gave charge of Islay to the earl of Argyle's son-in-law, John MacIan of Ardnamurchan, already tenant of Proaig and other lands in Islay. A charter of 1494 extended these lands, and by 1506 MacIan held more than three-quarters of the lay lands of Islay, as well as being bailie [local magistrate] of all Islay although the Rinns of Islay were disputed by the MacLeans of Mull. John MacIan was by now the most powerful chief in the western isles. Church lands occupied about one-fifth of the island and were the responsibility of various orders, including Iona Abbey, the Bishop of Isles, local churches, Oronsay Priory and Derry Monastery (Nerabus). MacIan was given the task of undertaking a valuation of Islay, creating bailie courts to replace Celtic law with feudal law and reforming the church. One of his earliest actions was the valuation of all church and lay lands which resulted in the 1507 list of the 'Fermes of Islay'.[34] This has become known as the 'MacIan Extent' and it continued as a basis for valuation and taxation into the nineteenth century. Between 1514 and 1516 MacIan took measures for the supply and defence of the castle of Dunyvaig in face of a MacDonald insurrection.[35]

When MacIan was killed in 1519, the earl of Argyll became guardian of his sons and the administration of his Islay estates was entrusted to Sir John Campbell of Calder or Cawdor, brother of the 3rd earl of Argyll, and the first Campbell to bear the Cawdor title, by marriage. By 1520 Alexander MacDonald of Dunyvaig and Sir John Campbell of Cawdor had entered into a bond of gossipry, fostering each other's children.[36] Cawdor also made bonds with tenants in Islay.[37] He was forced to give up guardianship in 1528 and Alexander MacIan took over. The new earl of Argyll fell out of favour in 1531, after which James V acquired most of the lay lands in the island, and the Crown rental of 1541 was used to establish feu duties. By 1542 Argyll was given a ten-year lease of Islay. The MacDonalds made one last bid to restore their lordship in the rebellion of 1545 led by Donald Dubh, grandson of the last lord of the Isles. But on his death, with no clear successor, Dunyvaig castle became a direct possession of the Crown but was, however, subsequently regranted to James MacDonald of Dunyvaig.[38] He married the earl of Argyll's sister, became closely allied to the Argyll Campbells and when he died in 1565 had received royal charters for widespread possessions covering almost all the lay lands of Islay, much of Kintyre and extensive holdings on Jura, Colonsay, Gigha and Ardnamurchan. James MacDonald's heirs engaged in quarrels with MacLeans over the Rinns of Islay, although in 1585 Angus married Lachlan McLean's sister. The feuds between the MacDonalds and the MacLeans finally reached their culmination in the Battle of Traigh Gruinart in 1598; the trouncing of the MacLeans is still a folk memory

that comes alive at each retelling, as well as being vividly brought to life
in William Livingston's poem.

Campbell tactics

The downfall of the MacDonalds and the loss of their hegemony left a
vacuum from which the Campbells were to benefit. Royal patronage and
judicious marriage through the fourteenth century had brought them
extensive lands; they were the sheriffs in the new sheriffdom of Argyll.
From 1383 they were also royal lieutenants of part, and eventually all,
of Argyll. By the early-fifteenth century they had developed from local
magnates into national ones. They held that position for centuries, but
also kept their grip on their local power base, indeed strengthening it
as much as possible, understanding that local and national power went
together. Colin Campbell was created earl of Argyll in 1457 and went
on to become Chancellor of Scotland in 1483.[39] The title earl of Argyll
itself is important; unlike the other new and honorific peerage titles of
the fifteenth century, it was a territorial designation like those of the old
provincial earldoms. It probably reflected the Rì Airir Goìdel, one of
Somerled's titles in the twelfth century, which was used until the early-
fourteenth century by his descendants. It has been suggested that when
the Campbells became earls of Argyll, they were claiming a place in the
Gaelic world roughly equivalent to that of Somerled's main descendants,
the MacDonald lords of the Isles.[40]

   The tactics of the Campbell family caused a further confusion of aims;
cadet MacDonald clans and others turned to them to intercede on their
behalf at court.[41] The Campbells found themselves 'colonial governors, torn
between going native and representing the values of "civility"'. They found
themselves trapped in the same set of pressures as the last lord, fluctuating
between their roles as agents of central government and natural spokesmen
for the values of local communities. Stewart government exacerbated rather
than solved the problems of the Isles; every reign between James II and
James VI faced a rebellion in the West.

   Clanship and kinship were supremely important in this tempestuous
period and the internal decline among the MacDonalds is a more satisfactory
explanation of their downfall than theories of Campbell manipulation,
although external influence was undoubtedly a factor.[42] By the middle of
the sixteenth century Campbell leadership and influence were on the way
to filling the vacuum created by the suppression of the lords of the Isles in
1493. This was so at all levels, cultural and intellectual as well as political
and military.[43] Through the sixteenth century the Cawdor Campbells
had built up extensive holdings in the north of Scotland. From the later-

sixteenth century the government of James VI was seeking to impose more political and administrative control on the Highlands, especially after the Union of the Crowns in 1603. The clans were then confronted by the naval and military might of an expansionist British state which could co-ordinate strategy much more effectively against the two Gaelic societies of the Highlands of Scotland and Ireland.[44] The government of James VI and I did not pursue wholesale annexation in the Highlands as in Ireland. Instead, wayward clans had their lands appropriated. The main victims included Clan Donald South and the MacIans of Ardnamurchan. The Statutes of Iona in 1609 were a comprehensive attempt to impose lowland values on Gaeldom.[45] Campbell cohesion was the key to their successful expansion as a clan and it provided a sharp contrast to the internecine quarrels which ruined the southern branch of the MacDonalds.[46] The Campbells continued to encroach and in the early-seventeenth century annexed the southern isles including Islay and only a rump of lordship remained in Crown possession.

The island, however, was devastated during the MacDonald-MacLean feud of the last quarter of the sixteenth century. Dunyvaig was besieged on at least one occasion after 1586, and James VI finally took the castle into royal custody a decade later. Early in 1606 Angus MacDonald was subjected to an act of caution for the maintenance of a royal garrison in the castle for a period of three months. However, direct royal control was considered to be the best solution and, under threat of siege in 1608, Dunyvaig was handed over to the royal lieutenants, Lord Ochiltree and Andrew Knox, Bishop of the Isles. A garrison consisting of a captain and 24 soldiers was housed there.[47]

By the beginning of 1612 Angus MacDonald was in financial difficulties and had to wadset or mortgage his lands in Islay for 6,000 marks to the then Sir John Campbell of Cawdor, though this was later redeemed.[48] Sir Ranald MacDonald, later earl of Antrim, acquired Islay on the death of Angus MacDonald of Dunyvaig in 1614, but he 'had not peaceable possession of it'.[49] 'The Scotch Privy Council . . . turned in search of someone, of power and means sufficient, to reduce the castle and island, and to pay a high rent to the Crown for the possession afterwards. The Thane of Cawdor offered the required rent, and satisfied the Council that he could perform the task of bringing the Islesmen to obedience . . . and set forth on his expedition to win his island kingdom'.[50] In 1614 a Crown charter was conferred on the second Sir John Campbell of Cawdor. The MacDonalds attempted to resist this and there followed much taking and retaking of the castle by various members of the family, especially Sir James MacDonald, Angus' son. In accordance with the terms of the charter issued to Sir John

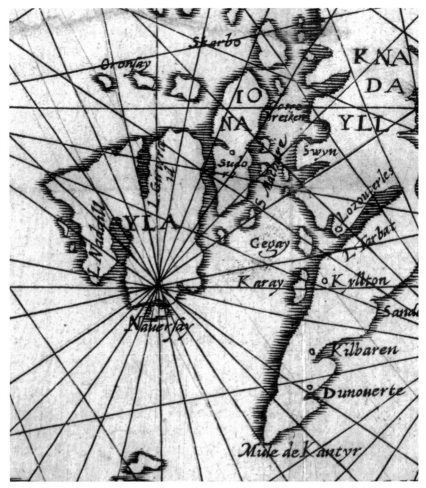

Even before Ortelius' map, the French geographer, Nicolas de Nicolay, produced a rutter or pilot guide for James V's voyage round Scotland about 1540 to quell the lords of the Isles. Not only did it provide the correct orientation of Lochs Indaal and Gruinart, but it was another two centuries before any other cartographer achieved or realised this (de Nicolay, *True Description*).

Campbell of Cawdor in November 1614 Dunyvaig Castle became the principal messuage of the newly erected barony of Islay. In October of that year Coll Ciotach, who then held the castle for Sir James, readily ceded possession of it to the earl of Argyll as a punitive royal expedition under the overall command of Sir John Campbell of Cawdor was planned. In order to avoid a protracted siege an additional force of 200 soldiers and heavy ordnance were shipped from Ireland. The besieging force under Sir Oliver Lambert completed their artillery platform at the end of January

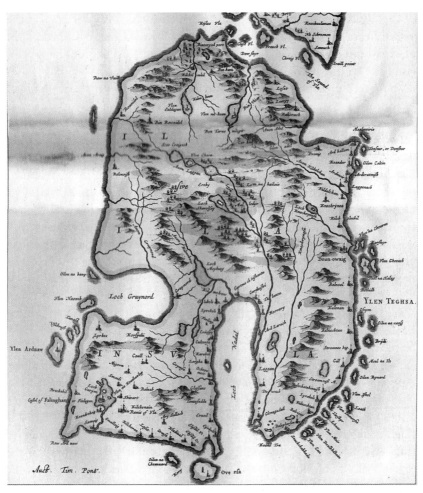

The first detailed map of Islay, compiled by Timothy Pont also in the 1580s, and published in 1654. The orientation of the main sea lochs is still uncorrected in the much later atlas publication. It took the mid 18th century for this detailed map to be superseded by that of Stephen MacDougall. Whilst the representation of the eastern part of the island is recognisable, the Rinns is not only truncated, but includes Finlaggan Castle.

1615 and on February 1 the bombardment of the castle began. Despite its nine-metre thick walls, 'three dayes batterye with the ordnance . . . was powerful to ruyne the whole howse'.[51] Sir John Campbell finally took possession of most of the island in 1615.

The house of Dunyvaig had finally fallen in 1615 to Campbell of Cawdor and over 450 years of MacDonald rule appeared to have ended, although feuding continued sporadically through the seventeenth century. The Campbells of Cawdor were especially important agents of the expansion of Argyll hegemony and the acquisition of Islay at the beginning of the seventeenth century thus continued an established policy of expansion on the west coast, although most of the Cawdor Campbells' lands lay on the opposite side of the country.[52]

Sources for place names comprise the written accounts that included Islay, from the sixteenth-century Boethius, Buchanan and Monroe to the later seventeeth-century Sibbald and Martin. Like the literary accounts, the mapping of the island was recorded by outsiders: 'The people living in the . . . Isles did not use maps [or written accounts] in their everyday lives but relied entirely on their cognitive maps' built up by a wealth of first-hand experience.[53] The earliest map showing the correct alignment of the two great indentations of Lochs Gruinart and Indaal was that of the Frenchman, Nicolas de Nicolay in 1546.[54] That Islay was a prized possession Ortelius had recognised in 1573, referring to it as the greatest and most renowned of the Hebrides, 'fertile for grain and rich in minerals'.[55] Timothy Pont compiled his map during the 1580s, although it is among the less accurate of his maps, since the overall shape of an island with large sea loch indentations had clearly been hard for Pont to establish with precision'.[47] Islay was depicted as a relatively densely settled land. It was the first to show some internal island names.[56]

Maps provide a rich source for mining island names and their changes, especially orthographic ones, although no individual source covered the entire island until MacDougall's mid-eighteenth century map. A rental of 1509, for example, provides around 140 names of landholdings (many of them quarterlands), churches and islands, identifiable as the main names that have survived the suceeding half millennium.[57] By 1614 when the Campbells of Cawdor from the north-east of Scotland were taking over the island, and settling many of their kinsmen therein, some of these landholdings had been subdivided as land use extended outwards and upwards, employing Gaelic, Scots and English for these divisions:[58]

Glenastells	Ochterach and Etrach	by 1722, Upper and Nether
Sannaig	Mor and Beg	
Ballenawchtane	Westir and Eister	by 1722, beg and More
Stenshawes	West and Eat	by 1722, Upper and Nether
Cragabolls	Over and Nether	
Glennagadill	one half; other half	
Dudil	Mor and Low	

Notes and references

[1] Grant, 'Scotland's "Celtic Fringe"', pp. 121–2.

[2] Ibid., p. 119.

[3] T. C. Smout, *A History of the Scottish People*, (London, 1969), p. 47.

[4] W. D. Lamont, 'Old Land Denominations and "Old Extent" in Islay', *Scottish Studies* 1 (1957), 1, pp. 183–203 and 2 (1958), pp. 86–106.

[5] D. H. Caldwell and G. Ewart, 'Finlaggan and the Lordship of the Isles: an Archaeological Approach', *Scottish Historical Review* 72 (1993), p. 160. See also David Caldwell, Islay. *The Land of the Lordship*, (Edinburgh, 2008), *passim*.

[6] Grant, 'Scotland's "Celtic Fringe"' p. 133.

[7] Clan Donald, *Ceannas nan Gàidheal*, p. 12.

[8] See Lamont, 'Old Land Denominations'.

[9] T. M. Devine, *Clanship to Crofters' War*, (Manchester, 1994), p. 4.

[10] Caldwell and Ewart, 'Finlaggan', p. 164.

[11] After the dissolution of the Lordship, they served the chiefs of Clanranald in South Uist. See D. S. Thomson, *The Companion to Gaelic Scotland*, (Oxford, 1983).

[12] J. W. M. Bannerman, *The Beatons*, (Edinburgh, 1986).

[13] J. W. M. Bannerman, 'The Lordship of the Isles', in J. M. Brown, (ed.), *Scottish Society in the Fifteenth Century*, (London, 1977), p. 228.

[14] See A. Macniven, 'The Norse in Islay', unpublished doctoral thesis, University of Edinburgh, 2006.

[15] RCAHMS, *Argyll Inventory*, 5, p. 35.

[16] *Idem*; Munro and Munro, *Acts of the Lords*, p. xxiv.

[17] J. W. M. Bannerman, 'Lordship of the Isles', p. 238.

[18] RCAHMS, *Argyll Inventory*, 5, p. 36.

[19] *Ibid*.

[20] Grant, 'Scotland's "Celtic Fringe"', p. 133.

[21] RCAHMS, *Argyll Inventory*, 5, p. 36.

[22] Grant, 'Scotland's "Celtic Fringe"', p. 126.

[23] *Idem*.

[24] Munro and Munro, *Acts of the Lords*, p. 293.

[25] W. D. Lamont, 'The Islay Charter of 1408', *Proceedings of the Royal Irish Academy*, 1960C, pp. 163–87.

[26] Grant, 'Scotland's "Celtic Fringe"', p. 127.

[27] Thomson, *Companion*, pp. 156–7.

[28] Grant, 'Scotland's "Celtic Fringe"', p. 129.

[29] Bannerman, 'Lordship of the Isles', p. 213.

[30] From 'Giolla Colum mac an Ollaimh', in the *Book of the Dean of Lismore*, quoted in Osborne, B. D. and Armstrong, R., *Scottish Dates*, p. 42. Gaelic orthography is variable.

[31] Lamont, *Sculptured Stones*, pp. 206–7.

[32] Caldwell and Ewart, 'Finlaggan', p. 165.

[33]   W. D. Lamont, *The Early History of Islay*, (Glasgow, 1966), p. 30.

[34]   *Ibid.*, p. 32.

[35]   RCAHMS, *Argyll Inventory*, 5, p. 274 .

[36]   E. J. Cowan, 'Clanship, Kinship and Campbell acquisition of Islay', *Scottish Historical Review* 58 (1979), p. 135.

[37]   *Ibid.*, p. 156.

[38]   RCAHMS, *Argyll Inventory*, 5, p. 274.

[39]   Grant, 'Scotland's "Celtic Fringe"', p. 121.

[40]   *Ibid.*, p. 122.

[41]   M. Lynch, *Scotland: A New History*, (London, 1991), p. 168.

[42]   E. J. Cowan, 'Clanship', p. 157.

[43]   J. Dawson, 'The Fifth Earl of Argyle', Gaelic Lordship and Political Power in Sixteenth century Scotland', *Scottish Historical Review* 67 (1988), p. 20.

[44]   Devine, *Clanship*, p. 12.

[45]   *Ibid.*, p. 13.

[46]   Dawson, 'The Fifth Earl of Argyle', pp. 11–12 .

[47]   RCAHMS, *Argyll Inventory*, 5, p. 274.

[48]   Lamont, *Early History*, p. 49.

[49]   Innes, *Thanes of of Cawdor*, p. 228.

[50]   Bannerman, 'Lordship of the Isles, p. 228.

[51]   RCAHMS, *Argyll Inventory*, 5, p. 274.

[52]   Dawson, 'The Fifth Earl of Argyle', pp. 12–13.

[53]   Macleod, F. (ed.), *Togail Tir. Marking Time. The Map of the Western Isles* (Stornoway, 1989), Preface.

[54]   Nicolas de Nicolay, *True and Exact Hydrographic Description of the Maritim [sic] Coasts of Scotland and the Orkney and Hebridean Islands*, (Paris, 1583).

[55]   Abraham Ortelius, *Scotiae Tabula in Theatrum Orbis Terrarum*, (Antwerp, 1573).

[56]   Timothy Pont, *Ila Insula* in J. Blaeu's *Atlas Novus*, (Amsterdam, 1654)..

[57]   MacDougall, Stephen. A few extant Ms. plans are in the Islay Estate Papers. The reduced smaller-scale *Map of Islay*, 1749, lithographed in 1848, is printed in *Book of Islay*, pp. 552–3; *A Map of Taynish . . . in Argyll*, 1747. The British Library Map Room, XLIX 28; *A Map of the Island of Giga*, 1747 loc. cit., XLIX 37 1.

[58]   Rentals, *Book of Islay*, Smith.

CHAPTER 5

The Cawdor Campbells in Islay

In the hundred or so years after 1615 Islay and other isles were at last being integrated into the life of Scotland as a whole. Motivated partly by exaggerated notions of the wealth of the Western Isles and partly by a desire to bring them effectively under the power of the Crown, James VI saw the problem from a number of different viewpoints.[1] When compared to other parts of the Hebrides, Islay may well have seemed of 'fabulous fertility' even in the seventeenth century.[2] As an economic investment, viewed from Edinburgh or the Moray Firth, it probably seemed much less desirable. To begin with, in any case, its possession was mainly for political rather than economic ends.

In the early-seventeenth century, the first Sir John Campbell of Calder or Cawdor, held 'large and still increasing' lands in Argyll.[3] With subsequent additions, the Cawdor Campbells came to own nearly all of Islay.[4] The main exception comprised the old Beaton lands centred on Ballinaby, bought in 1619 by Lord Lorne, afterwards Marquis of Argyll. In Lamont's view 'if Islay had to go to a Campbell, the Calder family was, on a short term view, the worst possible choice. Sir John was utterly reckless in accumulating land in widely separate parts of the country and it was impossible, quite apart from the financial difficulties in which he had become involved, to rule all these properties efficiently'.[5] The present Cawdor family's view is that 'Cawdor's new acquisition proved to be a millstone which all but drowned him in debt'.[6]

After Sir John's impecunious start in a devastated Islay, there were few times when any of the Cawdor lairds had long periods of effective management in Islay. They were frequently handicapped by family, as well as, financial difficulties. Although there were only six lairds in 112 years, there were long periods when lairds were minors and the lands were then managed or neglected by a succession of legal tutors, commissioners and administrators. Their residence on the island was also often sporadic. Only Sir Hugh, who came of age in 1660 and resigned in 1689, had a long-lasting adult lairdship; it was during that period that some changes were introduced that can still be seen. On a longer view, however, Lamont

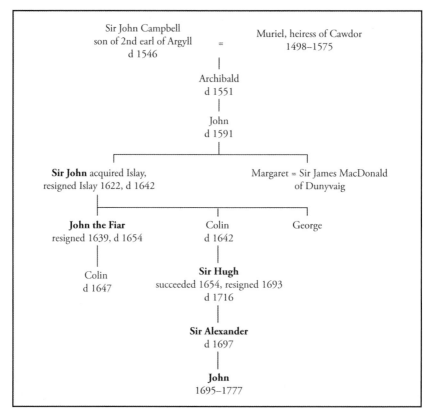

Outline genealogy of the Campbell of Cawdor lairds in Islay (Innes, *Thanes of Cawdor*).

argued that the grant of Islay to the Campbells of Cawdor was fortunate and 'was probably even an event of major importance in its economic history'.[7] This assessment was based on the belief that the more advanced farming methods around the Moray Firth may have proved useful examples for the Argyll lands. Despite their difficulties, the new proprietors became pioneers in the development of modern Islay and, among other innovations, Lamont mentioned the mine explorations of 1619 and the droves of black cattle through Jura to the mainland and England.

One deterrent was also the seventeenth-century background of little change in the agrarian economy of Scotland. With a restricted market for agricultural products, apart from cattle, at both local and national levels in the first half of the century, much of Scotland experienced low agricultural yields and high fixed rents, the latter paid mainly in grain. Records suggest that there were between fifteen and twenty seasons of grain failure in eastern Scotland between 1600 and 1660 when the price of grain was exceptionally high.[8] More often there were complaints of gluts or low prices. Stock-raising was more important in the west however, and during the century, farming for external sales increased at the expense of subsistence farming, particularly in the cattle trade. The Union of the Crowns in 1603 led to a growth in droving for the London market such that the black cattle sometimes accounted for more than half the total value of Scottish exports to England, in some years reaching tens of thousands of head.[9]

The early difficulties in undertaking agricultural changes on Islay in the first part of the seventeenth century are thus understandable. Capital accumulation was hard and results were limited. Most landowners were also undermined by their increasing state of personal indebtedness.[10] The Cawdor Campbells had to meet the expenses of winning and keeping the island, fighting Civil War campaigns, paying Crown and feu duties, appearing annually at the Privy Council in Edinburgh, as well as the administrative costs and family expenses included in living in style, with other establishments in London, Cawdor and Muckairn in Argyll. There was a growing dependence on lowland merchants for bonded loans and a more commercial approach to the management of lands.[11] Rentals in kind were gradually being converted to a cash value. Chiefs and their gentry had to extract more income from their lands and their wadsetting or mortgaging increased.[12]

Although Innes went so far as to aver that 'With the acquisition of Isla began the misfortunes of the family', Sir John's difficulties were not limited to the island, nor was he unusual for the times.[13] Numerous wadsets, or mortgages, also covered almost every portion of his northern estates. Creditors of every degree were clamouring for payment, the letters of the Edinburgh doer or agent 'mostly taken up with the pressing demands for money to satisfy them'.[14] The embarrassments on Islay were no less, as is evident in a letter to Sir John Campbell from his agent, James Mowatt, in March 1618, calling attention to the unpaid Crown Rents for Islay.[15] By that time 'The rebels hes spoilled mightilie the land that the poore tennents is almost undone'.[16] Some time between 1620 and 1622, a meeting of various of Sir John Campbell's friends made several suggestions to help resolve some of his debts; by 1623 these had reached the scale of a proposal to sell Islay or Muckairn.[17] The 'erll of Mar and the Clandonald' had expressed interest and several years later in 1627 there was renewed interest from the earl of Antrim.[18] But Islay remained in Cawdor hands.

Minorities and tutorships
The hands, however were different ones. Islay was given to the son of Sir John Campbell on the occasion of his marriage in 1622. Subsequently

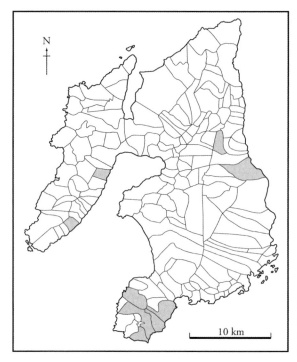

Holdings with two or more tenants named in the rental of 1633 are indicated here (Cawdor Papers).

By 1644 the numbers of holdings with two or more tenants had increased, and the numbers in these multiple tenancies had also tended to increase (Cawdor Papers).

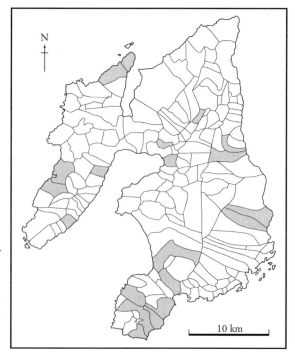

known as John the Fiar, he had been a heretic from his youth and in 1624 and 1625 welcomed an Irish Franciscan missionary, Patrick Hegarty from Louvain.[19] Two of Cawdor's sons and fifty other relatives were among over 500 islanders converted or baptised by Father Hegarty. There are some signs that John the Fiar also intended to take a more direct interest in Islay's other activities. Indications of this are to be found in the rentals and other documents relating to Islay that survive among the Cawdor records. 'With certain exceptions' it has been suggested that there is a general lack of material concerning the agrarian history of Scotland before 1760.[20] The Cawdor papers certainly form one of these exceptions and contribute to what has been referred to as a 'fine run of rentals' for Islay in the sixteenth and seventeenth centuries.[21]

Rentals for Islay survive in the Cawdor archives from 1626, although it is not until 1633 that they show in some detail the character of Islay's landholdings and agriculture. By then these holdings were probably held on long leases or tacks by men who were frequently Campbell kinsmen of the laird. Sir John's son explained that when Islay was acquired, it was 'not weel plenished with civile people' and his father had now 'peopled the said ylland with a nomber of his awne freindis'.[22] These tacksmen held the large grazing areas in the quartzitic hills of the north-east of the island as at Killinallan, in the south-east at Proaig, and in the western Rinns at Ardnave. A handful of holdings were leased as multiple tenancies, mainly concentrated in the Oa peninsula, each with up to four or five names responsible for paying the rent. On both tacks and joint farms there may also have been subtenants and possibly other families not responsible for any share of the rent, although they do not appear in the rentals. Cattle formed the major portion of the rental payments in kind; droves of cattle were collected and despatched annually to the south from Islay and Muckairn.[23]

Whatever the precise character of the domestic buildings such as the 'weill furnished duelling place at Mulindrie' described in 1586 by Dean Monroe, the incoming lairds of the early-seventeenth century seem to have brought with them a different attitude towards the style and setting of landowners' residences.[24] John the Fiar declared his intention of replacing Dunyvaig, the only 'sure place of residence' available to his father on acquiring Islay in 1614. Dunyvaig had remained a symbolic focus for local disaffection; this can be measured by the amount of destructive treatment it continued to receive, particularly during the first half of the seventeenth century. What survived the devastating siege of February 1615 and later attacks is now but a shattered fragment of the one-time fortified residence of the MacDonalds of Dunyvaig. April 1615 also saw the construction of a castle on the island in Loch Gorm and one at Dùn Athad near the Mull of Oa.

After another unsuccessful assault on Dunyvaig by a group of local rebels in 1630 the Privy Council agreed in the following year to John Campbell's petition to 'demloisce and cast downe the said hous to the ground, so as it serve not theirefter for a beild, resett, or starting holl to the rebellis of the Ylles', a recommendation that King James VI had previously made to the Fiar's father, Sir John.[25] In 1631 the Fiar talked of building 'a more commodious hous . . . in a more proper pairt of the yle'. The proposal remained unexecuted, and the Cawdors continued to use their Kilchoman residence until the long-cherished proposal to replace Dunyvaig as a dwelling was finally effected by Hugh Campbell in 1677.

John the Fiar had one son, Colin, and two daughters.[26] In 1639 John was pronounced insane and the island's management nominally passed to Colin, at that time a minor. The Fiar's brother, Colin Campbell of Kilchoman, became tutor in charge of the island, but he died in 1642 and another brother, George, took over. Both Colin and George, according to Innes, 'seem to have looked to Islay or their possessions in the far west, as their securest place of dwelling during the troubles of the civil war'.[27] Meanwhile the family continued to have its own troubles. The heir, Colin, died in 1647 whilst a student at Glasgow University and the Fiar himself died in 1654. Islay passed then to Hugh Campbell, son of Colin Campbell of Kilchoman, and again a minor. During these minorities and tutorships, financial difficulties were almost inevitable.

The rental for 1644 shows that the proportion of single tacksmen had declined to less than three-fifths and there was a consequent increase in the joint tenancies, and in their numbers of tenants.[28] The Oa again predominated but more multiple tenancies appeared in Kilchoman parish than in 1633. The real significance of these shifts is difficult to determine. Tacksmen as a group tended to inhibit agricultural change and their decline was often a desirable feature of Highland improvement. In mid-seventeenth century Islay many of the Campbell tacksmen had been 'planted' on Islay and should have brought to it their experience of farming in the better lands of the north-east of Scotland. More obvious as an indication of financial difficulty is the low rental which the Campbell family obtained from their lands in Islay and Muckairn. Innes averred that by the middle of the seventeenth century 'the troubles of the time affected the Highland and Island territories, even more than the rest of Scotland'.[29] Whereas the usual rent previously derived by Cawdor each year from Islay and Muckairn was about £20,000 to £22,000, in 1651 only one-tenth was collected, followed by one-third in 1652.

Due to Hugh Campbell's minority, his uncle George continued to act
as tutor, to be followed by another uncle, James of Kilbrandan. Hugh was
also a student of the University of Glasgow and as Innes put it;

> In this generation we arrive, as it were, by one step from a state of society
> and feeling which we cannot rightly appreciate, so different does it seem
> from ours; and find ourselves among the habits, manners, feelings and
> motives – even the language of our own time. To this effect the great
> Civil War serves as the line of demarcation between the old world and
> the new.[30]

Hugh came of age and was knighted in the Restoration year of 1660 and
two years later married Lady Henrietta Stewart, sister of the 3rd earl of
Moray. He served in several Parliaments as Member for the shire of Nairn
and lived a parliamentarian's life in Edinburgh during part of the year,
as well as embarking on major building work at Cawdor Castle. But Sir
Hugh also took an active interest in country occupations. In 1677, for
example, he set down instructions concerning a visit to Islay.[31] He was
concerned with stock and other estate affairs and his sporting interests
were apparent in his instructions concerning deer, rabbits and blackcock.
It was this visit that led to the construction of a new house at Lag Buidhe,
'a beautiful stretch of velvety sward at the head of Lochindaal, the first
portion of what is now called Islay House'.[32] Sir Hugh ordered that lime,
timber and all materials were to be got on the spot, but he proposed to
take skilled masons to the island.

After the 1660 Restoration the Scots became more active in escaping
agricultural stagnation. Acts of the Scottish Parliament to encourage better
husbandry were numerous after 1660, culminating in the enabling act of
1695 which made it relatively easy for individual landowners to divide
commons and to sort out land lying in runrig for the purpose of enclosure.
In the last decade of the century too, the first published Scottish tracts
on the improvement of farming methods appeared. Yet the fundamental
changes in agriculture that might have taken advantage of this permissive
legislation and technical advice were in fact delayed for many years, due
to successive gluts and famines.

Sir Hugh Campbell and his son, Alexander, were among the few
seventeenth-century landlords in the Western Isles who took a keen interest
in the general improvement of their island properties and were prepared
to invest heavily in it themselves, if necessary.[33] The later Cawdors were
also interested in the development of salt pans at Ardlarach and in lead
mining, bringing miners in from England.[34] The 'once troublesome island'

The earliest part of Islay House, to the left of centre, was started by imported masons around 1677 for Sir Hugh Campbell of Cawdor. 'Great' Daniel Campbell of Shawfield added the flanking wings with crow-stepped gables. The western tower, here hidden, belongs to Daniel the Younger's time, along with the eastern stair-tower, itself later replaced. In the 1840s Walter Frederick Campbell asked William Playfair to design 'offices' for Islay House.[35] This Victorian addition was later partially remodelled and screened by a mock-Georgian wing designed by Detmar Blow (MacNeill, *New Guide*).

gradually became less of a burden after Sir Hugh sent the 'tough and implacable' Sir Duncan Campbell of Ardnamurchan as his agent to sort things out and send 'huge droves of oxen, shod with horse-shoes' annually to the Falkirk Tryst.[36] In 1677 Sir Hugh had listed debts since 'I purpose to tak all the readiest wayes to clear my affairis. I find my selff infirm' and he wanted to arrange his succession.[37] There were further negotiations about the lead mines in Islay at the same time. The main contribution made to the landscape of today by Sir Hugh and his successor is in Islay House. On marriage in 1689 his eldest son, Alexander, took over the estates, although, despite his infirmities, Sir Hugh survived until 1716.

Further difficulties
In the mid 1690s, a hearth tax of fourteen shillings to raise monies for the Scottish armies, was levied on each household. In Islay in 1694 over three-quarters of the households had only one hearth, but 'mansions' such as those at Ballnaby, Kilchoman, Robolls and Smaull, each had five or six hearths.[38] Probably the most important development in Islay in the time of Sir Alexander Campbell was the gradual evolution of the 'town' of Killarow at the head of Loch Indaal into the administrative and commercial centre of the island.[39] In 1693 an Act of the Scottish Parliament conferred the right to hold free fairs there twice annually, for two days each in July and

in August, and a general weekly market on Thursdays. The same year, Sir Alexander became a member of the Scottish Parliament for Nairnshire, taking the place of his infirm father. In 1689 he had married Elizabeth, only daughter of Sir John Lort and co-heir with her brother of Stackpole Court in Pembrokeshire. They spent most of their time in London and Wales and left the Nairnshire and Argyllshire properties in the hands of agents. Very little is known of Sir Alexander's period in Islay except that financial difficulties continued and were not solved by raised rents, over which there was much complaint. When he died in 1697, his heir and second son, John, was only two years of age, and the estate was probably run by John's uncle, Archibald Campbell of Clunes and of Kilchoman. Between 1697 and 1716 when John came of age, matters deteriorated still further, with weather crises and famines frequent in the island and on the mainland. There were still, however, a few improvements in Islay during this period. By 1722 it was possible to say that 'Killchomman is a choice large good possession, having many parks and enclosures in it . . . a large malt kilne and change house and a good corne mylne upon it and many other improvements'.[40]

The Anderson Papers in the National Library of Scotland include many letters concerning the management of the Islay estate carried out for the later Cawdor Campbells by James Anderson, W.S., his son Patrick and son-in-law John Allan, sometimes referred to as the bailie of Islay.[41] By the second decade of the eighteenth century, much of the correspondence concerned the difficulties of rental arrears. In 1714–15 Patrick Anderson was writing to his father that as Mr Campbell had 'lodged the sole power in your hands it will make them repent they have been so backward and obstinat and I hope it will cause them pay their rents and arrears better'. In February 1715 James Anderson reported that Mr Campbell was 'mightily displeased at their backwardness' in delivering rents, but by May 1716 he was telling his son 'I approve of what you have done in the Sett and hope you have finished it to contentment. When that is done I hope money will be got in & a good Drove sent out'. By the following month he was even more approving. 'Considering the backwardness of people and the artful ways of the Chamberlains I think strange you have gott so much done & am persuaded if you had not been there I had gott nothing'. He next made further mention of weak tenants, the loss of income from the 1714 rent and the 1715 one only partly lifted. Patrick wrote to his father 'I'll take care rent for 1714 be made up by the Drove & for 1715. You won't lose'.

Despite this optimism, it is clear that when John Campbell succeeded in 1716 it was to a heavily-burdened property. The Islay rent was then supposed to raise £15,978 11s. Scots (about £1,332 Sterling). But arrears preceding 1714 had amounted to £4,875 18s. 8d. Scots, (£406.35) and those that accrued between 1714 and 1720 were £5,519 15s. 8d. Scots (£460) making a total of £10,395 14s. 4d. (£866.35). The Andersons' difficulties continued; in July 1716, in the aftermath of the Jacobite rebellion, Patrick Anderson was writing to his father:

> Yesterday the Act of Parliament for the better securing the peace of the Highlands was sent here by the Sheriff and published which has perfectly enraged the people here who would as soon part with their wives and children as with their arms but I hope it will be a means of humbling them'.

He then bemoaned 'weather cold and wett and I'm perfectly starved for want of Tea.

By December of that year John Allan was reporting to Patrick Anderson that he had 'sett Killerow and Kilhoman paroches; the crops had been gathered'. The year 1717, however, was to prove poor. There were many troubles with tacksmen and with the traik or cattle disease: 1717 became 'the worse paid rent that has been in Islay these 100 years'. Patrick Anderson described the dismal conditions in May 1717, when he wrote to his father 'these that were rich and had great flocks having lost more than the half and the small tenants are next to beggary'. Tenants had fed their meal to cattle that subsequently died and had no seed left to sow. Nor did they have any milk as they had sold their dairy cows to buy 'meall in order to preserve their families from starving. Of the main farmers or tacksmen, 'the Traik fell heaviest upon Archie and Lauchlane the latter, who had absolutely the best and the greatest stock in Isla, having lost both what he had in Ardneave and Kentra'. Anderson thought his father would scarcely believe him when he wrote that 'I cannot gett so much butterr and milk in this place as serves my tea and the muttons are not worth the eating and it's with difficulty we can gett as much bread as serves us. I would realy thought it impossible Isla could have been brought to such a low pass'.

Further lamentations included the observation of a higher than usual death rate which he attributed to the 'stench of the dead carcasses which the fields are overspread with'. After discussing how many of the tenants had left their lands altogether, Patrick tried to forecast that even when he did achieve a very difficult sett, the loss might be 'upwards of £6,000 sterling'. In a reply dated 20 June 1717, his father showed suitable distress at the state of Islay and her people; more practically he advised Patrick to send a boat to Ireland for wheat or bread. Two years later, things were not much better. There was 'not one cow out of Isla . . . not 30 were droveable . . . there is no money in this countrey just now'. In July 1722 the same phrase was being reiterated, though an addendum said 'the only fonds they have is Cattle which do not make money till the latter end of the next month that the trist holds at Falkirk'. There were complaints on Islay at that time of tenants having to pay raised rents, with the alternative of being removed.

Apart from these local difficulties the writing was on the wall elsewhere for young John Campbell. He was apparently in financial embarrassment outside Islay, for it was probably James Anderson who wrote to him in 1720 suggesting the sale of Muckairn to 'clear this Woman' – a reference to another subject.[42] This advice was probably not taken much to heart and in the summer of 1720 John Campbell was again being admonished by James Anderson, but the young laird was heedless; next he was writing to Anderson that he had a 'most pressing & unforeseen occasion to pay £300 ster: into the Exchequer tomorrow morning by eight a clock; I earnestly desire you if . . . possible to let me have it'.

Negotiations with the more experienced Shawfield

On 8 December 1721, John Campbell of Cawdor's doer again wrote a memorial for his consideration in which he talked of pressing debts, including a particularly large one to 'Mr Brodie', and made further suggestions about raising loans or selling off lands in Argyll (but not in Islay) and in the North of Scotland.[43] The memorial was clearly designed, also, to preserve the *amour-propre* of a difficult man. 'Nor can a sale be anyways dishonourable to him, being payment of the debts contracted by Sir Hugh and Sir Alexander . . . The sooner Mr Campbell Enters upon measures for settling matters with his Creditors, it's the better'.

By 1723 Daniel Campbell of Shawfield had acquired a wadset of Islay for £6,000 and in 1726 he purchased the right of reversion for a further £6,000.[44] These financial transactions were neither so prosaic nor straightforward as they appear at first sight. In November 1722, John Campbell had entered into some form of financial negotiation with Daniel Campbell of Shawfield, from whom he expected to receive 'the £1,500 which your obliging care has furnished me with. You may be perfectly easy about the people from Islay and Jura. Having gone so far with you, I shall, you may be assured, think myself bound in honour not to make any bargain . . . till you and I meet . . . Jura is the door to Islay and [I] shall reserve it accordingly'.[45]

A further letter from Cawdor to Shawfield on 7 March 1723, took the proposition further, with a postscript admitting that 'for one who knows so little of busyness as I it is better to receive than to make proposals, but I do assure you, Sir, that upon equall terms I had rather let it to you than to any other'. It is fascinating to conjecture a reconstruction of what may have happened between March 7 and April 9 in 1723. On the latter date, three advocates in Edinburgh wrote to John Campbell, noting his letters of March 26 and 29 to Mr Archibald Campbell W.S., which had asked him to raise from the bank, or through wadsets, 'The sum of £1,800 sterling to pay Shawfield punctually by the 5th May next and advising that you have received his proposals for a Leas of Isla'.[46] The advocates emphasised that there seemed no chance of raising a loan from the banks in Edinburgh unless the estate was clear of all debts. They also offered to act for Campbell in regard to the Shawfield lease. To gain time they suggested that Campbell of Cawdor should cover himself in the short term by raising the £1,800 on his own credit in London. In three months or so other arrangements could be made to pay this money back. The advocates strongly encouraged Cawdor to lease Islay only for one year at a time until a more stable solution to his affairs could be found. Unfortunately Campbell's actions seem to have ignored or overtaken such advice. He advised them on April 20 that he had concluded a bargain with Shawfield for a lease of his Islay lands for 21 years at £500 yearly, in return for Shawfield's advancement of the increased figure of £6,000, Shawfield taking interest 'out of the yearly duty'.

On April 30, after the advocates had indeed tried to raise some money by wadsetting lands elsewhere, somewhat miffed about not being consulted, they worded two very strong paragraphs to the hapless young man:

> You are certainly better acquainted with the gros of your affairs . . . than we can be presumed to be, and therefore however disadvantagious this bargain . . . may appear to us, We must submitt to what you have been pleased to determine in your own affairs. This far only we expect that before you finish the agreement in writing, which hitherto you say is only verball, you'll please to send to us a further particular of the articles, such as Shawfields terme of entry to the Estate, terme of payt of the duty and when interest is to commence upon the £6,000, when it is to be repaid him . . . in parcells or all at one terme, and with any other articles and powers in favour of Shawfield.
>
> It would likewise tend to the management of your affairs with greater advantage That we were apprys'd of the time when the money to be advanced by Shawfield, was to be paid, and to what use you design it should be applyed.[47]

It was, however, already too late to influence events; added to this letter was a postscript indicating that they had now learned that an agreement in writing had been completed with Shawfield, 'so we can say no further to it, but only desire you'd send us the original agreet. or a literal copie of it'. Further advice from Mr Archibald Campbell W.S. was contained in a letter from Edinburgh on 15 June 1723, in which Cawdor was told that his commissioners thought that the articles of agreement 'are most disadvantagious and destructive, and that you have been so greatly impos'd upon'. They suggested that he make a soft approach to Shawfield to try to reverse the process of law, otherwise Campbell of Shawfield could easily and rapidly reimburse his outlay.

So it appears that without recourse to his lawyers at all, young John Campbell of Cawdor, desperate for ready cash and, unable to raise any in London, must have met Daniel Campbell of Shawfield there. With the advantage of age and certainly with more business experience, the older Campbell managed a satisfactory business deal for himself. A wadset of Islay from John Campbell to Shawfield dated 3 August and 7 October, 1723, mentioned an 'agreement entered into betwixt the said John and Daniel Campbells of the date at London the Twenty second day of Aprile last' in which Daniel Campbell had advanced and paid John Campbell £6,000 (and £500 per annum); and John Campbell of Cawdor bound himself to repay the said sum, with interest. For Shawfield's security he agreed to deliver a wadset to all his lands for twenty one years or longer until the £6,000 was repaid.[48] Shawfield was also granted the rights to redeem other wadsets granted in the past on Cawdor property in Islay and Jura.

Three years later the Islay arrangement had changed in character from wadset to outright sale. The terms were clear and wholly to the advantage of Daniel Campbell of Shawfield:

> The disposition follows on a contract of wadsett, dated 3rd August and
> 7th October 1723, whereby the said John sold for £6,000, with power of
> redemption, all and whole of his lands and estate, "lying within the islands
> of Islay . . . as in the 1614 charter, with the addition of Knockransaill,
> Ardaright, Ardalisyn, and Ardagarie and Jura." The said Daniel became
> bound to pay £6,000, over and above the previous £6,000, as the price
> of the right of reversion of the said lands, and John thereby renounced
> the right of redemption and the feu-duty of £200.[49]

John Campbell retained his Cawdor and Pembroke lands and went on to enjoy a full parliamentary career before dying in 1777 at Bath.[50] Almost the whole of Islay and part of Jura had been acquired by Daniel Campbell for not much more than £12,000.[51]

Selling the island may have been the best thing that the hapless
or 'Joyless' John could have done at this time for Islay.[52] The Cawdor
Campbells had owned the island during a period when even the most
competent landlord would have found it difficult to make Islay prosper.
The Campbells of Shawfield were very different and, in Lamont's words,
'There is a sense in which the history of Islay as we know it today
begins with the purchase of the island by the Campbells of Shawfield in
1726'.[53]

Notes and references

[1]   F. J. Shaw, *The Northern and Western Islands of Scotland: their Economy and Society in the
      Seventeenth Century*, (Edinburgh, 1980), p. 4.

[2]   Innes, *Thanes of Cawdor*, p. 226.

[3]   *Ibid.*, p. xxiii.

[4]   Smith, *Book of Islay*, pp. 353ff and p. 380; Lamont, *Early History*, p. 60.

[5]   Lamont, *Early History*, p. 60.

[6]   *Cawdor Castle Guide*, (Cawdor, n.d.), p. 27.

[7]   Lamont, *Early History*, p. 65.

[8]   T. C. Smout and A. Fenton, 'Scottish Agriculture before the Improvers — an Exploration',
      Agricultural History Review 13 (1965), pp. 75–93.

[9]   Devine, *Clanship*, p. 15.

[10] Shaw, *Northern and Western Islands*, p. 43.

[11] Devine, *Clanship*, p. 15.

[12] Shaw, *Northern and Western Islands*, p. 43.

[13] Innes, *Thanes of Cawdor*, p. xxvii; F. J. Shaw, 'Landownership in the Western Isles in the
      Seventeenth Century', *Scottish Historical Review* 56 (1977), p. 45.

[14] *Ibid.*, p. 253.

[15] Innes, *Thanes of of Cawdor*, p. 245.

[16] Smith, *Book of Islay*, p. 343.

[17] *Ibid.*, p. 370.

[18] *Ibid.*, p. 378.

[19] C. Giblin (ed.), *Irish Franciscan Mission to Scotland 1619–1646*, (Dublin, 1964), p. 79.

[20] G. Donaldson, 'Sources for Scottish Agrarian History before the Eighteenth Century',
      Agricultural History Review 8 (1960), p. 87.

[21] R. Dodgshon, 'Mediaeval Settlement and Colonisation', in M. L. Parry and T. R. Slater
      (eds.), *The Making of the Scottish Countryside* (London, 1980), p. 61.

[22] Innes, *Thanes of Cawdor*, pp. 273-4.

[23] *Ibid.*, p. 278.

[24] RCAHMS, *Argyll Inventory* 5, p. 38.

[25] *Ibid.*, p. 274.

[26] J. Foster, *Members of Parliament, Scotland, including the Minor Barons, the Commissioners for
      the Shires, and the Commissioners for the Burghs, 1357–1882, on the basis of the Parliamentary*

Return 1880, with genealogical and biographical notices, (London, 1882), p. 53.

27 Innes, *Thanes of Cawdor*, p. xxxi.

28 Cawdor Papers, Bundle 655.

29 Innes, *Thanes of Cawdor*, p. 303.

30 *Ibid.*, p. xxxii.

31 *Ibid.*, p. xxxiii and p. 334.

32 MacNeill, *New Guide*, p. 67.

33 Shaw, *Northern and Western Islands*, pp. 160–1.

34 *Idem.*

35 Detailed architectural drawings, including designs of monograms intertwining his initials with those of his second wife, Catherine I. Coles, are in the Library of the University of Edinburgh.

36 *Cawdor Castle Guide*, p. 28.

37 Innes, *Thanes of Cawdor*, p. 338.

38 NRS, E 69/3/1, Heath Tax.

39 Lamont, *Early History*, p. 67.

40 Smith, *Book of Islay*, p. 541.

41 James Anderson Papers, NLS. The papers referring to Islay are catalogued under Advocates MSS. 29.1.2.

42 Ibid.

43 Cawdor Papers, Bundle 654.

44 Lamont, *Early History*, p. 68.

45 Smith, *Book of Islay*, pp. 424-26.

46 Cawdor Papers, Bundle 657.

47 Idem.

48 Cawdor Papers, Bundle 654.

49 Smith, *Book of Islay*, p. 429.

50 Burke's *Peerage, Baronetage and Knightage,* (London, 1967), p. 476.

51 This excluded Sunderland and Ballinaby farms. See Macdonald, *General View*, p. 615.

52 *Cawdor Castle Guide*, p. 28.

53 Lamont, *Early History*, Preface.

Shawfield House, Trongate, in Glasgow, first commission in 1711 for Daniel Campbell's nephew, Colen Campbell (Mitchell Library, City of Glasgow).

Woodhall, also showing Colen Campbell's influence, in an early-twentieth century photograph (University of Glasgow Archives).

CHAPTER 6

Hints of change: the first Shawfield Campbell

When Daniel Campbell of Shawfield came to Islay in the third decade of the eighteenth century, the landscape that he saw was one that had changed only slowly through the preceding centuries. He, and particularly his successors, introduced changes in the economy which profoundly affected the appearance of the island and the lives of those who lived there. These alterations did not take place all at once. Although the landscape changes were ultimately quite widespread, the new methods and ideas that constituted the agrarian revolution were initiated gradually, and at different times in different parts of the island. The old patterns and methods continued to exist alongside the new throughout the rest of the eighteenth century and well into the nineteenth.

The first Daniel Campbell of Shawfield and Islay was born about 1670, the second son of Walter Campbell, Captain of Skipness in Argyll; his mother had Islay connections.[1] In 1692, in his early twenties, he went to New England and became a shipowner and merchant, defying the English ban on Scottish transatlantic trade. On his return to Scotland he built up an exporting business with Sweden, exchanging American tobacco for iron ore. He also became involved in the slave trade, with the ill-fated adventure to establish a Scottish colony at Darien, on the isthmus of Panama, was then appointed collector of Customs at the new Port Glasgow and became one of the early Scottish financiers. By his first marriage to Margaret Leckie of Newlands he had three sons and three daughters. In 1702, when just over thirty, he was elected to the Scottish parliament as the Member for Inveraray Burgh in Argyll. Five years later, he was one of the commissioners in that parliament at the time of its dissolution. His vote was one of those in favour of the 1707 Act of Union and he continued to sit as the Member for Inveraray in the united parliament. He had purchased the Lanarkshire estate of Shawfield, on the banks of the Clyde between Glasgow and Rutherglen. Shawfield House, his fine town house in spacious grounds on the north side of the Trongate facing Stockwell Street, was the first commission for Colen Campbell, the nephew of Sir Hugh Campbell of Cawdor, and was finished by 1711. In the following year Daniel Campbell also became the owner of Woodhall estate in Lanarkshire.[2]

Allan Ramsay's portrait of
'Great' Daniel Campbell of
Shawfield and Islay (1670–
1753), who was 'a very canny
Scot. By his indomitable
energy and general shrewdness
. . . he . . . amassed a large
fortune' (Russell, 'A Canny
Scot').

Widowed in 1711, he married again three years later; his second wife
was Lady Katherine Erskine, daughter of Henry, 3rd Lord Cardross and
widow of Sir William Denholme. They had one daughter, Katherine. As
member for the Glasgow Burghs in the Union parliament from 1716 to
1734 and Deputy Lieutenant of Lanarkshire, he 'raised himself to . . . great
importance, not only in Glasgow . . . but also in Westminster, where he had
considerable influence', according to one of his descendants.[3] A Whig and
great personal friend of Sir Robert Walpole, he was called 'Great Daniel'
partly from his stature and build, partly from the position he achieved.
A biographical vignette summarised his abilities by saying that he 'far
surpassed all his brothers in business capacity, and proved himself a very
canny Scot. By his indomitable energy and general shrewdness, combined
. . . with a certain amount of what his countrymen call "pawkiness", he,
from a very small beginning, amassed a large fortune', with which he began
to acquire his estates.

In 1725 Shawfield House was severely damaged by a mob in reprisal
for Campbell's unpopular political action in voting for the 1725 malt tax,
which Scotland had been spared since the Union of 1707. He was not in
residence and had removed valuables beforehand, requesting General Wade's

help in anticipation of trouble. The £9,000 he received in compensation from Glasgow may have helped him to pay for the purchase of Islay and part of Jura. Daniel Campbell was then already 55 years of age. He remained a member of parliament for almost another decade, entailing considerable travelling between London, Woodhall and Islay, at a time when such journeys were measured in days. Even so, during almost three decades from the purchase of Islay until his death in 1753 he was probably much less of an absentee landlord on Islay than his Cawdor Campbell predecessors, in 1731 adding the flanking wings and a western part to Islay House.

Tacksmen and joint farmers

When Daniel Campbell came to Islay in the 1720s times had been hard. Much of the land had been mortgaged to kinsmen of the Cawdor Campbells, often distinguished from one another in rentals as Dallas, Calderach and so on, according to where they came from. The rental for 1733 in the *Book of Islay* shows that, in general, the large grazing lands were held by tacksmen in the north-east, the south-east and in the Rinns, whereas joint farmers were found on the mixed grain and stock holdings in more accessible and more productive areas along river valleys and on well-drained beach deposits.[4] There may have been tacksmen who were interested in farming for its own sake and there were tacks in Islay that had arable land of consequence. Some of these were enclosed and improved quite early, as shown in the mid-eighteenth century by Stephen MacDougall's maps of Coul, Cladavill and others.[5] But in most of the tacks, grazing areas were more extensive than arable land.

It is perhaps not surprising that tacksmen were among the first to be affected by the change in ownership. The 1730s saw the start of an emigration of some of the disaffected tacksmen from Islay. The colony of New York had advertised for Protestant settlers from Europe, with the promise of improved land for each family. Captain Lauchlin Campbell of Islay visited the colony in 1737 and returned there the following year with his own and thirty other families. A further forty families emigrated in 1739 and still more in 1740.[6] In all, he encouraged 423 people, perhaps about ten per cent, of the islanders to move there from Islay, many at their own expense. The venture was not a great success for Captain Campbell, although he was able to purchase a modest tract of land in southern Ulster, afterwards Orange County, N.Y., and erected a dwelling for himself and his family, calling it Campbell Hall. There he remained, except for a return to Scotland to fight for the Hanoverians in the 1745 rebellion. While some eventually settled in Washington County, others went their own ways, some joining North Carolina pioneers. Subsequent rentals of the century recorded a gradual decline in the number of tacksmen and their tacks became single farms or joint farms.

Tacksmen on Islay built conspicuous houses, such as this Georgian one at Ardnave.

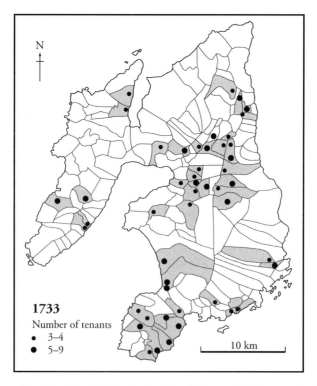

In 1733, just after 'Great' Daniel Campbell of Shawfield acquired Islay, much of the island was still in the hands of the tacksmen. Tenancies with more than two tenants responsible for paying the rent were concentrated in 'The Glen' and in the Oa (Smith, *Book of Islay*).

Apart from these large tacks or single farms, the other areas of the
island were farmed communally by joint tenants. Some of these had
subtenants and there were probably also some cottars or squatters who
had no formal share in the land. The tenants of the joint farms seldom
had equal shares of either rent due, or of the shares or soum of grazing
capacity or of arable land. The rental for 1733, for instance, shows that
Keppolsmore, with eight tenants each holding a six-pennyland directly
from the landlord was one of the few exceptions.[7] Even there, of course,
these equal shares may have hidden the existence of subtenants with
smaller subdivisions of the six-pennylands. Much more characteristic
was a joint township like Ballychatrican in the Oa, where two tenants
shared an eight-pennyland, two shared a four-pennyland and five a four-
pennyland. The rent was thus payable jointly by nine tenants, some of
whom may in turn have obtained part of their rent from subtenants.

As elsewhere in the Highlands and Islands, it was not until surveyors
were employed by the lairds during and after the eighteenth century
that landholdings were reckoned for rental purposes in terms of area
rather than by value, i.e. their capacity to support stock and to produce
crops. Long after such surveys were available, the old denominations or
assessments of worth sometimes continued to be used in Islay, as shown
in documents connected with the sale of parts of the island even in the
mid-nineteenth century. From the time of the colonisation of Islay from
Ireland in the sixth century until the end of the Norse connection in
the Western Isles in 1266, the chief land denominations in Islay appear
to have been the davoch, valued at ten marks and the quarter at two
and a half marks.[8] After 1266 an assessment subsequently known as the
Old Extent was imposed by King Alexander III, replacing the earlier
denominations with poundlands, marklands, ten-shillinglands and
cowlands. With the forfeiture of the lordship of the Isles to the Scottish
Crown in 1493, yet another system of land valuation was attempted. The
'bailie' of Islay, MacIan of Ardnamurchan, was ordered by the Crown
to bring the island into line with what was then the prevailing national
system of quarterlands valued at 33s. 4d. Scots. This reconciliation was
only partially accomplished in Islay and the local system of denominations
belonging to the Old Extent continued side by side with the newer
MacIan denominations right up to the early-nineteenth century. The
1733 rental, for instance, contained remnants of the Old Extent system,
although the majority of holdings were reckoned for rental purposes
under the MacIan system of quarterlands, and eighths. The picture was
still further complicated by the conversion of the Scots reckoning of the
MacIan system into sterling equivalents; the latter became known in Islay

as the False MacIan Extent. Subsequent division of the quarterland gave rise to several place names unique to the island; from half of a *ceathramh* or quarter, *ocdamh*, eighth, resulted the names Octomore, Octofad, and Octovullin. Other denominations for one-sixteenth, *leorhas*, and smaller subdivisions continued to be used into the rentals of the eighteenth and nineteenth centuries.

Early-eighteenth century farming
The way that the land of Islay was worked in the early-eighteenth century must for the most part be deduced from accounts written by visitors later in the century.[9] Although the term 'openfield agriculture' has been the subject of some controversy, it is an acceptable description of the system in Islay, as elsewhere in Scotland.[10] The eighteenth-century leases and tacks indicate that the land of the island was organised into wintertown, common pasture, muir and shielings or summer grazings. The term 'infield', frequently met with elsewhere and indicating the area of best soil that was cultivated regularly, was not often used in connection with Islay. It may in fact have been part of the wintertown, the latter phrase perhaps either an indication that the stock grazed the stubble in winter or a direct translation from the Gaelic '*baile-geamhraidh*'. It has also been suggested that the term 'wintertown' may describe the township settlement from which people removed in summer to shielings.[11] Another term that only infrequently occurs in Islay manuscripts is 'outfield'; elsewhere this indicates land of lower productivity that is normally grazed and cropped only periodically. It is possible that the pressure of population in eighteenth century Islay was not sufficient to require such periodic cultivation of the grazing area.

Surviving estate maps of Islay only occasionally show a well-marked division into infield and outfield. Instead, as in the township of Ballichlavan, the arable and pasture parts of each holding are shown as intermingled in the area near the settlement, depending on the topography, rocky outcrops and soils. The manner in which the openfield was cultivated in Islay up to the mid-nineteenth century is described in the *New Statistical Account* of the 1840s.[12] Mention is made several times in other sources of periodic reallocation of each tenant's strips in the openfield or commonfield, with the field itself probably enclosed by a dyke of turf or stone.

Apart from these areas of enclosed and improved land, each township possessed communal grazing on the muirs and hills, perhaps with temporary shielings on summer pastures. A small area of improved land around the house of the township's herdsman on the common muir of Ballichlavan is shown in Gemmill's plan. The number of stock that each of

In the 1770s Thomas Pennant reported that Joseph Banks had allowed his artist, Moses Griffith, 'to copy as many of the beautiful drawings in his collection, as would be of use' for Pennant's *Tour*. This one depicts 'sheelins' or temporary dwellings used after transhumance to summer pastures in Jura. Cheese from the cows' milk matured in baskets (Pennant, *Tour*). Ground plans of shielings in Islay conform to the same pattern (RCAHMS, *Argyll Inventory*, 5).

the joint tenants could graze on the muir was defined by share in the rent and was called soum. Earlier reference to shielings in Islay is found only in the rental of 1722, where Toradill's 'shielding in the muir' is listed.[13] Other indications can be found in the Gaelic *airidh* and its variants in the original namebooks of the Ordnance Survey and on the maps and plans from which these were compiled in the later-nineteenth century.[14] Their location can nowadays also be identified on air photographs and through observation. They were an important supplement to the grazing capacity of townships that depended on the sale of cattle for monetary income, but the use of common grazings and shielings in Islay appears to have ceased almost entirely in the nineteenth century.

The Welshman, Thomas Pennant, commented on the shielings in Islay and Jura which formed a prominent feature of the landscape. His account of one particular group is probably the best eye-witness account of the practice of transhumance in the Hebrides during the mid-eighteenth century. A drawing of shielings in Jura complemented Pennant's description: '. . . a bank covered with sheelins, the habitations of some peasants who attended the herds of milch cows. These formed a grotesque groupe; some were oblong, many conic, and so low that entrance is forbidden, without creeping through the little opening, which has no other door than a faggot of birch twigs . . . covered with sods; the furniture a bed of heath, placed on a bank of sod, and above, certain pendent shelves made of basket-work to hold the cheese, the produce of the summer'.[15]

Details of the productive capacity of the early-eighteenth century tacks and joint farms are given in the early-eighteenth century rentals in *Book of Islay*. The grazing capacity and the amount of grain sown on each 'town' or 'land' were supplemented by remarks on the nature of each holding and its suitability for grazing and crops. Some of the figures for the soum or grazing capacity and similar crop data were omitted for certain towns or lands in the Rinns not held by the Campbells. The remoter and hillier parts of the island in the north-east and south-east were mainly used for grazing. Adjacent to these areas were holdings that generally had more land capable of producing crops for human and animal consumption. Grain cultivation was more important than stock grazing in the larger river valleys, especially the Sorn and on the better-drained parts of the raised beaches around Loch Indaal.

The soum for Islay for 1722, excluding much of the Rinns, amounted to 6,645 cows and 'the product thereof yearly, such as thair two year old stirks and calfs with the cows'.[16] A rider was added to the effect that 'with each cow there are two sheep with their year olds and lambs to be grassed. As for extent ther, a toun is allowed to have fourtie cows: they are also there allowed to have eightie sheep with there product'. The number of horses or mares each land was allowed to graze, together with 'thair product also of two year olds and foals', amounted to 2,232, again with the Rinns excluded. Substitutions in the soums were permitted; usually two cows could be substituted for a horse and five or six sheep for a cow. Sheep were specifically mentioned only on three lands in Islay in the 1722 rental: Taycarmagan [*sic*], Ballevicar and on the Losset lands in the north-east. At that time, sheep were less important than cattle for rearing and export; their main use was probably to meet local needs for mutton and wool.

In 1722, again excepting the Rinns, the soum for 'corn' (Scots oats) amounted to 5,428 bolls, a boll being the size of container used in a particular area at a given time. The size of a boll varied from crop to crop, area to area and period to period. The rental mentions that this corn soum was sometimes exceeded on the island and this was also true of barley, for which the total soum was 798 bolls. Barley accounted for only about one-eighth of the cereal crops in the soum, which seems a low proportion on an island that was presumably already producing alcohol. 'Pees, ry, pottatoes, as they [sic] think fit, or thair convenience can allow them' were also mentioned as additional crops. Interesting remarks on the 'present capabilities' were given for each of the holdings with a few hints at potential capability. These included such phrases as 'Kilcherrans [Kilchiaran] a very good possession, alike for sowing and holding', 'Leack, Sannaigbeig, Grannard and Caspellen . . . the best land in the wholl countrie', 'Daill, Octonafreitch, Kilbrannan, & Surn a good wadset . . . the most of it lying exposed for good improvement'.

The rental of 1722 is some indication of the worth of the island that Campbell of Shawfield got for his £12,000; in 1722 the total rental was about £15,980 Scots, equivalent to about £1,332 sterling. Amortised at even ten per cent for ten years, he could easily have paid off the £12,000 (if all rents had been paid), and by 1733 the rental had gone up. It must, however, be remembered that the lands were not free of encumbrances and by the middle of the century many Islay lands were still wadset to various Campbells, as shown in the Valuation Roll for Argyll in 1751.[17]

Surveys and plans for agrarian change
An important legacy from the period of the first Daniel Campbell's lairdship of Islay comprises the estate documents of the time that still survive, including some of Stephen MacDougall's maps and plans. Immediately before going to Islay, MacDougall had in 1747 surveyed the estate of Taynish on mainland Argyll and the island of 'Giga' or Gigha, both owned by Roger McNeil of Taynish.[18] William Roy's Military Survey of Scotland did not include the islands, so the few extant MacDougall plans for parts of Islay are of considerable interest as they are smongst the earliest in the Hebrides. It seems likely that MacDougall was instructed by Daniel Campbell to determine the areal extent of the holdings, as a basis for assessing the improvements already carried out and to identify areas where other improvements could be initiated, such as draining for land reclamation. These surveys, showing the agriculture and settlement pattern before enclosure and sometimes also indicating the form of the intended reorganisation, are fascinating and valuable historical documents. The seventeenth-century enclosure acts of the Scottish parliament remained valid under the terms of the Union. Each landlord could therefore set about planning his estate with considerable freedom of action.

Although few maps or plans of individual holdings on Islay survive, those that do can probably all be ascribed to MacDougall's period and they are drawn at a scale of about 1:10,000. They show the marches or boundaries, enclosures, fields, buildings and areas capable of improvement for a few holdings in the Rinns. Also illustrated are the large houses in which tacksmen lived and the clustered houses of the subtenants or others. More of these

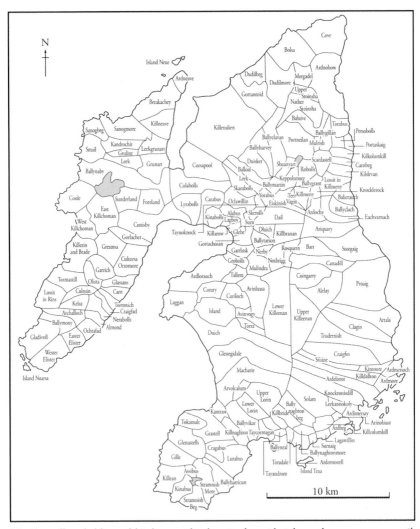

MacDougall probably used his large-scale plans in the mid-eighteenth century to compile a small-scale map of the whole island, although it was not to be published for another century. This redrawing omits the blocks used to represent settlement but locates many of the names of holdings mentioned in the text but no longer to be found on modern maps (Smith, *Book of Islay*).

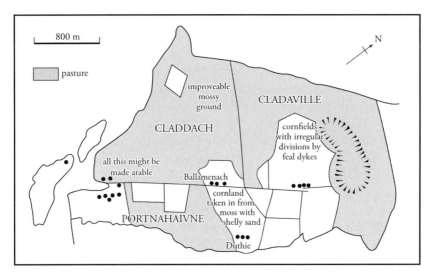

The surveyor, Stephen MacDougall, worked for various Argyll estates in the mid-eighteenth century. For 'Great' Daniel Campbell of Shawfield, he assessed present and potential land use in plans such as this one, redrawn, for the southern tip of the Rinns peninsula. Each dot may represent one occupied building, and pastures are shaded (Islay Estate Papers).

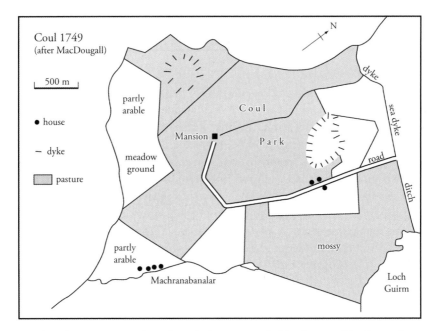

Simple realignments on tacks such as Coul were typical of 'evolutionary' landscape change (Islay Estate Papers).

maps may have formed the basis for a generalised, smaller-scale map that covers the whole island. This, though drawn by MacDougall between 1749 and 1751, was not published until a century later, when preparing for the sale of the island. Many townships that have disappeared from subsequent rentals can, however, be located on Stephen MacDougall's map.

Another kind of surveyor followed soon: Murdoch Mackenzie was engaged in hydrographic survey for the Admiralty and was the first to use triangulation with a good island base. He produced a one-inch to the mile map of 'Ila island' in 1757, concentrating on these coasts and those features of the island useful for navigation.[19]

For Islay it is unfortunate that only a few plans of this period remain. The possibility that additional ones were drawn is suggested in a surviving list of the contents of the Islay House library in 1777, which contains the entry 'Book of Maps of Islay'.[20] Much estate material relating to the island is also known to have been lost in a fire at Woodhall in Lanarkshire in the middle of the nineteenth century and at a later building owned by John Ramsay in Glasgow. John Francis Campbell, about the same time, also remarked that much of the family's collection of documents had been 'plundered'.[21] One map acquired by Sir Joseph Banks on his way to Iceland in 1772, may have been the same 'beautiful map of Islay' that Pennant saw the same year.[22] Another map that appears to have been lost is that to which Arrowsmith made reference in 1807 when he said that he had obtained a complete map of Islay by Robert Campbell, Esq.[23]

Great Daniel's tentative innovations
Although the main changes that were to transform Islay did not come until later, the first Daniel Campbell of Shawfield and Islay was responsible for a number of innovations during almost four decades as principal laird or landlord. Writing in 1777, more than twenty years after Daniel Campbell's death, his grandson and successor declared that from the time his grandfather had acquired the estate 'he immediately began, and zealously carried on, extensive plans for the improvement and civilisation of that corner. Every encouragement to Agriculture as the basis of his own and his tenants prosperity, was his great Object: To the branch of the flax husbandry and manufacture, he particularly turned his care and attention. He laid out in building Lint Milns, bringing to the Island, Manufacturers, Hecklers, Weavers etc. considerably above £2,000 Sterling'.[24]

The emphasis on flax for linen-making is significant. It was part of a general growth of the linen industry in Scotland at this time and was one of the characteristic ways in which individual landlords attempted to improve

Scottish agriculture. Islay became a laboratory for agricultural experiment and later in the century it was to become a showpiece. Daniel Campbell was an 'agricultural improver' and the Honourable Society of Improvers in the Knowledge of Agriculture in Scotland, the first of its kind in Britain, had been established in 1723 only three years before he acquired Islay. As his grandson pointed out in 1766, improvement was not only a matter of new crops and new techniques. It also involved social changes and alterations in the pattern of land management. His grandfather had introduced 'a Spirit of Industry into the Island of Isla, as the most proper means to Divert from, and if possible, to Eradicate the Idel-Loving and Clanish Spirit that prevailed, particularly he attended to the Raising of Flax, Built Flax Milns, Provided Flax Dressers, Hecklers, and Spinning Wheels, he encouraged Weavers, Gave Premiums to Importers of Flax Seed, and Dealers in Yarn, and to accelerate a Change to Industry, he gave his Tennants Leases for 31 years, a Term unknown to their Predecessors'.[25] Writing in 1808, Walker suggests that flax was probably the limit of Daniel Campbell's experimentation, whereas his grandson credited him with attempts to encourage agriculture in general, fisheries, as well as better education provision.

The use of leases was comparatively new in Highland Scotland. In the seventeenth century they were generally very long leases, usually for life and for nineteen additional years after death. By the eighteenth century, the normal period was between eleven and nineteen years, with most of the leases or tacks on one estate arranged so as to terminate in one year. Then the whole estate would again be 'sett' or let for another term. Walker mentioned that the Campbells of Shawfield had let all the estate in three nineteen-year leases from 1720 to 1777.[26] He perhaps meant that Islay had been let in 1720 by the Cawdor Campbells and Daniel Campbell had taken over the leases.

All of 'Great' Daniel's sons predeceased him. His eldest son, John, born in 1696 and later a Commissioner of the Inland Revenue, had married twice. His first wife, Lady Margaret Campbell, daughter of Hugh, 3rd earl of Loudon, died without issue a few years after their marriage in 1728. In 1735 he married Lady Henrietta (or Harriot) Cunninghame, daughter of the 12th earl of Glencairn, but died in 1746 before his father. So it was Daniel, the eldest of his four sons from this second marriage, who succeeded, still a minor, to the estate of Islay, part of Jura and to the mainland estate, when the redoubtable Great Daniel died at Woodhall in 1753, aged 83, having sadly bemoaned the 'Infirmatys attending old age'.[27]

Notes and references

[1] The Shawfield Campbell biographical material used for this chapter has been obtained mainly from the following sources: Burke, *Peerage*; J. B. Burke, *Genealogical and Heraldic Dictionary of the Landed Gentry of Great Britain and Ireland*, (London, 1843–9); L. Stephen (ed.), *Dictionary of National Biography*, (London, 1908); J. D. Duncan, 'Notes on an Inventory of Articles which escaped the hands of the mob on the occasion of the sacking of Shawfield Mansion, 1725', *Transactions of the Glasgow Antiquarian Society* 1 (1868), p. xxiv and pp. 388–97; Foster, *Members of Parliament*; S. Forman, 'Islay House', *Scottish Field*, 1960, May, pp. 37–40; K. Cruft, 'The enigma of Woodhall House', *Architectural History* 27 (1984), pp. 210–13; J. M. Reid, 'A New Light on Old Glasgow: The Shawfield Papers of Daniel Campbell', *Glasgow Herald*, 1, 2 and 3 June, 1959; Lady C. Russell, 'A Canny Scot', *Three Generations of Fascinating Women and other Sketches from Family History*, (London, 1905), pp. 154–82. J. Hill and N. Bastin, *A Very Canny Scot, Great Daniel Campbell of Shawfield and Islay 1670–1753, His life and Times*, (West Sussex, 2007).The Shawfield Papers in the Mitchell Library, Glasgow, mainly relate to the period before Islay was bought by Daniel Campbell of Shawfield.

[2] *Cawdor Castle Guide*, p. 28.

[3] Russell, *Three Generations*, p. 154.

[4] Smith, *Book of Islay*, p. 550.

[5] S. MacDougall's maps and plans of 1749–51: a few extant MS. plans are in the Islay Estate Papers. The reduced smaller-scale map of Islay, lithographed in 1848, is printed in Smith, *Book of Islay*, pp. 552–3.

[6] G. F. Black, 'Early Islay Emigration to America', *Oban Times*, 27 March, 2, 23 and 30 April, 1927; D. Barclay, 'Lauchlin Campbell of Campbell Hall and his Family', *Historical Papers of the Historical Society of Newburgh Bay and the Highlands* 9 (1902), pp. 31–6; D. Meyer, *The Highland Scots of Carolina, 1732–1776*, (N. Carolina, 1961); J. M. Patten, *The Argyle Patent and Accompanying Documents, excerpted from The History of the Somonauk Presbyterian Church*, (Baltimore, 1979); G. S. Pryde, 'Scottish Colonisation in the Province of New York', *Proceedings of the New York State Historical Association* 33 (1935), pp. 147–50. A. Murdoch, ' A Scottish Document' concerning Emigration to Carolina in 1772', *The North Carolina Historical Review* 67 (1990), pp. 438–41. J. G. Kyd, *Scottish Population Statistics*, (Edinburgh, 1975), p. 33.

[7] Smith, *Book of Islay*, p. 550.

[8] Lamont, 'Old Land Denominations', *Scottish Studies* 1 (1957), pp. 86–106 and (1958) pp.183–203; J. MacQueen, 'Pennyland and Davoch in South-Western Scotland: a Preliminary Note', *ibid.*, 1979, 23, pp. 69–74; B. Megaw, Note on the above, *ibid.*, pp. 75–7.

Pennylands were derived from subdivisions of quarterlands, which by the early-sixteenth century were valued at 33s. 4d. Scots, popularly known as 32/-. In sterling these became 32 pennylands and were divided viz:

Ceathramh	Quarterland	33s. 4d.	32/- 32d.
Ochdamh	Eighth or Auchtenpart	16s. 8d.	16/- 16d.
Lewirheis		8s. 4d.	8/- 8d.
Kerrowrane or Cota ban		4s. 2d.	4/- 4d.
Da Sgillin		2s. 1d.	2/- 2d.

[9] Pennant, *Tour*; Anderson, *Account*; Sinclair, *OSA*; Walker, *Economical History*.

[10] See also R. A. Dodgshon, *The Origin of British Field Systems: An Interpretation*, (London, 1980).

[11] Shaw, *Northern and Western Islands*, p. 91.

[12] *The Statistical Account of Scotland, by the Ministers of the Respective Parishes* (*NSA*), 33 vols. (Edinburgh, 1843-6), *Argyleshire*, (1845), p. 654.

[13] Smith, *Book of Islay*, p. 528.

[14] MS. name books, maps and plans of the Ordnance Survey, Edinburgh.

[15] Pennant, *Tour*, p. 246. ° Smith, *Book of Islay*, p. 473.

[16] Smith, *Book of Islay*, pp. 521–44.

[17] Islay Estate Papers, Attested Account of the Valued Rent of Islay, 1751.

[18] S. MacDougall, *A Map of Taynish . . . in Argyll, 1747*, The British Library, Map Library, K. Top. XLIX 28. Also, *A Map of the Island of Giga, 1747*, XLIX 37. 1. MacDougall may have been on Ileach.

[19] Murdoch Mackenzie, *The Maritim [sic] Survey of Ireland and the West of Great Britain*, (London, 1776), Chart XX.

[20] Smith, *Book of Islay*, p. 473.

[21] Reid, 'Shawfield Papers'; Ramsay, *John Ramsay*, pp. 50–1.

[22] Pennant, *Tour*, p. 261.

[23] A. Arrowsmith, *Memoir relative to the construction of the Map of Scotland published by A. Arrowsmith in the year 1807*, (London, 1809).

[24] Daniel Campbell the Younger petitioned the Annexed Estates Commissioners on several occasions for grants of money to aid his plans for the development of Islay. See NRS, E727/60 and E728/47. This particular reference is E727/60/1. The elder Daniel Campbell's plans over leases are illustrated in a lawsuit of 1760 between Donald Campbell of Killinalen and Colen Campbell of Ardnahow, NRS, CS 230/C/5/9.

[25] NRS, E728/47/4(2).

[26] Walker, *Economical History*, p. 68.

[27] Saltoun Papers, NRS, SB74. Silver in Bothwell Church is inscribed with Daniel Campbell's name and date of death.

Daniel Campbell the Younger (1737–1777) who succeeded to his grandfather's estates in
1753 (artist unknown, private collection).

CHAPTER 7

More comprehensive development

In virtually every European country in the eighteenth and nineteenth centuries, the rural economy had to produce more food to support growing towns and land was now seen as an asset to be managed for profit rather than for supporting rural population.[1] From the 1760s there was an increasing demand in the rest of Britain for such Highland produce as cattle, mutton, wool, linen, kelp, whisky, timber, slate and many other commodities.[2] Labour was required in Lowland agriculture, the Clyde herring fishery and in the bleachfields around the textile towns and villages. Recruitment into the army and navy for the Seven Years War, the American War of Independence and the Napoleonic wars also created a demand for labour. Rentals increased to capitalise on the surplus from rising prices. The traditional tacksman class was gradually reduced in number and social significance, with subtenure forbidden. Conventionally the eighteenth-century assumption was that a rising population was an economic benefit. Between the end of the Seven Years War in 1763 and 1775, however, there were further emigrations of about 1,300 people from Islay to North Carolina, perhaps encouraged by the Islay pamphleteer, 'Scotus Americanus'.[3] But the view of a correspondent to the *Edinburgh Advertiser* was that 'the loss of useful hands must soon impoverish any country'.[4] Another also pointed out that 'the poor deluded farmers that went away some years ago from Islay . . . wanted a passage back'.[5]

It was against this background of accelerating change in economy and society that Daniel Campbell the Younger, aged only sixteen, succeeded to the Islay estate on the death of his grandfather in 1753. After reaching his majority, he too became a member of parliament, representing Lanarkshire from 1760 to 1768. He is reputed to have been a 'great character in his day, but of a totally opposite sort to his grandfather. The first Daniel Campbell of Shawfield had a genius for making money and accumulated a large fortune which his grandson helped largely to diminish'. Daniel the Younger is described as 'living in great style . . . And he spent his money right and left, even more on others than on himself'.[6] A well-informed man, who travelled widely in Europe, he collected rare books and musical

instruments. Spending summers and autumns on Islay, he continued to
implement and expand many of his grandfather's ideas for agricultural
improvements, involving leases, stock and crops. In 1760, although still
only a bachelor of 23, he added two stair-towers, extending the south
front of Islay House.[7] Nearby, he also had the ornamental and octagonal
East Tower constructed, with his monogram alongside that of his king.[8]
Eight years later, one of the most impressive and enduring results of his
management was to be seen in the construction of Bowmore, one of the
earliest planned villages to appear in the Highlands and Islands. He was
an instigator and shareholder in the first regular sailing packet in the
Hebrides which plied weekly between Islay and West Loch Tarbert in
Kintyre.[9]

Such innovations were not merely far-reaching in their effects; they
were part of an overall vision that entitles Daniel Campbell the Younger
and subsequently his brother, Walter to be counted among those on whom
much of the success of the agricultural revolution in Scotland ultimately
depended. In his early twenties he was already thinking hard about his island
estate and by 1759 had begun 'particularly to inquire into the Situation of
Isla, the Disposition and Genius of its Inhabitants, whom he found still to
Retain a Bias to the Clanish manner of their Ancestors, averse to Industry
and Intercourse'.[10] So he 'Therefore Examined the Schemes Employed by
his Grandfather, and began to pursue them with more enlarged views In
regard to Agriculture, Manufactures, Trade and Police'.

Financing Islay's improvement

Daniel Campbell's vision was expressed implicitly; it did not constitute a
development plan in the modern sense of the term. He himself described
it as an 'Outline of a Plan, rather than a Minute and tedious detail'. But it
is significant that he used the term 'plan' at all and fortunately a substantial
amount of evidence survives in the landscape and in manuscript which
enables much of that minute detail to be reconstructed. Daniel Campbell
needed extra finance to accomplish his ambitions. Islay was not an Annexed
Estate, as its owner had remained loyal to the Hanoverians during the
1745 rebellion. Nevertheless, funds at the disposal of the Annexed Estates
Commissioners could be used in other parts of the Highlands and Islands
to promote 'the Protestant Religion, good Government, Industry and
Manufactures . . . to Erect publick Schools . . . for Instructing Young
Persons in Reading and Writing and English Language and in Several
Branches of Agriculture and Manufactures'.

The first application by Daniel Campbell the Younger for assistance of
this kind appears to have been made in February 1766.[11] His 'Memorial

and Petition', a more colourful forerunner of present-day application forms, showed that Daniel Campbell was an early advocate of development policies, jointly financed by public and private sources. He urged that to establish linen manufactures and fisheries in the Western Islands, 'the proper Plan is that the publick and the proprietors of such Islands, go Hand in Hand'.[12] He also reminded the Commissioners that duty of £500 had been paid annually to the Crown for many years back, arguing that some of this ought to come back to assist in the improvement of conditions on the island. Similar arguments are still frequently heard, as islanders calculate the excise duties accruing to government on whisky exported from Islay's distilleries! The laird maintained that, if encouragement were given, 'this island might soon become of infinite Utility to the Nation in General' and he requested £600 to carry on and complete the building of his parish church in what was to become the village of Bowmore, as well as a schoolhouse, an annual salary for the schoolmaster, a prison and a further £600 towards the establishment of linen manufactures and fisheries.

This first application was unsuccessful; the commissioners objected to giving aid for his suggested 'General purposes'.[13] Daniel Campbell apparently thought they had missed his point and renewed his request in further memorials.[14] These are much more interesting than the first and help to establish the position of both 'Great' Daniel and Daniel the Younger among leaders of change and improvement in the Highlands and Islands. The memorials discuss his 'Schemes and Plans of Improvements' under several headings: agriculture, fishing, linen manufacture, trade, roads, bridges, the sailing packet, fishing, religion, education, and law and order. He requested £1,000 in the first instance and added an assurance (the lack of which in his first memorial had apparently troubled the commissioners) that 'notwithstanding the large Sums he had already Expended, he would still advance out of his own pocket, a sum Equal to that which should be Granted'. The result on this occasion was more successful, the commissioners granting him half the sum that he had requested.[15]

A decade later, in 1777, Daniel Campbell again went in search of development aid. Writing to the Secretary of the Board of Trustees of Annexed Estates he recalled that after his previous successful application and the award of a grant for £500 he had 'assiduously pursued my plan of the improvement of that Island. Large sums have been expended, I may say at least £2,000 Sterlg, exclusive of what was laid out by my grandfather'. He then requested another £500 from the Board and promised to 'lay out a like sum for the improvement and prosperity of that Island'.[16] £300 was to send farmers to Northumberland and other parts of England to study the new practices there, and to give premiums to certain island farmers in the form of new and improved types of seed. £200 was to be spent on two mills, one for 'making' grass or barley, another for wheat. A further £200 would purchase a vessel for training fishermen and £300 to complete quays at Bowmore and Port Askaig.

This time the Board members were immediately sympathetic.[17] The public good, they decided, was best served by giving Daniel Campbell £500 to help promote the fisheries and improve the quays. They considered that the agricultural proposals were best left to Shawfield himself. It was the opinion of the commissioners that 'they have a gentleman to deal with, who, for activity and public spirit may be safely trusted with the management of the sum promised by them, without the least doubt of his being a faithful Stewart for the good of the public as well as for his own'.[18] It is sadly ironic that, having so successfully mastered the difficult art of obtaining government aid, Daniel Campbell the Younger died almost immediately afterwards, aged only forty. It was left to his successor to put the money to its intended use.

Optimistic agrarian plans

Daniel Campbell's thoughts and plans for agriculture, as they are set out in the memorials, are based on an optimism characteristic of the Scottish Enlightenment. He had gone so far as to suggest that nine-tenths of the surface of Islay was capable of improvement. The island, he added, contained 'most types of soils', which were able to produce 'Grains and Grasses, Cultivate in Britain, Comparative with the Continent. It has little Frost or Snow, so that Wheat and Sown Grasses, often make a Progress in Winter. It is a Country remarkably adapted for Flax, and bounds with Efficatious and lasting Manures, The hard and soft Marles, Lymstone and Shell Sand'. He also pointed out that he had been

> endeavouring to abolish certain Old hurtfull Customs, at the same time as he has been Introducing the most approved methods of the Old and New Husbandry, Summer Fallowing, the Use of the manures and laying down the Grounds in Good Heart, with Grass Seeds, Also has introduced the Turnip Husbandry, Wheat, the two Rowed Barley, White Oats, Beans, Pease, Hemp, Veitches, and Tare Seeds with Clover, Rye, St. Foin, Lucern, Burnet and Timothy Grasses, and has introduced all the different Ploughs, Machinery and Tools now used in the New and Old Husbandry, and has . . . experienced that all those Seeds and Grasses are Cultivate in Isla of equall perfection and Advantage with any part of Britain.[19]

Envisaging that there was good reason to expect that his tenants 'would soon become of very considerable Publick Utility, by exporting Great Quantitys of Wheat and other Grains', he also reminded the Commissioners that Islay's farmers would 'Rear up and export more Live Cattle, than at present, But also to Fatten for Export, and for the Use of Traders upon the Coast'.

Unfortunately there are few archives or published sources that can provide an objective review of Daniel Campbell's expansive claims. What seems probable is that some improvements were taking place, but that these were mainly confined to the larger farms, perhaps those on the best lands, those near the laird's mansion and those of the gentlemen farmers. Tacks or leases granted in 1768–9 by Daniel the Younger and in 1779 and 1802 by his successor, survive in archives.[20] Those for 1769 did not require tenants to make improvements; the 1779 leases, however, saw the introduction of 'improving' clauses. The absence of such clauses in the earlier leases was commented on in 1769 by Daniel Campbell's factor.[21] There was clearly scope for improvement and one way to do this, as both landlord and agent recognised, was through leases containing the new clauses 'productive of new and better effects'. At that time Islay was

> occupied by two classes of tenants – the gentlemen possessing several Quarterlands extending to three and four thousand acres and upwards. They mind husbandry very little, only the yearly sett of these large farms to a sett of poor people, whom they call their farmers. The small tenants, four, five, six or eight of them, enjoys a Quarterland promiscuously among them . . . These manner of holdings the proprietor is determined to alter.[22]

The word 'promiscuously' strikes oddly on the modern ear, but the basic problem was little incentive for an individual to attempt improvements. Reorganisation of landholdings was essential, but for this patience was necessary:

> In regard to the first class tenants . . . each is only to enjoy such an extent of land as may rationally fall under cognizance and management of a good improver. As to the second class or small tenants, their farms are to be new modeled, each to have an establishment for himself, and to occupy individually . . . But, as these cannot be carried into execution till the expiry of the current leases, that circumstance becomes the chief and principal argument for delaying the sett till the expiry of current leases . . . Shawfield has lately granted nineteen year leases of a considerable part of his estate from Whitsunday 1768 last, and part does not commence . . . till Whitsunday 1779, the period when all his tacks of the Argyllshire state expires.[23]

The later-eighteenth century period of renewal in many aspects of Scottish life included similar events, albeit different in scale, such as the creation of Edinburgh New Town and Islay's village of Bowmore, both started in the late 1760s. 'Designed street by street, house by house, with certain social, economic and architectural considerations always in view', Bowmore's wide Main Street is dominated by the unusual round church with its conical roof. In the 1980s the prize-winning Ayrshire herd returns for milking to McKerrell's Dairy.

The fishermen's buildings beside Bowmore harbour were partially remodelled in the late-twentieth century, but the staircases seen in nineteenth-century watercolours still remain.

It is ironic that this major obstacle to Daniel Campbell's improvements was probably caused by the nineteen-year leases that had been one of the earliest agricultural advances made before his grandfather's time. Since the existing nineteen-year leases on his estate did not expire until 1777, not much could be done until then. It was therefore not Daniel the Younger who would achieve the reorganisation and agricultural improvements meanwhile could be only piecemeal.

Village planning

Daniel Campbell was not the first to envisage a new element in the eighteenth-century landscape in Scotland, but he was one of the first and, as it turned out, one of the very few to act on this vision in the Highlands and Islands. Throughout Scotland as a whole, in little more than a century from about the time his grandfather had bought Islay in 1726, over 150 completely new planned villages were established at the instigation of individual landlords. They were developed 'in response to and also to assist a revolution in the economy of the estate and of the nation'; and they were 'expected to provide a completely new framework for human life in the countryside . . . part of a still larger ideal of promoting economic growth in the kingdom'.[24] The movement also had its social and aesthetic aspirations: replacing the long established core of the estate at Kilarrow,[25] the village was designed 'street by street, house by house, and garden by garden with certain social, economic and architectural considerations always in view'. The landowner generally exercised control over the appearance and layout of the village but the houses were seldom built at his expense. He was normally responsible for providing facilities such as inns, a church and sometimes also a courthouse and a school. Daniel Campbell's Bowmore, begun in the late 1760s, seems to have followed this general pattern. Often, the landowners also exercised complete control over the affairs of the village through a baron bailie who was frequently also their agent or factor.

Like many others of its kind, Bowmore was based on a geometric plan, with a broad main street, running south and uphill to the newly-constructed church. Daniel Campbell had applied in particular for financial help in building Bowmore's church, as 'a very necessary and expedient measure, upon an Island so populous and extensive as Isla, for civilising and promoting the protestant Religion amongst the present Inhabitants, exclusive of the great increase that may be reasonably expected, in a very short time, from the Encouragement offered by the Memorialist to Settlers and the plans of Improvement now under execution'.[26] He added that plans of this church as well as of the proposed schoolhouse and prison could have been exhibited with his memorial, but he did not consider it imperative as he 'must necessarily contribute largely to this work himself'.

The church conspicuously dominates the top of the wide Main Street. Its architecture is unusual, but it stands in good proportion to the rest of the street and the village. It was probably inspired by the various projects for a circular church at Inveraray designed between 1747 and 1760 by William Adam and his son John, in particular John Adam's scheme of about 1758, not carried out in the end.[27] This undermines the belief that a 'French architect who, doubtless influenced by tradition, was determined to eliminate any corners for the devil to lurk in'.[28] Another suggestion has been that 'its exterior was in imitation of a church in Rome', seen by Daniel on his Grand Tour, or at Hamilton.[29] The simple internal layout, with a central pillar supporting the roof-structure, was constructed by a Fife man, Thomas Spalding, for £1,000.[30]

Over a short period, Daniel Campbell spent £1,660 on church matters, compared to an annual income from Islay rents of about £2,700.[31] The new church and manse at Bowmore cost about £500 (a restoration appeal launched in 1980 was for £200,000) and two new manses for the other parishes had become necessary at £200 each. There were also other expenses including the yearly stipend for a minister of £32 6s. 2d.[32] Daniel Campbell also maintained a school in each parish 'for instructing Youth in Reading and writing the English language', clear emphasis being placed on what, for Islay, was then a foreign language. He also wanted 'One Schoolmaster at least Qualified in teaching Grammar, Arithmetic, Book-keeping and practical Mathematics', for whom a school or schoolhouse was necessary, and whose salary the public should pay. A prison was required on Islay 'especially in a Country where the partiality of Family Attachments does in part still prevail'.

The main street in Bowmore was intersected by another and along the wide streets single-storey or two-storey houses were constructed, built directly on to the street with no front gardens. To encourage people away from the land and to make subsequent land reorganisation easier, whilst also recognising that those so displaced retained an attachment to land, he planned his village so that each family had a 'feu' consisting of a house site and a little land for a 'garden', potatoes, oats, flax and cow's grass. The village was thus intended for farmworkers or day-labourers and also for non-agricultural workers. Creation of suitable non-agricultural employment was apparently as difficult then as it is now, perhaps even more of a problem for island than mainland landlords. Fishing was not yet as important in Bowmore as Daniel Campbell had perhaps implied in his first memorial that it would be and the main national drive to reorganise and improve the fishing industry was still fifteen years or so in the future. Apart from an incipient service sector, distilling and other industries based on agriculture were the only possibilities. Linen-weaving in particular had to be introduced and encouraged if Bowmore was to succeed economically. Half a century later, when another phase of village-building on Islay was undertaken by Daniel Campbell's successors, there were more opportunities.

Linen manufacture, fishing and mining
In Daniel Campbell's memorials there seemed to be a tacit assumption that flax-growing was required, not merely to provide a basis for village industry, but that it represented in itself a significant agricultural improvement. In 1777 he claimed that 'Agriculture and the Flax husbandry in particular, have been my favourite objects.'[33] By 1776 he had contracted a Linen Manufacturer from south of the border to settle and carry on 'the Branches of Weaving and Bleaching, to whom he hath promised to advance a Considerable sum of money . . . and . . . hath already set up above Twelve Looms'. The laird also laid out ground which he offered rent-free for seven years to persons 'skilled in any Branch of the Linnen Manufacture as an Encouragement to Settle there'.[34]

This enthusiasm for flax-growing, before cotton from the American colonies reduced its importance, was apparently shared by someone else on Islay. Even before Daniel Campbell's first memorial, Mrs Margaret Campbell of Lagganlochan petitioned the Commissioners and Trustees for Improving Manufactures in Scotland for assistance in January 1765. Her request was sent the following month to the Commissioners of Annexed Estates as 'this Board's Funds are too narrow even for the low Countries'.[35] In passing on the request, the Board recommended 'the Island of Islay as remarkably fit for Flax Raising and Spinning' and also recommended Mrs Campbell as a 'proper person to be intrusted with the Distribution of any Encouragements the Commissioners may think fit to bestow'. In Mrs Campbell's opinion, for £60 to £80 per year for three years, it could be practicable 'to have Sixty Girls annualy taught Spinning, as many Wheels & Reels given them – and a Competent Allowance of good Flax seed given to the Farmers'. Thereafter she hoped 'they would be able to carry on the trade themselves'. Whereas the spinning was usually an occupation for the womenfolk, weaving was more likely to have been done by men, since it was much heavier work. Finishing, washing and drying would probably also have been done by women. The finished product was probably intended at first mainly for local consumption, although in 1772 Pennant noted that £2,000 worth of flax yarn was exported, which

A noted Scottish silversmith, Adam Graham, made this goblet about 1780 from Islay silver, mined from Dalradian limestone veins (Glasgow Museums).

Lead-smelting furnace at Freeport, 1772 (Trustees of The British Library).

'might be better manufactured on the spot to give employ to the poor natives'.[36] In 1777 Daniel Campbell could claim that 'Manufacturers have been brought, public marketts for the sale of yarn have been instituted and large quantities of Yarn sold'.[37]

As with other developmental opportunities, the scope for improvement in fishing seemed almost unlimited to Daniel Campbell. His first memorial in 1766 declared

The Shoars of this Island abound with most kinds of Fish known in the Scotch Seas; There are Several Rivers abounding with Salmon, and in Lochindale . . . great quantities of Herrings have been taken. There are Cod Banks on every side of the Island, most of which were of late discovered by Fishing Vessels from Liverpool and other parts of England. The Inhabitants know no Art of Fishing but by the Hand Line and Rod; wherewith they take Cod, Haddock, Whiting, Flounder; and a great Variety of other kinds particularly a Delicious Fish which they call the Merry Fish . . . But for want of method no great quantities are Caught.[38]

On his own initiative, he offered house sites and other attractions such as three acres of land, peat rights and free rent for seven years to encourage those 'skilled in the Cod and Herring Fishing, willing to settle in the said Island'. He had introduced the 'Long Lines, Salmon and Herring Netts', instead of the simple hand rods. The fish resources within and adjacent to the island had been explored and this suggested that there was 'very great Encouragement towards a profitable and lasting fishing'.

The most successful mode of fishing was buss fishing which depended on bounty paid. Daniel Campbell remarked that Islay already had ten busses, but that they were used only in the herring fishery from September to January. For the remainder of the year some or all of these were taken out of the water and the 'hands return to work on the land or are idle'. Daniel Campbell's intention was to convert this activity from a convenient off-season supplement to agriculture to a full-time occupation. He proposed to establish other branches of the 'Curable Fish that fall from January to September and thereby to secure Employment for the whole year and a Moderate Degree of profits on such as will Engage to Continue the Fisheries, when the Bounty is withdrawn'. But he had scarcely had time to effect much progress before his premature death.

According to Pennant as many as 700 men were employed in mining and fishing in Islay in 1772. Islay's mineral resources had been recognised by the Cawdor Campbells and they seem to have been of at least equal interest to Daniel Campbell the Younger, although government assistance was not available for mining and there is therefore no mention of it in the memorials addressed to the Commissioners. In July 1770 a report on the 'State of the Mines in Isla' was prepared for Daniel Campbell.[39] At that time there were eight mines open, all fairly near to each other and near the present village of Ballygrant. Seven exploited lead-ore veins (Mulreesh, Portnealon, Shenegart, North and South Ardachie, Ballygrant and Gartness) and one a copper vein at Kilslaven. Technical problems of drainage and power were described in each case, as well as the apparent richness of each mine. The general tone of the report was optimistic; the mines could be worked 'with considerable profit both to the Proprietor & Undertaker'.

This optimism was echoed by Pennant in the 1770s:

> The ore is of lead, much mixed with copper . . . the veins rise to the surface, have been worked at intervals for ages, and probably in the time of the Norwegians . . . The lead-ore is good; the copper yields thirty-three pounds per hundred; and forty ounces of silver from a ton of the metal. The lead-ore is smelted in an air-furnace, near Freeport . . . Not far from these mines are vast strata of that species of iron called bog-ore, of the concreted kind: beneath that large quantities of vitriolic mundic [iron pyrites].[40]

Pennant's enthusiasm, however, was not shared by Shawfield, who claimed that mining on Islay was only about half as profitable as it was in the better-known and richer veins at Leadhills in Lanarkshire, a view endorsed by John Williams in the 1780s.[41]

The first half century of Shawfield Campbells

For the Campbell of Cawdor period of management in Islay, the main problem for us today is a relative shortage of material and evidence. But from 1726 to 1777, when the first Daniel Campbell of Shawfield and his grandson were making their improvements and planning others, the problem is rather an excess of enthusiasm, most evident in the boundless optimism of the memorials. In assessing the extent to which the Shawfield Campbells had brought real benefits to Islay, it seems reasonable to conclude that, taking population increase into account, the island was economically more advanced in 1777 than it had been in 1726. A flax industry had been established and was apparently thriving; the mines near Ballygrant provided substantial employment and fishing was entering a phase of expansion. The new village of Bowmore offered a lifestyle and opportunities immensely different from the old village of Kilarrow at the head of Loch Indaal, removed for the development and enhancement of the 'policies' surrounding the stylish Georgian mansion available to the islanders before the 1760s. Encouragement of religion and education was scarcely more important than the institution of a pacquet to the mainland; all changes brought Islay and its inhabitants into closer contact with a Scotland that was itself in the ferment of the eighteenth-century 'enlightenment'.

This exchange of ideas was exemplified in the visit to Islay in July 1772 of the distinguished topographer, Thomas Pennant. He was a native of Flintshire, an antiquarian and naturalist with an 'unusual flair for accumulating historical information about whatever places he visited'.[42] The Islay visit took place during his second tour of Scotland; his first had taken him no further than the Lowlands. Even Samuel Johnson awarded Pennant a good mark: 'He's the best traveller I ever read; he observes more things than anyone else does'.[43] Thomas Pennant was far less critical of things Scottish than was Dr Johnson and was duly rewarded. Both Edinburgh and Glasgow made Pennant a Freeman of their cities, an honour that Glasgow has not felt called upon to accord to any other Welshman except David Lloyd George.

Travelling with Pennant on his second tour was the draughtsman Moses Griffith. It was he who drew or copied the illustrations that, engraved by Mazell, were included in the published account of Pennant's tour; some of the original drawings survive in the British Library.[44] The two men visited Islay from the 2nd to the 6th of July 1772 and, despite unpleasant sailings, they found much to interest them and thoroughly enjoyed the hospitality of various Campbell lairds. Apart from Shawfield himself, with whom they dined at Islay House, Pennant eulogised over Campbell of Sunderland's northern part of the Rinns:

> The improvements of his lands are excellent, and the grass so good and the fields so clean, as to vie with any place. Near the house, in a well-sheltered nook, is an apple-orchard, which bore plentifully: these with strawberries, are the fruits of these remote islands; the climate denied other luxuries of this nature: and even in these articles, Pomona [Roman goddess of trees and fruit] smiles but where she finds a warm protection.[45]

From Sunderland, he explored 'the unspeakably savage' scenery to the north and west and rode into the 'fine cave of Saneg-mor . . . of an august length and height'.

He similarly commented on Campbell of Ballinaby's estate:

> His land is quite riante [pleasing]; his pastures in good order; and his people busily employed in hay-making: observed one piece of good grass ground, which he assured me was very lately covered with heath, now quite destroyed by the use of shell-sand. Perhaps it may seem trifling to mention, that some excellent new potatoes were served up at dinner; but this circumstance, with the forwardness of the hay harvest, shows what may be effected by culture in this island, when the tenure is secure, for both Sunderland and Balnabbi are proprietors.

The cruck-frame cottage illustrated in Pennant's *Tour* could still be recognised in Islay's rural buildings, both ruined and occupied in the last century. (Pennant, *Tour*).

Spinning and weaving of flax into linen was one of the major innovations of the Campbells of Shawfield. The interior of a weaver's cottage, however, merited Pennant's description of the Ilich as 'lean, withered, dusky and smoke-dried' (Pennant, *Tour*). Depicted are grandmother, weaver and wife, with six of their children.

Because of the size of Islay, it was scarcely possible for the visitors to cover the entire island in four days and they do not appear to have ridden anywhere south of Bridgend. Pennant only mentions that he looked across the loch to Bowmore. Not everything that Pennant observed on Islay could be described as 'riante'. He also recorded

> . . . a set of people worn down with poverty: their habitations scenes of misery, made of loose stones; without chimnies, without doors, excepting the faggot opposed to the wind at one or other of the appertures, permitting the smoke to escape through the other, in order to prevent the pains of suffocation'. He continued 'The furniture perfectly corresponds: a pothook hangs from the middle of the roof, with a pot pendent over a grateless fire, filled with fare that may rather be called a permission to exist, than a support of vigorous life: the inmates, as may be expected, lean, withered, dusky and smoke-dried.

This picture, Pennant hastened to add, was one that was not limited to the island of Islay.

It is easy to forget that famine was still never far off even in the eighteenth century, whether from overpopulation, bad weather, crop disease or other causes. Pennant himself mentioned that in the summer of 1772 famine had only just been averted by the arrival of a ship, bearing part of the £1,000 worth of meal annually imported to the island. He described the natural effects of bad food and the related epidemics on the island, together with 'dropsies and cancers'. Other comments, for example on social customs and superstitions, reinforced his general picture of an island still only in the early stages of an economic and social transformation.

The rural squalor that Pennant described is, paradoxically, probably the best testimony to the vision of the first Daniel Campbell of Shawfield and even more to that of his grandson. 'I have assiduously pursued my plan of the improvement of that Island', wrote Daniel Campbell the Younger just before he died in 1777.[46] The social, economic and educational gap between the Shawfield Campbells and the vast majority of Islay's inhabitants was great. Although, or even because, the island offered better physical resources than many parts of the Highlands and Islands, it would not have been surprising if the Shawfield Campbells had seen improvement wholly in terms of economic benefit, especially to themselves, and resorted to the technique of clearance used elsewhere. It was Islay's good fortune that its owners saw improvement in social as well as economic terms and that they set out to improve the quality and condition of Islay's inhabitants. When Daniel Campbell the Younger died

in 1777, aged only forty, the main task of landholdings reorganisation
was still in the future, but the humanitarian character of the changes had
been established as the pattern to follow. The step from Pennant's cottages,
'scenes of misery', to the fine new village of Bowmore was a magnificent
beginning and Bowmore continues as a fitting memorial to the humanity
of its founder.

Notes and references

[1]   Devine, *Clanship*, p. 39.

[2]   *Ibid.*, p. 42.

[3]   I. H. Adams and M. Somerville, *Cargoes of Despair and Hope*, (Edinburgh, 1993), p. 211
       et seq.; W. R. Brock, *Scotus Americanus: a survey of the sources for links between Scotland and
       America in the eighteenth century*, (Edinburgh, 1982); Meyer, Highland Scots, 1732–1776,
       p. 84.

[4]   *The Edinburgh Advertiser*, 17 July 1772.

[5]   *The Edinburgh Advertiser*, 5 May 1772.

[6]   Russell, 'A Canny Scot', p. 176.

[7]   Forman, 'Islay House', *Scottish Field*, p. 40; NLS, Glasgow Testaments, 13 February
       1778, 604.

[8]   RCAHMS, *Argyll Inventory*, 5, p. 294.

[9]   Smith, *Book of Islay*, p. 469.

[10]   Daniel Campbell the Younger petitioned the Annexed Estates Commissioners on several
       occasions for grants or money to aid his plans for the development of Islay. These requests
       are in NRS, Annexed Estates Papers, E727/60 and E728/47.

[11]   NRS, E728/47/2 (2).

[12]   NRS, E728/47/l.

[13]   NRS, E728/47/4 (2).

[14]   NRS, E728/47/2(2).

[15]   NRS, E727/60/1.

[16]   Ibid.

[17]   NRS, E727/60/2.

[18]   Ibid.

[19]   NRS, E728/47/4(2).

[20]   Islay Estate Papers, Leases to tenants.

[21]   Smith, *Book of Islay*, pp. 469–71.

[22]   *Idem.*

[23]   *Idem.*

[24]   T. C. Smout, 'The Landowner and the Planned Village in Scotland, 1730–1830', in N. T.
       Phillipson and R. Mitchison, Scotland in the Age of Improvement, (Edinburgh, 1970),
       p. 76.

[25]   See RCAHMS, *Argyll* 5, pp. 184–5.

[26]   NRS, E 728/47/3.

27 William Adam had designed a circular church at Hamilton in 1732. His son's plan of 1758 was never executed. I. G. Lindsay and M. Cosh, *Inveraray and the Dukes of Argyll*, (Edinburgh, 1973), pp. 165–7.

28 Weir, *Guide to Islay*, p. 34.

29 Forman, 'Islay House', p. 38.

30 The *Ileach*, 36, 8 November 2008, p. 14.

31 Rental in 1779, according to Macdonald, *General View*, p. 619.

32 NRS, E728/47/4(2).

33 NRS, E727/60/1.

34 NRS, E728/47/1.

35 NRS, E728/19/7.

36 Pennant, *Tour*, p. 261.

37 NRS, E727/60/1.

38 NRS, E728/47/ 1.

39 Professor John Walker Papers, Edinburgh University Library, MS. D.c.i.57.

40 Pennant, *Tour*, p. 249.

41 J. Williams, *The Natural History of the Mineral Kingdom*, (London, 1789).

42 Pennant, Tour, pp. 249–68; G. V. Jones, 'Pennant, The Observant Traveller', *Scottish Field*, 1971, June, p. 23.

43 Jones, 'Pennant', p. 23.

44 According to Pennant, 'Joseph Banks, Esq. . . . permitted my artist to copy as many of the beautiful drawings in my collection, as would be of use in the present work'. The originals are in the British Library Map Library K. Top XLIX. 37. 3a and b.

45 Pennant, *Tour*, p. 254 *et seq*.

46 NRS, E727/60/1.

Sketch of Walter Campbell of Shawfield and Islay (1741–1816) who succeeded his brother, Daniel, in 1777. His first marriage produced five sons and six daughters, his second, one son and two daughters (artist unknown, private collection).

CHAPTER 8

Momentous times

When Daniel Campbell the Younger died in 1777, he left a large amount of personal and heritable debt, though perhaps little was directly related to the Islay estate. He also left closets full of dandy clothes and well-stocked cellars and libraries.[1] His next brother, John, had died a year or so earlier, also a bachelor. The succession of the Shawfield and Islay estates therefore passed to the third son, Walter Campbell of Skipness, born in 1741 and an advocate. Under the 1770 Law of Entail, Walter was initially unable to sell off parts of the estates to help clear debts of over £90,000. His difficulties were summarised in a petition sent to Parliament by Walter and some of his cousins, and a private Act enabling them to sell and realise some of the money was passed.[2] The Shawfield and Jura estates were sold, but Islay was retained in the family, along with Woodhall, Skipness and Ardpatrick. This decision was almost certainly in the best interests of Islay's inhabitants.

Walter Campbell unexpectedly became laird of Islay at the age of 36, beginning with considerable difficulties and only slightly fewer responsibilities, as he never became a Member of Parliament. He spent more time on his Islay estate than did many other Highland lairds, between three and four months each year and in 1788 extended it by purchasing the Sunderland estate in the Rinns for £10,000.[3] In almost four decades from 1777 to 1816 when he was responsible for Islay, changes in the island's economy and, to a certain extent in the landscape, continued, although perhaps the greatest number of changes that remain visible today did not occur until after his death. He came to be much admired by other improvers, travellers and visitors interested in the agriculture and changing social economy of the Highlands and Islands, in times that were often difficult for the nation as a whole. Walter Campbell shared his predecessors' concern for the islanders. In this Islay was fortunate: there were enough landlords elsewhere in the Highlands during this period who possessed vision and drive in abundance, but who were notoriously lacking in humanity. Walter's elder brother had set a pattern that seemed to require consolidation and extension after his death. In regard to agricultural improvements, for instance, it was becoming clear that the system of improving leases could only bring results if, instead of the older communal method of farming, every tenant had his own holding. This inevitably meant that fewer people should be dependent on agricultural employment, at a time when the population as a whole was growing. Sources of non-agricultural employment were therefore needed.

Relentless population growth
Innovation and improvement in a rural landscape are seldom easy to achieve on a large scale, though the more kindly environment and less acute population pressure in Islay at first may have made them easier and more rewarding than in many other parts of the Hebrides. Nevertheless, as elsewhere in the Highlands and Islands, the increasing population of villagers, tenants, subtenants and landless cottars was making a reorganisation of the system of agriculture simultaneously both more essential and more difficult to achieve. The Rev Dr Webster undertook the first comprehensive estimate of the population of Scotland in the middle of the eighteenth century. Alexander Webster was born in 1707 and was elected Moderator of the General Assembly of the Church of Scotland in 1754. Acting on behalf of the government, he persuaded the Society for Promoting Christian Knowledge in the Highlands and Islands to require every minister in those presbyteries where the society had erected charity schools, to enumerate his parishioners. In default the minister was threatened with withdrawal of the school. The total for Islay in 1755 was 5,344 persons, a figure that was to increase considerably over the next half century.[4] Dr. Webster's 5,344 islanders of 1755 had risen by the late 1760s to over 7,000. The clerical authors of *The Statistical Account* provided details of each Scottish parish in the early 1790s and estimated that the total population of Islay was then about 8,400, comprising the parish of Killarow with 2,500, Kilmeny 2,000, Kilchoman 2,300 and Kildalton 1,600.[5] One of the ministers even gave a total of 9,500 for the island; the laird himself claimed over 10,000, while the figure at the first official census in 1801 was to indicate an island population of 8,364.[6] Using this latter figure, there had been a growth of between fifty and sixty per cent in less than forty years.

With some justification the rise in numbers was universally regarded for much of the eighteenth century as a sign of progress and Daniel Campbell the Younger and his brother Walter looked forward to further growth. The latter claimed about 1791 that there had been no emigration in his time, 'though there are more inhabitants than are industriously employed. 'My great object has been . . . to retain at home and render usefully employed those hands that have heretofore been less productive than they ought to have been'.[7] At the end of the century Malthus published his *Essay on the Principle of Population* and national census-taking was instituted.[8] There were serious food crises in 1782–3, 1795–6, 1806–7 and 1816–17.[9] By then on Islay the concern had changed to the problem of relating the island's population to available resources and to creating non-agricultural means of employment. Here, as in other respects, Islay's main landlord reflected, or even slightly anticipated, national trends.

In the latter part of the eighteenth century and the early years of the nineteenth, similar increases in population had occurred for several reasons over most of the West Highland seaboard: the cessation of civil warfare after the 1745 rebellion; the spread of the potato as a human foodstuff that could be grown in increasingly marginal environmental conditions; end-of-century inoculation and vaccination against smallpox; and the existence of supplementary sources of income in linen manufacture, fishing, whisky distilling, mining, the manufacture of kelp from seaweed and employment in the military. The full reason for this rapid population increase is still not completely understood. The rate of increase varied from one part of the region to another and in Islay the lack of a substantial kelp industry, together with the relatively greater ease of outward migration to the mainland and emigration beyond Scotland, meant that the rate was not so great as elsewhere, or as it might otherwise have been.

Nevertheless the minister of the parish of Killarow and Kilmeny was able to comment in the early 1790s that 'the whole population of Islay has increased greatly within these 40 years, owing principally to the tenants, who are in possession of large farms, dividing their possessions among their children, which encourages marriage. Some, however, who are reduced in their circumstances, are obliged to emigrate'.[10] There were years of food crisis and wartime shortages. This theme of emigration was further developed by the writer of the Kildalton parish account, when he observed that 'the females are more numerous than the males, a great number of young men having left the parish, and gone to the Low Country [i.e. the Scottish Lowlands] for employment. Some have gone to America and other places; so that the number of inhabitants has diminished within these forty years'.[11] With the institution of regular decennial censuses in 1801 it becomes possible, despite defects in the early censuses, to be more precise about changes in numbers, age structure, occupation and other characteristics, though not in detail about migration.

While the Islay population increased dramatically during the second half of the eighteenth century, agrarian and other changes maintained, and even improved, standards of life. But it was often achieved by the exodus of people. Highlanders and islanders had left for Europe, England and

Ireland for centuries long before the 1700s and from the 1730s transatlantic emigrations to New York and North Carolina involved substantial numbers. Others left for army and navy service, and after the Seven Years War there was a renewed increase in emigration in the years between 1763 and 1775.[12] More left from the Highlands and Islands than from any other British region except the London area.[13] Almost one-fifth of all British emigrants in these years came from the Highlands and Islands of Scotland, one of the most sparsely populated areas of the United Kingdom.

Transatlantic emigration all but ceased during the American War and when it resumed, was less frantic. After the outbreak of war with France in 1793 emigration again slowed down, but after peace in 1801 the exodus rose to the high levels seen before the American War. Landowners and government were concerned about the potential loss of labour and army recruits and rushed through a Passenger Vessels Act in 1803 to increase the costs of transatlantic voyage.[14] The number of emigrants fell drastically again, though individuals and parties of Highlanders continued to leave during the Napoleonic wars.

These waves of emigration, consisting mainly of able-bodied men and small tenants with some means, were a reaction to the many changes in land settlement, rentals and tenure which were threatening the old way of life. The reasons why so many people should seek to emigrate are far from clear. The 'pull' factors involving 'chain migration' to the expanding settlement and economies of the transatlantic colonies were important. The 'push' of Malthusian population pressures in a rising population may have led to the outflow of 'surplus' people. Population loss was inevitable because the Highland and Hebridean economy could not always generate enough work. However, the picture between 1769 and 1815 is considerably more complex and it is by no means certain that the demographic explanation is entirely satisfactory for that earlier period. Economic activity was often expanding, despite years of crisis. This was not an exodus born of the stress of hunger and destitution. Rather it was a movement which involved a degree of choice in which the the Highlanders and islanders chose to go to the New World to improve their situation, as 'makers and masters of their own destiny'.[15] This emigration was one of rising expectations.

Changes in the rural scene
The three main aspects of the agrarian revolution in Scotland were enclosure, consolidation of holdings into single farm units and the separation of agricultural and industrial activities. Depending on population pressure and other factors, these occurred at different times in different areas of the Highlands and Islands. The general enclosure acts

enabled the Scottish lairds to make these improvements more informally and not necessarily all at once. It has been claimed for Islay that 'towards the end of the seventies . . . the dominant personality, Campbell of Shawfield, a landowner with control of almost the whole island, had driven through a complete agrarian reorganisation with the aid of a band of farmers who combined elegant manners with professional assiduity'.[16] However, other writers had different views and from archive evidence it seems clear that such a sudden and wholesale reorganisation did not take place. One of Walter Campbell's inherited difficulties was that many leases did not expire until 1796.[17]

However, by 1785 James Anderson was reporting that it was difficult to imagine the degree of improvement that could be achieved in the islands. They had been 'hitherto so entirely neglected [except] for the island of Islay which has been for a few years past under the care of a judicious proprietor, who has studied to augment his own revenue by promoting the prosperity of his people'.[18] Walter Campbell himself described what he had achieved by the beginning of 1791.[19] Over thirty miles of good roads had been built, with bridges and milestones, two quays erected, small inns built, regular packet and post established, and the two villages of Bowmore and Portnahaven begun. Land was being reclaimed, Shetland sheep imported (with plans for Spanish sheep as well), and exports included horned cattle, horses (including one 'bred by me' which was being ridden by the Prince of Wales), fish, kelp, yarn and even grain.

The writers of *The Statistical Account* in the last decade of the eighteenth century were local ministers who compensated for their lack of wider experience by their ability to give precise information about specific places in their parishes. The Rev Archibald Robertson of Kildalton bewailed the lack of attention given to agricultural improvements by the small tenants and the gentlemen farmers of his parish alike. He contrasted this situation with the parish of Killarow where people 'are encouraged to improve a little in agriculture, by the example of Mr Campbell of Shawfield, who is one of the best farmers in the west of Scotland: and perhaps his Islay estate is capable of as much improvement as any in the kingdom'.[20] Only a small part of the Kildalton parish was described as being enclosed and this deterrent to improvement was emphasised. Less favoured physically, Kildalton's relative isolation from the main centre of activities at the head of Loch Indaal was probably another factor delaying improvements. The only route from this parish to the others was along the beach of Laggan Bay; no roads over the peat bogs had yet been built.

The Rev John Murdoch, minister of the united parishes of Killarow and Kilmeny, also paid tribute to Mr Campbell, who 'has improved large tracts of moor ground, within view of his own house, which lies about three English miles from the village; and from his method of cultivation, they have produced large crops. He spares neither pains nor expence; and in this respect several of his tenants attempt to imitate him'.[21] Mr Murdoch estimated that about £700 to £1,000 annually was spent by Walter Campbell on improvements, compared to an island annual rent several times that amount.[22] The same approving attitude was adopted by the Kilchoman writer: 'Within these dozen years, the present proprietor has more than doubled his rents; yet the tenantry, as well as himself, are better off than ever. They have given him, as it were, an addition to his estate, by rescuing many acres of moor and moss, from a state of nature, and bringing them to yield good crops of corn and grass. On the other hand, the proprietor has given the tenants such advantageous leases, that they have greatly bettered their circumstances, as well as increased their numbers, and are enabled to live much more comfortably than formerly'.[23]

One might suspect that some of this praise by the Islay ministers was generated by the knowledge that the proprietor was not only responsible for their appointment and for paying their stipend, but was likely to read their comments when the *Account* was published. Their accuracy is, however, evident from the independent appraisals of more expert witnesses. Contemporary writers and analysts, experienced in assessing estate management, recorded the improvements that had taken place despite population and other difficulties. The general impression that improvements were taking place in some areas of Islay but not in others is also corroborated by contemporaneous estate documents and rentals. Leases and rentals indicate that by the end of the eighteenth century, the earlier pattern of large single holdings and joint farms had been altered in several respects, particularly in their relative distribution. There is also evidence that tenants were becoming mobile, going within the island from one township to another, or from townships to single holdings. They were also moving into the village of Bowmore and were migrating to the mainland, especially to the Scottish lowlands and emigrating abroad.

Even more striking was the small number of large areas rented by a single farmer: by 1798 there were only 32.[24] Some of the large tacks had become single farms. Others, instead of being worked by subtenants, had become joint farms with tenants who rented directly from the laird but still farmed in common. The large holdings were still in the north-east and south-east and there were some medium and small-sized holdings near the laird's mansion at the head of Loch Indaal. But the distribution of joint holdings with more than two tenants had considerably expanded in area. Multiple townships existed over the whole of the Oa peninsula and in the interior valleys of the eastern hills. Indeed between 1779 and 1802 the leases showed an increase of about one-third in the numbers of legal small tenants per holding. Subtenants too may have increased, although the new leases were supposed to debar tenants from subletting.

The Hebridean model

Into the new century, Robert Fraser recorded that the improvement of Islay had been going on ever since Anderson's time, in an 'accelerated ratio in every kind of improvement'.[25] During his tour in the following decade, the surgeon-geologist, John MacCulloch, considered that Islay retained 'so few of the Highland manners, as scarcely to excite any feelings different from the Low Country'.[26] During Walter Campbell's lairdship the most complete record of the agricultural situation in Islay, however, compared to the rest of the Hebrides, is that of James Macdonald.[27] Born in North Uist in 1777, Macdonald later gave up the struggle to be a sedentary minister of a Fife parish church and became a much-travelled companion to the Clanranald heir at the turn of the century.[28] He was commissioned by Sir John Sinclair to write a *General View of the Agriculture of the Hebrides* and in 1808 spent the months of May to September gathering information in the islands. His payment was £300 in three instalments and his work was highly praised over forty years later: 'No better report has ever appeared on any special subject'.[29] Macdonald recalled the time spent on Islay in 1808 as one of the happiest periods of his life, 'and equally interesting, whether recollected as dedicated to the contemplation of a sequestered island in a state of rapid improvement, and unlooked for approaches to a high state of refinement; or as enjoyed in the conversation and company of a most polished and hospitable class of his Hebridean countrymen'.[30] He reckoned the island to be 'the most improved of the large Hebrides, and as the leader and model of the other isles, [it] deserves particular attention'.[31]

Macdonald's systematic analysis and text of 700 octavo pages, covering the Hebrides as a whole, are accompanied by an appendix of regional Hebridean descriptions, adding another 200 pages. Throughout both parts there are recurrent references to Islay as a Hebridean model. His use of sources and attempts at quantification, analysis and explanation are impressive. In his preliminary references to Islay and to Walter Campbell, Macdonald inserted a careful disclaimer, that as he was going to 'make frequent mention of this gentleman, and always to his advantage, it is but justice to him and to myself to state (in order to prevent the imputation of partiality), that, at the time of writing this, I have not the honour of his acquaintance, and have never as yet even seen him'.[32]

Macdonald also paid due and sometimes considerable praise to other improvers in Islay and elsewhere. These included the other main improving proprietor of the island, Campbell of Ballinaby, as well as some of Shawfield's tenants, 'thirty gentlemen farmers'. Concerning Campbell of Ballinaby's efforts, he explained: 'Mr Campbell of Ballinaby, in Islay, is fast improving both soft peatmoss and hard hill ground, for the purposes of aration. He rears excellent horses of the real west or Hebridian breed on his own property, rather larger than the common gearran [gelding], but with the same properties of strength, activity, durability, and hardiness. A pair can draw the plough, with proper management, for twelve hours every day in the week. Three pairs of these ploughed regularly, each working day, from the 6th till the 24th of May 1808, and with singular vigour and correctness, without any driver or leader but the ploughman. They had done the same for months before. We have never seen a more beautiful furrow in Norfolk, East Lothian or Holstein than behind the Gearrans, bred in Islay, and conducted, both plough and horses, by one Islay boy'.[33] A decade earlier, the Kilchoman minister had noted that the Islay folk were said to keep too many horses at the expense of 'the system' of black cattle. There was a lively trade in horses across the North Channel, culminating in the annual Ballycastle Fair.

Macdonald set out clearly his reasons for emphasising the roles of individuals in the island, rather than that of their environment. He argued that the state of property was neither very favourable nor very adverse to agricultural improvements. More depended on the landlord's disposition: every improvement of consequence owed its origin and success to 'some spirited and intelligent' proprietor, especially one who resided regularly on the spot and who understood business. Although Macdonald seems to have regarded Walter Campbell of Shawfield as the most impressive improver in all the Hebrides, many of the other southern islands, including Gigha, Colonsay and parts of Mull, were farther ahead than most of the Outer Hebrides. This was attributed mainly to the influence of the landlords, but Macdonald suggested that there were other more complex reasons, such as the lairds' interest in, or an area's ability to produce profitable, if labour intensive, kelp from seaweed. He was particularly impressed that at that time there were never any arrears of rent on the estate of Islay, although he subsequently contradicted himself on this point.

In Macdonald's comparisons, Campbell of Shawfield found himself in distinguished company of the great estates of 'Lord Macdonald, Shawfield, Clanranald, Seaforth, Duke of Argyll, Hamilton, &c.', managed by resident stewards or factors, who usually lived on the spot. Lord Macdonald and Campbell of Shawfield were able to demonstrate that 'a large rental is not incompatible with the other duties of a landlord'. He claimed that Shawfield had always distinguished himself since he succeeded to the Islay estate as 'the first of the Hebridian improvers. Residing in that island for three or four months of the year, 'he spends among a tenantry, who love and respect him, a very large portion of the rents which they pay'. He planted trees, and they grew where 'it was supposed none could thrive'. He enclosed, drained, embanked, and 'shut out the sea' from several hundred acres of fine land. Employing nearly one hundred labourers all the year round, and teaching 'practically regular industry, good order and perseverance . . . He encourages, in the most judicious and effectual manner, all those tenants who exhibit active industry, and a desire for improvement'. Macdonald claimed that by these means Walter Campbell had within thirty-four years tripled the rents, and the intrinsic value of his fine islandas well as bettering the situation of his tenants 'beyond description', at the same time doubling their numbers. This outcome he attributed to the fact that most of the other great proprietors are at present non-residents, and spent very little of their time upon their estates'.[34]

Macdonald did allow that the environment of Islay may have encouraged experiments in agricultural improvements. His field observations of the soils, for example, led him to conclude that substantial areas of the island showed 'judicious management, rational industry, and rapid improvement. The principal proprietor, as well as Mr Campbell of Ballinaby, sets a good example, which a very respectable tenantry are anxious to follow. Green crops are generally introduced – lime stone is burned for manure with peat fuel, even by the small tenants, who pay no more than eight or ten pounds of rent; and inclosures, roads, and draining, give the soil an air of sheltered richness and comfort rarely witnessed on this side of Scotland'.[35]

This contrast with other parts of the Hebrides could be measured in different ways. Macdonald reckoned that Islay had just over 8,000 hectares of arable and meadow land, after the Uists and Barra (16,000), Skye (12,000) and Harris and Lewis (10,500).[36] Islay had twelve per cent of the arable and meadow in the islands, although the island represented a much smaller proportion of the total area. Rents for part of Islay represented about 30s. (£1.50) per year for each person, compared to 23s. (£1.15) for the Hebrides as a whole, or 120s. (£6.00) for Berwickshire.[37]

The agricultural system that gave such encouraging results was an interesting blend of the traditional and the novel; the major visible changes in landscape and agrarian reorganisation in Islay were yet to happen. Though there had been some changes in landholdings, the prosperity was based more on new crops and new methods. Among the novelties was wheat cultivation, in which Macdonald noted a 'fair experiment' had been made, but he also recognised that some years must elapse before the results of the experiment might be good enough to warrant encouragement. It may seem to modern eyes an unlikely crop for Islay, but this was the period of the Napoleonic blockade.

Barley, used for cattle food and for whisky distilling, was a different matter. Macdonald reported that barley was grown from improved strains, instead of the old, low-yielding 'bear' or 'bigg' barley. Lime, spread to destroy the grub worms to which barley was very prone, helped to give good yields. Oats of course were grown both for human consumption and for animal fodder, as were potatoes. The latter were important also as a cash crop for export; as in Bute, Gigha and Colonsay, the potato fields were usually drilled and then hoed, in contrast to the lazybed digging of the Outer Hebrides. Similar improvements were evident in green crops. The first field of clover in the Hebrides had been sown in Islay as far back as 1761 and new grass strains had been introduced for both hay and pasture. The flax that was among the earliest innovations of Daniel Campbell was the basis of the yarn-spinning and linen-weaving, producing what Macdonald described as the staple commodity of the island of Islay.

Despite such crop improvements, the mainstay of agriculture on Islay remained livestock and, as in the past, this meant cattle rather than sheep. Some of the wealthier farmers had introduced new breeds, but black cattle still represented a large proportion of the total. While touring the Highlands in 1803, James Hogg, 'the Ettrick Shepherd', claimed that 'Campbell of Islay, and he only, hath long disputed the field with [the duke of] Argyll for the best breed of Highland cattle . . . it is truly amazing the prices that these two houses draw for their cattle, it being much more than double the average price at Dumbarton Market'.[38] The lack of sheep – Macdonald claimed there were no sheep farms as such on Islay – was unlike the situation in many other parts of the Highlands and Islands where clearances were already substituting sheep in the previous rural economy. In Macdonald's view, Islay and some of the other smaller islands could not afford room for sheep walks and were better under black cattle. Wool and mutton were imported to Islay and instead of sheep, Macdonald noted that hogs were reared in great numbers. These, like potatoes, were apparently intended partly for export to Ireland.

This pattern of slow but perceptible change, based as much on improvements to the old order as on its replacement by new techniques, became the characteristic feature of the agricultural 'revolution' on Islay. In the types of crop and breeds of animal, in the system of rotation and the patterns of landholdings, old and new methods continued to coexist until at least the middle of the nineteenth century. This evolution was in contrast to many parts of the wider West Highland region where swifter and more uniform transformation of the landscape of any one estate, resulting in a pattern of large sheep farms and lotted crofting townships, was a true revolution.

Non-agrarian change

Unlike his predecessor, and especially his successor, Walter Campbell did not establish further new villages to accommodate the growing island population. Nor did the Campbell seat at Islay House change much. It was, however, probably during this period that the source for much of the agricultural innovation was created, the Home Farm in Islay House Square. Bowmore, established in 1768, continued to develop as the main administrative centre for the island. Shore, Jamieson (reputedly named after a drover) and High Streets had been laid out to the west of Main Street and School and Flora Streets east of it. It is possible that some of the single-storeyed cottages in these streets that remained thatched as late as the 1960s were among those referred to in *The Statistical Account* of the 1790s, although much altered internally.[39] In the first decade of the nineteenth century Bowmore's population, according to the village schoolmaster, was about 670.[40] Along the broad Main Street and a number of the cross streets, are some of the survivors of the Georgian houses and cottages of the late-eighteenth century, extensively remodelled inside. A watercolour of a Fair Day in Bowmore in the 1830s shows the slate-roofed houses along the main street and there is today much similarity.[41]

One of the Shawfield Campbells' enthusiasms was the development of linen manufacture and this was a main stimulus to employment in Bowmore, along with day-labouring. With each house and garden the Shawfield landlords granted nineteen-year leases for feus of five or ten acre lots outside the village 'to be reclaimed from a wild state, the first 6 years gratis and the other 13 years at a very small rent . . . many hundred acres . . . which a few years ago were used as peat mosses, and not worth 6d. an acre of rent, are now covered with flourishing crops'.[42] These lots remain clearly visible today on either side of School Lane. Around £7,000 was raised annually by the manufacture of linen, some of it exported. Little flax was grown elsewhere in the Hebrides; Islay produced three times as much as all the other islands combined.[43] One Scots acre on Islay produced thirty-two stones of lint, bringing the farmer a profit of two guineas and providing three months' employment for twelve people in its manufacture. Whatever the importance of linen manufacture to Bowmore in its first half-century, it declined subsequently as cotton and wool replaced linen and as large factories in the Lowlands and England replaced the handloom weavers of the villages. By 1841, when detailed employment information became available for the first time, in the copies of the census returns there was only a handful of handloom weavers then in Bowmore, half of them making linen cloth, the other half using wool.[44]

The British Society for Promoting the Fisheries of Scotland was established to encourage landlords to set up villages expressly for fishing. Tobermory on Mull and Ullapool on the Wester Ross mainland were the two main results of this endeavour.[45] It is rather surprising that the response was not greater, in view of the importance of fishing on Scotland's east coast and the comparative shortage of land-based resources along the west coast. In 1785 the economist, James Anderson, suggested that part of the explanation was to be found in the restrictions caused by the laws on salt; he also emphasised the latent aversion to the sea of most inhabitants of the West Highlands. Anderson recommended subsidies that would encourage landlords to establish fishing villages and he argued that these villages would have to be planned on a relatively large scale if they were to be successful.[46]

On Islay, the arguments for fishery development had been heeded by Daniel Campbell the Younger. It was his brother Walter who was left to make the first significant experiments in this direction, after his purchase of the Sunderland estate in 1788.[47] At this time Portnahaven, on the southern tip of the Rinns, was already a thriving fishing harbour and settlement. According to the Kilchoman minister, writing in *The Statistical Account*, Portnahaven was famous for its cod fishing and Walter Campbell had encouraged its development by providing boats, land and timber for houses.[48] The main problem was the lack of a market. By the first decade of the nineteenth century both local and distant markets for Portnahaven fish had expanded. Macdonald described the industry as he found it in 1808: 'The inhabitants of the village were furnished with fresh fish at a halfpenny per pound; and each of the fishermen cleared £2 sterling by one night's industry . . . they frequently run over with cargoes of [fish] to . . . Ireland, and sell them under the name of wild salmon'.[49] But development of this resource still lay in the future; it depended not merely on infrastructure and the encouragement of Islay fishermen but required parallel development of transport facilities and marketing arrangements.

Although less evidence survives of Walter Campbell's activities outside the agrarian sphere, he did report in 1779 to the Commissioners of the Annexed Estates on the use of the grant that they had made to his brother two years earlier. Walter had spent £250 of the grant, matched by a similar contribution himself, on the Port Askaig pier and on various unspecified coastal fishing experiments. Work on Bowmore pier had not yet begun

Fishermen's cottages nestle around Portnahaven harbour; the village was renowned for its many seafaring captains. Nowadays many of the houses are occupied, mainly in summer, by families based in Glasgow or beyond. (Eric Thorburn).

and he asked for the remaining £250 of the grant in advance: 'Besides the Pier at Portaskeig a much larger and more expensive one is proposed to be erected at Bowmore the principal village in the Island situate upon the first harbour in the West the estimate whereof amounts to £420 Str and is to be begun the 1st of March next, part of the materials being already provided and laid down. It is therefore hoped the Honourable Board will now find it convenient to advance the other £250 . . . towards erecting the Quay at Bowmore'.[50]

By the time of *The Statistical Account* in 1794, the Rev John Murdoch was able to describe the fine quay at Bowmore which could take vessels of three metres' draught. In the late-eighteenth century, however, fishing was still mainly for local consumption. Every farm around the head of Loch Indaal was alleged to have a boat, but James Anderson noted that there was little attempt to utilise this resource except for family needs. Around Islay, shellfish were to be found 'in very great quantities; crabs and lobsters of the largest size, and finest quality Great quantities of oysters of different kinds . . . also great plenty of mussels, cockles, clams, rasor or spout-fish, limpets, wilks, shrimps and several other sorts'.[51] Similarly there was no shortage of what he described as 'finny fish'; shoals of mackerel, the abundant haddocks, whitings, skate, halibut, sole, and flounders. As for herring, 'the quantities that might be catched on these coasts between the months of June and January, were the inhabitants in a situation that permitted them to follow that business, are so great as would appear altogether incredible to such as never have been on those coasts'.

At the turn of the century Walter Campbell and other neighbouring landowners, including Archibald Campbell of Jura and Messrs McNeill of Colonsay and of Oronsay, approached another source of public finance. They prepared an application in 1804 to the recently-established Commissioners for Making Roads and Building Bridges in the Highlands of Scotland, asking for help with their planned improvements to the mainland through Islay and Jura.[52] Walter Campbell wanted financial help for the survey and construction of the extension to the existing road from Port Askaig to Bridgend that had been made at his expense. The proposed extension to Portnahaven was surveyed in 1805 by George Langlands and built the following year at a cost of just over £60 per kilometre for its 22 kilometres. The section through Jura suffered various complications, but was eventually built at Archibald Campbell's expense by about 1810, by which time the stone piers at Feolin and Lagg, still extant today, were also 'of the most substantial kind'.

Although kelp manufacture was never so significant to Islay's economy as it was elsewhere in the Hebrides, there was some activity, especially in the south-east where conditions for growth were more conducive than on the other Islay coasts. Even there was less than the five or so metres regarded by Macdonald as being favourable for seaweed growth.[53] A letter from Campbell of Ardmore in 1820 described some of the difficulties of reaping seaweed in Islay, including the lack of 'experts' who could increase the harvest.[54] In 1821 the Islay factor paid out £413 in about 400 individual payments, so the scale was indeed small. The individual producer retained only about one-third of the price from the mainland dealers, the other two-thirds going equally to Walter Campbell and to freight charges. Nor did mining contribute much to the island at this time; MacCulloch's report in the second decade of the century was that the lead mines had been abandoned for some time.[55]

Brewing and distilling, however, were increasing. It is difficult to estimate either the amounts of spirits produced or the numbers employed. But when the 1795 Act was passed which prohibited illicit distilling in Britain, the 'in farm' supervisor of the excise on Islay was supposed to have 'taken up' about ninety stills some with a capacity of over eighty gallons.[56] But the islanders were not to be outdone and replaced them almost as quickly, only to have these confiscated in turn. The reverend authors of *The Statistical Account* frequently referred to the evils of alcohol, while other less prejudiced writers observed the existence of many distilleries on the island. Macdonald, for instance, remarked that the islanders were 'fond of ardent spirits . . . They might, however be gradually weaned . . . from their obstinate prejudices in favour of whiskey, were a few breweries established among them'.[57] Walter Campbell had 'with his unwonted activity and beneficence, built a brew-house', and established 'a complete brewing apparatus at Bridgend, near Bowmore . . . some years ago'. Macdonald described its output, on the basis of his own acquaintance with it in 1808, as being 'very good strong ale and table-beer' which appeared 'already to have effected a laudable change in the taste of the whiskey-drinking classes on that island, many of whom now prefer good ale to bad whiskey, and have relinquished the detestable habits of drunkenness in which they were formerly too apt to indulge'.

Running like a thread through many of the contemporary accounts was the growing realisation that, however desirable or remarkable were the improvements in agriculture and other traditional activities, the growing pressure of population demanded other solutions. Macdonald noted that although spinning of yarn and weaving of cloth were carried out in Islay for local use, it was not the basis of an industry that served many markets beyond the island. There were no bleachfields in the Hebrides, 'not even in Islay, where great quantities of flax are manufactured into yarns and linens, and whence these are sent to the Firth of Clyde and Dumbarton for bleaching'.[58] There were also growing opportunities for employment in the service sector, especially through increasing transport of imports and exports to and from the mainland and Ireland. Nevertheless there were still too many people on Islay for the available work. The government assistance provided in the 1770s was not repeated in very large sums. Macdonald claimed that 'government has done nothing in Islay to promote the improvements carried on by the patriotic and enlightened proprietor, who . . . has done much; but he cannot do everything'.[59] Campbell of Shawfield and Islay, Macdonald indicated, was willing to sacrifice rent increases and land improvements and was willing to carry arrears of rent, to avoid clearing people from the land. But it was impossible for them all to be accommodated on the island in a manner 'consistent with his general system'. The quandary was handed on to Walter Campbell's successor.

In 1814, two years before he died, Walter Campbell gave the Sunderland estate that he had acquired in 1788 to his second surviving son, Walter, while the estates of Skipness and Ardpatrick went to his remaining younger sons, Robert and Colin.[60] Walter Campbell, 'the most zealous improver of all', died at Islay House on 19 October 1816, at the age of seventy five; his monument is in the round church at Bowmore. His first marriage, at the age of twenty seven, to Eleanor Kerr of Newfield had produced ten children. His heir, John, had latterly been a Member of Parliament for Ayr Burghs until, in what had almost become a family tradition, he predeceased his father in 1809. John Campbell's marriage in 1796 to Lady Charlotte Campbell, youngest daughter of the fifth duke of Argyll, had produced a male heir, Walter Frederick Campbell, who was eighteen when his grandfather died.

John, known as Jack, and Lady Charlotte had developed a peripatetic and expensive lifestyle revolving around his regiment, then Argyll militia commitments, followed by parliamentarian ones, as well as producing nine children in as many years. Even before he died in 1809, Jack and his father, Walter, had tried to reschedule his debts, which by Jack's death amounted to almost £8,000. Walter Campbell, himself the father of fourteen children, was hard-pressed and had arranged long loans from relatives. His grandson, Walter Frederick, thus inherited personal as well as estate encumbrances and difficulties.[61]

Notes and references

[1] Islay Estate Papers, Inventories.

[2] Macdonald, *General View*, p. 63 and p. 619.

[3] J. G. Smith, *The Old Country Houses of the Old Glasgow Gentry*, (Glasgow, 1880).

[4] Kyd, *Scottish Population Statistics*, p. 33.

[5] Sinclair, *OSA*, pp. 276–302.

[6] W. Campbell to Earl Bathurst, 26 January 1791, Historical Manuscripts Commission, *Report on the Manuscripts of Earl Bathurst*, (London, 1923), p. 20.

[7] *Idem.*

[8] T. R. Malthus, *An Essay on The Principle of Population*, (London, 1798).

[9] Sinclair, *OSA*, p. 293.

[10] *Ibid.*, p. 301.

[11] *Idem.*

[12] Alexander Campbell of Balole or 'Scotus Americanus', published a tract for potential emigrants to North Carolina, in 1773 and had also spent some years in the West Indies. See A. Murdoch, 'A Scottish Document', pp. 438–49.

[13] B. Bailyn, *Voyages to the West*, (New York, 1986), p. 95.

[14] Devine, *Clanship*, p. 179.

[15] J. M. Bumstead, *The People's Clearance*, (Edinburgh, 1982), p. 221.

[16] M. Gray, *The Highland Economy 1750–1850*, (London, 1957), p. 81.

[17] Smith, *Book of Islay*, p. 469.

[18] Anderson, *Account*, p. 145.

[19] Campbell to Bathurst, 26 January 1791, HMC, *Bathurst*, pp. 20–1.

[20] Sinclair, *OSA*, p. 287.

[21] *Ibid.*, pp. 298–99.

[22] By 1808 the annual rental was £11,000. Macdonald, *General View*, p. 613.

[23] Sinclair, *OSA*, p. 284.

24   Islay Estate Papers, Rental for 1795.

25   R. Fraser, *A Letter to the Right Hon. Charles Abbot, Speaker of the House of Commons, containing an Inquiry into the most effectual means of improvement on the coasts and western isles of Scotland, and the extension of the Fisheries*, (London, 1803).

26   J. MacCulloch, *The Highlands and Western Isles of Scotland . . . Founded on a series of annual journeys between . . . 1811 and 1821*, 4 vols. (London, 1824). 4, p. 419.

27   Macdonald, *General View*: Islay is referred to throughout the text; the main Islay account is on pp. 612–63.

28   Biographical material on James Macdonald is from A. Gillies, *A Hebridean in Goethe's Weimar*, (Oxford, 1969).

29   J. Donaldson, *Agricultural Biography*, (London, 1854), p. 103.

30   Macdonald, *General View*, p. 633.

31   *Ibid.*, p. 614.

32   *Ibid.*, p. 64.

33   *Ibid.*, p. 66.

34   *Ibid.*, pp. 63–4.

35   *Ibid.*, p. 21.

36   *Ibid.*, p. 27.

37   Macdonald, *General View*, pp. 549–50.

38   James Hogg, *A Tour in the Highlands in 1803*, (Paisley, 1888), pp. 25–6.

39   Sinclair, *OSA*, p. 301.

40   Macdonald, *General View*, p. 637.

41   Forman, 'Islay House', p. 38.

42   Macdonald, *General View*, p. 630.

43   *Ibid.*, p. 532.

44   Copies of the Census enumerators' schedules for 1841 to 1901, NRS.

45   Lewis, *Topographical Dictionary*, 2, p. 546.

46   Anderson, *Account*, p. 67ff.

47   See Campbell of Sunderland Papers, NLS, Acc. 6233, 11. The Sunderland estate had had to be sold after bamkruptcy and death of its owner, Robert Campbell.

48   Sinclair, *OSA*, p. 281.

49   Macdonald, *General View*, pp. 630–1.

50   NRS, E727/60/3 (1).

51   Anderson, *Account*, pp. 10–11.

52   See *Reports of the Commissioners for making Roads and Bridges in the Highlands and Islands of Scotland, BPP*, 1805, III; 1807, III; 1810, IV and 1812–13, V.

53   Macdonald, *General View*, pp. 621–2. About twenty tons of seaweed produced one ton of kelp.

54   Islay Estate Papers, Factor's note about payments to kelp gatherers in Ardmore, 1820.

55   MacCulloch, *Highlands and Western Islands*, p. 419; see also R. Forsyth, *The Beauties of Scotland*, 5 vols. (Edinburgh, 1805–8), 5 (1808), p. 517.

56   A. J. Youngson, *After the Forty Five* (Edinburgh, 1973), pp. 115–6.

[57]   Macdonald, *General View*, p. 207.

[58]   *Ibid.*, p. 53.

[59]   *Ibid.*, p. 631.

[60]   Islay Estate Papers, Disposition of the Estate of Sunderland, 1814.

[61]   Perth and Kinross Council Archives, Threipland Papers, MS 169/2/3/16.

CHAPTER 9

Designing the landscape

Almost a hundred years had passed between the purchase of Islay by 'Great' Daniel Campbell in 1726 and the death of Walter Campbell in 1816 and during this time the basic task facing a landlord on Islay had changed. The initiative and perseverance of the Campbells of Shawfield, their factors and tenants, had yielded results that deserved and received widespread recognition among agricultural experts and social observers throughout and beyond Scotland.

By the second decade of the nineteenth century and with recession after the end of the Napoleonic wars, the need for further agricultural improvements still remained, but it had ceased to be the primary problem. Prosperity had brought its own difficulties in the form of a population that was continuing its rapid growth, despite migration. If agricultural reorganisation was to be pursued to its logical conclusion in terms of maximising revenue, then a large number of families would have to find their primary income from non-agricultural sources. There was, in fact, no real choice: a reduced dependence on agriculture was as necessary, on a long-term view, for the tenants and cottars as for the landlord.

The scope for influence and initiative on the part of the principal laird, however, was still enormous and Walter Frederick Campbell grasped the opportunity, despite inherited and escalating financial problems. Succeeding his grandfather at the age of only eighteen, over the next thirty two years he initiated many of the changes in agriculture and settlement that have contributed to the present appearance of Islay. The period of Walter Frederick Campbell's lairdship of Islay was probably one with greatest evidence of change that Islay ever witnessed, as far as landscape and settlement were concerned.

In his personal life, Walter Frederick Campbell repeated several of the Shawfield characteristics. He was a member of parliament, for Argyll, between 1822 and 1841 and was married twice.[1] His first wife and cousin, Lady Eleanor Charteris, daughter of the eighth earl of Wemyss, was the inspiration for the names of two of the villages that he established, Port Ellen and Port Wemyss. The death of Lady Eleanor in 1832, after mental

The artist, William Heath, recorded the Islay scene in the 1830s, executing a large volume of highly romanticised watercolours for the laird. The Paps of Jura form the backdrop to this distant view of Islay House (*Scottish Field*).

A different view by Heath of Islay House and Square from the garden in the new policies established during the gentrification of the estate (private collection).

The East Tower folly, moat and monkey puzzles, as depicted in a postcard of 1904 (Valentine Collection, St. Andrews University Library).

Islay's Highland Games latterly took place in August instead of December, but the shot putt, hammer throw and caber toss are the same activities as John Francis Campbell depicted in one of his watercolours, dated 1842 (Trustees of the National Galleries of Scotland).

illness, was a profound shock to her husband: in a black-edged letter to
Campbell of Melfort in March of the following year, Walter Frederick
wrote that he was as yet 'little able to attend to anything I am not in good
health and it will be along ere I recover the shock both health and spirits
have received'.[2] The lighthouse at the entrance to Port Ellen harbour
commemorates Lady Eleanor's death with a rather pious inscription. She
is buried in one half of a sombre black marble sarcophagus in Bowmore
Church: the other half has remained empty.

Walter Frederick did recover, and his second marriage in 1837 to
another cousin, Catherine Coles, produced further children. During his
lairdship, considerable additions were made to Islay House, including the
rear extension 'of offices' designed in Scottish Baronial style by William
Playfair.[3] A second residence in the south-east, Ardimersay Cottage, was
also constructed; a map of 1821 includes a vignette of a proposed *cottage
ornée*.[4] In 1820 Foreland House was finished and surrounded with gardens
and plantations by his uncle, Captain Walter Campbell as the centre of
his Sunderland estate. Walter Frederick Campbell's main contributions
to Islay, however, were of much wider significance, taking the form of
changes in agricultural extent, further separation of agricultural and
other employment (including the creation of several new villages) and
improvements in internal and external communications and transport.

Pressures in the agrarian economy

This was the period when the population on the island was increasing to
its maximum of around 15,000 about the time of the 1831 census (1841
and 1851 in Kildalton and Oa).[5] How did this happen? In the parishes
of Killarow and Kilmeny for example, the numbers of marriages recorded
in the old parish registers increased at a growing rate in the first decades
of the nineteenth century. These were followed by similar increases in the
numbers of births. As long as births were more numerous than deaths,
and despite net out-migration, the population continued to increase.
Between the 1750s and the 1790s, population had increased by between
fifty and sixty per cent; between the 1790s and the 1830s it increased by
eighty per cent to just under 15,000.

The number of multiple tenants was also at its highest. In 1824, just
under fifty tenants had large and medium-sized holdings, twenty had
small single holdings under £20 annual rent, but 670 tenants occupied
95 townships.[6] Land pressure and the upper limits of cultivation in Islay
therefore were also approaching their maximum in the 1830s. Townships
were divided into Upper and Lower, or West, Mid and East or whatever
was appropriate. In the low sun of winter and spring or under snow,

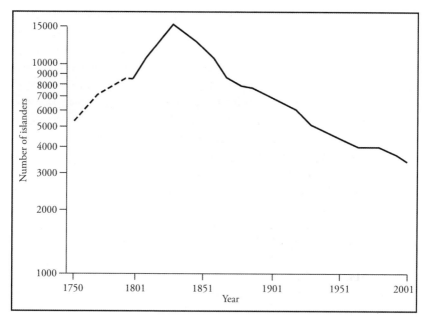

Islay's population, 1755–2001. Numbers of islanders increased by over one-half in the second half of the eighteenth century; but in the next three decades it almost doubled. A figure of 14,992 was recorded in the 1831 Census. The subsequent decline from this peak was almost as rapid, as the semi-logarithmic graph shows. For the past century, the rate of decline has been more gradual (*Census of Scotland*).

the lazybed and ploughed ridges which accompanied this expansion of cultivated land can still be seen in the glens as well as the edges of upper hills and moors. Because of this land pressure, and also due to national decline in cattle and crop prices after the Napoleonic wars, arrears of rent mounted steadily. Tenants were not evading payment of their rents, but were simply not able to pay.

Recognising this, some of Walter Frederick's views on the mounting problems were expressed in 1826 in a report to the Select Committee investigating the possibility of encouraging emigration as a means of alleviating overpopulation in the western Highland and Islands, in itself a change of emphasis.[7] He preferred to solve land pressures by persuading the surplus population to move to villages, with enough land for potatoes and cow's grass. But some people had refused to give up their tenancies and, in such cases, he would have been 'very glad to have got those people to emigrate, and would have advanced a moderate sum of money'. He did try to make changes without moving islanders compulsorily from their birthplace. Walter Frederick Campbell's objective was not the clearance of people from the land; his purpose, like that of his Shawfield predecessors,

These West Highland oxen were prizewinners for Campbell of Jura at the Highland Show in 1838, the year in which the local agricultural association was established (Royal Highland and Agricultural Society of Scotland).

Dairy farmers and cattle were introduced by Walter Frederick Campbell in the 1870s Ayrshire cows were in their heyday in the 1950s (*Scottish Farmer*, 1958).

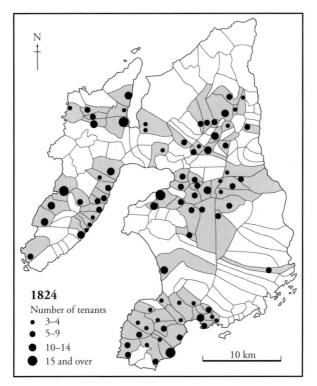

1824

Number of tenants
- 3–4
- 5–9
- 10–14
- 15 and over

10 km

Approaching the time of maximum population and land pressure, and, Bowmore and Portnahaven apart, with village building still to absorb people from the land, the extent of the numbers problem facing Walter Frederick Campbell is shown here in the map of holdings with more than two tenants in 1824 (Islay Estate Papers).

was the improvement of agriculture and an improvement in the returns from farming for his tenants and himself for further investment. But such agricultural reorganisation almost always involved a reduction in the number of tenants.

In the Scottish Highlands and islands landlords had virtually complete freedom of action. An Act of the Court of Session of 1756 had clarified the legal procedures for removal of tenants, which could relatively easily be accomplished through the application to a local sheriff court at least forty days before Whitsun. Most of the Highland population had no absolute legal right to land and this made the reductions in numbers possible. Gradual and relentless displacement rather than mass eviction was the norm; most clearances before 1815 were not designed to expel people. Most removals probably only involved a few people at a time until the more drastic episodes of the mid-nineteenth century, when some Highland landlords seem to have equated agricultural improvement with total clearance of tenants. On Islay total clearance was still rare, perhaps partly because the pressure of population on resources had not been so great as elsewhere, but also because the Campbells of Shawfield were both humane and perceptive enough to realise that total clearance was not a prerequisite for improvement.

During this period the laird employed the Renfrewshire surveyor, William Gemmill, to produce maps and plans of the holdings on the island, with a view to their further improvement or reorganisation.[8] Together with other surviving estate material such as annual rentals and factors' reports the maps and plans make it possible to reconstruct the nature and progress of planning and achievement of reorganisation. While it followed the family tradition of estate improvements, this period of major reorganisation by Walter Frederick Campbell during the 1820s and 1830s to be the last of such enterprises on Islay. 'Policies' were laid out, farms and villages built. Subsequent Victorian changes were slower and more sporadic, variations on a Georgian landscape theme that was established during Walter Frederick's lairdship and one that is still clearly recognisable.

The changes continued in the 1830s and were exemplified in the development of what is still an important element in Islay life. The Islay, Jura and Colonsay Agricultural Association was inaugurated in 1838, the first such to be established in the islands.[9] By the 1830s one of the principal objectives was 'the improvement of Highland breeds of cattle and sheep' on the three islands. The Annual Show that was instituted has become one of the principal events of the Islay calendar, with a spectacular array of silver trophies presented to winners of many classes of entry.[10]

Evolutionary rural change

Some of the processes of change were gradual and evolutionary. For example, evolution from eighteenth-century tacks to single farms was characteristic of some grazing areas. In Islay, some improvements had taken place from the early-eighteenth century onwards. For instance, the manuscript estate plan by Stephen MacDougall of the Islay tack of Coul shows that, even before 1749, the land had been reorganised into arable and pasture fields, enclosed by dykes or walls of stone or turf. Around the entire holding ran a stone dyke.[11] In a rental of 1795, Coul was mentioned as forming part of a larger tack comprising the six holdings of Coul, Coulererach, Foreland, Cultoon, Corgortan and Buninuilt. But by Walter Frederick's time in 1819, Coul had become a single farm with an individual tenant.

Tenants in 1803	Tenants in 1824	Rent in 1824
J. Leitch	J. Leitch	£8 13s. 4d.
	A. Leitch	£8 13s. 4d.
J McCannell	J. McCannell	£8 13s. 4d.
	A. McCannell	£8 13s. 4d.
J. Smith	M. McCannell	£17 6s. 8d.
A. Smith	J. McCannell	£10 16s. 8d.
	Heirs D. Leitch	£6 10s. 0d.
A. McCannell	A. McCannell	£17 6s. 8d.
D. McCannell	D. McCannell	£8 13s. 4d.
	G. McCannell	£8 13s. 4d.

Changes in tenancies in Kendrochid between 1803 and 1824. Proportional shares of total rent indicate communal working of the joint farm. Halved or shared portions of rent indicate subdivision of individual shares (Islay Estate Papers).[12]

Another process of change occurred with increases in numbers of tenants and the consequent subdivision of their holdings. The late-eighteenth century had seen a rapid increase in the number of legal agricultural tenants, as for example in Kendrochid.

Continued subdivision of multiple holdings, often already too small to provide an adequate living, hindered the introduction of new agricultural techniques and provided an immediate reason for reorganisation. To remedy the deteriorating situation, a reduction in the number of tenants and an informal reorganisation of the holdings so as to enlarge the individual holdings were undertaken. The total number of tenants in Nereabolls in the Rinns, for example, was reduced from eleven to eight between 1824 and 1833. From the rentals it seems that most of the eleven tenants, all of whom had been in arrears of rent, were replaced by others from surrounding townships. The equally-apportioned rents indicated for the year 1833 perhaps represent an attempt to re-establish an earlier division into eight shares that had become subdivided with population increase. Such reorganisation does not appear to have been accompanied by a physical reorganisation. The lack of any regular pattern on subsequent maps of Nereabolls, or at the present day, tends to confirm this and to imply that the creation of consolidated holdings for each of the tenants was a more informal process.

Tenants in 1824	Rent	Tenants in 1833	Rent
A. MacDonald	£6 5s. 0d.	A. Mackenzie	£18
J. MacArthur	£6 5s. 0d.		
A. MacEachern	£12 10s. 0d.	A. McLergan	£18
Heirs Macmillan	£12 10s. 0d.	J. McDermid	£18
A. Brown	£6 5s. 0d.	D. & A. Campbell	£18
A. Johnston	£6 5s .0d.		
J. Mackinnon	£12 10s .0d.	J. Mackinnon	£18
D. Macmillan	£12 10s. 0d.	A. McDonald	£18
D. McQuarrie	£6 5s. 0d.	C. Campbell	£18
D. Lamont	£6 5s. 0d.		
A. Johnston	£12 10s. 0d.	D. Mitchell	£18

Reductions in tenants and tenancies in Nereabolls between 1824 and 1833 were perhaps to re-establish an earlier number of holdings (Islay Estate Papers).

The old system of joint farms had involved annual or periodic reallocation of a large number of cultivable strips among the tenants. It seems probable that in places like Nereabolls, where small tenants persisted and clearance did not take place, the first stage in consolidation of holdings may have been an agreement to abandon periodic reallocation in favour of a fixed pattern of strips.[13] This would in time be succeeded by an exchange of strips among tenants, a process of consolidation which could be initiated either by the landlord or by the tenants themselves, as their numbers began to decline. Usually a rather irregular pattern of field boundaries resulted, following the irregular limits of the former cultivated fields. Only rarely in the Islay townships where reduction of tenants took place is there evidence that a rigid system of small holdings or crofting townships was imposed by the landlord. By the gradual processes of delayed marriage or celibacy, emigration or death, informal rearrangement of the land into single consolidated holdings took place, at least when there were no more than, say, ten tenants in a township.

Revolutionary plans
There had been occasional clearances in late-eighteenth century Islay to make way for a single farm, as at Ballyclach sometime between 1779 and 1795. Similarly Octovullin had eleven tenants named in a rental of

Echoing the round church at Bowmore were the D-shaped plans of the farmsteading at Kilchiaran, built in the mid-1820s, and similar to the steading at Maam near Inveraray in Argyll; and of the village of Port Wemyss, started a decade later.

1812, but by 1824 there was only one. Only in a few cases on Islay was clearance as sudden and revolutionary as it was in the more notorious 'cleared' areas elsewhere in the Highlands and Islands. Of the few that did take place, Kilchiaran is perhaps the best example. Numbers of tenants on this holding rose in the late-eighteenth and early-nineteenth centuries, so that by 1825 there were seventeen direct tenants named in the rental. The rental for the following year gives only the names of two Ayrshire brothers, Duncan and James Campbell. Many of the removed tenants' names can be traced in later rentals for nearby holdings and villages. Eleven became tenants in the adjacent townships of Gearach, Olistadh and Conisby, or moved to the new village of Port Charlotte. The remainder migrated further or left the island.

Walter Frederick Campbell's role as landscape planner is more evident in the planned or formal reorganisation of holdings. This type of reorganisation was carried out first by Walter Campbell of Shawfield and Walter Campbell of Sunderland, but was repeated by Walter Frederick, through his factor or agent. Its hallmark was the regular field patterns that it produced, often with a dispersed settlement pattern, and it is most evident around the shores of Loch Indaal, near Walter Frederick's Home Farm. One of William Gemmill's maps of the lands of 'Isla House', the proprietor's mansion, shows the layout characteristic of the

An engraving by Thomas Dick
of Walter Frederick Campbell,
laird of Shawfield and Islay, after
a painting by Kenneth McLeay
(Trustees of the Scottish National
Portrait Gallery).

Walter Campbell's son, John (Jack),
here portrayed by Edridge in the early
1800s, did not live to succeed to the
Islay and other estates. Colonel Jack's
wife, Lady Charlotte, daughter of the
5th duke and duchess of Argyll, was
a renowned beauty, notorious Court
diarist and 'Silver-Fork' novelist.
The eldest of her nine surviving
children, Walter Frederick, named
Port Charlotte after her (Russell,
Three Generations).

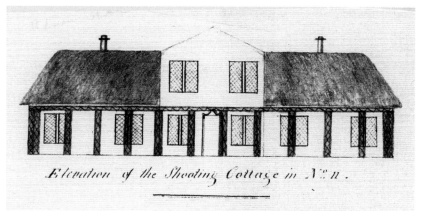

Elevation of the Shooting Cottage in N:° 11.

The elevation of the 'Shooting Cottage' as suggested on A. Henderson's survey of Ardimersay in 1821 (National Library of Scotland, Gordon Cumming Papers).

It had become more fanciful by the time that Lumsden, in his *Steam Boat Companion* of 1825, reported that 'Mr Campbell has lately built a very pretty shooting cottage, situated in a romantic part of the coast'. The *cottage ornée* at Ardimersay, as depicted by Heath, was superseded later in the century by Kildalton House nearby (Private collection).

Tenants in 1802	Tenants in 1815–16	Tenants in 1824–25
J. McEachern	J. McEachern	J. McEachern*
J. McEachern Jr.	J. McEachern Jr.	J. McEachern D. McIntyre
R. McEachern	P. McEachern	P. McEachern*
A. McEachern	A. McEachern	A. McEachern
A. Bell	D. Bell D. & A. Gillespy	D. Bell (To Gearach) A. Gillespy*
D. McNeill	D. McNeill J. McNeill	N. McNeill J. McNeill ** A.McAllister**
A. Currie	P. Currie	D. & J. Currie L. Currie
	D. McLachlan	P. Currie & D.Gillespie*
D. McLellan	D. McLellan	J. McLellan J. McArthur

Seventeen tenants in Kilchiaran made way for one large farm. Their names can be traced in subsequent rentals to other holdings and Rinns villages. Those marked with an asterisk moved to Conisby, while those marked with two asterisks moved to Olistadh (Islay Estate Papers).

Romantic approach to designing lairds' policies and estate buildings; this has remained almost unchanged to the present day. The House, garden, plantations, drives and Home Farm Square are all shown as part of the new landscape.

The pattern on Islay is very different from the formal reorganisation elsewhere in the Highlands, where the establishment of lotted or regular crofting townships was more typical. In Islay, the former joint townships were reorganised into several individual small holdings, generally with no common pasture. Unlike joint farms, where the shares of rent were usually equal divisions or subdivisions, the rents on the reorganised small holdings were not usually proportional. The rental for Ballitarson in 1824 indicated this uneven apportionment of rent. Gemmill's plan of Ballitarson showed the new individual holdings bounded by stone dykes, each with its own farmstead. Indications of the old order are shown by phrases such as 'old turf dykes not shown'.

Another form of reorganisation was that of lotting, through the creation of small blocks or strips of land, perhaps with common pasture, which

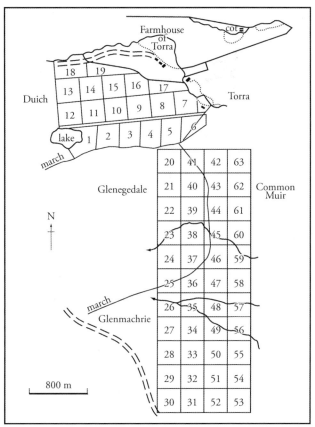

Peaty moorland was surveyed by William Gemmill in 1828 for laying out 'twenty acre' holdings or lots, for tenants displaced elsewhere (Islay Estate Papers).

were laid out for part-time or non-agricultural workers near villages, or on waste land or muir. These village lotments form a distinctive feature of the Islay landscape; they were planned by the lairds to enable those who worked as day-labourers or in non-agricultural employment to produce their own potatoes and milk. The lots were essentially a type of land-reclamation scheme, involving drainage of the unimproved land, followed by dressing with shell sand, no rent being payable at first.

Around the edges of the villages of Bowmore, Port Charlotte and Port Ellen, for example, the peaty muir was reclaimed in lots or compact blocks by village tenants. Some of these were agricultural tenants displaced from the townships, who had now become agricultural day-labourers or craftsmen with no other access to land. Each plot of reclaimed land was intended to produce potatoes for a family as well as oats and grass for a cow's milk. A less elaborate scheme was set up around the lead-mining area of Ballygrant. The fishing village of Port Wemyss in the 1830s, however, showed a pattern more reminiscent of Outer Hebridean townships laid out for crofter-fishermen much later in the nineteenth century. Each individual tenant's lot or holding was a narrow strip of land running back from a road to the hill or to the shore.

The reclamation of such land in regularly shaped lots by village tenants was paralleled elsewhere on the peaty muir or moorlands of Islay by schemes of lots for other agricultural tenants who had been displaced from joint farms. Schemes of this kind were started on the Glenegedale, Duich, Glenmachrie and Torra muirs between Bowmore and Port Ellen. The schemes were planned in 1828, based on a map of William Gemmill. They do not appear to have been settled completely as planned and, in view of the generally poor quality of the land, were probably among the least successful of the various experiments in reorganisation. It is worth remarking, however, that even these muir lots in Islay took a different form from those conceived by most Highland and Hebridean lairds. The absence of common grazing is noticeable, despite the vast areas of adjacent hill grazing. The principle of one piece of land for each tenant was maintained; the small tenant was limited to his lot and hill pasture was used for cattle and sheep farms, as well as deer.

Villages proliferate
Although most of Islay's villages were founded several decades later, they all owe much to Daniel Campbell's first experiment with his model village of Bowmore. Walter Campbell of Sunderland redeveloped Portnahaven in the 1820s and four new villages were established in the 1820s and 1830s by Walter Frederick Campbell as part of his overall plan for the island. Port Ellen, Port Charlotte, Port Wemyss and Kiells were all designed to provide non-agricultural employment, in fishing, distilling, weaving and the provision of services. In 1821, three-quarters of the 2,285 families in Islay were listed in the census as being employed in agriculture.[14] By 1831, when several of the villages other than Bowmore were just beginning, this proportion had already dropped to two-thirds. The villages were to help reduce the rate of population decline thereafter on Islay, in comparison to that being experienced in many other parts of the Hebrides. In most of the villages, tenants had moved from the 'country' and built their single-storeyed or two-storeyed houses that are for the most part still standing, albeit renovated.

As a substantial early example of village creation, Bowmore is really *sui generis* on Islay, the more so because of its diversity of function: the other villages tended to have a more specific economic base, though diversity has often come with the passing of time. Just as Bowmore had its counterpart on the Scottish mainland in weavers' villages like Eaglesham, so the creation of villages based on fisheries reflected a more widespread movement. During the first quarter of the nineteenth century the fishing industry seemed potentially prosperous enough to encourage the creation of fishing villages in Islay. In 1825 Portnahaven fishing boats, 'probably the finest on the west coast of Scotland', were reported to be going to the Giant's Causeway, thirty miles away in Antrim, to fish for a 'rich harvest of cod, ling and turbot'.[15] In the early 1820s Walter Campbell of Sunderland formed his new village around the creek of Portnahaven, as was later described by Lord Teignmouth, 'on the basis of an old one, which he found in a poor and wretched state'.[16] Cottages were built 'on a new plan, arranged in rows on either side of the creek, neatly slated, and furnished with windows, fire-places, and sometimes with grates'. Some of them became shops, which were well supported: bakers, grocers, and other tradesmen. The same author added that the girls of the villages were introduced to 'plain embroidery' and 'execute it skilfully'. A school for the Society for Promoting Christian Knowledge, one of Telford's parliamentary churches, with a glebe donated by Walter Campbell and a 'neat . . . and orderly' public-house were all included in the new community of Portnahaven.

The next village to appear was started about 1821 around Leodamus Bay in the south-east of the island. Named in happier circumstances after Walter Frederick Campbell's first wife, a list of the 1821 'founders' of Port Ellen, originally Port Eleanor, was published in a later guide to Islay.[17] A distillery was established in 1827. Though partly concerned with provision for rural migrants and for fishermen, it has also been claimed that the 'building boom' of the 1830s in Port Ellen was only partly the result of deliberate village planning, and that it was also connected with the property qualifications required for parliamentary franchise after the 1832 Reform Act.[18] Lord Teignmouth noted that 'the expectation of a fishery at Port Eleanor produced by the appearance of the herrings, has been disappointing' and this is confirmed by occupation structures of Port Ellen in 1841.[19] Then the major sources of employment were agricultural labouring, services and distilling.[20] Some of the street names in the village retain the family names given to them, such as Frederick Crescent, after the laird and Charlotte Street, after his mother.

The plans for another fishing village, Port Wemyss, are dated 1833. Despite the apparent association with east coast ports of Fife and recalling the Fife fishermen brought to Islay many decades earlier by the younger Daniel Campbell, the name is almost certainly a tribute to the family or to the memory of Walter Frederick Campbell's first wife, who was a

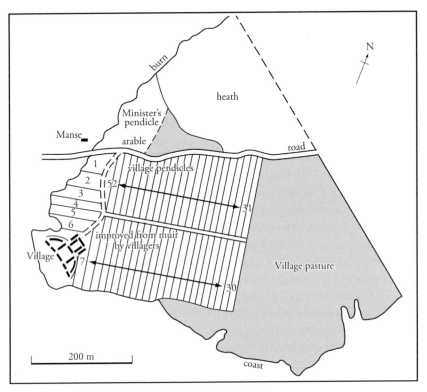

This redrawing of Gemmill's plan of Wemysshaven or Port Wemyss in 1833 shows the D-shaped plan of the village, narrow lots and common pasture; incomers were from nearby holdings affected by clearance or reduction of tenants including Kilchiaran, Lossit and Nereabolls. Individual names were noted, with the state of progress of house building (Islay Estate Papers).

daughter of the eighth earl of Wemyss. The D-shaped plan of the village at Port Wemyss with its accompanying lots, was drawn up by William Gemmill. Many of the tenants were encouraged to engage in the fishing industry whose outlook seemed prosperous. The factor's superscriptions on Gemmill's map demonstrate the progress of house construction in the new village: 'finished', 'building', 'commenced', or 'nothing done'.[21] Several of the new tenants came from rural areas in the Rinns and by the time of the 1834 rental there were thirty four names.[22] A few years later Lord Teignmouth noted the success of those Islay fisheries, (though not herring) despite opposition to Campbell of Sunderland's plan to convey the cured fish to market quickly in a single vessel, instead of each boat making its way to Ireland.[23]

Whereas both Portnahaven and Port Wemyss were villages in which fishing was the dominant activity, in Port Charlotte fishing was from the start only one element in the economy. Begun in 1828 on the western side of Loch Indaal, expanding the site of the earlier changehouse and malt mill at Skiba or Sgioba on Port-na-Dronnaig, in several respects Port Charlotte resembled Bowmore. The village plan and buildings were similar, though Port Charlotte's architectural focus was provided by the school rather than a church. Like Bowmore also, Port Charlotte was intended to accommodate agricultural day-labourers and craftsmen; many of these came into the new village from the surrounding townships, as happened at Port Wemyss. By 1829 a distillery had been established. The village continued to live up to Lord Teignmouth's description of 1836, when he remarked that one's attention was easily drawn from Bowmore to the 'showy village called Port Charlotte which Mr Campbell has erected on the opposite side of the Bay'.[24] Walter Frederick Campbell's mother was commemorated in the name given to the new village. Lady Charlotte Campbell had inherited her beauty from her mother, the duchess of Argyll, one of several renowned Gunning sisters of Anglo-Irish eighteenth-century society. Widowed at the age of 34, and with nine children to support, Lady Charlotte kept a diary, later published notoriously and anonymously, of her life as lady-in-waiting to Princess Caroline, wife of the Prince Regent, from 1810 to 1815.[25] Later, while living in Italy, and much to her family's disgust, she then married her son's tutor, the Rev Edward Bury, by whom she had two further daughters, before being widowed a second time. She wrote a score of 'silver fork' novels to supplement her income from a Shawfield annuity and editions and new novels continued to appear even until after her death in 1861, aged 86.

It is not known exactly when the village of Kiells was begun, though the factor in 1826 noted that a stone dyke was built around the 'weavers lots' in Kiells, and there is mention in 1829 that £750 had been spent on houses there.[26] The weavers were listed then, from east to west, as William Walker, John McLelland, John Stewart, Robert White, John McLellan, William Brownlee, Andrew Young, ? Hamilton, Robert Crawford and John Stewart. These probably comprised the ten heads of families that Lord Teignmouth reported as having been brought from Glasgow by Walter Frederick Campbell 'to introduce the book-muslin into Islay . . . in the hope of forming a manufacturing colony, which might be recruited from the native population. It has proved not altogether unsuccessful'.[27] The original house designs for Kiells village contained no distinctive windows like those found in weavers' villages elsewhere, though they did have small attic windows. Modernisation grants have resulted in some exteriors and interiors being considerably modified.

The Kilmeny village of Kiells was built in the 1820s to house immigrant linen weavers and their families from Glasgow, in five pairs of cottages. With house improvement grants in the early 1970s, the uniformity of the cottages disappeared and the intervening spaces were filled by pairs of local authority houses.

The small, straggling and essentially unplanned settlement of Ballygrant had very different functions in its early days. When the principal link with the Scottish mainland was the drove road through Port Askaig and Jura, Ballygrant was a staging post on the journey from Killarow, Bowmore's predecessor at Bridgend and, later, from Bowmore itself. Ballygrant Inn is the modern version of that 'changehouse'. Ballygrant also served in the eighteenth and nineteenth centuries as the focus of sporadic lead, copper and silver mining in Islay: the scars and residues are still visible in the landscape, especially around Mulreesh. In Ballygrant itself, some of the former miners' houses remain as 'Miners Row', now much renovated.

The Hebridean exception
Walter Frederick Campbell's few clearances, the considerable planned reduction in the numbers of joint tenants on the farms, physical changes to the pattern of landholdings, his attempts to attract people from the land into the villages for day-labouring and non-agricultural employment, and even the muir reclamation schemes, all resulted in a decrease in the number of joint tenancies and joint tenants after the early 1830s. Whereas in 1821 three-quarters of the agricultural families on Islay were joint tenants, by 1831 only one-third of the smaller number of agricultural families were joint tenants.[28] This reduction in the number of joint tenants was sometimes accompanied by reorganisation of holdings as in the case

of the cleared townships or reorganised groups of smaller holdings. But in other cases, the old organisation and morphology tended to remain, or changed gradually and informally. Relics of the older order of tacks and joint farms continued to exist side by side with the newer pattern of laird's policies, single farms and small holdings. Teignmouth averred that 'of farmhouses and cottages Isla attends an infinite variety'.[29] This varied landscape was, and is, in strong contrast to many other areas of the West Highland seaboard, where changes were abrupt and all-embracing.[30]

The more gradual aspect of change in Islay is also unlike the reorganisation that took place in many parts of lowland Scotland. There, earlier in the eighteenth century, revolution of the landscape had often occurred much more completely and suddenly. Even in nearby Cowal and Kintyre on mainland Argyll, sheep farming was established as early as the mid-eighteenth century by the clearance of tenants, many of whom moved relatively easily to Glasgow and the other lowland industrial centres. Islay was an exception and has remained so to this day. Though it is undeniably part of the Highlands and Islands in very many elements of its physical appearance and social character, there is also a lowland aspect of the landscape, created mainly in the second quarter of the nineteenth century through the establishment of a varied pattern of agricultural holdings and the establishment of a number of villages, with later Victorian replacements or additions.

Notes and references

[1]   Foster, *Members of Parliament*, p. 62.

[2]   Campbell of Melfort Papers, Edinburgh University Library, MS. E59/2 Dk.73.151; also Islay Estate Papers, MS. Pedigree of Campbell of Skipness, Shawfield and Islay, 1886.

[3]   W. H. Playfair, Drawings of Islay Estate Offices 1841–42 (and also of East Lodge 1845–6), The Library of the University of Edinburgh, Special Collections Catalogue 30.
      William Heath (1795–1840) was commissioned by Walter Fredrick Campbell to record scenes of Islay and Islay life. Dated from 1829 to 1836, the rather romanticised watercolours are bound in a volume presented by Mr Ian Hunter of Laphroaig to Mr James Morrison on his coming of age in 1951. The volume was bought from the sale of the effects of Rosneath Castle, the home of Princess Louise, Duchess of Argyll. See also RCAHMS, *Argyll Inventory*, 5.

[4]   Plan of Ardimersay, 1821, NLS, Deposit 175, Box 62, Gordon Cumming Papers.

[5]   *Census of Scotland* 1951, (1953), Table 3.

[6]   Islay Estate Papers, Rental of 1824–25.

[7]   *Report of the Select Committee appointed to inquire into the Expediency of encouraging Emigration from the United Kingdom, BPP*, 1826, IV, p. 75.

[8]   The maps and plans by or attributed to William Gemmill are in the Islay Estate Papers and photocopies are in NRS, Edinburgh. Other contemporary documents amplify them, such as the lengthy and much annotated List of Offers of Farms in 1833 in the Islay Estate

Papers. Gemmill married and lived and worked on the island for almost two decades. See M. Storrie, 'Designed Historic Landscape' *Scottish Archives* 7 (2001), pp 59–77.

[9]   Macdonald, *General View*, p. 561; M. Storrie, *Continuity and Change: The Islay, Jura and Colonsay Agricultural Association, 1838–1988*, (Islay, 1988).

[10]   Following the demise of the creamery and changeover from dairy to beef cattle (one farm, Esknish, apart) the silver cups for dairy sections in the annual show were loaned to the museum for display there.

[11]   Islay Estate Papers, Stephen MacDougall's MS. Plan of Coul Park.

[12]   This and subsequent tables are based on various estate rentals in Islay Estate Papers.

[13]   M. C. Storrie, 'Landholdings and Settlement Evolution in West Highland Scotland', *Geografiska Annaler* 47, (1965), pp. 138–61.

[14]   *United Kingdom Census* 1821 and 1831.

[15]   Lumsden, *Steam-Boat Companion*, p. 69.

[16]   C. J. Shore (Baron Teignmouth), *Sketches of the Coasts and Islands of Scotland and the Isle of Man*, 2 vols. (London, 1836), 2, pp. 315–6 and p. 331.

[17]   MacNeill, *New Guide*, pp. 113–4.

[18]   C. M. Macdonald (ed.), *The Third Statistical Account of Scotland*, Argyll (Glasgow, 1961), p. 345.

[19]   Shore, *Sketches*, 2, 314.

[20]   Copies of each census enumerator's schedules for the censuses in Scotland from 1841 to 1911 are at NRS, Edinburgh, and available online. Those for Islay were discussed in M. C. Storrie, 'The Census of Scotland as a source in the Historical Geography of Islay', *Scottish Geographical Magazine* 78 (1962), pp. 152–65.

[21]   Islay Estate Papers, William Gemmill's MS. map of Wemysshaven, 1833.

[22]   Islay Estate Papers, Estate rentals for 1833 and 1834.

[23]   Shore, *Sketches*, 2, 317.

[24]   *Ibid.*, p. 311.

[25]   Biographical material from various sources. See *Diary Illustrative of the Times of George the Fourth*, attributed to Lady C. S. M. Bury or Campbell, 4 vols. (London, 1839).

[26]   Islay Estate Papers, Factor's note on tenancies at Kiells.

[27]   Shore, *Sketches*, 2, 324.

[28]   Islay Estate Papers, Estate rentals for 1821 and 1831.

[29]   H. A. Moisley, 'Some Hebridean Field Systems', *Gwerin* 3 (1960), pp. 22–35; 'The Birth of a Crofting Landscape; North Uist in 1799', *Scottish Geographical Magazine* 77 (1961), pp. 89–92.

[30]   Shore, *Sketches*, 2, 308.

CHAPTER 10

Crisis and solution

The decades of the 1820s and 1830s in Islay were very busy ones, in which the population soared to between four and five times the present population, despite net out-migration. As well as the activities in weaving, fishing, mining and distilling, construction of roads, piers, villages, dykes, farmhouses and out-buildings, distilleries and public buildings were all going on apace. But in the recessionary aftermath of the Napoleonic wars, the balance between income and expenditure deteriorated, both for the landlord and for his tenants and other islanders. The immediate consequence of the post-war price collapse was a dramatic surge in rent arrears and the need for greater income to service debt charges. There were difficult years of harvest failure, particularly in 1816–17, 1821–2, 1825, 1835–6, while potato disease in the decade after 1845 was yet to come.[1] It became virtually impossible even for the best laird and his agents, to manage the growing crisis. Many of the early-nineteenth century activities had been bolstered by temporary wartime conditions. With the coming of peace, the export economy of areas such as the Highlands and Islands of Scotland faltered. Cattle prices halved between 1810 and 1830.[2] Fishing encountered both erratic herring migrations and withdrawal of herring bounties. Duty on imported barilla was reduced and cheaper alkali could be obtained using common salt, so both the price and production of kelp fell drastically. Only sheep prices suffered less. The making of illicit whisky was threatened by excise changes. Peace also led to the return of soldiers and others. The 1820s decade began the process of disintegration of the economic fabric in the Highlands and Islands. In Devine's view:

> The experience of the western Highlands is a salutary reminder that economic change is not necessarily for the better . . . The Highlands became a "problem" region where economic transformation had produced difficulties rather than benefits . . . Whether more effective management of the resources of the region by the landlord class would have resulted in a different outcome is an interesting question. Several landlords, particularly on the kelping estates, seem to be more interested in profit

than in investment yet others such as Campbell of Shawfield and Islay did try to fund relatively ambitious fishing and industrial developments. But after doing well to start with, they often came to little, suggesting that even the most imaginative of schemes, using not inconsiderable finance, faced major problems. Highland landlords were confronted with more formidable obstacles than their counterparts elsewhere in Britain.[3]

External threats

The relentless rise in population had continued and population growth outstripped traditional agricultural productivity. The old agrarian economy had been balanced annually on a knife-edge between a meagre sufficiency and periodic shortage, particularly in a climate that was almost marginal for successful grain cultivation. After the end of the Napoleonic wars the economic and demographic pressures notably increased as sources of employment and income became less certain. A large population had been vital to the labour-intensive economy of the later-eighteenth century. In Argyll and particularly in Islay, agrarian change maintained and even improved standards of life, along with the outward movement of people from the region.

As the post-war recession deepened, most people learned to subsist on potato cultivation, fishing, labouring and earnings from family members temporarily in the Lowlands, or further afield. Out-migration did not keep up with the decline in employment and income. Viewed from the present-day perspective, the improvements made by Walter Frederick Campbell in the 1820s and 1830s, despite all the difficulties, were considerable. But the external world began more and more to influence the economy of Islay, as well as the lives of its inhabitants and even of the landlord himself. The pace of innovation slackened.

Further development of the landscape in Islay after the mid-1830s proceeded at a much slower rate than in the previous decade. Overall, the numbers of agricultural tenants in multiple tenancies were declining fairly dramatically. In the 1833 rental there were 95 holdings with 539 joint tenants named. Twenty years later the corresponding numbers were 65 and 305.[4] Decrease in the number of tenants per holding was accompanied by an increase in the average size of the individual holdings. Only in a few areas, such as Cragabus in the Oa, did the holdings remain unconsolidated. Rentals show that the number of agricultural tenants in most parts of Islay continued to decline except in the Oa, the 'Glen' and the northern Rinns.[5] Lord Teignmouth confirmed that all was not well when he wrote in the 1830s of the continuing existence of subletting with its 'usual mischievous effects' and also of the continuing presence of runrig tenure, especially on the 'frequented shore of Lochindal'.[6] He nevertheless paid the usual tribute to the 'meritorious exertions' of Walter Frederick, his uncle Walter, of Sunderland and their agents, Mr Chiene, the factor, and Mr Webster, the overseer.

In the normal state of affairs the problems noted by Lord Teignmouth would not have been of much importance; indeed the gradualness of landscape and social change is one of the virtues of the Islay evolution. But the times were becoming anything but normal. As in Ireland and other areas, excessive reliance increased on the potato, which had spread rapidly throughout the west Highlands and Islands after the middle of the eighteenth century, tending to replace barley and oats as a human foodstuff. By the 1830s lazybed cultivation for potatoes had extended cultivation limits to their maximum. But, in 1835 the potato crop throughout the region almost failed.[7] The disease was caused by the fungus *Phytophthora infestans* and there was no contemporary understanding or cure for the blight. Maritime regions were especially at risk. The spores spread most rapidly in the moist environment during the spring and summer months. 1835 was an exceptionally cold and wet season and the crop continued to have difficulties during the next decade.

The leavers

Despite Walter Frederick Campbell's attempts to create employment in his reorganised landscape of farms and villages through the 1820s and 1830s, the mounting arrears of rent and the farming difficulties already appearing in the 1830s made out-migration inevitable. The previous chapter showed that, despite net out-migration from the island, Islay's population continued to increase dramatically to around the time of the 1831 census and even to that of 1841 in Kildalton and Oa, where numbers of marriages and births remained higher. But thereafter it began to drop as rapidly as it had risen. In the most populous part of the island, Killarow and Kilmeny, the numbers of marriages and births fell in the 1830s, and young single people and recently-married people left. For the island as a whole, net out-migration added to the fall in births. Temporary migration for seasonal work off the island partly helps explain why mass emigration did not necessarily occur when population growth was outstripping available resources. Agriculture, fishing, industry, construction, transport and domestic service in the Lowlands all required increasing amounts of temporary and even permanent labour. Part of the income earned there helped to support many island households, indirectly discouraging further migration in the short term.

Emigration was increasingly being seen by Highland and Hebridean lairds and their agents as the necessary short-term and immediate cure for the perceived problem of 'overpopulation', although some like Walter Frederick Campbell inclined also to the view that the problems derived from economic difficulties as much as demographic forces. Migration is not easy to measure, but references to its size or impact are often found when population change was considered to be threatening. The enumerators of the census in 1841 attributed the decrease in Killarow not only to 'young persons leaving during the summer months for the Low Country, in search of employment', but also 'to extensive emigration, amounting to about 720 persons since 1831'. The minister for nearby Kilmeny also noted that the decrease there was to be accounted for by emigration. This theme of migration and emigration was further developed by the writer of the Kildalton parish account in the 1840s, when he observed that 'the females are more numerous than the males, a great number of young men having left the parish, and gone to the Low Country for employment. Some have gone to America and other places; so that the number of inhabitants has diminished'.

Between 1737 and 1740 423 islanders of the then population of about 5,000 had emigrated from Islay to New York and North Carolina.[8] Further individuals, groups and 'chain' emigrants continued settling in the Carolinas and Georgia while others subsequently pioneered in Upper Canada and the West. Many Argyll and island names appeared in the cadastral surveys and in the cemeteries of the New World, including Islay, Ontario and Islay, Alberta (there is even an Islay in Peru, named however, after a desert cactus, *Islaya Lindleyi Paucispina*). Other local names included Bowmore (later, Duntroon, Ontario) and Campbeltown (renamed Fayetteville, North Carolina). Inscribed on a plaque in the cemetery of Simcoe County in Ontario is a map of numbered plots: 'This plaque stands at the centre of seventy-five acre lots laid out by the government in 1833 for the use of needy immigrants. Pioneer families, Islay Scotch, some Irish and German, settled here but soon found these "free" lots too small and moved to larger farms. Many of them and their descendants are buried in this cemetery'. The road which passes to the south was part of the old mail road from Bowmore (Duntroon) to Owen Sound on Georgian Bay.

Migration was not wholesale or planned, but took the form of trickle, step and chain migration. The population became more mobile. Perhaps the first move was by rural displacement into an island village. The next move was perhaps to Glasgow, Paisley, Greenock or Ulster and thence perhaps further afield, particularly to Upper Canada, i.e. what is now Ontario, the United States of America and subsequently to South Africa and the Antipodes. Most emigrants in the 1820s and 1830s probably travelled in family units or small parties of around one to two dozen people. *Oran le seann Ileach*, the song of an exiled Islay pioneer, describes the way in which, despite hardships, these settlers eventually controlled their own lives in the townships of Ontario.[9] Some pioneer graveyards in the townships of Oro and Nottawasaga on Georgian Bay, in Lake Huron, have many headstones for islanders such as Campbells from the Oa, who sailed from Loch Indaal in 1831 with their family of six. Other families were the Bells, Curries, Dallases and many Macs. Descendants of a family of Gilchrists who had pioneered and settled Islay in Victoria County in Ontario in the 1830s, were later to move west, homesteading and founding Islay in Alberta.[10]

The conventional wisdom of the eighteenth century against emigration did not change quickly, but with the very serious subsistence crisis in the 1830s, worsening in the 1840s, a new consensus began to emerge. It came to be regarded as axiomatic that the Highlands were 'overpopulated' and that only through extensive emigration could the problems of the area be alleviated. In 1841 a Select Committee of the House of Commons solemnly concluded that there was a population surplus in Highland and Hebridean parishes of 45,000 to 60,000 people. For Islay it was suggested that one-fifth, or 3,000, of the population ought to be removed.[11] But the most significant change occurred in the attitudes of many Highland and Hebridean lairds. Some became interested in 'assisted emigration', although for the most part the state was at first unwilling to play a major role in this. A scheme of assisted emigration to Australia was established, using colonial land revenues to help cover emigration costs.[12] In 1837 Walter Frederick Campbell was one of the parliamentarians involved in promoting colonisation and settlement of New Zealand.[13] But perhaps the most remarkable aspect of the period from the end of the Napoleonic wars to the 1840s is that many more did not leave Islay.

Problems mount for the stayers
One of the problems that faced Walter Frederick Campbell during these unhappy decades was that Islay's suffering was usually less than that in other areas, partly due to the earlier exertions of himself and his forebears. This meant that Islay did not perhaps receive as much government or other assistance as provided elsewhere. The 1841 Select Committee was told by one witness that Islay was a comparatively fertile island 'in . . . as good a state as to provisions as Arran, and the great proprietor there has the character of being at all times disposed . . . to attending to the people's wants . . . Owing to the liberality of the proprietor and to the exertions of his principal tenants in affording employment, no public assistance

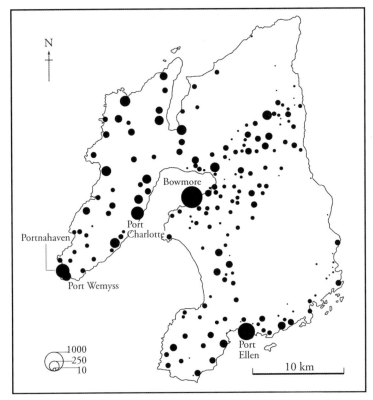

At present, most of Islay's population of around 3,500 lives in villages: rural settlement is predominantly dispersed. However, around the time of maximum population in the 1830s, settlement was usually clustered (Compiled from copies of Census enumerators' schedules for 1841, National Records of Scotland, Edinburgh).

will be required'.[14] By this time the landlord was scarcely in a position to share this view, but was reluctant to acknowledge it.

Charles Baird, the Honorary Secretary of the Glasgow Committee for Highland Relief, reported that in 1841 the Committee had sent Islay some 576 bolls of meal and 90 barrels of potatoes.[15] He added that the landlord had given donations, especially in Bowmore parish which was 'in a state of extreme misery'. Baird believed that Campbell could give no more and the Committee thought it right to send some supplies to Islay, to aid him in his exertions. Walter Frederick, in a letter on 28 March 1842 to Sir George Clarke, asked what had become of his petition to the Treasury for a grant to help work the mines in order to relieve unemployment. He even misleadingly exaggerated Islay's population by about twenty per cent while saying that without such a grant he certainly 'should not attempt to work these mines, my great object being to give employment to the

Large Population (seventeen thousand Souls) resident in my Highland propriety'.[16]

When compared to similar reports on most other areas of the west Highland seaboard, it does seem that the destitution and poverty on Islay were not so great as elsewhere, little though this can have comforted the laird or his tenants. The policy of reducing the dependence on agriculture, and in some parts of Islay a real reduction in the size of the agricultural population, saved the island from the most extreme pressure on the land experienced elsewhere. An interesting survey of the agricultural situation in Islay in 1843 was presumably an effort to try to get to grips with the rental situation which was becoming less and less favourable to the landlord.[17] The amounts of barley, oats and potatoes sown were shown against their yields and the proportion expected to be sold for cash; similar data was collected for the horses, cattle and sheep kept by the 529 tenants, 499 cottars and 105 workmen engaged in agriculture.

The island could not, however, escape the effects of the potato disease that spread from Ireland in the middle of the 1840s. Walter Frederick reported that the disease had first been observed during August 1845 in Islay in the stems, leaves and tubers of potatoes in a south-facing field near Port Ellen.[18] He added that the Rinns were still quite free, as also were the sandy areas of the island, but that the disease was spreading. Ministers of the parishes who were asked to report on the situation at the end of 1846 wrote varying accounts.[19] In Kilmeny, the Rev Donald Macdonald observed the 'failure' of the potato crop and went on to say that although the average crop of oats and barley had been better that year, much of the barley was destined to the distilleries to pay for the rent owed, so that 'want, and extreme destitution, and starvation press hard on a great proportion of our people already . . . there are in the villages and other locations in Islay, upwards of 5000 souls whose pressing wants and impending starvation demand immediate relief'. If his estimate is to be believed, this meant about forty per cent of the Islay population was on the brink of starvation by that time.

The Rev James Dewar, writing about his parish of Kilchoman, was less specific, but equally alarmed. He asserted that the laird was doing 'every thing in his power . . . to alleviate our present distress, and to meet the grievous calamity with which it has pleased the Almighty as a judgment to visit us'. But prospects for the following summer were 'dark and gloomy'. Draining at Loch Gruinart to reclaim land had begun, but Dewar believed it would bring only a brief respite. A government grant of the large sum of £30,000 over three years helped with the Gruinart reclamation, using tiles manufactured in the works still visible at Foreland.[20] Over in

Kildalton, the Rev Archibald McTavish agreed that the following spring and summer would be critical, 'for their small stock of oats and bere will soon be consumed'. For the present, however, McTavish felt that Islay was surviving the crisis better than many other areas. The most telling illustration of the intense pressures unleashed on a population by failure of the potatoes was the increase in mass migration: Jura lost almost one-fifth of its population between 1841 and 1851, while Islay's declined by nine percent.[21]

Unfortunately the slight relative advantage of Islay continued to keep it well down the list of priority areas for such government assistance as was available. The latter was of course, not great and the appalling problems in Ireland, where perhaps a million people died of starvation or disease between 1846 and 1851, made it easier to neglect the problems on Islay. Cattle numbers were run down by sales to pay for meal or to pay some of the rent. Landowners were hit by rental arrears and rising payments for the poor. Both the *New Statistical Account* of the 1840s and the registers kept by the Superintendent of the Poor after the Scottish Poor Law Act was passed in 1845 indicate the growing problems in Islay.[22] Unfortunately, the landlord himself was perhaps unwilling to admit his increasing inability to control the island's affairs. Sir Edward Pine Coffin was appointed by the Treasury to inquire into the need for government relief measures, and was sent to the Highlands in September 1846 to report on the extent of the potato failure and its social consequences. After active service in the Napoleonic wars, Coffin had taken part in famine relief operations in China and Mexico, and had just been knighted for his services in the administration of relief at Limerick. Regular tours of inspection were carried out by Sir Edward and his officers in the powerful steam vessels of the Royal Navy which were also used to convey vital supplies in virtually all weathers. Sir Edward reported that he had been in touch with Walter Frederick's Edinburgh agent, who 'expresses his belief, that although severe privation must inevitably be caused by the failure of the potato crop in that island, the measures taken or intended by Mr Campbell's order will suffice, without Government interference of any kind, to prevent any absolute destitution'.[23]

During previous food shortages, emergency meal supplies had been imported into the western Highlands to avert starvation. But what has been termed the 'Highland Famine' or 'Great Hunger' of the later 1840s was of a quite different order of magnitude from past scarcities.[24] The failure of the potato in 1846 finally removed the principal part of the food supply in many areas. But disaster might not have happened if other economic resources had been available to purchase food supplies from elsewhere.

Cattle prices were depressed and herring fishing was in difficulty. Migrant family members brought or sent back remittances but after the nationwide depression of 1848, there were fewer jobs available in the lowlands. Even so, the failure of the potato in the Scottish north and west did not lead to a crisis of Irish proportions. The problem was both more manageable and containable albeit accompanied by malnutrition, disease and financial hardship.

After serving in the East Indies, Charles Trevelyan had been appointed Secretary to the Treasury in 1840. He was a member of the evangelical 'Clapham Sect', a man of intense religious beliefs, renowned for his integrity, strong principles and commitment to duty. By September 1846 he unequivocally stated government policy to be that 'the people cannot, *under any circumstances*, be allowed to starve'.[25] It was the duty of each landowner to provide for the subsistence of his tenants. The latter, in turn, had to pay for help or carry out work of some kind in return. Public loans continued to be made available, under existing legislation, for fisheries, drainage and public works.

A visit to Islay by Sir Edward Pine Coffin's deputy, Captain Pole, found Walter Frederick Campbell more sympathetic to the notion of assistance than Walter Frederick had suggested, though he evidently shrank from any help to his people that brought any authority in competition with his own plans. Pole in fact proposed that some assistance should be given to enable the twenty-kilometre road from Port Ellen to Bridgend, begun in the previous year, to be completed (the 'High' Road). This road was to replace the existing link between the two points which was over 25 kilometres long, of which almost half were 'on the seashore and not passable in storms' (a reference to the Big Strand along Laggan Bay). Sir Edward was apparently unconvinced; he thought that Walter Frederick was 'very imperfectly informed of the real extent of the destitution . . . This seems to be a case in which it is difficult to interfere, but which it would be at the same time dangerous to consider as provided for'.[26] Sir John McNeill later also percipiently noted that he had been aware all along that Campbell of Islay was 'quite confident of the sufficiency of his own means and measures to supply the necessaries of life to all his people . . . Mr Campbell is a man of kind heart and generous nature, and if he fails, it will be from want of available means or of efficient management'.[27]

Campbell's own thoughts on the matter of governmental assistance are contained in a letter that he wrote to Sir George Grey, the Home Secretary, in October 1846.[28] As they stand, his views are unexceptional by the standards of his peers and his predecessors. He suggested that government aid might include loans for public works if these were on a large scale, small grants for smaller works, promotion of fisheries, assistance for emigration, the establishment of depots for food (Indian corn) in different localities and amendments to the drainage acts. Apart from the reference to emigration, there is little to indicate a realisation that the problems were beyond the capacity of a single landlord to overcome.

Debts escalate – sequestration

1848 was a year of national financial crisis and European upheaval. Borrowing reached sixty per cent and the bankruptcies of many 'such small game as . . . Lord Bellhaven and Campbell of Islay' were gazetted.[29] There is little evidence in any other region of Britain, however, of a financial catastrophe on the scale which overwhelmed the West Highland landowners. They were partly responsible for their plight with over-ambitious expenditure and undermanagement of their estates and they did not live within their means. Sir James Riddell had spent over £50,000 on his Ardnamurchan and Sunart estate by 1848, without the expected returns; Lord MacDonald owed over £140,000, while the debts of Walter Frederick Campbell of Shawfield and Islay eventually amounted to over £800,000, equivalent to almost £50 million by the second decade of this century.[30] Some of these debts were incurred for reasons of conspicuous consumption, such as the improvement of estate mansions, the acquisition of town houses and the purchasing of fine furniture, as well as a parliamentary lifestyle and large families. But many were inherited and others were due to unsuccessful investments in the infrastructure of the estates and the provision of relief for destitute tenants during bad seasons, all of which failed to bring in income.

As with tenants, whether a landed family survived or not, when all other resources failed, was mainly dependent on the balance between debt and income. When the cost of servicing interest charges became greater than annual income, debts quickly accrued. It was difficult for landowners to economise and reduce absolute levels of expenditure because much debt was inherited. Estates were also entailed and burdened with annuities, life-rents and other portions for relations, especially for younger sons and daughters. There were three aspects to attaining solvency: income had to be increased, costs lowered and management improved, but none seemed likely to produce the required changes in the short term.

Since the death of his grandfather in 1816, Walter Frederick Campbell had changed the face of Islay. In April 1847, however, a visitor to Islay left a very dismal account. In the course of a survey of possible harbour improvements for Islay, Jura, Colonsay and the adjoining coasts, Joseph Mitchell, Engineer to the Fishery Board Commissioners, stayed with

Campbell and his family for a fortnight. He later wrote that 'the poor laird . . . appeared despondent beyond measure. We attributed this to the dreadful potato blight, so disastrous to the country and his people; but he was depressed by what was to him a more serious calamity. Owing to the general distress, the rents were not forthcoming, and the holders of bills and bonds were not paid their interest. The banks also became alarmed, and stopped further advances. Hence in a few months after this the creditors seized the property of Islay, and Mr Campbell was declared bankrupt . . . These pecuniary difficulties . . . arose mainly from previous embarrassments on the estate, but unfortunately Mr Campbell was no man of business', a percipient comment.[31]

As can be seen in the archives, from the rash of meetings and paperwork over the summer months of 1847, the financial difficulties had been mounting for years. Already in 1826 Walter Frederick had returned a list of tenants heavily in arrears to his factor with the comment 'Being as you know extremely distressed for money myself, I must positively request you to use all legal means to obtain payment of these enormous arrears and from the state in which I am myself placed, although I say it with sorrow, I must insist on summonses of removal being served on many if not all of the above list'.[32] This unconscious echo of the Cawdor Campbells a century earlier is one of the first indications that the growing pressure on the island's income was already having its effect on the laird. His request to the factor was, of course, largely unproductive: the tenants were not evading payment of their rents but were simply not able to pay. The 1828 'Black Book of Islay' had been one indicator of attempts to monitor the increasing problems of arrears.[33] How difficult this might prove appears in a letter from the office clerk, Robert Cross, to the laird in October of that same year, in which he confessed that his 'accts are all made up. But it has baffled me hitherto to make them ballance . . . When I came to Islay first i did not understand accts well . . . but still thought I wd learn & if I was carefull I should save as much of my wages as enable me to ballance . . . I hope to be able to meet you without the murdering thought of Being in your debt'.[34] £210,000 was raised between 1837 and 1839 from the Scottish Widows Fund and Life Assurance Company and sundry bequest funds, using bonds secured heritably on different parts of Islay. Second charges were subsequently resorted to on some of these. By 1847 £300,000 was being requested from the Royal Bank of Scotland to pay off heritable debts of £125,000 on Woodhall estate and personal debts of £170,000, using Woodhall and almost all of Islay as security. The arrears of rent in Islay alone amounted to some £32,000 by the end of October 1847,[35] the net rental being £17,000.

Sorting out the financial chaos was to prove difficult and time-consuming. William Webster, the factor at Woodhall and overseer in Islay, was praised for his accounts of Woodhall from 1841 to 1845, but the situation in Islay was less satisfactory.[36] By the middle of 1847, almost after the horse had bolted, the distiller and farmer, John Ramsay, was advising the Campbells, and wrote to the Islay factor, George Todd Chiene, that he had been thinking about the general management of the island since Walter Frederick Campbell either personally or through those acting for him, 'desires in future to exercise a stricter rule over his own affairs'.[37] He urged the factor to update the accounts to provide Walter Frederick Campbell with a balance sheet exhibiting the actual state of the receipts and expenditure to Whitsunday 1847. Such a past 'satisfactory analysis of the whole' would allow lessons for guidance in the future to be deduced. 'From the little time you are yourself enabled to devote to your accounts, with your present clerk, I confess I have my fears . . . these fears I admit cause the disinclination on my part to interfere, in any way with Mr Campbell's affairs'. The subsequent view of the heir, John Francis Campbell, was that Chiene was 'an honest man though not fitted for the situation'.[38]

By October 1847 the debts were thought to include heritable bonds of £490,000, banks were owed £310,000, there were personal debts of £107,000, debts in Islay of £20,000 and an annuity for Lady Charlotte Campbell, now Bury of £1,500, although some of the estimates were probably on the high side.[39] The net rentals for Woodhall and Islay were £11,000 and £17,000 respectively, though when they were used to calculate assets, gross rentals were used. It was estimated that twenty years' purchase at £12,300 for Woodhall would yield a sum of £246,000, while thirty years' purchase for Islay at £20,000 would provide £600,000. The demands from the bank were becoming more and more urgent, as Walter Frederick Campbell's Edinburgh agent, James McInnes, pointed out in October to the Islay factor. Signing off 'yours in tribulation', he emphasised that 'the Bank of Scotland has become more & more urgent for a payment to account, which I cannot give, indeed I am as I told you quite exhausted, and look with the utmost anxiety to hear from Islay – For my sake hasten relief, surely something <u>may</u> be done – something <u>must</u> be done. The <u>interest</u> term is close at hand'.[40]

John Ramsay then tried to get more return from Islay. In writing to Chiene, he pointed out that 'Mr McInnes has produced a statement showing that your remittances for the last nine years amount only to £234,000' although this was, in fact more than the rental income. It was expenditure that had escalated out of control.[41] Without mincing words, he told the factor that it was imperative that nothing was to hinder him from getting to Edinburgh 'by Friday's steamer', or sending 'the whole Books, Vouchers, accounts, receipt Books, rentals and all other letters or documents whatever that will enable us to make up or form a general estimate of the expenditure for the period above named'.

By then Walter Frederick Campbell's affairs were in the hands of his son, John Francis Campbell and John Ramsay for, 'being advised to go abroad for some time for the recovery of his health', Walter Frederick Campbell had left for his property near Avranches in Normandy on October 21, accompanied by his wife, younger children and some of their Islay House silverware.[42] With the income insufficient to meet the annual interests on the heritable and personal debts and other burdens, John Francis Campbell and John Ramsay asked counsel for guidance on immediate procedures to pay interest, recover arrears, advise creditors, possibly sell parts of the estates, and on the uncertain financial arrangements for various family marriage contracts.

Within days, and after repeated consultations with John Francis Campbell, John Ramsay and James McInnes, Counsel had given his opinion 'that it would be altogether . . . prejudicial to make any unnecessary delay in meeting the Creditors; and that any schemes of tiding over the approaching term by raising money to pay, not Interests only, but some of the more pressing debts, partly at least in principal, would not be not only unadvisable but of very questionable propriety'.[43] He strongly advised 'young Islay', John Francis Campbell, not to act as his father's commissioner, but to be prepared to come forward as a creditor, as heir of entail and under his mother's marriage contract. Nor did he see any advantage in John Ramsay acting as commissioner in the circumstances, acting simply as agent for Islay. His main recommendation was to execute a Trust Deed on behalf of all the creditors and to name trustees. He added that a great deal would depend upon the forbearance and even the indulgence of creditors and recommended not postponing 'even for a day the duty of taking the creditors into Counsel'.

A meeting of creditors in Edinburgh on 5 November 1847 indeed recommended that Walter Frederick Campbell's affairs be handed over to a Trust and that he be formally asked to agree to sequestration. Chiene was soon writing a 'private' letter to John Ramsay saying that Islay was in a sad state and that he was beset 'by all who think they may suffer directly or indirectly . . . the Poor people in many cases are afraid of the Bank and are drawing their deposits from the National Bond'. John Francis Campbell was in Edinburgh, still hoping that the situation was retrievable, writing to John Ramsay, also in Edinburgh, that the creditors seemed very much inclined to put a low value on Islay and wanted to sell it 'now to anybody for anything

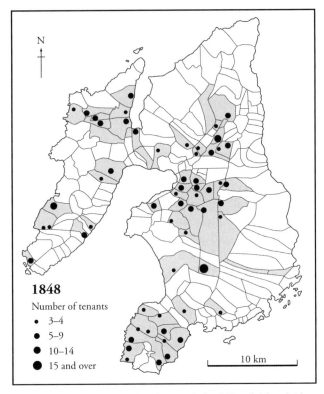

1848

Number of tenants

• 3–4
• 5–9
● 10–14
● 15 and over

10 km

1848 was the year in which Walter Frederick Campbell of Shawfield and Islay was sequestrated, and administrator James Brown was appointed to act on behalf of trustees and creditors. Potato disease, crop difficulties and rent arrears had resulted in a further reduction in
multiple tenancies and tenants, concentrated in the 'Glen', the northern Rinns and the Oa
(Islay Estate Papers).

it will fetch'. He hoped that in that case he could find a purchaser 'who will
let me make what I can out of the place for [the rental of] £17,000 a year.
What think you of my bright idea? I fear it is a castle in the air but it is a
very pretty one and I shall live in it till it tumbles down'. The castle did not
materialise and by 22 November, his father, Walter Frederick Campbell,
was dispiritedly writing from Avranches, to lawyers in Edinburgh. 'As I now
learn by your Letter that it is the wish of my Creditors that I should be
sequestrated (though it is a bitter Pang) I at once yield to their wishes and
I send herewith the proper form to enable you to take out a Sequestration
before the Courts. I trust that the Creditors will not use unnecessary
harshness – as I have done all in my power to do justice to them'.

By the time sequestration was awarded on 2 December 1847, the debts
exceeded £800,000. In keeping with the mood, Webster told of the very
stormy weather being experienced in Islay: 'the loudest Peal of thunder

was this morning betwixt 1 and 2 o'clock I ever heard, the houses in the neighbourhood "they say the beds on the earthen floors" shook as if they had been in a Steam boat'. Tax personnel had almost effected a sale of the cattle and crops in Islay, which Webster managed to stall until 'we may expect to hear something of a Trustee being appointed'. After thirty years with Walter Frederick Campbell as laird and after 120 years in Shawfield ownership, the laird of Islay estate had been declared bankrupt: he was not yet fifty. From 5 January 1848 until the end of August 1853, it was administered by an Edinburgh accountant, James Brown.[44]

Many Highland estates were in trust by mid-century. They were administered by the agents of trustees for the creditors of the landowners and their responsibility was to treat the property as an asset, run it efficiently, increase rental income and, if possible, increase its solvency for quick disposal. Financial imperatives were ahead of most other considerations. It was not therefore surprising that trustees resorted to clearances in Islay. During the interregnum in Islay, James Brown was responsible for clearances, for instance in many of the townships in 'The Glen' as seventeen-year leases expired in 1850.

The main concern of James Brown, of course, lay not in agricultural improvements, but in the management and disposal of the estate on the best terms for the creditors. Times were hard although the sporting opportunities provided by the Highlands were coming to be appreciated by those who were growing rich on the commercial and industrial revolutions of the nineteenth century. One talked-of purchaser for Islay would perhaps have put Islay clearly on the map, as James Crawford, who had taken over from McInnes, gossiped to John Ramsay that 'Prince Albert being so fond of Highland Sports, the Queen has resolved on purchasing Islay, where her husband will have all kind of Sports, fishing, Shooting &c &c. Of course "Islay" would be appointed "Ranger of the Island". I wish the news were true. When I mentioned them to old McInnes today he smiled – which I have not seem him do for 3 months'.[45] A very different outcome would have resulted had a scheme mooted by the Tontine Association in 1850 come to fruition. It was proposed that Islay be sold off democratically in 3,000 lots each of twenty hectares to islanders and 'others engaged in town-business, who find their health giving way in consequence, and . . . the plan here proposed would be the very thing for their case'.[46] Over £700,000 might be raised by the sale of Islay alone.

Early in February 1848 John Francis Campbell was still dreaming in a letter to John Ramsay, though realism was more to the fore, saying that he had had a letter from his father saying that John Ramsay had told him that Islay would then sell at £400,000. 'I think you had better not tell

them such disagreeable facts. It only sets them thinking all manner of
plans which have no chance of success'. He argued that '£400,000 at five
per cent is £26,000, the Islay rental is £17,000 and Chiene's books shew
only £15,000. What good then would <u>borrowed</u> money do? and who
is to lend it? A gift of £50 or £100,000 might do but who is to give it?'
He instructed John Ramsay to send any plans direct to himself 'for I can
consider them calmly but my Father takes them at once as . . . concluded
and writes to people in such a strain that they are provoked . . . and this
may do harm'.[47] By May of 1848, on being advised that he was likely to
succeed in his claims as a creditor, he was speculating on buying the personal
debts and obtaiing the reversion of Islay. 'The worst is that I hear a rumour
that young Mathieson has long been on the look out for Islay and that
he has a million and a half'.[48] In the autumn of 1848 he was reduced to
asking John Ramsay if any scheme could be contrived 'that would yield
me an income and give me the Cottage' [at Ardimersay].[49] A few months
later on return from visiting his parents in France he was still showing
concern but 'unless some windfall comes my way I have little chance of
recovering any considerable portion of Old Islay as for a small favour I
would rather remain as I am than set up there as a "Lack Laird" with all
the bother and none of the advantages of my former position'. He pressed
for any information John Ramsay might 'chance to pick up. Who knows
what may turn up . . . If I had the funds . . . I would venture a great deal
for a footing in the old place'.[50] By then 'he was pounding away every day
and beginning to understand legal jargon a little as the first step towards
learning law'. He was just thirty years of age.

For sale
Meantime, Brown's difficulties on getting a good price for Islay to raise
monies may account for the elaborate overstatements in his descriptions
of the Islay estate.[51] It was advertised for sale at £540,000 in November
1848.[52] In March the following year John Francis Campbell was still hoping
for wonders: 'I must not think of buying either "farms or districts" I have
all the will to do wonders in that line, but the power is sadly deficient.
However who knows what may turn up? I little thought of the down
come'.[53] Standing aside, he praised Brown's wisdom 'in not allowing people
to starve for want of work, and in giving useful work [on the roads] to
employ them, new men have new measures and I have no doubt but that
much more in the way of rent can be got, than ever was got before, by
simply having the determination to demand it. I fear I never would have
the heart to screw folk if I had the chance but I take it, it is better for all
parties to keep clean books and no large balances one way or the other'.

But his pipedreams were thwarted and in April 1849 he surmised: 'all my schemes for buying land without money are about to be fairly swamped'.[54] He had heard that 'Morrison who bought Fonthill Abbey was going down to buy Islay. He began the world as his Father-in-law's foreman and has now an enormous fortune. I am told he is both dour and a good man of business, so if he does as he intends he will probably succeed in adding to his fortune perhaps at the expense of the present inhabitants'. He added that Morrison meant to take his wife and family to Islay to live there for two months 'so you will have a chance of studying the man'. But he warned John Ramsay not to talk too much about this, 'for reports spread rapidly in Islay and I don't want to spread the news till I am sure that he has made up his mind – at present it seems he has only determined on looking. I take it however he won't hesitate long for by all accounts he has the means at his disposal'.

With estates of Basildon Park in Berkshire and Fonthill in Wiltshire, James Morrison was 64, had been member of parliament for Inverness Burghs from 1840 to 1847 and was, like Walter Frederick Campbell, a member of the original committee of the Reform Club. In the words of his descendant and biographer, Richard Gatty, he had long 'had a weakness for the west coast of Scotland'.[55] This London 'merchant prince' took some of his family on holiday to Islay in July 1849. They 'stayed at the inn at Bridgend and in spite of bad weather spent the inside of a week seeing something of the island'. They admired the setting of Islay House, including the 350 different rose varieties in the garden. But they did not spend two months and were not yet persuaded to part with the then upset price of £540,000.

The accountant, James Brown, might have been permitted a wry smile, had he discovered that, 'while he <u>did</u> sleep in Islay House on the night of 30th March 1851', the census enumerator had omitted recording him, the indignant supervisor having personally checked the fact.[56] John Francis Campbell was still trying to do his sums, using Scottish interest rates of $2\frac{1}{2}$ and $3\frac{1}{2}$ per cent, writing to John Ramsay: 'Islay will be the grand point on which to found . . . a loan for there the land is the thing . . . at Woodhall it is the coals. Tell me then whenever you hear anything about the state of affairs in Islay & if there be any prospect of receiving rents there were I once in a position to ask for them'.[57] By September 1852, after several fruitless advertisements, the asking figure for the Islay Estate had been reduced to £440,000. Who was likely to buy it, and why? Highland estates were in great demand from social groups outside the Highlands; despite the economic and social crisis, land prices rose and the west Highland region began to attract very wealthy purchasers, not only from the Scottish Lowlands but from further afield. Larger properties did prove more difficult to sell but even they eventually found purchasers. By mid-century, the Romantic Movement and the ideas of the sublime and the picturesque which could be applied to the grandeur and scenery of the remote Highlands and Islands appealed to the English upper and middle classes. The region rapidly developed as a major centre for the physical sports of hunting, shooting and fishing, which required space empty of people.

The revolution in communications paved the way: the replacement of sailing ships by steamers and improved road transport. But the exceptional availability of Highland estates also helped to satisfy other more powerful needs of the wealthy. It was difficult even for the most affluent members of the new merchant and industrial classes in England to buy a great deal of land there in Victorian times because few large estates ever came to market. In the western Highlands, it was possible to buy up many thousands of acres of wild and beautiful country for an outlay which would have purchased only a small country estate elsewhere. By the 1850s the pattern of landownership in the western Highlands and Islands had been revolutionised.[58] All of the Outer Hebrides had been sold by the hereditary proprietors and large parts of Skye, most of Mull, Raasay, Ulva, Islay, Lismore, Rhum and Eigg in the Inner Hebrides had new owners. Of the Inner Hebrides, only Coll, Tiree, parts of Skye and Jura remained under the control of their traditional possessors. The scale of land transfer in this region was exceptional when compared to the land market elsewhere in Britain.

The Morrison purchase

James Morrison, with Scots forebears, was possibly the richest British commoner in the nineteenth century.[59] In James Brown's words, 'At last, Mr Morrison of Basildon Park, who had formerly made special inquiries, came forward, through his eldest son, and after much negotiation, it was arranged, that on his becoming bound to offer the upset price, the Estate should . . . be exposed to public sale on the 31st August [1853] at £440,000'.[60] In the meantime, enquiries with a view to purchase had been made by a wealthy coal and iron manufacturer, Mr James Baird of Gartsherrie in Lanarkshire, the arrangement with Mr Morrison being kept private, and 'on the day the Estate was knocked down to Mr Morrison, after competition with Mr Baird at £451,000'. Entry was at Martinmas 1853, with money payable at Whitsunday 1854. £451,000 was a far cry from the £12,000 that Daniel Campbell of Shawfield had paid for Islay in the 1720s. But the trustees did not have to split up the estate into separate lots to facilitate a sale and, in the event, Morrison only acquired Islay after Baird's intervention, which slightly pushed up the price. James

Brown still had difficulties selling Woodhall, the other Campbell estate in Lanarkshire, despite the fact that this mineral-rich property lay in the very centre of the booming industrial area of west-central Scotland. It was apparently the Hebridean estate, with its stricken population and uncertain rental which proved more attractive than the lands in Lanarkshire which were richly endowed with coal and iron-ore measures and situated close to manufacturing industry.

In 1850 John Francis Campbell had asked John Ramsay if he could point out to the Islay commissioners and trustees that they were doing no good 'in screwing my father . . . he did not screw them when he might . . . this confounded Discharge has made poor Mrs Campbell fret so that she is reduced nearly to blindness . . . crying has brought on the old illness'.[61] Early in 1853 the personal creditors agreed to his father 'being personally discharged under the Sequestration Statute from all debts contracted by him before the Sequestration of his Estates'. The list of creditors was long and varied, including banks, agents, lawyers, landowners, relatives, friends and neighbours. Walter Frederick's affairs – in the end the debts amounted to some £815,000 – were not finally wound up until late in 1858 for Islay; Woodhall was sold in 1862 for £175,000.[62]

Perhaps the saddest émigrés of all, Walter Frederick Campbell and his family, continued to live in exile in France, aided by an annuity from friends.[63] Silver from Islay House had been 'taken by Mr Campbell' on 21 October 1847, but much of the remaining superb and valuable 'gold and silver plate . . . paintings, sketches, books on the fine arts' were sold at auction in Edinburgh in November 1854.[64] Walter Frederick survived only till 1855, dying at Avranches overlooking Mont St Michel. He is buried there, not lying beside his first wife in the sarcophagus in the round church in Bowmore. French obituaries testified to his continuing lack of realism as far as money was concerned. To the small community in which he then lived, 'Mr Campbell gave with both hands . . . to their wants and distresses his hand was ever open'.[65] Islay had passed to the Morrison family and the Shawfield link with the island had apparently been severed.

What did James Morrison get for almost half a million pounds in 1853? One description is contained in the detailed, if overblown, prospectus that was prepared in 1852 to entice prospective buyers. As one reads through the *Particulars of the Barony and Estate of Islay*, the whole of the island except the 'Properties of Sunderland and Ballinaby' being offered for sale, there is a gradual escalation of its virtues.[66] 'This very extensive and valuable Estate' becomes 'This magnificent Property' and then an estate that 'can nowhere be excelled'. The last sentence in the prospectus reads 'On the whole, it may be safely said, that whether as regards present or prospective inducements, an Estate superior to Islay has seldom, if ever, been offered for sale'.

The mansion and the sporting attractions were given precedence over the island economy: this was scarcely flattering to the work of the Shawfield Campbells, but it was a buyer's market. The 'Mansion House of Islay' was described as large and commodious, a great part of it being entirely new, [the Playfair extension] 'in the best style of architecture and finishing . . . and surrounded with far spreading plantations; and the Gardens, Pleasure Grounds, Private Drives, and Walks around and connected with it, are very extensive and varied, and laid out with great taste and judgment, for convenience and recreation. Considerable streams, uniting in the grounds in their course to the sea, add much to their ornament and beauty'. This is a recognisable description of Islay House and some of its grounds today.[67]

Not so the other residence for the laird in the south-east of the island, a 'Marine Residence at Ardimersay, beautifully situated amid woodland and rock scenery, and containing, with offices, and other appurtenances, suitable accommodation for a genteel family. This delightful retreat, the singularly picturesque features of which are well known, affords an agreeable variety from the principal residence of Islay House'. This area of Kildalton certainly provides a contrast with the head of Lochindaal, but it is not today quite so agreeable: only the outbuildings of the former *cottage ornée* survive and the Victorian mansion of Kildalton House, built later on an adjacent site, stands empty and derelict.

Despite the attempt to catch the eye of those interested in shooting and fishing, the sporting opportunities of the island are summarised in a few short sentences. All kinds of field sport, and shooting both on land and water were to be enjoyed 'in the highest perfection. Game of every description, four-footed and winged, is plentiful: and fishing, either in the sea, in lakes or in streams, is always at command; and salmon, with every variety of sea fish, is in abundance'. In the Ardimersay area in the south-east there was an extensive stock of wild fallow-deer, and the woodcock shooting was 'believed to be unrivalled in the kingdom'. The climate was described as 'mild and salubrious' and the soil and climate as 'favourable to all kinds of agricultural crops, and the pasture . . . luxuriant'.

The economy of the island was discussed under various heads. The rental, excluding Islay House, the factor's residence at Eallabus House and the shootings and fishings, woods and plantations, was 'about £19,045', and was expected to increase progressively due to 'the Improvements in Drainage and otherwise that have been effected within these few years'. Such a gross return at less than 5 per cent on the reserve, or upset, price at £440,000 suggests that the purchaser was not expected to buy Islay for its agricultural profitability, unless he was prepared to take a very optimistic view about the scope for such progressive increases. The previous twenty years were described as a period in which 'much improvement' to agriculture had taken place and 'the capabilities of the Estate for further improvements are very great'.

Among the attractions mentioned were the distilleries, drove routes for cattle through Jura, the cattle themselves, ferries and regular steam or sailing vessels: in each case these were put in a favourable light and any difficulties in freight and ferries were of course glossed over. Apart from the distilleries, 'there are plenty of powerful Water Falls fit for all kinds of manufactories', a remark that was not merely naïvely optimistic but perhaps rather archaic at mid-century. So, via the partly constructed High Road, the estate tile and brick works at Foreland, the harbours, ports and villages, the account concluded with the coastal fishery and the 'great variety of minerals' on Islay. Or rather, it concluded with the cautious understatement, 'By an extended application of capital, all these natural productions might be brought to yield valuable capital returns'.

Although he never went to the island again, James Morrison took a great interest in it and was reputedly keen to improve the peat lands with shell-sand. Jointly with John Ramsay he bought and ran the steamship *Islay*. Gatty supposed, on the basis of family tradition, that James Morrison 'seems to have had some definite scheme in mind for Islay. Unfortunately there is no record of what it was'.[68]

Notes and references

[1]   *Appendix to First Report of the Select Committee appointed to inquire into the Condition of the Population . . . and into Emigration, BPP*, 1841, VI, 212.

[2]   Devine, *Clanship*, p. 52.

[3]   *Ibid.*, p. 49.

[4]   Islay Estate Papers, Sundry rentals.

[5]   Islay Estate Papers, Estate rentals for 1835 and 1836; see also Kildalton Papers, List of Tenants in the Oa, 1839, TD1284.

[6]   Shore, *Sketches*, 2, 308.

[7]   R. N. Salaman, *The History and Social Influence of the Potato*, (Cambridge, 1949, reprint 1970), p. 374. The potato's complex DNA was established in 2011, with the potential of eradicating blight.

[8]   See Chapter 6, fn. 6.

[9]   M. MacDonell, *The Emigrant Experience*, (Toronto, 1982), pp. 36–7.

[10] A. F. Hunter, *A History of Simcoe County*, (Canada, 1909), 2 volumes, II, pp. 134–58 and 232–60. A. Ronaghan, *There'll always be an Islay*, (Islay, Alberta, 1977).

[11] *BPP*, 1841 *Emigration*, VI, 30.

[12] Devine, *Clanship*, p. 186.

[13] W. P. Reeves, *The Long White Cloud*, (London, 1956), p. 189.

[14] *BPP*, 1841 *Emigration*, VI, 30.

[15] *Ibid.*, p. 53.

16 Clerk of Penicuik Papers, NRS, GD18/3470.

17 Islay Estate Papers, *Statistics of Lands, Occupiers, Stock and Crops in Islay 1843*, (1890).

18 Anon, 'Appendix to Report on the Disease of the Potato Crop in Scotland in the year 1845', *Transactions of the Highland and Agricultural Society of Scotland*, New Series, 16 (1845–47), p. 460.

19 [McLeod, Dr N.], *Extracts of letters to Dr [N] McLeod regarding the famine and destitution in the Highlands and Islands of Scotland*, 1847, (Glasgow, 1847), pp. 26–31. It has been estimated that one-third of the crop was lost in 1845. (Salaman, History *and Social Influence*, p. 476).

20 J. Brown, *Report to the Creditors and General View of the Funds Realised*, Campbell of Jura Papers, NRS, GD64, p. 1.

21 *Census of Scotland 1951*, Table 3.

22 Poor Records, Argyll and Bute Council.

23 *Correspondence . . . relating to the Measures adopted for the Relief of Distress in Scotland*, BPP, 1847, LIII, 37.

24 Devine, *Clanship*, pp. 146 et seq.

25 *Ibid.*, p. 158.

26 BPP, *Distress*, LIII, 71. Plans for this road 'the High Road' are in Islay Estate Papers.

27 *Ibid.*, 187.

28 *Ibid.*, 81–3.

29 R. Blake, *Disraeli* (London, 1966), p. 257.

30 Devine, *Clanship*, p. 68, and Brown, *Report to the Creditors*, p. 4.

31 J. Mitchell, *Reminiscences of My Life in the Highlands*, 1 (London, 1883–4), 2 vols. pp. 299–300.

32 Islay Estate Papers, List of tenants heavily in arrears in 1826.

33 Kildalton Papers, The Black Book of Islay, 1828.

34 Islay Estate Papers, 31 October 1828.

35 Kildalton Papers, Correspondence, 22 October 1847; Brown, *Report to the Creditors*, p. 1.

36 Ibid., 6 September 1845.

37 Ibid., 23 June 1847

38 Ibid., 30 May 1847.

39 Ibid., 22 October 1847.

40 Ibid., 10 October1847.

41 Ibid., 26 October 1847. This figure presumably included income other than rental.

42 Ibid., List of Islay House Silver, August 1846, with List of Silver taken by Mr Campbell on 21 October 1847.

43 Ibid., 27 October 1847.

44 Islay Estate Papers, Disposition by Walter Frederick Campbell of Islay in favour of James Brown.

45 Kildalton Papers, Correspondence, 7 January, 1848.

46 J. Murdoch, 'A New and Ready Way of Disposing of that Interesting Island Which would pay the debt, restore the late proprietor, and give the best return to large and small capitalists', in W. MacDonald, *Descriptive and Historical Sketch of Islay*, (Glasgow, 1850), p. 30. For further writings of J. Murdoch, see also J. Hunter, (ed.), *For the People's Cause*, (Edinburgh, 1986).

47 Kildalton Papers, Correspondence, 2 February 1848. The Far East entrepreneur.

48 Ibid., 9 May 1848. Sir James Mathieson of Jardine had bought the Isle of Lewis for £2.5 million a few years earlier.

49 Ibid,, 27 October 1848.

50 Ibid., 17 January 1849.

51 Islay Estate Papers, *Particulars of the Barony and Estate of Islay*, 1852.

52 Brown, *Report to the Creditors*, p. 1.

53 Kildalton Papers, Correspondence, 10 March 1849.

54 Ibid., 6 April 1849.

55 J. B. Burke, *Genealogical Dictionary*; Burke Peerage; R. Gatty, *Portrait of a Merchant Prince: James Morrison 1789–1857*, (Northallerton, n.d. [1977]), pp. 288–90 and p. 300; W. D. Rubinstein, *Men of Property*, (London, 1981).

56 Copy of Census enumerator's book, Census of Scotland 1851, 536/13.

57 Kildalton Papers, Correspondence, Undated, probably 1851/2.

58 Devine, *Clanship*, p. 64.

59 *Ibid.*, p. 82.

60 Brown, *Report to the Creditors*, p. 2.

61 Kildalton Papers, 25 February 1850.

62 Brown, *Report to the Creditors*, p. 4.

63 NLS, Sale Catalogues, 16, f, 2 (12).

64 Attributed to Walter Frederick Campbell in his exile, and edited by his son, J. F. Campbell, are two volumes published in 1863. Written in 1848, *Life in Normandy*, (Edinburgh, 1863), consists of 'vignettes in the life of Mr Cross who . . . with a small independence, found himself the great man of the quiet little town where he lived . . . poverty in England being wealth in Normandy'. Watercolours executed by John Francis Campbell while visiting his father in Avranches, are in the National Galleries of Scotland, Edinburgh.

65 J. F. Campbell collected French obituaries of his father: Special Collections, Glasgow University Library, Mu43-c. 17.

66 Islay Estate Papers, *Particulars of the Barony and Estate of Islay*.

67 Storrie, 'Recovering the Historic Designed Landscape of Islay Estate', *Scottish Archives*, 7 (2001), pp. 59–77.

68 Gatty, *Portrait*, p. 289.

Charles Morrison (1817–1909), who brought new management and invested in Islay Estate for more than half a century until his death in 1909 (Gatty, *Portrait*).

Victorian additions in the 1860s included estate workers' cottages, as at Bluehouses, Bridgend, first occupied in the 1860s. Photograph before a large house was added behind.

CHAPTER 11

'This very extensive and valuable Estate' after 1853

The Campbells of Shawfield were gone from Islay after 120 years; for a longer period of time after 1853 the Morrisons were to be the principal lairds in Islay. Innovation and improvement that four generations of Shawfields had initiated was not maintained at the same rate by their successors but the need and scope for such zeal was considerably reduced as the nineteenth century went on. By 1850 the essential steps had been taken that had transformed Islay into a more varied economy and society that had the potential to provide a better life for the majority of its inhabitants. Although the certainty of this was clouded at mid-century by the potato disease and islanders being on the brink of starvation, what Islay needed in the future was not so much more change, as a period of tranquillity in which the initiatives that had been taken in the first half of the nineteenth century could come to fruition; this the Morrisons and other lairds provided. Their wealth gave more freedom of action than their increasingly impoverished predecessors and, like their counterparts throughout the Highlands and islands, they rebuilt farmhouses and out-buildings, adding Victorian cottages, schools and churches.

It was early in 1856, after a full decade of misery, that the first optimistic reports of recovery began to appear in the Highlands and Islands, but the potato was never again so important in the Highland diet. Indeed, in Islay drought was to cause problems for the potato that year. The majority of the population of the western Highlands and Islands became less dependent on the land for survival and entered more fully into the cash economy, selling their labour for cash wages and buying more. Prices for Highland black cattle rose and fishing and whisky distilling expanded in the 1870s and 1880s. There was a relative improvement in living standards although the majority of inhabitants of the region continued to endure an existence of poverty and insecurity. Life was still precarious and there were still bad seasons: at best, then, 'recovery' was modest.

Already by 1854 James Morrison had been advised to take things easier for his health and the management of his estates was taken over by his two elder sons, Charles and Alfred. At the time, Charles demurred to his brother, Alfred: 'as I am an unmitigated Cockney it will be much better that you should be the man'.[1] But Charles was the one who took the main financial role as far as Islay was concerned. Of his father Charles wrote 'he does now wish, never to be troubled by anything being said about it . . . he does not like to be troubled at all about the place, and only looks at his investment ledger to see how much of his capital he has spent on it'.[2] Like his father an 'outstanding businessman and financier', Charles Morrison was well read and artistically appreciative. It was also in 1854 that his political economy text, *The Relations between Labour and Capital*, was published.[3] Despite a taste for exotic waistcoats, he was of what used to be described as a 'retiring disposition'. He travelled and invested extensively in America and 'turned the fortune he had inherited into an even more substantial one', while amassing a substantial art collection.[4] A later commentator also noted that Charles Morrison lived a 'bachelor life, devoting himself to business in the city; and as he is no sportsman or agriculturalist, the administration of the estate is given over to factors'.[5]

Charles Morrison had indeed made the successful bid for Islay and not only went there from time to time, but carried on a copious and regular correspondence with his commissioner and factors until his death in 1909. The minutiae of estate business dealt with harvests, sales, rents and arrears, construction and ornamentation, as well as the perennial problems of steamer provision. There was no intention of living on the island. Despite Charles Morrison's view of the soft furnishings in Islay House being 'a parcel of old, faded, unfashionable shabby . . . rubbish', there was talk of Islay House being rented to a hotelier as it 'would make one of the most attractive houses anywhere to be met with . . . with sport for a fortnight or month'.[6] Charles Morrison emphasised that 'we must make all arrangements as if we were never going to visit the island except in flying visits and at long intervals and . . . we shall in all probability always use the Inn'.[7] His father appeared to think otherwise, saying that he or his son 'should some day build a House for some of the family to have always ready for Use'.[8] While dismissing Islay House as 'inconveniently large' and the Inns as 'fit only for drovers', he wondered whether it might be possible to use 'Webster's House' [Daill], which would be 'just the thing' for a few months at a time. Islay House was let seasonally to shooting tenants, and it was not until 1892 that it was used by the Morrisons when Mrs Alfred Morrison and the next generation began to visit more frequently.

Charles Morrison wanted to see how things went for the first year after entry. He often referred to his father in the early correspondence with John Ramsay and William Webster. In June 1854 he wrote to his new commissioner and factor, John Dickson, subsequently also factor to

the duke of Buccleuch in Dumfriesshire, 'I think I had better leave you
and Webster to manage the estate at least for the present'.[10] The question
of buying the arrears was finally settled, James Brown 'having used every
means to extract the last farthing from the tenants that he could'.[11]
Approaching the first rent collection the new laird was venturing the
opinion that the tenants might try 'experiments with their new landlord,
to see whether he will let them get into arrears, & we must begin at once
to show them that he will not'.[12] The euphoria was beginning to wear thin:
after harvest and at rent collection time Charles Morrison was writing:

> I begin to fear I was mistaken in thinking there were not too many people
> on the island. If the present aspect of our collections is any specimen of
> what we are to expect, there are a great deal too many. Our rental must
> be independent of the potato or it will be a lame affair . . . the failure of
> the potato crop . . . was a circumstance which we could not foresee . . .
> it must materially modify our views as to the extent of the diminution
> of population which may be requisite to make the rental a clear one, or
> the population manageable when a bad time comes again . . . While I
> wished to avoid anything like wholesale clearance I never intended to
> keep men who did not try . . . it is my father's money & my father's land
> which I have to deal with – we must keep down the outlay [to assuage]
> his desire for immediate returns.[13]

In a letter to John Ramsay there is a tantalising reference to an enclosed
'Memorandum on the management of the population in Islay', but it
has not surfaced.[14] In any event, as envisaged as a possibility as early as
1849, one of the first results of the Morrison purchase was the sale of
several parts of the island. Although the sale of the Kildalton, Dunlossit
and other areas represented a substantial transfer of land, the Morrison
family continued to own the main core of the island, whether measured
in terms of acreage, agricultural value, or population. The era of Charles
Morrison added further plantations, Victorian farm buildings, cottages
and lodges to the Islay landscape. It was proposed at first to spend several
thousand pounds a year on such improvements for a return of over five
per cent, and a thousand pounds annually on philanthropic affairs,
including the poor and knitting schemes.[15]

But by the spring of 1856 Charles Morrison was writing to John
Dickson that he had 'at least hoped to be able to pay the £7,000 interest
on the mortgage of £176,000 from a nominal estate income of £16,000',
but was appalled to discover not only 'the illusory character of income of
Islay' but an 'actual loss of revenue on account'.[16] Again he wondered what

the state of the Islay cash account would be 'when a <u>bad time</u> for farmers comes, since it is so unfavourable after a good time'. By then he was 'very glad' he had made a sale of part of the estate to John Ramsay.

James Morrison died in 1857, 'the richest commoner in the South', leaving several million pounds as well as estate in the United States of America, and having settled landed estates on all of his sons. There is a much more business-like approach to the monitoring of expenditure and revenue on the Islay estate, with proto-spreadsheets being sent regularly to Charles Morrison, unlike the chaotic state of affairs a decade earlier. After the fascination of reading through half a century of the correspondence between Charles Morrison and John Dickson in the archives of Islay Estate, it was a considerable shock to this author to read that John Dickson was to attend the funeral in May 1909 of the nonagenarian Charles Morrison.[17] This was followed shortly after by a telegram on 23 November announcing John Dickson's own demise.[18]

After Charles Morrison's death in 1909, the estate passed to his nephew, Hugh, Alfred's son. Hugh Morrison brought his new bride, Lady Mary Leveson-Gower, to Islay in the autumn of 1892 when there was a great bonfire celebration on the estate.[9] From then on, Hugh Morrison and his descendants regularly visited Islay. By Hugh's marriage to Lady Mary the Shawfield connection with Islay revived, for she was a granddaughter of Walter Frederick Campbell.[19] In 1910 a two-storey mock-Georgian wing designed by Detmar Blow, and set back from the main Georgian tower, was added to Islay House's frontage. By 1921 it was proposed that some more parts of the estate be sold, with preference to sitting tenants, but little came of it. A decade later, John Granville Morrison succeeded to the Islay estate and to other family possessions, including the Fonthill estate in Wiltshire. Sitting as member of parliament for Salisbury in Wiltshire from 1942 to 1964 and later becoming Lord Lieutenant of that county, he was for a number of years chairman of the 1922 Committee of Conservative backbenchers. Created Baron Margadale of Islay in 1964, he took his title from a favourite sporting area in the remote north-eastern part of Islay. As elsewhere, the economics and management of sporting and agricultural estates have undergone many changes with many more external influences shaping them than even in the last of the Shawfield days. But the Islay Estate of today is still very much a recognisable, if areally reduced, successor to the agricultural and sporting estate purchased in 1854, although Islay House was sold in 1985.

The other estates

Shortly after the 1853 Morrison purchase, John Ramsay, merchant in Glasgow with lowland whisky distilling connections, tenant of Cornabus and Ballevicar and distiller in Islay, relieved the Morrisons of the parish of Kildalton and Oa in three separate purchases. The first of these, consisting mainly of the lands north-east of Port Ellen, was effected in 1855.[20] The sale included all the land within the parish of Kildalton from, in the south, the lighthouse in Port Ellen bay to the northern boundary of Proaig on the Sound of Islay. The offer also contained a promise that, in addition to the purchase price of £70,765, John Ramsay would pay a further sum of £500 towards the fund 'required to finish the road now being made between Port Ellen and Bridgend in Islay'.

After James Morrison's death, John Ramsay, now 'of Kildalton', offered Charles Morrison £9,500 for part of the parish of the Oa, near Port Ellen in 1858.[21] Charles Morrison wanted to dispose of the rest of the south-eastern part of his estate, particularly the Oa. Sir Smith Child, MP, of Stallington Hall in Stone, Staffordshire, a banker who had married of Miss Campbell of Jura, was also interested and he and John Ramsay were corresponding on the matter. Smith Child did not, however, go ahead and purchase the Oa, though he did become an Islay landowner shortly after. By 1861 John Ramsay, for another £45,000, had added to his lands the rest of the over-populated Oa peninsula and other holdings as far north as Laggan and Island.[22] He clearly recognised the main problem of too many tenants on the land, particularly in the Oa. Ramsay's view of the Oa expressed to Smith Child claimed that 'if people were removed and some improvements made on the better part of the land, it could be made a good sheep grazing. My views, however, regarding such removals are so much in unison with your own that I could not like to meddle with any improvement which involved the removal of any tenants'.[23]

Sir John McNeill was the third son of the laird of Colonsay, who trained in medicine and served in the East India Company, then as a diplomat in Persia, before being appointed the first chairman of the Board of Supervision of the Scottish Poor Law, a post which he held for over three decades after 1845. It was McNeill's *Report* of 1851 to the Board which finally discredited charitable relief as the solution to Highland destitution, as opposed to emigration. This led to the passage of the Emigration Advances Act which provided loans at low rates of interest to proprietors who wished to assist the emigration of the destitute population of their estates. Both McNeill and Sir Charles Trevelyan then became deeply involved in the formation and administration of the Island and Highland Emigration Society.

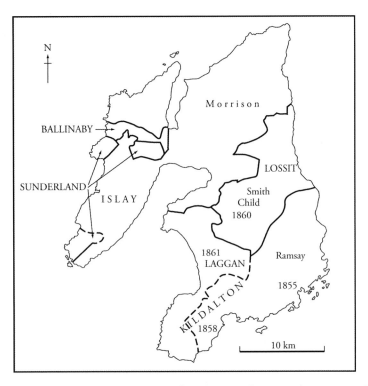

After James Morrison bought Islay in 1853 for £451,000, there were three major and two smaller estates: a reduced Islay Estate, and those of Lossit (Dunlossit), Kildalton, Sunderland and Ballinaby (which had never been in Shawfield ownership).

Some suspected that the eagerness of lairds and officials to support emigration derived ultimately from the fact that the costs of assisted passages were in the long run much lower than either famine relief or extension of the Scottish Poor Law. Reduction in numbers or clearance of small tenants and cottars and assisted emigration schemes all became integrated into coherent programmes of action on several Hebridean estates. After 1848 the volume of summonses of removal granted to landlords in west Highland sheriff courts dramatically increased. In a sense, the distress in some areas brutally solved the social problem of too many people on the land, which had long confronted estate landowners, thus accelerating emigration.

Elsewhere in the Highlands and Islands the new richer landlords financed emigration schemes on a massive scale and whole areas were rapidly depopulated. Even Sir Edward Pine Coffin was concerned about the intensity of clearance, very concentrated in space and time after mid-

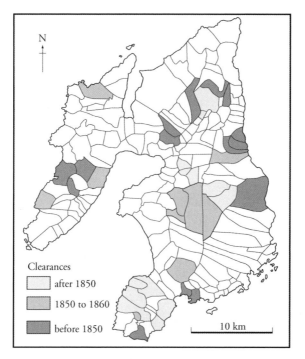

N

Clearances
☐ after 1850
▨ 1850 to 1860
■ before 1850

10 km

Revolutionary agrarian changes included some clearance of tenants to make way for single farms, sometimes physically reorganised. More formal reorganisation took place in other holdings, particularly for village and muir lotments (Islay Estate Papers).

century. Many became destitute and for the first time the poorest made up the bulk of the migrants. Increasingly, the incentives for the new landlords to promote assisted emigration became stronger. In Islay, one solution for John Ramsay lay in financial assistance for emigration from the Oa to Canada. This began in 1862 with clearance of tenants from Killeyan and their assisted emigration: it is plain however, that John Ramsay found this distasteful. Discussing his moral dilemma with Charles Morrison, he expressed the hope that the latter would not sell more land on Islay: 'it is not many of the Highland proprietors who direct their personal attention to the moral and intellectual improvement of the people on their land and were you to sell I should dread the risk of your estate coming into the hands of one who would buy it only for sport or profit and carry out plans in utter disregard of the interests and feelings of the people'.[24] In a paper read in Edinburgh to the National Association for the Promotion of Social Science he tried to explain his feelings and actions:

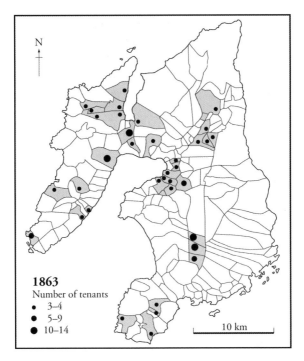

N

1863
Number of tenants
• 3–4
• 5–9
● 10–14

10 km

The policies of James Brown on the sequestrated estate and of Charles Morrison and John Ramsay after the estate was broken up, are evident in this map for 1863. Since 1848, the decline of holdings with more than two tenants is particularly pronounced in the 'Glen', the northern Rinns and the Oa (Islay Estate Papers).

> The cause of periodical destitution in the Highlands . . . has been the excessive dependence of the people upon the produce of the soil, and the lack of sufficient application and effort to procure supplies from other sources for the increase in their number: and if so the remedy as plainly appears to be the local development of industry, so as to provide a greater supply of remunerative employment: the removal of obstacles which hinder people in their efforts to help themselves — the promotion for increased facilities for intercourse with the mainland: the aid and encouragement of spontaneous migration: and chiefly and above all and with a view to attain all, the diffusion of the blessings of a sound English education.[25]

Notwithstanding, he then went on to persuade entire communities to emigrate to Canada as entities, cancelling arrears of rent, buying their stock and negotiating reduced steamer fares. In 1862–3 about 400 people may have emigrated abroad from John Ramsay's lands in the Oa, while in the decade of the 1860s, net out-migration from Islay may have amounted to

about one-quarter of the population.[26] John Ramsay sincerely believed that
'voluntary' emigration to Canada, as opposed to migration to other parts
of Britain, was the right solution to Islay poverty and lack of opportunity.
He was more than ever convinced of this when he visited the Islay people
in their Ontarian homes in 1870, documenting this visit in his *Diary*.[27]
He also referred again to the socio-political dilemma while speaking at
the annual meeting of the Islay Association in Glasgow in 1878:

> 'I went . . . to visit the residents from Islay who are located on the bank of
> Lake Simcoe, Georgian Bay, and Lake Huron . . . and what I saw there fully
> satisfied me that whatever people thought of the fact of people emigrating
> to Western Canada, I came home with the solid conviction that it was
> certainly the people who had occasion to be benefited by their removal
> from the Western Isles. I know I am subjecting myself to the criticism of
> those who deprecate the removal of a single soul from the Hebrides'.[28]

For the islanders who did not emigrate, Charles Morrison and others,
with some government assistance, tried hard to provide other means of
employment in constructing new farms and houses, ornately-decorated
cottages and steadings, in draining and planting, completing the 'High'
road, building the 'Low' road and helping to run the island steamer
connections with the mainland. Ardimersay Cottage had proved difficult
to keep weatherproof and in 1870 a Scottish baronial mansion was built
on ground above Ardimersay and named Kildalton House. Surrounded by
plantations of exotic trees, it was to be a home for John Ramsay and his
second wife Lucy, daughter of George Martin of Auchendennan on Loch
Lomondside. By this time John Ramsay had become another member of
the Islay contingent at the Palace of Westminster, sitting as member of
parliament for Stirlingshire in 1868 and for Falkirk from 1874 to 1886.[29]
He achieved some importance through his interest in education, being
a member of many boards and commissions and also an author on the
subject.[30]

After his father's death in 1892, Captain Iain Ramsay succeeded as
laird of Kildalton estate; but it was gradually broken up. In the 1920s
the area around Kildalton House came into the hands of a colourful
family. Talbot Clifton was a war correspondent in South Africa in 1901,
an Arctic explorer, horseman, marksman, motor-car enthusiast and an
expert on orchids. His marriage to Violet Mary Beauclerk in 1907 was
widely reported in society journals; she also became a well-known writer
of their travels.[31] This estate has subsequently been broken up into several
units, including Ardtalla estate. Much of the Oa formed the Kinnabus

Estate where considerable farm amalgamation occurred before purchase by the Royal Society for the Protection of Birds in 1984. The rest of the Oa remained longer in Ramsay possession, but is now in the hands of various owners, including several continental Europeans. The northern part of the former Kildalton estate became the Laggan Estate.

Although Sir Smith Child did not take on the Oa's problems in 1860, he did purchase a substantial part of the lands around Port Askaig, for £53,960.[32] The estate was known in turn as Losset, Lossit, Glen Lossit and Dunlossit. After less than a decade, however, Smith Child's son and heir died suddenly in 1868 and the estate was sold to Kirkman Finlay of the Glasgow tea-importing firm, and of Toward on the Firth of Clyde.[33] Kirkman Finlay was the eponymous grandson of the famous cotton manufacturer and merchant who had been lord provost of Glasgow in 1812 and MP for Glasgow from 1812 to 1818. For more than two decades after 1868 the new owner did much of the tree planting that became such a distinctive feature of Dunlossit estate. He also incorporated the existing small shooting lodge into an enlarged Dunlossit House or Castle, before selling the estate in 1890 to Donald Martin of Auchendennan, John Ramsay's brother-in-law. After a serious fire at the mansion, Martin built the present Scottish baronial Dunlossit House, which figures so prominently in any view of Port Askaig from the Sound of Islay, over which it commands an equally impressive view to the Paps of Jura, to Colonsay, Mull and Ben Nevis.

The Dunlossit estate changed hands three times thereafter.[34] In 1911 it passed to W. A. Bankier and about 1918 to Nathaniel Dunlop. The latter died in 1931, but in the uncertain times of the Depression, the trustees did not sell the estate until 1939. The purchaser then was Helmut B. Schroder, a London merchant banker who died in 1969. In the mid-1960s about 1,000 hectares of the Dunlossit estate in the upper part of the Laggan valley were the first of several Forestry Commission plantings on Islay, since cleared, with the lands reverting to the estate. In successive Schroder lairdships, further plantations were establised, many improvements were made to agricultural land and farm buildings and the innovative estate was much favoured for shooting and fishing.

Like the Islay estate in the middle of the nineteenth century, the affairs of the Sunderland estate were also in difficulties.[35] In 1846 the estate was purchased for £28,000 from the trustees of the late Walter Campbell of Sunderland by Alexander McEwan, a Glasgow merchant. The McEwans, however, encountered various marital and settlement difficulties, McEwan being declared bankrupt in 1858. The estate passed into the management of a trustee, Mr Balderstone, who initiated the breakup of the Rinns into

several smaller estates. In 1861 The Cladville area came into the hands
of the Baker family, while Coul formed a separate small estate which
remained in the McLaughlin family until the 1970s. The Sunderland
part of the Rinns was owned by the Morrison family, until it in turn was
divided and sold in the 1970s. The southern portion around Ellister has
since been further divided into individual owner-occupied farms, the
Forestry Commission acquiring Ballimony. The northern portion, based
on Foreland House, was the last piece to be sold and while reduced in size
comprises the Foreland Estate. The first decade of the present century saw
considerable investment in Foreland House, policies and gardens. Part of
Ballinaby was managed by the Department of Agriculture and Fisheries
for Scotland, but is now in several private hands.

Evolving landscape
Although in the Islay, Kildalton, Dunlossit and other separate estates, the
enthusiasm or conservatism of different lairds has been evident in the rate
and character of landscape change, the main pattern of change was the
filling-in of detail. By about 1870 the present agricultural landscape and
settlement pattern of Islay had largely been established and the population
then numbered about 10,000.[36] Although reflecting wider concerns of
national policy and conditions in agriculture and the economy as a whole,
Islay continued to remain a Hebridean exception, especially in those
activities that were based on land resource. For this reason, some of the
main events in the subsequent history of the Highlands and Islands during
the last century proved of less importance on Islay than elsewhere. In 1884,
for example, the Napier Royal Commission of Enquiry into Crofting
Conditions listened to evidence but recommended little change in Islay.[37]
There is only one lotted township, Claddich, in Islay, although other areas
have been designated as crofts. Much the same was true of the so-called
'Deer Forest Commission', appointed in 1892 'to inquire whether any land
. . . now occupied for the purposes of a deer forest, grouse moor or other
sporting purposes, or for grazing, not in the occupation of crofters or small
tenants, is capable of being cultivated to profit or otherwise advantageously
occupied by crofters or other small tenants'.[38] The commission took an
optimistically short-sighted view of 'profitable cultivation' and none of
their recommendations was implemented in Islay.

After the First World War, well-intentioned resettlement schemes
for returning servicemen had some impact on Islay, though again such
schemes were much more common elsewhere. Additions were made to the
village lands of Port Wemyss and Port Charlotte (in Wester Ellister and
Lorgbaw respectively); the two former farms of Cladville and Ballimony

in the Rinns were also converted into small holdings. This did little to counter the gradual decline in the numbers on the land: the trend towards assimilation and amalgamation continued. Most of the settlement schemes initiated after the First World War subsequently re-amalgamated into larger single units.

Clearances and depopulation

At the time when Islay was purchased by the Morrisons, its population had already fallen from the peak of almost 15,000 recorded in 1831 to about 12,000.[39] Characteristic of the whole of the next hundred years was a gradual decline in the number of tenants. The interior valleys of the eastern hills and the peninsula of the Oa witnessed the greatest population changes after the middle of the century, with reduction in numbers of tenants and clearances. Migration to the villages, to the Lowlands and assisted emigration abroad took place, especially from the Oa. Elsewhere on the island the numbers of tenants continued to decline more gradually.

The decline in numbers was accompanied by a gradual change in the rural-village balance, in age composition, gender ratios, and changing patterns of employment. In the twentieth century the widespread reduction in agricultural employment and the opportunities in the major urban centres of the Lowlands and beyond, caused this population decline to continue on Islay, as in many other places. From a population of 12,334 in 1851, the island's population numbers declined to around 3,500 by 2001.[40] The part of the island with the largest population has always been the central parish of Killarow and Kilmeny. This was the area where improvements came first, on the relatively large area of tillable land in the island around the laird's mansion at the head of Loch Indaal. This region today includes Bowmore, the major service centre of the island, the two distillery villages of Bunnahabhain and Caol Ila and three other villages at Bridgend, Ballygrant and Kiells. The presence of these centres and their sources of employment is one reason why this parish has had a slower rate of population decline than the others.

The Rinns parish of Kilchoman was the second most populous in the early nineteenth century, reaching 4,822 at the 1831 census.[41] At that time most of the population lived on farms or in joint townships. As the decades passed, an increasing proportion was recorded in the three villages of Port Charlotte, Port Wemyss and Portnahaven. In Port Charlotte the main employment was in agriculture, fishing and distilling; in the others, the emphasis was mainly on fishing. After some clearances of joint farms and more gradual reductions in the number of tenants and others dependent on the land, and as line fishing became less successful, the population

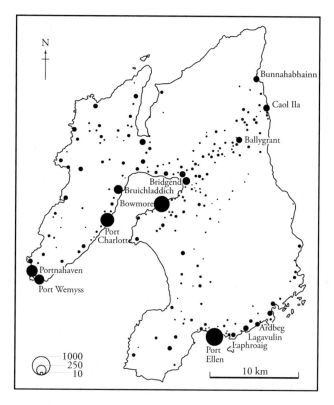

Considerable thinning out of the population clusters had taken place by 1891 with a legacy of deserted buildings: several new distillery villages had been established. (Compiled from copies of census enumerators' schedules for 1891, National Records of Scotland).

in the Kilchoman peninsula began to decline after the 1830s. However, herring fishing increased in importance and for much of the second half of the nineteenth century there were around two hundred boats engaged in fishing from Islay, each manned by perhaps a man and a boy.[42] In the 1880s a curing station at Tayovullin on Loch Gruinart was established, still partly visible today. A distillery was created at Bruichladdich in 1881, and the population of Kilchoman parish rose again for the next decade or so. The First World War interrupted the trade with the herring markets of Germany and Eastern Europe and by 1921 only fifty boats were registered in Islay. The later 1920s and the 1930s witnessed the virtual disappearance of the herring shoals. The closure of the distillery in Port Charlotte coincided in 1930 with the almost complete disappearance of fishing and the rate of population decline in Kilchoman became severe, exacerbated by an unbalanced age structure. In this century, distilling has been revived at Bruichladdach and another small distillery established at Kilchoman.

The ruins of the township of Lurabus on the southern slopes of the Oa peninsula testify to the emigrations of many hundreds of islanders from the Oa to Ontario in the 1860s (University of Cambridge).

In Kildalton parish in the south-east, the population was never particularly numerous, since most of the land was originally in large grazing tacks and no eighteenth-century villages were established on the model of Bowmore. But in the Oa peninsula, the interior valleys and basins came to support a very high population in the first half of the nineteenth century, even though there was only a restricted amount of agricultural land. This increase in the Oa, together with nineteenth-century expansion of Port Ellen and in the smaller distillery villages in Kildalton, accounts for the increase in population of Kildalton and Oa parish which continued until after the census of 1841. Subsequently the decrease in numbers of people in the Oa and of the farmworkers in Kildalton, was only partially offset by continued growth in the industrial villages which contained five whisky distilleries in all. External influences on population change during the nineteenth century included the California gold rush, emigration to the Antipodes and to South Africa, together with the labour required for the central lowlands of Scotland and the importance of Britain as a maritime and trading empire.[43]

Apart from the published census data, the copies of individual census enumerators' returns are available for research for the Scottish censuses from 1841 to 1911.[44] From these can be traced the movements of individual people from one agricultural holding to another or from agricultural holdings into industrial villages. They also throw light on changing densities and distributions of population and settlement and changing age and occupational structures. As a result of the major land reorganisation extending from the 1820s to the last quarter of the nineteenth century, much of the clustered settlement on Islay gradually disappeared. It was replaced by a pattern of single dispersed farmhouses and service or industrial villages. In 1841 rural settlement was still predominantly in a clustered form, but by 1891, apart from a few of the original clusters in the northern Rinns and the Oa, which were still occupied, the rural settlement pattern was predominantly the dispersed one that it is at the present day. The area of settlement had retreated, especially in the interior valleys of the south-eastern hills and in the Oa. This retreat has continued and the evidence is easily visible in the clustered ruins in the Oa, the Glen and in the northern Rinns.

The remains that one sees today are often all that is left of 'swollen clusters deserted almost immediately after a period of vigorous but unhealthy growth'.[45] Some of those that were abandoned, such as those at Braid, now part of Kilchiaran, indicate a loose, unplanned grouping. Others were more regularly laid out or spaced on the ground, such as at Olistadh in the Rinns; they may have been partially reorganised some time during the agrarian revolution. Most were occupied into the second or third quarter of the nineteenth century. Some have been reconstructed, as at Carnduncan. Associated with many of these settlements are signs of former cultivation, particularly clearly seen at certain times of the year when either the light conditions, or the state of the vegetation cover, or more rarely, snow cover, enable the outline of the cultivated ridges to be more easily recognised. This is also true of the former shielings and summer pastures.

As elsewhere in Scotland and beyond, a significant factor in the overall decline in population was the gradual decrease in family and household size. Average size tended to remain higher in the rural areas than in the villages for some time, but household size everywhere declined during the nineteenth century. Changing age structures and gender ratios were also noticeable; by the end of the century and well into the next, the greatest imbalance in gender ratios and age structures was in the rural areas and in

Islay House was enhanced with 'policies' of plantations, gardens, a 'lake', aviaries, and Home Farm Square. Even before the Forestry Commission started planting in Islay in the 1960s, there was thus more woodland than is usual in the Hebrides. Islay House and the Home Farm Square beyond, are set in the kindly Sorn valley where it drains into Loch Indaal (Eric Thorburn).

the remoter villages of Portnahaven and Port Wemyss. The Oa in particular had an excessive imbalance of old to young people and of men to women. Other areas showed an almost complete reversal of the 1841 age pyramid. But the imbalance between old and young and between males and females has rarely been so extreme as in many other parts of the West Highland seaboard.

The unspecialised employment structure of the early-eighteenth century in Islay changed gradually through the nineteenth to a more specialised and more varied one. The male employment recorded in the census from 1841 to 1911 can be grouped into several main types, led by the primary occupations of agricultural tenants, farmers and crofters, farmworkers, estate workers and labourers. A second group comprised craftsmen (quarriers, millers, blacksmiths, joiners, plumbers, tailors, shoemakers and weavers), together with other non-agricultural workers such as fishers. A third group consisted of services for the population such as merchants, professional people, clerks and others in burgeoning local and national government and quangoes.

Employment of women on Islay was important in the nineteenth century, although even then only a small proportion of the total number of women of working age were actually in paid employment. These were essentially connected with the house or the land, acting as domestic or nurse maids, seamstresses, spinners, knitters, teachers, dairymaids, fieldworkers, postwomen and, occasionally, as nurses or midwives. In the twentieth century many of these occupations have become redundant so that retail or hotel work became the main category of female employment. Other alternatives such as public relations and secretarial work in the distilleries and the professions provided year-round occupations, and the present century has seen a substantial escalation in public sector employment for women. Growing numbers of jobs in quangoes, health and educational support have offered more female employment and the potential for more two-income families.

Architectural Heritage

The majority of Islay's buildings are not outstanding. But to both islanders and visitors, the buildings, churchyards, monuments and other man-made elements provide visible and harmonious links between the past and present in Islay. Some buildings are statutorily listed as of architectural or historical interest, such as Islay House or the round church in Bowmore.[46] Others, particularly in the villages, are being reconstructed or rehabilitated. In addition, ruined settlements decline in visibility as they are 'rescued' for development. All form part of the settled ecumene. Because many of the buildings are in the vernacular or traditional style, few architects' names or plans are known. Apart from the occasional village house there was little development during the twentieth century until the later 1960s, though sometimes a building's function changed.

Different stones were quarried or gathered locally for most of the island's buildings; few building materials were brought in from the mainland until about the time of the Second World War. Brick, concrete, timber-frame and prefabricated techniques are now all used in new buildings, particularly since changes in the ferry system in the late 1960s made awkward and large loads less of a problem to get to the island. Roofing slates were generally locally quarried, but now, as elsewhere, other imported roofing materials are normally used.

There are only a few large houses. Apart from the remains of medieval castles, the main legacy of the Cawdor Campbells is in the earliest part of Islay House, begun in 1677 by Sir Hugh Campbell when he started his new 'Killarow House'.[47] Its window openings were later enlarged, but the original building is still recognisable (see p. 76). What else remained of the Campbell of Cawdor and earlier periods has mostly been overshadowed by efforts of the Shawfield Campbells and later owners. Daniel Campbell of Shawfield extended Islay House with two wings in 1737 and his grandson built the eastern staircase in 1760.[48] By this time the entire house was beginning to look very grand, with its Palladian windows and splendid Georgian interior. It was almost a hundred years before the Victorian additions designed by William Playfair were built in the early 1840s. In 1910, Detmar Blow designed the present two-storeyed mock-Georgian wing on the east of the house, for Hugh Morrison, but the back remains turreted in distinctly Victorian fashion.

The only other houses in Islay comparable in style, if not size, are Eallabus and Foreland House. Eallabus was built as a factor's residence, probably in the time of Daniel Campbell the Younger, and was gutted and restored in the 1980s as the laird's residence after Islay House was sold.[49] Foreland House was built about 1820 around the core of an earlier one, by Walter Campbell of Sunderland when he retired from the East India Company.[50] The other big houses were those at Ballinaby, demolished in the 1950s after a 1933 fire, Cairnmore near Port Ellen, Kildalton House built in 1870 by John Ramsay but unoccupied for many decades past, and Dunlossit House, now a home of the Schroder family. The latter three houses were typical Victorian gothic-baronial shooting estate houses.

Tacksmen's houses that survive from the eighteenth century include those at Ardnave, Gartmain, and perhaps also at Coul; others were constructed later in much the same style, with rounded staircases at

'Great' Daniel Campbell of Shawfield and Islay built the Whin or Meal Mill to grind flour from spring and summer wheat. Other mills ground barley and oats. The nearby Wauk Mill still produces woollens and a unique Islay tweed worn by Islay Estate personnel.

Archibald Cameron recorded many Islay scenes at the turn of the nineteenth century, such as the herring curing station on the west side of Loch Gruinart (Museum of Islay Life).

the front. Large single farmhouses of varying dates of construction are at Sanaig, Kintra and Leorin for instance. Several were designed with integral farm buildings; others had separate outbuildings such as in Islay House Square, or in the more unusual semi-circular farmsteading at Kilchiaran.

Throughout the past two centuries change has also taken place in the occupance and character of the rural vernacular buildings. The traditional cruck-framed 'black house' cottages drawn for Thomas Pennant in the 1770s have been replaced through time by the dressed stone, separate dwelling and stock byres such as those seen on Glenegedale and Duich muirs. Many of Islay's smaller buildings today reflect the period of intense estate activity connected with the agrarian and village plans of successive Campbells of Shawfield. Apart from the farmhouses and their outbuildings, there were the agricultural workers' cottages, tenants' cottages and estate lodges, some, for instance, with the intertwined initials WFC designed by Playfair for the East Lodge at Bridgend. Later Morrison landlords and the Ramsays of Kildalton added other farm buildings, cottages and lodges, those in the south-east being in a highly decorated style.

Industrial buildings include many of the earlier mills associated with the rural economy of the island that are no longer used, such as the Starch Mill at Mulindry and the Meal or Whin Mill at Bridgend.[51] The Wool Mill near Bridgend was powered until 1979 by a water-wheel and produced Islay tweeds, blankets and the like. Since 1981 it has been revived as the Islay Woollen Mill and although no longer powered by water, its tweed and other products are sold world-wide. It constitutes a veritable museum, with the only slubbing billy left in the world, two of the few remaining spinning jennies and much else besides. Remains of kilns for burning limestone for agricultural purposes can be found throughout the limestone belt from Bridgend to Port Askaig. Other buildings, such as smithies, have by now generally been converted to other uses. Little clear evidence remains of linen-weaving times, except in the village of Kiells or in the retting dam for the lint mill at Sunderland. For the late nineteenth-century fishing expansion, a few derelict structures on the western shores of Loch Gruinart are the best evidence, apart from the fishing villages themselves. The remains of mining activity are more obvious; ruined buildings, remains of tip heaps and shafts are easily recognisable in the Robolls, Mulreesh and Shenegart areas around Ballygrant. There are many disused local stone quarries, and several slate quarries.

It is of course with the distilleries that most of the remaining industrial buildings of Islay are associated. Apart from the reconstruction of some distilleries in the late 1960s and early 1970s, the tall Maltings at Port Ellen and the gradual addition of extra warehouses for storing the whisky as it matures, many of the buildings connected with Islay whisky-making are recognisably old. Relics of illicit distilling in the past are on display in the Museum of Islay Life at Port Charlotte.

The most obvious attempts to change the face of Islay in infrastructure and public buildings were in the village of Bowmore. Much of the core of the present village was built in the late-eighteenth century and has remained little modified externally. Elsewhere, construction activity in the second quarter of the nineteenth century has left legacies in the domestic architecture of the villages of Kiells, Port Charlotte, Port Wemyss and Port Ellen. Some of the roads, piers, lighthouses, bridges, schools and churches also date from this period. The churches and manses at Risabus in the Oa and Portnahaven, and the manse at Kilmeny were built in 1828 to plans by Thomas Telford, as part of his work for the Parliamentary Commissioners appointed in 1823 to build additional 'Places of Worship' in the Highlands and Islands. How difficult it is today, standing in the desolate ruins of the church in the Oa, to imagine it in 1831 being 'always well filled; so much so, that at present 55 heads of families are unable to procure accommodation'.[52] The chequered religious history of Scotland is reflected in the many churches of different denominations, except Roman Catholic, whose adherents celebrate mass in the Scottish Episcopal Church at Bridgend.

By the late-eighteenth century Daniel Campbell the Younger was encouraging education with his schools and schoolmasters. After that, schools multiplied and in Walter Frederick Campbell's time there were four 'parochial' schools under his patronage in Bowmore, Kilmeny, Kilchoman and Kildalton.[53] In addition there were twenty-eight other schools, including those supported by the Scottish Society for Promoting Christian Knowledge and by the Gaelic Society in Edinburgh. The teachers of the smaller single-teacher schools were 'young men . . . engaged and paid by the parents of the children under instruction, which never exceeds 2s. 6d. [12½p] per quarter. At these small schools, without salary, the instruction afforded is not all that could be wished'. Nevertheless the numbers of readers and writers for this and other parishes were quite creditable. Many of the teachers had been educated outside Islay, the Bowmore schoolmaster in Penrith, for example. There is no mention in the early-nineteenth century of women teachers, but by the middle of the century they had become assistants. John Ramsay of Kildalton founded several schools, including a 'female' one, education being one of his main interests,[54] and other vocational 'female' schools appeared.

The landowners were eventually overtaken by local government and schooling became more centralised. Schools at Kiells, Newton, Port

Charlotte, Portnahaven, Bowmore and Port Ellen catered for local primary children while all senior schoolchildren travelled to Bowmore by bus. Bowmore school, up on the hill above the village and harbour, was much extended in the 1960s and in 1974 local parents successfully petitioned for it to have sixth form status to obviate the need to send children to the mainland. It was then re-named Islay High School and subsequently extended, and there have also been several new primary school buildings as well as closures of the smaller rural schools.

With the breakup of the main estate and the harder times in the island during the middle of the nineteenth century there was a lull in the changing appearance of the island. But the new landowners later in the century and the county council gradually effected change by adding housing to the edges of the villages, widening roads and so on. New industrial villages were created around the distilleries at Bruichladdich and Bunnahabhain. There was renewed activity in the estates, with much tree planting, particularly in the Islay, Dunlossit and Kildalton estates, new farm cottages and estate lodges. Many of the hotels, shops, banks and other buildings of the period remain little changed externally to this day. The beginnings of substantial change in the villages really dates only from the end of the Second World War. This was initiated primarily by Argyll County Council; until the 1970s there was little private building on the island, in contrast to the scores of houses built by the county council, and its successors, and housing associations. Changes in the ferry system led to substantial improvements to ferry terminals, roads and bridges, with successive upgradings. The airport runway and passenger handling facilities at Glenegedale have also been upgraded several times.

Islay's many villages are not merely distinctive when compared with the settlement pattern of the remainder of the Hebrides, they are very different from one another. All of the Islay villages are calendar villages, amongst the most attractive anywhere in the Hebrides. For over two centuries, they have housed an increasing proportion of the island population and this trend continues. Not all of them provide expanding opportunities for employment and the tendency towards concentration of services in Bowmore is fairly clear. Nevertheless, the villages and the limited facilities that they offer, have probably been an important factor in accounting for the relative stability of Islay's population in recent decades, when compared with the rapid decline in many other islands.

One source that deserves renewed and critical attention comprises the late-nineteenth century galaxy, some brighter, some less so, of antiquarians and topographers who wrote volumes (literally) on the island's place names. One has to empathise with Captain Frederick Thomas who studied the place names of the Hebrides from Valuation Rolls, since the large-scale Ordnance Survey maps had not yet been published, and in the case of Islay, he was perhaps unaware of manuscripts maps such as those of William Gemmill.[55] Others followed, including MacNeill (1890), Johnston (1892 et seq.), Maxwell (1894), MacKinlay (1904), Gillies (1906), Henderson (1910), MacBain (1922), Watson (1926) and Gray (1939).[56] Traditionally in the Gaelic world there has been a strong drive to provide explanantions for names and this developed into a tale category called sheanchas, combing a knowledge and entertainment function. The Scottish Place Name Survey of the University of Edinburgh recorded a score of reels including Islay place names, mainly in the 1960s; these have now been digitised as part of the *Tobar an Dualcahis* project, but most still await transcription and translation.[57]

The final phase in the detailed naming and mapping of Islay occurred between 1875 and 1878. This was late in the day as far as the Ordnance surveyors were concerned, having had a major diversion to Irish mapping for half a century. Amongst others, Andrews criticised Brian Friel's depiction in *Translations* (1981) of the conflict between local people's knowledge and mental maps of Irish place names and their subsequent transliteration and translation by the English military surveyors.[58] The same problems had faced the Ordnance Survey in Scotland, as recorded by Colonel Sir Charles Wilson: 'Very great care was originally taken in the collection of names – three authorities were obtained for each name, and the orthography was determined by men with a good knowledge of Gaelic'.[59] He continued percipiently, 'I am afraid however, that there was too great an inclination to attribute a Gaelic origin to all names, and that in some places, more especially in the west coast, the OS orthography is sometimes at fault'. Many of his caveats are borne out in the resultant Islay maps. The Ordnance Survey Object or Name Books accompanying the map sheets, mostly on the scale of 1:10,569 or six inches to the mile, provide the largest numbers of names.[60] If repeat names for rivers, hills and so on are subtracted, some 3,000 individual names were recorded in the 1870s. These have been transcribed into the online Islay Cultural Database, along with other relevant sources such as monumental inscriptions, while The Ordnance Survey has an online index to the names on its *Pathfinder* 1: 25,000 series.

Many, many hours must have been spent by the officers and sappers of the Royal Engineers, the local informants and the orthographers 'with a good knowledge of Gaelic'. In each Islay parish, several dozen local informants included tenant farmers, shepherds, teachers (including Hector MacLean of Kilmeny) and fishermen, as well as non-Gaelic speaking agents of the laird. The orthographic 'specialists' comprised the ministers and the schoolmasters (most of whom were Gaelic-speaking although teaching only in English). Over the same period a dozen different officers and sappers did the paperwork to produce the name books which were then scrutinised in the directorate. Others, including islanders, were involved in the actual triangulation and chain surveying. Registration records tell of one sapper dying of pneumonia in January 1875, while an asthmatic labourer died a couple of months later. At least five children were born to wives of the Ordnance Survey men, including little Georgina Islay Jones, born to the wife of surveyor George Jones, at 9.30 in the evening of 28 August 1876 on board the steamer *Islay* in the Sound of Islay![61] One reader of the *Scots Magazine* in 1963 claimed that Glen Logan was so named because the surveyor involved, Kenneth Campbell, had been unable to spell the Gaelic name given by the three local informants, and had instead inserted the name of the officer collecting his work.[62]

During the second half of the twentieth century even as population declined, extensions to the villages were named by the local authority. In Bowmore, adjacent to Hawthorn Lane on the former Hawthorn Park (or field) the new Beech Avenue, Birch Drive and Elder Crescent arose; an older name, Stanalane, was bestowed on a later development, while in Port Ellen, North Bay, Cnoc na Faire and Ardview were established. Sporadic Gaelic street signs began to appear. In Port Ellen, above the name Charlotte Street incised in stone and used for almost two centuries, there was now fixed a council street sign, 'Sraid Thearlaig', while Frederick Crescent in the same village became 'Corran Fhreadaraig'. Yet the different segments of the latter named on an estate map of the late 1820s might have proved more interesting. Road signs and maps still differ as to Keills or Kiells. So far in Portnahaven and Port Wemyss there are no street signs at all, whether Church, High, King or Queen. The politically correct re-gaelicisation continues with perplexing signs proclaiming 'Skiba' (Old Norse *Sgioba*, ship crew or *Skipà*, ship water) for Port Charlotte (after the then laird's mother) or 'Bun na Othan' (Gaelic, mouth of the river) for Port Wemyss (after the then laird's wife). In a corrective, Stahl noted 'It is understandable that the overwhelming pressure of English in Gaelic territory forces Hebrideans to protect their language and culture. This, however, should not be carried out in a desperate attempt at artificial gaelicisation, which not only wipes out English names but renders some Norse names beyond recognition.[63]

From the romantic, if rather ghoulish, study of kirkyard headstones[64] through the manuscripts to the more prosaic electoral registers of the present day, similar influences have changed the composition and sources of islanders' surnames; and also of forenames, although the latter are more susceptible to changes in fashion. From about the twelfth century surnames developed from Clan Donald and its branches. By the time of the sveenteenth-century Campbells of Cawdor and after Daniel Campbell of Shawfield became laird of Islay in 1726, the surname of many of the larger tenants or tacksmen was Campbell, while many of the islanders were still Macdonalds or from related clans. At the end of the eighteenth century there was already more variety and the first complete list of every person in the island to which there is access, the copies of the census schedules for 1841, carried this process further. By then there were more extraneous names, although they still formed only a small proportion of the total. Since then, however, the wholly Hebridean and Highland names have been further eroded and present electoral registers and the *Islay and Jura Phoney Book* show much less dominance of one name or group than ever before. In earlier days the use of nicknames to distinguish different people with the same forename and surname was common. The habit still persists today, but the use of more varied forenames from different sources and societies gives less justification.

Notes and references
[1]   Gatty, *Portrait*, p. 30.

[2]   Islay Estate Papers, 8 December 1853.

[3]   C. Morrison, *An Essay on the Relations between Labour and Capital*, (London, 1854).

[4]   C. Williams, *Basildon, Berkshire*, (Reading, n.d., [1994]), p. 132.

[5]   Mitchell, *Reminiscences*, p. 300.

[6]   Islay Estate Papers, 18 February and 24 April 1854.

[7]   Ibid., 3 June 1854.

[8]   Ibid., 6 July 1854.

[9]   Ibid., 15 September 1892.

[10] Ibid., 30 June 1854.

[11] Ibid., 24 November 1854.

[12] Ibid., 28 October 1854.

[13] Ibid., 17 November, 27 November and 8 December 1854.

[14] Ibid., 7 December 1854.

[15] Ibid., 8 December 1854 and 20 January 1856.

[16] Ibid., 10 May 1856.

[17] Ibid., 25 May 1909.

[18] Ibid., 23 November 1909.

[19] Ibid., various biographical sources.

[20] Ibid., missives.

[21] Idem.

[22] Idem.

23 Ramsay, *John Ramsay*, p. 34.

24 *Ibid.*, pp. 37–8.

25 *Ibid.*, pp. 38–9.

26 Calculated from census and registration changes.

27 Ramsay, *John Ramsay*, p. 48. See also an emigré's corroboration in Meek, *Coran an-t Soghail*, p. 41.

28 *Report on the Proceedings at the Annual Meeting of the Islay Association*, (Glasgow, 1878), p. 29.

29 Foster, *Members of Parliament*, p. 293.

30 J. Ramsay, *A Letter to . . . the Lord Advocate of Scotland on the State of Education in the Outer Hebrides, in 1862*, (Glasgow, 1863).

31 V. Clifton, *The Book of Talbot*, (London, 1933).

32 Islay Estate Papers, Disposition by Charles Morrison, 1860.

33 C. Brogan, (ed.), *James Finlay and Company Limited manufacturers and East India merchants, 1750-1950*, (Glasgow, 1950).

34 Information from Dunlossit Estate.

35 *BPP, Distress*, 1847, LIII, 75.

36 *Census of Scotland*, 1951. (1953), Table 3.

37 *Report of Her Majesty's Commissioners of Enquiry into the Condition of the Crofters and Cottars in the Highlands and Islands of Scotland, BPP*, 1884, C.3980.

38 *Minutes of Evidence, Royal Commission (Highlands and Islands, 1892)*, 1895, *BPP*, C.7668-1, II.

39 *Census of Scotland 1951*, (1953), *BPP*, 1895, C.7668-1, II. Table 3.

40 *Census of Scotland 1991*, Small Area Statistics.

41 *Census of Scotland 1961*, Ar*gyll County Report*, (Edinburgh, 1964), Table 4B.

42 *Appendix C to Second Report of the Tidal Harbours Commissioners, BPP*, 1848, XXXII; *Annual Reports of the Fishery Board for Scotland*.

43 Macdonald, *Third Statistical Account*, pp. 343-4.

44 Storrie, 'Census of Scotland'. See Storrie, M. C. 'The Census of Scotland as a source in the Historical Geography of Islay, *Scottish Geographical Magazine* 78 (1962), pp. 152–165.

45 H. Fairhurst, 'The Archaeology of Rural Settlement in Scotland', *Transactions of the Glasgow Antiquary Society* New Series, 15 (1960), p. 144.

46 Statutory List of Buildings of Architectural or Historic Interest, Historic Scotland. Killarow or Bowmore Church is category A (of national as well as local interest) and Islay House is category B (of more local than national interest, but also of special interest). The older parts of most of the villages in Islay have been designated 'conservation areas'.

47 Innes, *Thanes of Cawdor*, p. xxxiii.

48 Forman, 'Islay House', p. 38 and p. 40.

49 *NSA, Argyleshire*, p. 651.

50 RCAHMS, *Argyll Inventory*, 5, p. 290.

51 *Minutes of Evidence, Royal Commission (Highlands and Islands) 1892, BPP*, C.7668-1, II, 832.

52 *Sixth Report of the Commissioners appointed for building additional Places of Worship in the Highlands and Islands of Scotland, BPP*, 1831, XI, 30.

53 *Abstracts of Education Returns (Scotland) 1834, BPP*, 1837, XLVIII, Argyll, 68–101.

54 J. Ramsay, *Letter* (1863).

55 Thomas, F. W. L., 'On Islay Place Names', *Proceedings of the Society of Antiquaries of Scotland* New Series 4 (1881–2), pp. 241–76.

56 Gillies, H. C., *The Place Names of Argyll*, (London, 1906); Gray, A., *The History of Islay Place Names*, (Glasgow, 1940); Henderson, G., *The Norse Influence on Celtic Scotland*, (Glasgow, 1910); MacBain, A., *Place names of the Highlands and Islands of Scotland*, (Stirling, 1922); MacKinlay, J. M., *The Influence of the Pre-Reformation Church on Scottish Place Names*, (Edinburgh, 1904); MacNeill, J. G., *The New Guide to Islay*, (Glasgow, 1900) and Watson, W. J., *The History of Celtic Place Names of Scotland*, (Edinburgh, 1926).

57 Edwards, E. (ed.), *Seanchas Ìle*, (Glendaruel, 2007).

58 Andrews, J., 'Notes for a Future Edition of Brian Friel's *Translations*', *The Irish Review* 13 (1993), pp. 93–106; Friel, B., *Translations*, (London, 1981).

59 Wilson, Sir Charles, 'Methods and Processes of the Ordnance Survey', *Scottish Geographical Magazine* 7 (1891), p. 257.

60 Object or Name Books of the Ordnance Survey; microfilm, RCAHMS.

61 Registration of Births and Deaths, NRS.

62 Nicolaisen, W. F. H., 'OS Folklore', *The Scots Magazine*, May 1963, p. 115.

63 Stahl, A.-B., 'Norse in the Place Names of Barra', *Northern Studies* 35 (2000), p. 111.

64 McWee, R. and Ruckley, N. A., *Guides to some of the old Graveyards in Islay*, (North Carolina, 2002 *et seq.*).

CHAPTER 12

Islay and whisky

Islay and whisky come almost as smoothly off the tongue as Scotch and water. Why should this particular small island off the west coast of Scotland have become one of the principal manufacturing centres for a product with a world-wide reputation and demand? Or, as the Islay resident might be inclined to ask, how has it happened that the island of Islay should account for such a disproportionate share of national revenues, through the excise duty on whisky? The reasons depend partly on historical accident but are not complex.

The main reason is to be found in geography. Although Irish whiskey is much less important in world markets today than 'Scotch', *uisge-beatha*, (pronounced 'oosh-kay-bay') or *aqua vitae*, the 'water of life', was introduced into the Highlands and Islands of Scotland from Ireland at some unknown time. Across the narrow, if at times tempestuous, North Channel, the peninsula of Kintyre and the island of Islay were well placed to benefit from this transfer of technology, especially as the necessary raw materials were readily and plentifully available – barley, peat and suitable water. Both Kintyre and Islay had relatively good and plentiful cultivable land, peat was abundant and water supplies varied and copious. The 'art' of making the spirit spread to the rest of the Highlands and Islands and further afield; especially in areas where greater supplies of grain were available, distillers became larger producers. Small pot distilleries gave way to those with large patent stills; single malt whiskies to blended whiskies, and Scotch became a national drink rather than a Highland one and subsequently an international one.[1]

Today, with energetic, skilful marketing and legislative controls, a commodity that is both attractive to world-wide tastes and also capable of continuing adaptation to changes in taste, Scotch is universally renowned, though the total quantity of Scotch whisky and Irish whiskey produced is far less than that of other whiskies, let alone other spirits. Unlike products which are now manufactured in many places far from their original area, true Scotch whisky is still produced solely in Scotland. Scotch is not a homogeneous product: while *aficionados* often prefer a single malt whisky from a favourite distillery, most Scotch whisky is consumed in blended form, a single bottle containing the products of several distilleries. The possibilities of blending are infinite: there are many thousands of different blends on sale throughout the world, in a diverse number of brands and bottles.

Illicit distilling

Such subtleties did not trouble those who developed the skill. Produced in small pot stills on farms and grain mills in many glens and along the coasts of the Highland seaboard the raw materials used were locally-grown bere barley, a four-rowed type suited to West Highland conditions, water that had flowed through peat, and peat itself, used both in the barley-malting process and as a fuel to heat the crude distilling apparatus. Barm or yeast was slow to multiply. The resulting spirit varied in quantity and quality from season to season and year to year and was consumed locally. The amount produced depended to a considerable extent on the amount of local barley available in excess of that needed as human and cattle food. Distilling was usually a seasonal occupation during the agriculturally inactive months of late autumn, winter and early spring, when water was plentiful in the small burns.

Taxation and excise duties have been as much a part of whisky as the barley, water and peat. If barley had to be imported from Ireland or England before the Act of Union, it was dutiable. Customs and excise duties were levied through Boards of Commissioners, but in Scotland they were 'in farm', i.e. the duties and taxes were collected by middlemen under contract.[2] After the Union, the Crown assumed direct responsibility for their collection throughout Scotland, except in Islay where the excise levy apparently remained 'in farm' to the laird almost to the end of the eighteenth century. This seems to have led to less than efficient collection of excise dues on Islay and to much illicit distillation or 'smuggling'. The word 'smuggler' was not one used by the earlier distillers and their carriers who thought of themselves as free traders. 'Smuggling' was coined and used romantically by others for the whole process from production to sale.[3] How ironic that Islay had been purchased in 1726 by Daniel Campbell of Shawfield, with compensation for the damage done to his Glasgow mansion by rioting maltsters and other protesters after he had supported the increased Malt Tax of 1725.

The rapid expansion of illicit whisky manufacture and distribution after the middle of the eighteenth century was also a response to market opportunity.[4] Traditionally, locally produced beer and imported wine had been favourite drinks in Scotland. In Islay, 'brewhouses' were specifically mentioned at Killarow near what is now Bridgend in the 1686,[5] but the consumption of malt spirit was already becoming more popular. Elsewhere, urbanisation and an increasing population stimulated an expansion in demand for all food and drinks, including spirits. Duties were levied on malted cereals, on the distilling of spirit and on the finished products. The incentive to cheat the revenue by avoiding payment of duty coincided with the increasing consumption of whisky; Highlands and Islands illicit spirits, when marketed in the Lowlands, fetched a substantial premium. The apparatus for pot-still distillation could be made or purchased for a few pounds and 'distillation was well suited to the socio-economic communalism of the Highlands where social links at local level preserved fellow feeling against the law so vital to the success of the illicit trade'.[6] Consequently the law was defied on a widespread scale.

Rises in the malt tax always encouraged illegal production, but particularly after 1786, when a system of still licensing was adopted throughout Scotland, albeit with a differential favouring the Highland zone with its higher costs. It was then forbidden to transport Highland whisky across a 'Highland line' from the Sound of Jura to the Moray Firth, thereby encouraging smuggling. Licence duties rose dramatically, and even stills below forty gallons' still-content were declared illegal. Previously, every person who had a still whose contents were limited to twelve gallons could distil legally for his own use and the outlawing of such small stills drove private household and family production underground. In nearby Campbeltown, for instance, no official still licences were issued between 1797 and 1817, although there were perhaps hundreds of illicit stills in the Kintyre region.[7] As one writer put it 'from the late seventeenth century until the early nineteenth century smuggling was a major crime conducted on a colossal scale' adding that all of society was complicit and some officers of the excise were venal'.[8]

The Church of Scotland minister who wrote the Kildalton parish survey in *The Statistical Account* in 1794 was not, of course, a sympathetic witness: 'This island hath the liberty of brewing whisky, without being under the necessity of paying the usual excise duty to government. We have not an excise officer in the whole island. The quantity therefore of whisky made here is very great; and the evil, that follows drinking to excess of this liquor, is very visible in this island'.[9] He described how poverty-stricken farmers sold their barley to the distillers, then had to pay one-third more to purchase barley for their stock. The 'gentlemen' of Islay gathered together to assess or stent individual contributions or cess towards the running expenses of the island, such as the sailing packet, the surgeon and the schoolmasters and schools. (Included in the levies were considerable quantities of whisky punch and whisky toddy consumed at their dinner, along with rum, port, porter, sherry and brandy). At their meeting on 1 April 1796, alarm was voiced at the grain being diverted to illicit distilling at a time of great shortage during the Napoleonic war:

> This Meeting Considering the great Exertions of the legislature in Suppressing the Distilling of Spirits & the great revenue given up by Ministry for the purpose of providing a Sufficiency of Grain for the use of the nation, which in many parts in threaten'd with a Famine, and Considering that great exertions have already been made in suppressing the Distilling in this Island, This meeting unanimously Resolve Individually and Collectively to exert themselves in putting a total stop to the said Illegal Practices, in case they hear or know of any person within the Island attempting to distill privately after this date. And they further Resolve that they will not only give Information to the Capt or officers of Vol^{rs} of any person they know or hear of privately distilling, But that they will themselves assist personally in Suppressing the Same.[10]

Five years later, the Stent meeting on 26 March 1801 was again expressing concern, given the 'State of the Island as to Grain & provisions' until the next harvest came in, they recommended that no exports, and they were, each and every one, to 'use their utmost exertions for preventing any of the Grain of the Island being destroy'd by Illegal Distillers', again encouraging informing against this 'Illegal and Destructive Traffic'.[11]

Since 1797 the excise had no longer been 'in farm' and gaugers, the colloquial term for excisemen, who carried gauges to determine the alcoholic content, had arrived on the island,[12] so any reports of ill-doing could now be reported to an official Customs and Excise presence. One zealous Collector of Excise was Angus Campbell. In 1801 he issued summons against fifteen per cent of families in Islay: 229 men and four women (together with nineteen in Jura and eleven in Colonsay) had to appear in the Justices of the Peace court.[13] Accused of malting or distilling privately, selling spirits without a licence (also tea and tobacco), 56 of the accused were absolved while the rest were fined. The majority had to pay up to £2, but some were fined up to £10, and if unable to pay, were imprisoned in Inveraray. The 229 were, however, those who had been caught; how many others went undetected can only be surmised. Moreover, the number of women on the list appears suspiciously low, since mothers, wives and sisters, even daughters, were often involved in aiding and abetting in malting and storage, if not in distribution.

Being in the employ of the Customs and Excise was not a particularly enviable position. Most were incomers, unfamiliar with the terrain and nature of the people and often endangered. For long the pay was poor, to incentivise recoveries, since officers received a proportion of the value of the seizures.

One tidesman,[14] Archibald Currie, was drowned on 10 January 1804 when 'proceeding to the Island of Colonsay on the Service of the revenue', his widow receiving the salary due to him for the quarter up to 5 January, £6 5s., plus six shillings and eleven pence farthing for the additional five days prior to his death.[15] Although the salary of the tidewaiter at Bowmore, Donald McLean, was less per quarter (£2 10s.), when he died on 16 April 1810 he was due his proportion of seizures amounting to £50 17s. 10$^1/_2$d.[16] A former captain of the customs cutter, the *Prince of Wales*, was due the portion of his annuity or pension of just over £40 per annum.[17] The extant parish marriage registers for the first half of the nineteenth century are witness to Islay's attractions for incoming revenue bachelors who found island brides. An excise officer at Bowmore, Robert Hamilton, married Elisabeth Douglas, 'a young girl' in Bowmore, on 27 November 1811.[18] But since there are no records of any Hamilton children, he may have been moved on before 'going native', and this is typical of others.

However, the excise acts were probably still being evaded on a substantial scale in Islay as elsewhere, with illegal whisky being produced despite the gaugers and grain shortages of the Napoleonic times. During the wars, imports of French brandy and claret were also threatened by rising tariff duties and interrupted trade. Distillation was forbidden in many years of the first decade of the century, and then occasionally up to 1813. Even so, when he visited Islay in 1808, James Macdonald reported that 'considerable quantities of barley' were being sent to Campbeltown and other Argyll distilleries. He also considered that 'the proprietor . . . does all on his power to prevent smuggling and illegal operations . . . he has accordingly built, in the heart of Islay, the only brewery in the Western Isles . . . for gradually weaning off his tenants from a taste of ardent spirits, and accustoming them to the more nourishing and wholesome beverage of ales'.[19] Subsequent legislation, however, merely confirmed and strengthened the trend towards illegality while the vastly inflated revenue demands of the Napoleonic wars produced a marked rise in all of the taxes. From 1814 stills of less than 500 gallons (later reduced to 200 gallons) were banned in the Highland area, thus outlawing all but a tiny minority of licensed distillers in the north.

Post-war regulation

The dramatic expansion of illicit distillation after the end of the Napoleonic wars concentrated government attention. In 1816 the 'Highland line' was abolished, revenue was raised from duty on spirits rather than from annual licence fees and penalties against smaller stills were revoked, but the resurgence in the fortunes of the legal sector was short-lived. English and Scottish duties on barley were equalised in 1819; in reality this represented a tax increase in Scotland and another incentive for farmers to dispose of their grain to illicit whisky-makers. Two major investigations in 1821 and 1822 exposed the extent to which the law was being flouted and the revenue cheated.[20] To bring the situation under control, an Act in 1823 required legal distillers to use stills with capacities of over forty gallons; for such distilleries the excise duty was then reduced from its previous high levels. By offering inducements for larger-scale commercial production it was hoped that the industry could be brought under control and illicit distillation reduced or eliminated. There was one fixed rate of duty throughout Scotland and the fee to become a licensed distiller was a relatively modest £10. This substantially eroded the illicit producer's cost advantage over his licensed rival. While the decade after 1823 still witnessed a series of violent incidents between the revenue service and groups of illicit distillers, the new policy appears to have worked quite well. The amount of duty-paid whisky almost doubled between 1823 and 1824 and the quality of the product improved markedly.[21] In 1821 Islay accounted for ten of the 114 official distilleries listed in Scotland, although there were still presumably illicit ones as well, some of which came to be registered after the Act was passed.[22] By 1833 two additional distilleries had been recorded in Islay and the official amount of whisky produced had risen from 29,731 to 169,718 gallons (some 765,000 litres).[23] Several of these distilleries have survived to the present day – Ardbeg, Bowmore, Lagavulin and Laphroaig – but many of the others operated only for relatively short periods, including Ardenistle, Ardimore, Bridgend, Daill, Lossit, Mulindry, Newton, Octomore, Octovullin, Scarrabus and Tallant.

Although the 1823 Act did much to bring illicit distilling under control, there were inevitably some who were still unable or unwilling to meet its requirements. For much of the first half of the nineteenth century there was a continuing game of hide-and-seek between the farmer-distillers on the one hand and the excisemen or gaugers on the other. Extant official correspondence in the excise records from 1837 to 1849 contains many accounts of seizures of stills, malt and wash (the fermented liquid from which the spirit is distilled) from 'hovels in the muir' or from 'caves on the shores at Proaig and Ballychatrigan'.[24] Excise officers patrolling the coast in their cutter were reported to have scaled cliffs near Glenastle in the Oa to investigate distillers manufacturing in cave systems. Flight across the muir enabled the moonshiners to evade arrest, but usually at the cost of losing their stills and raw materials. One such still from a cave on the

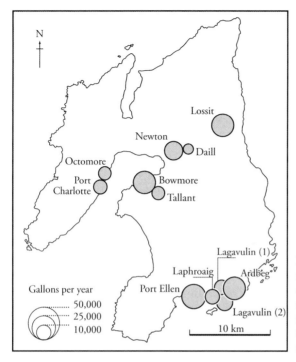

In the 1830s distilleries fluctuated in output by season, both in numbers and output. The total production from twelve Islay distilleries in 1833 was 170,000 gallons (*BPP*, 1835, XXX).

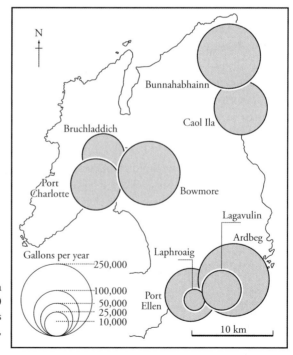

Alfred Barnard recorded a production of 1,250,000 gallons for Islay's distilleries in the 1880s (Barnard, *Whisky Distilleries* 1887).

The process of condensing vapour in a coil immersed in cold water has to be conjured up for this illicit still now on display in the Museum of Islay Life.

Barnard painstakingly toured all the United Kingdom distilleries in the mid-1880s. The pot stills used today are almost identical to those of Barnard's time, each distillery having differently shaped stills to produce their particular whiskies. Peat is still used in malting, but other power is diesel or electric (Barnard, *Whisky Distilleries*, 1887).

Sound of Islay is in the Museum of Islay Life. But since there were less than a dozen excise officers identified in the censuses of 1841 and 1851, it must have been something of a losing battle, and illicit distillation perhaps continued longer in Islay than in many other areas.

The enthusiasm with which distillers were pursued was perhaps in the long-term interest of Ilich, as well as that of the British exchequer. Lord Teignmouth referred to the alcohol problem in the 1830s: 'whisky follows the Highlander from the cradle to the grave, and often accelerates his progress from one to the other . . . To try to prevent further illicit distilling, Mr Stewart Mackenzie of Lewis, the duke of Sutherland, some of the proprietors of the Orkneys, as well as Mr Campbell of Islay, erected distilleries. This provides a more adequate, cheap and legal supply of the spirit'.[25] In his evidence to the Poor Law Inquiry in 1844 the Kildalton minister endorsed Teignmouth's views while also displaying much more tolerance than his predecessor half a century earlier, saying that the distilleries 'afford a great deal of employment . . . the people . . . are very temperate and industrious . . . the more distilleries they have the more temperate they become. There is not one gallon of whisky drank now for fifty that were drank when [I] came to the parish [twenty-one years before]'.[26]

The customs, and particularly the excise, establishment in Islay became substantial after the middle of the century. Detailed census returns illuminate the strict hierarchy, classes and terminology of controllers (customs), supervisors (excise) and various officers such as riding or divisional, only rarely from Islay, and born in other parts of Scotland, England and Ireland. Some were single men, who 'lodged' locally. Houses had to be provided by each distillery company for the married men, most of whom appear to have been moved around frequently since their wives and most of their children had also been born elsewhere. An exception was John Holmes, born in Edinburgh, listed in the 1871 census as Inland Revenue Officer in Bowmore, and who, in 1873 at the age of 32, married sixteen-year old Agnes Kirk, the daughter of a local builder and hotelier on Bowmore quay. By the time of the next census ten years later they had five children and he had been promoted to Divisional Officer. However, a year before he could be counted in the 1891 census, and by then Supervisor, he had suffered from nervous exhaustion for over a year, and succumbed after a heart attack.[27] With the addition of distilleries at Caol Ila in 1846 and Bunnahabhain and Bruichladdich in 1881, there were then normally between twenty and thirty officers on the island.

Victorian Scotch

While these regulatory measures were taking effect, a fundamental technical change had taken place in whisky production. In Dublin in the early 1830s Aeneas Coffey patented the still that bears his name and this laid the basis for the production of grain whisky, a less potent product than the Highland malt whiskies. The Coffey still process used only a small proportion of malted barley to unmalted cereals and new grain distilleries could therefore be established wherever there were plentiful supplies of barley or other cereals, even if these were distant from peat sources. The character of the water was also less important since the process itself produced whisky with fewer impurities through more efficient distillation than that of malt pot stills. During the remainder of the nineteenth century, the skill of blending these grain whiskies with one or more malt whiskies gradually developed. Blending was itself a logical extension of the old process of vatting, the mixing of malts from different seasons or different distilleries. Scotsmen spread across the expanding Victorian empire and the world, creating a steadily rising demand for Scotch in overseas markets. Continental *phylloxera* affected supplies of wine, brandy and cognac, to the advantage of other spirit producers. Of the many new distilleries built in Scotland Islay's three new ones at Caol Ila, Bunnahabhain and Bruichladdich, were all coastal to ship their imports and exports.

A detailed record of the distilleries on Islay at the height of the 1880s boom was provided by Alfred Barnard in his amply-illustrated book, *The Whisky Distilleries of the United Kingdom*.[28] The title, it should be noted, was deliberately precise. Legislation had not yet limited British whisky production to Scotland and Barnard's survey included a number of remote outposts of the industry, including one distillery beside Regent's Canal in east London. He produced distillery sketches and descriptions of the historical development, production methods, quantities, personnel and other details of each of the distilleries visited. It is evident from the twenty-seven pages devoted to Islay that very little in the external appearance of the distilleries or their villages changed during the following hundred years. Nine distilleries, then producing over a million gallons (over 4.5 million litres) of malt whisky annually, were described for Islay: Ardbeg, Lagavulin, Laphroaig, Port Ellen, Bowmore, Lochindaal (Port Charlotte), Bruichladdich, Caol Ila and Bunnahabhain, six of which still produce over twelve million litres (over 2.5 million gallons) today, along with a small farm distillery at Kilchoman, first distilling in 2005. This stability contrasts with Campbeltown in nearby Kintyre; of twenty-one distilleries listed by

Barnard in 1887, only two survive today. Overproduction, compounded by declining quality, did not serve Campbeltown well in the industry's booms and busts of the twentieth century.[29]

Barnard claimed that 'isolated' Ardbeg was not officially established until 1815 but had for long been a haunt of smugglers. With access to the waters of Lochs Airighnambeist and Uigeadail and to sea transport on the south-east coast, the original owners, the MacDougalls, subsequently built the main distillery buildings, pier, school and houses that are still there today. Even in Barnard's time, Ardbeg was producing one-quarter of a million gallons (over one million litres) of whisky each year. The peat used had to be brought only about three kilometres, its chief characteristic being the absence of 'sulphur or other offensive material'. As with most Islay distilleries then, the annual output of 'pure Islay Malt' was 'taken up by the . . . wine and spirit merchants in Glasgow, Liverpool and London'. Half of the spent grain or draff, left after the distilling process, was used on local farms for cattle feed, the remainder being exported to Ireland.

According to Barnard, Lagavulin had begun in 1742 when it also 'consisted of ten small and separate smuggling bothies for the manufacture of "moonlight", which . . . were all subsequently absorbed into one establishment', probably in the 1830s. Some of the mystique and hyperbole that can still pervade malt whisky publicity is evident in his description: 'the Lagavulin water has a hundred falls before it reaches the Distillery and . . . travels over moss and peat lands all the way down, which is said to give the pronounced flavour to the Lagavulin whisky'. At the beginning of the nineteenth century Lagavulin produced only a few thousand gallons a year and even in Barnard's time the annual output was only 75,000 gallons (340,000 litres). In quality, however, 'we tasted some eight years old . . . which was exceptionally fine'. Most was used for blending, but not all: 'there are only a few of the Scotch Distillers that turn out a spirit for use as single Whiskies and that made at Lagavulin can claim to be one of the most prominent'.

Almost next door to Lagavulin was Laphroaig distillery, started in 1820. According to Barnard it looked from the distance like a 'cluster of ruins, but on nearer inspection we found it to be a Distillery of a very old-fashioned type'. Personally entertained by the proprietor, Mr Johnston, Barnard agreed that the whisky made at Laphroaig was of 'exceptional character . . . and is a thick and pungent spirit of a peculiar "peat reek" flavour'. He explained that the small annual output of just 23,000 gallons (about 100,000 litres) then rendered it of high value in the market. He also recorded more of the lore and myth that surrounds the making of Scotch:

Although the Distillery is of small dimensions, the proprietors would not attempt to disturb the present arrangements, as thereby the character of the Whisky might be entirely lost. The distilling of Whisky is greatly aided by circumstances that cannot be accounted for, and even the most experienced distillers are unable to change its character, which is largely influenced by accidents of locality, water and position. No better instance of this can be given than the case of Lagavulin and Laphroaig Distilleries, which, although situated within a short distance of one another, each produce Whisky of a distinct and varied type.[30]

Barnard's painstaking researches then took him on to Port Ellen, Bowmore and the two distilleries in the Rinns: Bruichladdich and the Lochindaal distillery at Port Charlotte. Port Ellen distillery started as a malt mill in 1825 situated on the shore half a kilometre from the eponymous village. In Barnard's time the annual output was 140,000 gallons (some 630,000 litres). The party 'found the coach drive from Port Ellen to Bowmore one of the most uninteresting that we had ever experienced . . . in all our wanderings we have never travelled by such a dismal and lonely road'. Their mood, however, revived when staying at the 'picturesque hotel' in Bridgend, 'the best and only one of any importance in Islay, possessing gardens and grounds of most enchanting loveliness'. Bowmore was allegedly founded in 1779 by a local merchant and farming family, the Simsons. A long lade had to be constructed to bring water from the Laggan river and barley was shipped from north-east Scotland. The distillery, owned at Barnard's visit by the Mutters, had its own steamship to import the grain and to export its 200,000 gallons (900,000 litres) of whisky.

Bruichladdich, (pronounced 'brew-ich-laddy'), on the shores of Loch Indaal, was deemd by Barnard to be 'quite an aspiring and tastefully built village . . . planted on one of the finest and most healthy spots in Islay'. Using new concrete technology, the new building of 1881 was 'a solid handsome structure in the form of a square, and entered through an archway, over which is a fine stone-built residence for the use of partners staying on the island' (this was still in use over a century later). Bruichladdich's 94,000 gallons (about 400,000 litres) of malt whisky left 'by the steamers which leave the quay every Tuesday'. Port Charlotte or Lochindaal distillery was established earlier in the century than Bruichladdich, perhaps based on an earlier mill at Skiba or on a still at Octomore farm and taking its water from Lochs Gearach and Octomore. Its 127,000 gallons (over half a million litres) in Barnard's day went either from Bruichladdich pier, or were 'floated out to the ships in casks, ten casks being lashed together by iron pins and a chain called "dogs" and towed out by boatmen'.

The workforce at Bulloch Lade's Caol Ila distillery over a century ago (Royal Commission on the Ancient and Historical Monuments of Scotland).

Finally, Barnard arrived on the Sound of Islay, where he was suitably impressed by the setting of Caol Ila ('cull-eela'), 'standing in the wildest and most picturesque locality we have seen'. He described the site and locality romantically, and the factory technically, noting that 'comfortable dwellings have been provided for the employees, forming quite a village'. The water, 'said to be the finest in Islay, comes in the form of a crystal stream from a lovely lake called Torrabus'. Annual production of just under 150,000 gallons (some 675,000 litres) could not satisfy the demand for this 'favourite Whisky', the output having to be rationed among buyers. The distillery and the earliest of the houses for its workers are crammed together at the foot of a very steep cliff that cuts the village off from much direct sunlight, especially in winter. In Barnard's day, and until the 1960s, Bunnahabhain ('Bonnahaven') was only accessible from the sea or via a rough hill road: 'This portion of the island was bare, and uninhabited, but the prosecution of the distilling industry has transformed it into a life-like and civilised colony . . . The Distillery proper is a fine pile of buildings in the form of a square, and quite enclosed . . . entering by a noble gateway'. Despite extensive remodelling outside and inside, the present-day visitor can confirm that Bunnahabhain does indeed have the appearance of an impressive walled fortress. It was built in 1881 and the distillery owners also constructed the road link with the Bridgend to Port Askaig road,

Most of Islay's distilleries were remodelled in the 1970s, on a scale inconceivable before the transport revolution of 1968. Some changed their external appearance almost beyond recognition, as for instance, at Caol Ila, on the Sound of Islay.

('as good as it was costly') as well as a 'commodious pier' (for £3,500), at which chartered steamers and the *Islay* called. Villas were erected for the excise officers, houses for the workers' families, as well as a reading room and a school room. Fifty to seventy workers were then employed in the distilling season, in contrast to a few operators today.

In the earlier distilleries such as Ardbeg, almost all of the 130 people in the village by 1891 were local, apart from the three revenue officers and the schoolteacher.[31] In contrast, almost half of Bunnahabhain's residents were incomers. The Highland Distillery Company gave prizes to each of the Bunnahabhain pupils at the end of the school year, whether or not children had had to miss lessons for fast days, potato or nuts gathering, winter storms or childhood epidemics.[32] Queen Victoria's Diamond Jubilee was celebrated by the children at Islay House, and although the sports had to be cancelled due to rain, mugs were duly presented. The highest number on the school roll was 39 in 1896, and Lady Mary Morrison donated prizes in 1909 for Dux boy and Dux girl, as well an midday cocoa. All ages were taught in one classroom by one teacher, usually female, who put up with a lot from older lads, but also recorded how much she would miss some children returning to Ireland, presumably with their father, Samuel Downey, a 'First Class Inland Revenue Officer'.[33]

The twentieth century and beyond

Even for an industry characterised by huge swings in demand and therefore in estimating supply, years ahead after maturation, the whisky industry of the twentieth century had more than its usual share of boom with overproduction, decline, takeovers, mothballings or closures. After the late-Victorian and early-Edwardian boom in demand, the consequences of World War I, the depression, American Prohibition between 1920 and 1933,[34] then World War II and its long aftermath all contributed to great uncertainties.[35] Since its whiskies contributed to the blends, the Islay whisky industry was affected by all of these. Laphroaig contrived to export its whisky to America as medicinal, obtained by prescription, and the Bahamas and Canada also supplied bootlegged 'Scotch'. The main blending firms had coalesced into Distillers Company Limited (DCL) by 1920, and by the start of the second war, had taken over and mothballed or closed down many distilleries in Scotland.[36] Port Charlotte distillery finally closed down in 1930.[37] Some of the buildings continued to be used for maturing whisky in casks for others. Part of the premises were occupied by the Islay Creamery, producing cheeses of the Dunlop type, until in 1981 new premises for the Creamery were built farther north. In the 1990s some of the warehouses were imaginatively converted for use as a youth hostel and field centre, lecture hall and museum for the Islay Natural History Trust.

Soon after the start of the the Second World War, with grain and manpower scarce, the Islay distilleries were mothballed, with the exception of Bowmore which was taken over as an RAF Coastal Command base. Loch Indaal was used by Catalina and Sunderland flying boats patrolling the Atlantic convoys and looking out for enemy U-boats.[38] As well as the maltings being commandeered as dormitories and the offices as heaquarters, a camp of Nissen huts was erected above Bowmore. Together with the airbase at Glenegedale (which also housed the Royal Canadian Air Force 422 Squadron), the population of Islay was perhaps doubled or more at times during the war. Afterwards, whisky production resumed and continued at a fairly low level, with long breaks during the summer months. Demand, however, increased during the 1960s with more and better advertising, and all the distilleries were developing and renovating by the 1970s. Overproduction once again produced a 'whisky loch' and the industry turned to promoting single malts as a panacea and to compete with other spirits and wines. For a time only Lagavulin and Laphroaig had been available as bottled single malt. The first single Bowmore malt was marketed in 1972 and the then owners, Stanley P. Morrison Ltd put a special bottle on the market to celebrate the distillery's bicentenary in 1979. An attractive reception centre was also created out of some of the older buildings, and this was subsequently repeated by some of the other distilleries, in time adding well-stocked and well patronised retail outlets and some cafés. One of the Bowmore bonded warehouses became the equally well patronised island swimming pool, heated ingeniously as a by-product of the whisky manufacturing process. The fortunes of Ardbeg, Port Ellen and Bruichladdich were more mixed; it was not till the late 1990s and after, that Ardbeg and Bruichladdich were re-established as ongoing concerns, while Port Ellen was irrevocably closed in 1983 with its distilling machinery dismantled.

By the turn of the 21st century the explosion of world marketing publicity resulted in many of the Islay whiskies appearing in top rankings whether by numbers of bottles, favourite tipples or extravagant claims in trade journals or events such as whisky festivals, including Islay's own Malt and Music Feis. Despite the level of excise duty, demand soared in the rest of the United Kingdom; other markets boomed in Northern Europe and Germany, the Americas, then Japan and the rest of Asia. Aficionados may be of malts in general, or of one specific bottling of one particular distillery.[39] Fans' clubs, such as the Ardbeg Committee or the Friends of Laphroaig, grew into tens of thousands. To the uninitiated, the production at one distillery may look much the same as any other. But there are still differences, some of which may be more substantial than others. Still important are the peatiness of the malt, shapes and sizes of the copper stills, length of fermentation, the duration and 'cutoff' timings to get the required phenol content,[40] the types and lengths of maturation depending on different casks and whether in warehouses by the Atlantic or in inland Scottish lowlands, and the marryings or cask blendings of the malts themselves. Whisky is produced at between two and three times the volume in Barnard's day. Half comes from just two distilleries, Diageo's[41] Caol Ila and Lagavulin; Laphroaig, Bowmore, Ardbeg, and Bunnahabhain contribute most of the rest. Privately owned Kilchoman, producing some 25,000 litres, and Bruichladdich, at about quarter of a million litres annually, target niche (and expensive) markets, stressing particular attributes such as using organic and locally grown barley, specially malted on the mainland. Bruichladdich bottles on site with local spring water, and in 2010 distilled an Islay gin, flavoured with over a score of herbs mainly sourced on the island. These, including bog myrtle and juniper, had been used in earlier times to flavour ales (including heather ales), as Pennant noted on his 1772 tour.[42] Aiming to recreate the idea of the farm distilleries of the nineteenth century, Kilchoman is Islay's smallest, distillery, and not to be outdone, has produced a bramble liqueur.

Only Bowmore, Laphroaig and Kilchoman malt a proportion of their own requirements on site. When Port Ellen distillery was finally closed down in 1983, a thirty-metre tall malting plant was subsequently added to the landscape under an agreement of 1987 called the Islay Concordat. Barley is brought in from East Anglia or elsewhere to the pier at Port Ellen and moved by road to the Maltings, where it is converted into the specific type of malt required for each customer. For almost quarter of a century smoke regularly belched out from the Maltings, probably to the detriment of the health of islanders living nearby. In 2010 an even taller smoke extraction unit was added to the skyline. Perhaps for the first time in over three centuries, commercial brewing was re-established on the island. Islay Ales was started up in 2004 in an old tractor shed in Islay House Square, itself being gradually renovated by Islay Estate to provide small craft and retail outlets. Producing mostly bottled beers with evocative Islay names, Islay Ales are exported far and wide.

Islay Malts
Malt whisky production nowadays forms only a small part of the total business of 'Scotch', a business that involves malting, distilling, maturing, bonding, blending, bottling, cooperage, promotion, sales and other activities. Yet within the trade the Islay Malts have a separate and distinguished place in the classification of Scotch whiskies, due to the higher degree of peatiness or 'heaviness' in their bouquet or flavour. The visitor to Islay can normally see round a working distillery. Malt whisky production begins with the making of malt, nowadays mostly using barley imported from elsewhere in Britain or abroad. Barley is soaked in water for two or three days until it is moist enough to allow germination to

begin. After the water has been drained off, the grain is spread out on the malting floor to allow germination. It is turned over from time to time during the next week and is then transferred, as 'malt' to perforated racks above peat-fired kilns where it is dried and permeated with smoke from peat fires. This dry malt contains enzymes and starch necessary for the next process, mashing.

After the malt has been ground into a rough meal or 'grist', it is again mixed with water to form a 'mash' which is in turn heated. The enzymes help to convert the starch into various sugars such as maltose, sucrose, dextrins and other substances. The resulting sweet solution or 'wort' is subsequently run off and the process is repeated several times until the wort solution is too weak to use. The spent grain or 'draff' is then used as an important source of cattle fodder. Meanwhile the worts are cooled slightly and led to very large tuns or 'washbacks'. Here brewer's yeast is added and its enzymes ferment the worts to form alcohols and certain other by-products. Many of these impurities are removed in distillation, but a few traces remain to give the Islay whiskies their distinctive flavours and bouquets. The resulting liquid, known as 'wash', is heated in a still, a copper vessel with a distinctive shape. Copper is not only a good conductor of heat, but helps to remove some of the undesirable sulphates, while adding sweeter, fruity esters. The amount of contact with copper affects the 'lightness' or 'heaviness' of the product, so stills are of varied sizes and shapes, and while some are squat, others are pear-shaped or tall, and the lyne arms at the top are also of varying lengths and angles.

It is here that the distillation process begins. Crude ethyl alcohol and its various volatile associates are separated or cut off from the remaining matter and are cooled in a pipe or 'worm', to condense into a liquid form known as 'feints' or 'low wines'. The residue is later redistilled to produce more low wines and the low wines themselves are then redistilled in smaller spirit stills. This separates the potentially potable crude whisky from the other products. A colourless liquid at this stage, it flows through a locked spirit safe into a spirit receiver. The glass-walled, but otherwise very secure, spirit safe provides the official measure of production: it was introduced to Islay by John Ramsay of Kildalton and was used at Port Ellen distillery for several years before its general adoption by HM Customs and Excise.[43] In the spirit receiver the whisky is mixed with water to reduce its strength before being pumped to the filling store. The raw whisky is then poured into oak casks or barrels that have normally been been used previously for sherry (declining, since sherry itself has declined in popularity), wines or bourbon. The whisky must then remain in duty-free bonded warehouses for at least three years to mature. During this period the liquid volume

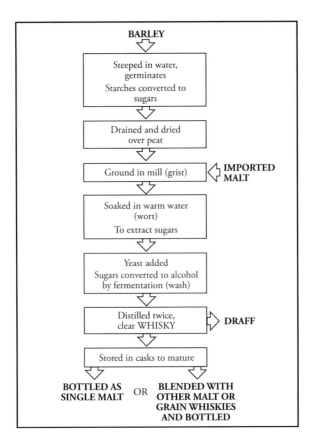

The local 'bere' barley has been replaced by barley from north-east Scotland, eastern England and elsewhere; and the distilleries may be considerably automated, but the basic process of producing malt whiskies remains the same. The golden colour is achieved during maturation in former sherry casks, or by adding caramel.

decreases by evaporation through the cask staves (the 'angel's share' is more prosaically reckoned to be about two per cent). The casks help to give the characteristic colouring to the spirit. It is claimed that coastal maturation impregnates the whisky with its saltiness; however, the amount of whisky matured in the coastal bonds of Islay varies from none to one hundred per cent.[44] If the final alcohol is below 46 per cent by volume, it is chill filtered to prevent hazing when diluted. Most of the marrying and bottling takes place on the mainland, after which some cases have to be returned to the retail outlets at the individual distilleries and elsewhere, though sadly there is no duty free at the airport or on the ferries. Multifarious awards are regularly chronicled in the main industry magazines and fanzines.

With increased production, too much draff is produced for the requirements of the island farmers and it is exported as cattle feed to the mainland. With increasing environmental awareness, instead of being flushed into the sea, the pot ale and spent lees were collected by road tanker from all the distilleries except Caol Ila and Bunnahabhain, and taken to a plant at Caol Ila before being discharged into the fast flowing Sound of Islay. But energy and its costs being of increasing importance, in 2010 Bruichladdich introduced an anaerobic digester, aiming to produce all its future electricity needs from its pot ale and spent lees, avoiding transport.

Most of the whisky distilleries in Islay have been renovated or redeveloped. Caol Ila's external appearance changed strikingly: the tall chimney stack and pagoda-like malt kiln chimneys disappeared. Most produce more whisky than ever, but with a smaller direct labour force in charge of automated systems and processes, even the exciseman being replaced by automated recording. The increased production led to the construction of some large new bonded warehouses. Water supply, both as regards quantity and quality, is a critical factor for some, as the distilling season is being stretched nearer a twelve-month operation. Most of the whisky produced leaves the island as casks in road containers for blending into world-renowned brand names. Few of the several thousand blended whiskies on the world market have no Islay malt in them: Ballantynes, Black Bottle, Cutty Sark, Famous Grouse, Long John, Teachers and White Horse amongst them.[45] Changing tastes and aggressive promotion, however, have encouraged most of the distilleries to market an increasing, though still small, proportion of their output as single malts. Islay Mist, probably better known than any of these, is not in fact a single Islay malt. It is an unusual de-luxe blend of three malt whiskies from three distilleries – Laphroaig on Islay and Glenlivet and Glen Grant on Speyside. It was specially inaugurated for the 1st Lord Margadale's coming-of-age in 1928. As with the marketing of many other products, special and expensive editions of single malts, new blends of malts such as the 'Islander' and new brands of blends such as 'Black Bottle' have multiplied and are able to be purchased in many mainland off-licences, supermarkets and airport duty-free malls, along with imaginative descriptions of their different 'bouquets' and other attributes.

The whisky landscape

Islay, the Hebridean exception, is in no respect more distinctive than in the scale of its whisky industry. Distilleries are found in many parts of the Highlands and Islands, including the Northern and Western Isles and Arran. There are also both malt and grain distilleries in the Lowlands. Only

in the 'golden triangle' of malt whisky distilleries on Speyside is there a
concentration that can match Islay's in quality of product: or, perhaps,
in an annual contribution to the exchequer in excise duty equivalent to
over one thousand pounds for every Ileach of whatever age.

The contribution to employment that distilling has provided directly
and indirectly is a significant element in Islay's comparative prosperity,
although the distinctive customs and excise designations and the gaugers
have gone, to be replaced by automated recording and unannounced
monitoring visits. Particularly with increased use of internet, whisky
tourism had burgeoned and has become an important addition to the
traditional visitor season. The distilleries and their associated villages
have been an equally important element in the visual landscape. They
remain so today, despite changes that are not all as aesthetically pleasing
as they are economically desirable. The tall and distinctive boiler-house
chimney stack from the coal-firing days now only remains in a few
instances, replaced by smaller flues during conversion to oil-burning
furnaces. The pagoda-like structures of the malt-drying kilns have been
especially distinctive, but some of these were threatened when malting
gravitated towards the mainland in the 1960s, or was centralised at Port
Ellen in the following decade. The rows of distillery workers' houses are
still characteristic elements of the landscape, especially in the more isolated
distillery villages, although many have been converted for visitor letting.
Other activities related to distilling are to be seen around the island, such
as the peat cutting on the muirs, now mechanised. Containers conceal the
empty casks arriving by ferry on Islay and the casks of mature, unblended
whisky leave the same way, less noticeably than when they were stacked
on the distillery piers, awaiting shipment by coaster or puffer. Juggernauts
negotiate the winding road from Port Askaig to Bunnahabhain and Caol
Ila. Perhaps the most memorable contribution, apart from several hundreds
of millions of pounds to the Exchequer annually, is not even a sight but
a smell: the 'peat reek' surrounding the distilleries, accompanied by the
smell from domestic peat fires. Only in a few other areas of Scotland or
Ireland can that particular blend be found.

Notes and references

[1]   See e.g. H. C. Craig, *The Scotch Whisky Industry Record*, (Dumbarton, 1994); M. S. Moss
      and J. R. Hume, *The Making of Scotch Whisky: a history of the Scotch Whisky distilling
      industry*, (Edinburgh, 2000) and N. Wilson, *Scotch and Water*, (Glasgow, 1998).

[2]   R. O. Jarvis communication, 1959. A. J. Youngson *After the Forty Five*, (Edinburgh,
      1973).

[3]   There is an extensive literature on many aspects of illicit distillations and smuggling,

beginning with S. Morewood, *An Essay on the Inventions and Customs of both ancients & moderns in the use of Inebriating Liquors*, (Dublin, 1824). See also S. Sillett, *Illicit Scotch*, (Aberdeen, 1965), *The Whisky Smugglers*, (Glasgow, 1990) and many of the writings of G. D. Smith, including *The Secret Still. Scotland's Clandestine Whisky Makers*, (Edinburgh, 2002) and *A to Z of Whisky*, (Glasgow, 2009).

4   T. M. Devine, *Clanship to Crofters' War. The social transformation of the Scottish Highlands*, (Manchester, 1994), p. 119.

5   Smith, *Book of Islay*, p. 519. In 1811 Walter Campbell's Islay brewery was still the only one in the Hebrides (Macdonald, *General View*, p. 621).

6   Devine, *Clanship*, p. 123.

7   *Ibid*, p. 122.

8   G. Smith, *Something to declare. 1000 years of Customs and Excise*, (London, 1980), p. 37.

9   Sinclair, *OSA*, p. 296.

10   Smith, *Book of Islay*, p. 145.

11   *Ibid.*, p. 158.

12   N. Wilson, *Scotch and Water*, p. 18. Gauger was the official title until 1831 when it was renamed division officer (urban) and riding officer (rural).

13   These are all named in F. Bigwood, *Justices of the Peace in Argyll; processes etc. of the JP Courts 1686–1825*, (North Berwick, 2001).

14   See L. F. Hobley, *Customs and Excise Men*, (London, 1974). For the Customs, tidesmen or tidewaiters met vessels 'on the tide', boarded them and ensured that all dutiable goods were given into the custody of landwaiters, who assessed the appropriate duties. Goods were not released until duties were paid. The superior officers were tide surveyors. The Excise officers were directed by supervisors, divisional officers, land surveyors in a strict hierarchy of officers; riding officers were responsible for smuggling on land; others were allocated to the Excise cutters.

15   Commissariot of the Isles Register of Testaments 1802–20, NRS, CC12/3/7, 38.

16   Ibid., 161.

17   Ibid., 113.

18   Old Parochial Registers of Births and Baptisms, Killarow, 536, NRS.

19   Macdonald, *General View*, p. 621.

20   Reports from Committees, *BPP*, 1821, VIII.

21   S. Morewood, *Essay*, pp. 324–8. Reports of Commissioners of Inquiry into the Mode of Charging Excise, *BPP*, 1823, VII and 1835 XXX.

22   M. C. Storrie, 'The Scotch Whisky Industry', *Transactions of the Institute of British Geographers*, 31, 1962, pp. 97–114; *Fifth Report of the Commissioners . . . Excise Duties*, *BPP*, 1823, VII, 253.

23   *Appendix to Seventh Report of the Commissioners of Inquiry into the Excise*, *BPP*, 1835, XXX, Appendix C.

24   Official Correspondence of HM Customs and Excise, Port Ellen District, Argyll South Collection, NRS, CE 81.

25   Shore, *Sketches*, 2, pp. 203–5.

[26] *Minutes of Evidence, Poor Law Inquiry Commission for Scotland, BBP*, 1844, XXI, p. 155.

[27] Censuses of Scotland, 1871, 1881, 1891; manuscript copies of enumerators' books, NRS.

[28] A. Barnard, *The Whisky Distilleries of the United Kingdom*, (London, 1887); Islay is described on pp. 87–113.

[29] See D. Stirk, *The Distilleries of Campbeltown. The Rise and Fall of the Whisky Capital of the World*, (Glasgow, 2005).

[30] Barnard, *Whisky Distilleries*, p. 95.

[31] Census of Scotland, 1891, NRS.

[32] Argyll and Bute Archives, CA5/179, Bunnahabhain School Log Book.

[33] Census of Scotland, 1891, NRS.

[34] By the start of the First World War, almost half of the American states were 'dry', the temperance movement having grown to such an extent that the National Prohibition Act of 1919 enabled federal enforcement of the 18th amendment to the Constitution. It 'banned the manufacture, sale, or tranport of intoxicating liquors . . . to reduce crime and corruption, solve social problems, reduce the tax burden created by prisons and poorhouses and improve health and hygiene in America'. It came into force on January 1, 1920 and was not repealed until 1933, after ale consumption, criminality and bootlegging had all increased dramatically.

[35] See Craig, *Record*, (London, 1994). Company records in the archives of the University of Glasgow amplify many of the fluctuations.

[36] See R. B. Weir, *The History of the Distillers Company 1877 to 1939* (Oxford, 1995).

[37] B. Townsend, *Scotch Missed. The Lost Distilleries of Scotland*, (Glasgow, 1997), pp. 169–70.

[38] Crown Film Unit, *Coastal Command*, video DD985.

[39] Exemplified in the writings of Michael Jackson, such as *Malt Whisky Companion*, (London, 2010).

[40] Phenols are the umbrella term for the peaty aromas and flavours of chemical compounds. The ppm (phenol parts per million) indicate the peatiness of a spirit, from just a trace in the light whiskies of Bunnahabhain to the 46.4 ppm of Bruichladdich's Octomore, although most are around half of that.

[41] Diageo, with its wide range of mainland distilleries, concentrates on a more restricted range of Islay whiskies for blending with its other products.

[42] Pennant, *Tour*, p. 221.

[43] F. Ramsay, *John Ramsay of Kildalton,* (Toronto, 1988), p. 18.

[44] See A. Jefford, *Peat Smoke and Spirit. A Portrait of Islay and its Whiskies*, (London, 2004) for technical summaries of individual distilleries.

[45] Archives such as those of Diageo at Menstrie near Stirling illustrate the changing advertisements for many of their distilleries and blends.

CHAPTER 13

The perennial grouse

Whether central in a seafaring lordship or later more peripheral, Islay has been characterised by the gradual integration of its economy and society with the wider world beyond its shores. Not all of this involved direct contact with that world: ideas and technology travelled as effectively as people. But the establishment, maintenance and improvement of links between Islay and the outside world were both a necessity for the success of the social and economic changes, especially from the eighteenth century, and also one of the most tangible measures of that success.

The drovers' route through Jura
Before the agricultural and other improvements of the eighteenth century, Islay, like other Hebridean islands, had of necessity to be largely self-reliant. Relatively few Islay residents ever left the island; what they could not obtain or make from their own resources had normally to be gone without. There were of course minor exceptions, such as tea and other luxuries. Contemporary letters recorded the difficulties of obtaining these, but those who were most burdened by such afflictions were the few at the top of the social scale. The fact that they were able to commit their complaints to paper obscures the fact that literacy was almost as rare as tea.

Black cattle were sent each year in their thousands from Islay to the market at Falkirk in the lowlands, most of them ultimately finding their way to England.[1] One route to the mainland before the late-eighteenth century was through Jura. It is now normally referred to as 'the overland route', although the alignment did vary slightly from one period to another. It included two sea crossings: across the Sound of Islay and then across the Sound of Jura from Lagg to Keills in Mid Argyll. This route remained in use until early last century and one of the last drovers was Dugald MacDougall who died at Minard, Loch Fyne, in 1957.[2] The spring and summer found him out in the islands buying young cattle as 'the Islay Trysts in May and June offered the finest cattle in the West'. The Islay cattle were driven on foot from all parts of the island to Port Askaig, ferried across to Feolin in Jura and again walked via the inland Market loch to the ferry at Lagg. There they were cajoled into

Many views in Islay are enhanced by the backdrop of the mountainous Paps of Jura, as depicted here by Schetky. The road formed part of the 'overland route' for cattle, folk and mails.

another boat, carried over the Sound of Jura to Keills and unloaded on to the jetty. The herd made its way by Tayvallich and Bellanoch over Crinan Moss to Kilmichael and up the glen to Barmolloch. There they grazed until they were ready to be sold at the Falkirk Tryst on the second Tuesday of October.

The ferry controversy of the 1960s was evidence that many Islay residents were still inclined to look back on the period of the overland route as a golden age which might return, but there were problems associated with it that led to frequent difficulties and recriminations, especially in the early-nineteenth century. Complaints about the quality of the jetties and of the roads through Jura and on the mainland from Keills were numerous. Even the right-of-way was in question. The new mainly coastal road to Lagg in Jura was still incomplete in 1805 and the chief proprietor, Archibald Campbell of Jura, challenged the right of Walter Campbell of Islay to use the new road for the passage of his cattle to the ferry at Lagg, alleging that the droves were only entitled to use the old hill-track.[3] Direct, if rather unreliable and irregular, links between south-eastern Islay and the mainland were later initiated and in time the overland route fell into disuse. This reflected a basic shift in technological advantage towards sea transport and away from land routes.

Sailing packets and steamers

As early as 1764 the problems and costs of maintaining a mail-carrying ferry to the mainland were preoccupying the attention of Islay's gentlemen and tacksmen and were duly recorded at their twice-yearly Stent meetings. Up to that time the financial risk involved in providing this service appears to have been borne by several of the landowners including Campbell of Shawfield, Campbell of Jura and McNeill of Colonsay, as well as mines' operator, Charles Freebairn, and the packet owner.[4] In 1767 the Stent provided £40 2s. 6d. towards the packet from one Hallowday (November 1) to the next. This sum was to cover both the expenses of the vessel and of the postmaster and runners, with the provisos 'that no postage be payd for Leters from Tarbert to Ilay or from Ilay to Tarbert, And That the Baggs containing the Leters Are not to be opened at Portaskog, Or any where else in Ilay, But at Killarow'.

The man responsible for running the service, also acting as postmaster, was the merchant, David Simson. The packet was to make a return sailing every week, wind and weather permitting. Some complaints about the service were noted in 1769 but the improvements demanded then were still apparently lacking in 1771: 'the Pacquet Master & Owners must get . . . four Beds lade in the Cabine and four new Mattresses in them and . . . there [must] be locks on two of them and none but Cabine passengers admitted to them . . . there [must] be three sufficient Sailors & a Boy always in the

Pacquet'. Part of the Stent subsidy for the service was withheld until the improvements were made. Even this was not effective and by October 1775 Simson was faced with an ultimatum from the committee appointed to run the packet and post:

> The present Pacquet belonging to David Simson, Mercht in Isla, & Colin Campbell, present Pacquet Master, shall be continued for the space of two months from this date, within which time the said Pacquet is to be repaired and made fitt in Masts, Sails, Rigging, & Ground Tackle, also the Cabin to be properly repaired. That while the Pacquet is repairing the Contractors shall Find a proper Boat to the satisfaction of the said Committee to ply during the absence of the other.

In the end Colin Campbell of Carnbeg was given a seven-year contract and his vessel apparently gave more satisfaction. But he did not renew his contract when it expired and the packet master, John Hill, of Port Askaig, took over responsibility.

By 1794 the main complaint at the Stent meeting was that, since the then packet master was residing at Tarbert and not in Islay, 'he is thereby Induced to remain at Tarbert when he coud [*sic*] make a good passage to Islay. It is hereby recommended . . . that his residence shall be henceforth in Islay'. The supervisory committee met every quarter, more frequently than the Stent body itself. Over the years fares gradually crept up: the annual subvention also increased, especially after government subsidy was withdrawn in 1812. The most persistent complaint concerned the apparent inability of the packet master to prevent steerage passengers from invading the cabin. The temptation was probably considerable: not merely was the sailing ship dependent on favourable winds but the vessels used were very small. Colin Campbell of Carnbeg had contracted to provide a vessel of at least thirty tons, but this was reduced to twenty for his successor.

However, a major revolution was on its way. The Stent meeting in May 1822 looked forward to the replacement of the sailing ship by a steam-driven 'packet'. Such an innovation would bring more than merely technical advantages, for 'the Packet shall at all times be provided with food for the passengers, to Consist of Porter – Ale – Cheese – Biscuits – Teas and Sugar – and at times Cold Salt Beef'. However, such luxury had to be anticipated for a while longer: the first steam-driven vessel did not arrive on the Islay service until 1825.[5] A nine-year-old wooden paddle steamer. the *Waterloo*, she was renamed the *Maid of Islay*. Sailing from West Loch Tarbert, she provided a connection with Clyde steamer services to the East Loch, establishing a pattern that was to endure for almost a century and a half.

Two years later a second vessel was acquired and named *Maid of Islay No. 2*. In summer *No. 2* took over what had been *No. 1*'s schedule: a Tuesday outward run to Port Askaig, and a similar run on Thursday extended to Oban, Tobermory on Mull and Portree on Skye, returning to West Loch Tarbert on Monday. Meanwhile *No. 1* provided the Clyde link from Glasgow to Greenock, Rothesay and East Loch Tarbert. In winter *No. 1* was laid up, but *No. 2* appears to have made one trip a week from Greenock to Islay, West Loch Tarbert, Oban, Tobermory, Isle Ornsay, Portree and certain other intermediate points. *No. 1* was sold in 1831, but *No. 2* continued to serve Islay as before until 1845. Her successor, between 1846 and 1849, was the *Modern Athens* and a slightly altered service was adopted. She sailed from Glasgow on Mondays for Port Ellen and then made two trips to West Loch Tarbert and back, connecting with the Clyde steamers to the East Loch, before starting her return journey to Glasgow on Fridays. The Kilchoman minister noted the 'great' improvement with satisfaction, with an additional pier at Port Ellen: 'a powerful steam packet plies regularly between the island and Tarbert . . . the mail is received and despatched four times weekly, twice by packet, and twice through Jura by the ferries'.[6] Two routes to the mainland were steadily growing in importance: from Port Askaig or Port Ellen to West Loch Tarbert, with nearby connections to Clyde services on Loch Fyne; and a less frequent and more circuitous route round the Mull of Kintyre to Glasgow. These two routes continued to dominate the Islay traffic scene for well over a century until the late 1960s.

West Loch and Mull of Kintyre routes
The earliest iron paddle-steamer on the Glasgow to Islay route appeared in October 1849. This was the first completely new vessel to serve the island since the sailing ships of the previous century; she was appropriately named *Islay*, later *Islay I*, and was 'powerful and fast-sailing'. Her route extended beyond Islay to Oban and Skye, with occasional calls in Ireland. She ran ashore at Port Ellen in 1857, but a greater mishap occurred when she was wrecked completely in 1866. Charles Morrison, John Ramsay and T. G. Buchanan replaced her with the single-screw *Islay II*. Later taken over by David Hutcheson and Company, the precursor of David Macbrayne's company, she was stranded on Rathlin Island in 1875, and subsequently wrecked in Red Bay, Cushendall, Antrim, in 1890.[7] The third vessel to bear the name, *Islay III*, took over the Glasgow to Islay service in 1890. She was not a new ship: as the *Princess Louise* she had already spent eighteen years shuttling between Stranraer and Larne. Serving Port Askaig, Bruichladdich and Jura twice-weekly from Lancefield Quay in Glasgow, *Islay III* survived sundry mishaps. As *The Oban Times* reported from Port Askaig in 1900:

In 1825 the paddle steamer, the *Maid of Islay*, replaced the sailing packet and William Heath's drawing suggests familiar congestion at Port Askaig (private collection).

The PS *Glencoe* was built in 1841 as the *Mary Jane*, and was introduced on the West Loch to Islay crossing in 1857. For almost half a century, while a succession of vessels on the Mull of Kintyre route was coming to grief, this iron paddle steamer served the Islay folk. She then went on to other routes until she was sold in 1931, aged 90! (Duckworth and Langmuir, *West Highland Steamers*).

On the Mull of Kintyre run, three successive steamers called *Islay* foundered. After surviving sundry mishaps, the *Islay III* was wrecked in 1902 on Sheep Island, not far from Port Ellen (Duckworth and Langmuir, *West Highland Steamers*).

The custom-built PS *Pioneer II* arrived in Islay in 1905, 'materially different from any of her predecessors, and [she] struck a distinctly modern note'. She remained on this run until 1939 when superseded by the then modern TS *Lochiel*. The *Pioneer II* ended her days as a floating laboratory, the *Harbinger*, in Portland harbour, but her name was resuscitated in 1975 for a new Caledonian MacBrayne ferry on the Islay service (Museum of Islay Life).

Quite a thrill of delight passed through the village hearts on Saturday morning
when, after six weeks of absence, the *Islay* sailed into harbour under her own
steam with salutes of cannon from MacArthur's Rock ... Battered and rusty
she looked certainly; but now she is safely in dock we hope to see her ...
back at an early date.[8]

But *Islay III* also came to grief, this time on Sheep Island outside Port Ellen,
in 1902.

The next ship designated to maintain the service (there were of course
several short-term and seasonal replacements) was even older. Over the
previous twenty-seven years she had borne the names *La Belgique*, *Flamingo*,
and *Paris*. In this last incarnation she had spent thirteen years on the
Newhaven-Dieppe service but, 'though an excellent boat ... her main
fault seems to have been with respect to speed'. Perhaps to avoid the fate
of her predecessors, she became not *Islay IV* but *Glendale*. The device was
unsuccessful; within three years, in July 1905, she was wrecked on Deas
Point, Kintyre, due to 'an error in navigation'. For the next fifteen years
various ships, including the *Clydesdale II*, a single-screw vessel, maintained
the service. Thereafter a succession of workhorses for David Macbrayne's
company, including the *Lochdunvegan I*, *Lochbroom I*, *Lochbroom II* and
finally the *Loch Ard* took over the Mull of Kintyre route. The vessels all had
provision for a few passengers, but were essentially for freight. Introduction
of ro-ro services from the West Loch in the late 1960s removed even the
freight advantage and the last regular sailing from the Broomielaw in Glasgow
to Islay round the Mull of Kintyre was in March 1970.

The route from Islay to Glasgow and the Lowlands via West Loch Tarbert
was the inverse of the overland route. The latter had used the ability of the
principal users, cattle, to provide their own motive power and sea crossings
were reduced to a minimum. The steadily increasing flow of human beings
was less manageable and they, together with mail and other urgent freight,
switched to the route that maximised the advantage that steamships in the
nineteenth century had over land transport beyond the railway net. For this
reason the pier in the West Loch was placed so close to the head of the loch
that Islay ferries were traditionally shallow in draft and were wapped on
their bow rope to turn in the confined space. From there to the pier at the
East Loch was only a few kilometres and then the travellers used the Clyde
steamers to Glasgow or to the railhead at the Tail of the Bank.

For almost fifty years, while successive vessels on the Mull of Kintyre
route foundered, one iron paddle-steamer was the mainstay of the West Loch
Tarbert service. Introduced as the *Glencoe* in 1857, she had in fact been sailing
elsewhere since 1841, smaller in size and under the name of *Mary Jane*. She

remained on the Islay run from 1857 until 1905, then went on to other tasks in the same fleet before being sold in 1931 when ninety years old. The *Glencoe*'s replacement in 1905 was the *Pioneer II*, newly-built for the Islay mail service. She was described at the time, as 'materially different from any of her predecessors and [she] struck a distinctly modern note'. For the next sixty-five years, the West Loch service remained little changed, except for the replacement of the *Pioneer II* in 1939 by the rather squat but new twin-screw vessel, the *Lochiel* (really the *Lochiel IV*) and the service continued more or less unchanged until the end of the 1960s. Sailing outwards from Islay six mornings a week to West Loch Tarbert, it connected with the morning sailing from the Clyde to the East Loch, this latter service also maintained almost unbroken by the MV *Loch Fyne*, then back to Islay in three hours during the afternoon. A Sunday sailing was unthinkable.

During the Second World War *Pioneer II* made a brief reappearance while the *Lochiel* was transferred to the Clyde, but the *Pioneer II* was then transferred to Portland Harbour where, as the *Harbinger*, she ended her days as a floating laboratory. The 1960s were not a happy time for the *Lochiel*. The decade began disastrously when the ship struck a submerged rock at the entrance to the West Loch and settled, fortunately in shallow water and without injury or loss of life. This incident can again tactfully be described as 'an error in navigation'. The *Lochiel* was raised, somewhat remodelled and returned to the service.

Three ships, the *Glencoe*, *Pioneer II* and *Lochiel*, had served Islay from the West Loch for over a century. It was misfortune for the *Lochiel* to end her Islay service at a time of strong public debate about the reorganisation of ferry services, when the *Lochiel*'s inadequacies were very obvious. Nevertheless she and her predecessors had served the island well. Many Islay residents and visitors remember her with nostalgia, perhaps best expressed by a visitor from Bletchley. Finding her gone from her normal station, he wrote to the *Scottish Field* in July 1971 to inquire 'Where has the dear, dour, old ruin gone?'[9] The answer for the present author and family, one balmy May evening in 1980, was a nostalgic aperitif on deck before an enjoyable meal in the dining saloon of the *Lochiel*, riding high without engines and in new livery, in Bristol harbour. She was finally broken up in 1996.

Debate, competition and reorganisation

The main problem facing the West Loch Tarbert route in the 1960s was that it was served by a conventional ship, whereas the growing number of vehicles that was transported to and from the island required something else. Using wheel nets, cars and small vans were winched aboard and stowed in the *Lochiel*'s hold, but this was unable to cope with the demand. As an

The squat TS *Lochiel* did good service for Islay until the 1960s. The decade began disastrously when she sank at the entrance to West Loch Tarbert, Despite subsequent remodelling, her winching gear for handling a small number of cars was not suitable for the era of the car ferry. Many, including a nostalgic English visitor, missed the 'dear, dour old ruin'.

In the late 1960s Islay became the first of the Hebrides to have competing state and private ferry companies, and the fare structure was more favourable to Ilich than to other Hebrideans. A ro-ro ferry, MV *Sound of Islay*, was introduced by Western Ferries in April 1968 and could carry container vehicles as well as cars. The days were also numbered for the few remaining coasters or 'puffers', one of which is seen here at Port Askaig (Eric Thorburn).

interim measure a second vessel was added to the service in summer, but this was clearly only a stop-gap solution. The initiative clearly lay with Macbrayne. The firm was nominally a company in the private sector, but in fact it depended on government assistance (especially where new capital investment was concerned) and it included Scottish Office nominees on its board of directors. Elsewhere in the Hebrides similar problems were evident and in the early 1960s Macbrayne took delivery of three large car ferries, the *Clansman, Columba and Hebrides*, serving the Outer Isles, Mull and Skye. Had a fourth vessel been ordered at the same time for the Islay service the *Lochiel*'s replacement might never have become a real issue.

By the time Macbrayne did announce an order for such a car ferry, to carry 400 passengers and forty-six cars, costing £750,000, there were many on Islay and beyond who argued that this was not the best solution. One reason why these early car ferries were relatively large was that they were intended to encourage tourism in the Hebrides by providing sleeping accommodation in areas where hotels were few and often small. Since hotels were reasonably plentiful on Islay at the time, why such an elaborate vessel and high fares? Why not, in fact, return to the old pattern of very short sea crossings via the overland route through Jura? An Islay Transport Users' Committee was created with the support of the Islay District Council and a Norwegian transport expert delivered a favourable report on the overland scheme for the Highland Transport Board in 1966.[10] The latter in turn recommended that the *Lochiel*'s service to the West Loch be abandoned in favour of the overland route. For several years the controversy raged through open meetings, closed committees, newspaper columns and, no doubt, also through the corridors of St Andrew's House in Edinburgh. Macbrayne, it seems clear, had not done much investigation of alternative solutions to the *Lochiel* replacement problem. A large car ferry like the others seemed the obvious answer to them. In fairness to Macbrayne, its social responsibility, reflected in its government subsidy, was to provide services to Gigha and Colonsay as well as to Islay and Jura, and flexible vessel deployment; this was conveniently minimised by proponents of the overland route.

While the debate continued, experimental new links developed. In 1966 a small company, Eilean Sea Services, began to operate a landing craft of thirty-five tons between Port Ellen and the mainland. Its first main contract was to bring in construction materials and equipment for the reconstruction of Port Ellen distillery. The service by the *Isle of Gigha* appeared to be thriving when the vessel suddenly capsized four miles off the Islay coast, with the loss of two lives and cargo. This incident seemed to many to indicate that small simple ferries, on the overland or any other route, were not the answer and once again the controversy appeared to be on the brink of resolution in favour of a new Macbrayne vessel. In 1968, however, with a minimum of advance publicity, Western Ferries, a company that had grown out of Eilean Sea Services, began operations with a much firmer financial basis and with a new, purpose-built, ro-ro ferry named the *Sound of Islay*.[11] This vessel created a transport revolution on Islay almost overnight. She was faster than any used previously, so that two and even three round trips a day were possible between Port Askaig and the new simple terminal lower down West Loch Tarbert at Kennacraig. Loading and unloading were only a matter of drive-on, drive-off, and the fares charged were well below those of Macbrayne: in some cases little more than half the vehicle rate on the *Lochiel*. There was even a service on Sundays: the islanders enthusiastically welcomed the reading of Sunday newspapers that day.

The most profound change, however, was brought about by the ability of the *Sound of Islay* to take large vehicles and trailers. Instead of having to import barley and export whisky by coasters or puffers (including the familiar *Pibroch* and *Moonlight*), the distilling industry reorganised on a basis of road-hauled containers and much of Islay's retail trade and agricultural supply industry did the same. The first lorry drivers from the mainland had to contend with the precipitous climb out of Port Askaig (the bends were smoothed out in 1971, and again early this century) and with a decorative stone footbridge linking two parts of Islay Estate at Bridgend, which had subsequently to be removed.

So successful was the *Sound of Islay* that she was replaced in 1970 by a larger vessel built on the same principle, but with more deck space and a few more comforts, the thirteen-knot *Sound of Jura*. The *Sound of Islay* went off to a run between Campbeltown and Cushendall in Antrim, while the *Isle of Gigha* reappeared as the *Sound of Gigha*, in Western Ferries' livery and with improved seaworthiness, plying across the Sound of Islay on the short crossing between Port Askaig and Feolin in Jura. Macbrayne replaced the *Lochiel* with the Clyde car ferry *Arran*. So successful was the Western Ferries' competition, that for a time it seemed that Macbrayne might withdraw completely from the route. Their planned large new ferry was, however, built and named the *Iona*, but she did not arrive on Islay. Argyll County Council saved the cost of the new terminals on Islay and in the West Loch, as well as the cost of rebuilding the road on Jura for an overland route, which went into limbo.

Nevertheless it was evident in the early 1970s that a stable pattern of service was yet to be achieved. Macbrayne did announce its intention of withdrawing completely, but then changed its mind when absorbed into the Scottish Transport Group. The latter made a takeover bid for Western Ferries whose directors at first recommended acceptance. A capital reconstruction of Western Ferries averted bathos, but by the mid-1970s the future was still uncertain. Macbrayne-STG had converted the *Arran* to a drive-on, drive-off ferry, but only at the cost of making it difficult for the vessel to use the piers at Gigha and at Craighouse in Jura. In due course the *Arran* was succeeded by a new sixteen-knot vessel, the *Pioneer*, that served Port Ellen and eventually Gigha, but avoided Port Askaig. Western Ferries continued to use Port Askaig, with the link to Feolin on Jura, Colonsay henceforth looking northward to Oban. Western Ferries argued that, if the government subsidy were transferred from Caledonian MacBrayne, as it was now called, to Western Ferries, the firm could carry vehicles and passengers free to Islay ever after. Sadly, this desirable development did not take place and competition in speed and fares (together with rapidly-rising fuel costs after 1973) meant that the *Sound of Jura* had to be sold in 1976. The *Sound of Islay* took over again until October 1981, when general and whisky recession forced suspension of service. Traffic was taken up by the *Pioneer*; Kennacraig was bought by Caledonian MacBrayne to save time and fuel consumption in the West Loch and the terminal was extended.

Eventually, in February 1979, the larger *Iona* at last arrived on the Islay run, after pier modifications at both Port Ellen and Port Askaig. She provided a thrice-daily return service from the mainland to Islay on summer weekdays, a twice-daily service on summer Sundays and winter weekdays and made a single round trip on winter Sundays. It would be difficult to deny that, for Islay, this proved a vast improvement on the situation of the mid-1960s, when a pattern that had survived almost without change for a century finally broke down. Pier alterations in the 1980s and 1990s for MV *Claymore*, MV *Isle of Arran* and *Hebridean Isles* brought ro-ro facilities and the reinstatement of a once-weekly link in summer to Colonsay.

During the first decade of this century a more frequent service was maintained by the latter two vessels. The new century, however, was characterised by renewed dilemmas and controversies regarding the future provision of what were now termed 'lifeline' services. Increased demands of distillers and other commercial operators, visitors and islanders required more sailings. Uncertainties were prolonged by government and European Union directives, while the provision of piers and vessels became the concern of a separate company, Caledonian Maritime Assets Limited (CMal). A new vessel, MV *Finlaggan* was built in Poland for which substantial pier and terminal alterations on the mainland and island had to be undertaken in 2011. At that time a major Ferries Review was conducted by the Scottish government to examine the provision of all Scottish ferry services, but given the financial constraints of the second decade of the century the outcome was once again uncertain. Meantime the Islay service was of a standard and frequency unimaginable in the 1960s, and, apart from the cost, despite islander concessionary fares, 'the perennial grouse' much less justified.

In 1842 John Francis Campbell of Islay sketched the rescue activities at Geodh Ghille Mhòire, west of Sanaig, of bodies and wreckage from the Irish emigrant ship, the *Exmouth of Newcastle*. He recorded that 'the ship struck on the rocks to the right and no fragment more than six feet long could be recovered . . . the most of the ship was smashed into fragments a few inches square on the 23d of May. 113 bodies had been recovered and buried by Campbell of Ballinaby and Henry Rockside . . . only 3 out of 230 were saved' (Trustees of the National Galleries of Scotland).

The *Harald*, wrecked off the Oa in 1909, was only one of over 250 mishaps known around Islay's shores (Museum of Islay Life).

In peril on the sea

Sea travel to Islay has never proved easy. For instance, several boats were recorded as being shipwrecked in 'tempestuous weather' in December 1718. Many of the basic navigation aids and safety regulations were only developed during the nineteenth century. Islay has an honourable record of help to those stranded along its coastline. In 1785 James Anderson expressed his opinion that 'in no part of the world, would a man who had the misfortune to suffer shipwreck, have a better chance to meet with every possible assistance, than there, or at a smaller expence'.[12] He described how a vessel loaded with linen yarn from Ireland had run aground on Islay a few years earlier. Despite the obvious value of the yarn to Islay's own domestic industry, over the next few weeks hundreds of islanders washed the salt out and dried the yarn so that only a few hanks were missing, 'to the utter astonishment of all the parties concerned'.

By the mid-nineteenth century, the 300-ton brig, the *Exmouth of Newcastle* was thirty years old, and after whaling and general trading, had been adapted to provide accommodation for about two hundred emigrant passengers. In late April 1847 she was loading in Londonderry or Derry before setting out for Quebec and Montreal on the St Lawrence.[13] One Islayman, Donald Ferguson, had sailed over to try to find seed potatoes (very scarce on both sides of the North Channel because of the potato blight), and talked to some of the *Exmouth* passengers as well as watching them partying with dance and song. This was not the iconic 'coffin' ship with starving catholic peasants driven into exile, but a mixed complement of catholic and protestant families. with some capital, setting off for new lives with greater promise than seemed possible in the famine conditions. They were setting off in a surveyed ship under the command of the sober and honest Captain Booth. A day or two later, however, Donald Ferguson was back in Islay recognising many of the bodies washed ashore after the vessel had struck rocks in wild seas at Geodh Ghille Mhòire on the north-west coast of the Rinns due west of Sanaig. 220 had been drowned, many of whom were buried by the islanders in the sands below the spot where a monument was erected in 2000. The latter gave the figure of 241 drowned, but official listings are of 208 emigrants, three cabin passengers, the captain and eight crew. The English inscription on the stone describes 'emigrants', translated into the Irish transcription as *deorai* ('exiles') as opposed to *eisimirceacha* ('emigrants'), a distinction as often ignored in Scotland as in Ireland.

Long before Compton Mackenzie's *Whisky Galore* entered global vocabulary, Islay had its own tragicomic version. In May 1859 the brig, *Mary Ann of Greenock* was wrecked in Machir bay at Kilchoman and was fast breaking up, some of the cargo floating ashore. Some two hundred boxes were 'saved', containing bottles of brandy, whisky and gin, as well as at least six puncheons or large casks of whisky, brandy and wine. *The Argyllshire Herald* reported that 'the wildest scenes of drunkenness and riot than imagined took place. Hundreds came, especially the Portnahaven fishermen who turned out to a man. Boxes were seized as soon as landed, broken up, and the contents carried away and drunk'.[14] The police sergeant and constable tried to keep order but were defeated by thirty or forty men, and retreated from the mayhem to the sanctuary of Coul farm. They were followed there by about 'thirty of the natives yelling like savages. Mrs Simpson of Coul gave the police firearms and the mob dispersed. But by next morning the scene presented was still more frightful to contemplate'. One Portnahaven fisherman, Donald McPhayden was considered to be 'the strongest man on Islay, but the brandy proved to be still stronger'. As his coffin was being carried for internment, 'groups could still be seen fighting or dancing – or craving for drink'. Two others died subsequently.

Of a very different order and still remembered distressingly in Islay and America is the very dark last year of the First World War when SS *Tuscania* and HMS *Otranto* came to grief off Islay.[15] While it was normally the horrors and deaths in the trenches that affected many island families as elsewhere, the Ilich were involved in two of the worst World War I disasters at sea in 1918, the *Tuscania* by enemy torpedo and the *Otranto* through navigational error and collision. The United States had become involved in the war in April 1917; tens of thousands of American troops had to be moved over the Atlantic in seas often wild, as well as patrolled by German U-boats. The transporters were requisitioned liners with British officers and crews outnumbered by the American military, white and black. Devastating Spanish influenza added to the miseries of the ocean, the convoys having to slow down for burials at sea.

The new Clyde-built Cunard-Anchor liner of over 13,000 gross tons, the SS *Tuscania*, had sailed from Glasgow via Liverpool to New York on her maiden voyage in February 1915; cabin class accommodation was for 271 passengers, second class 246, and steerage 1,900. Requisitioned in 1917 as a troop carrier, and painted olive grey, she left New Jersey early in 1918, bound for Le Havre; from Halifax, Nova Scotia she was part of the escorted HX20 convoy of eight troop and provision ships, 23 ships in all, zigzagging across the Atlantic. Under Captain Peter McLean, her officers and crew numbered just under two hundred, the rest of the complement of 2,401 comprising US troops. Fifteen years later, at a dinner organised by the Tuscania Survivors Association, the guest speaker was one Captain Wilhelm Meyer who had been in command of the German U-Boat UB77. He described how he had been patrolling for several weeks without diving in the approaches to the

North Channel between Ireland and Scotland, when, about seven miles north of Rathlin island, in the late afternoon of 5 February, he could not believe his 'good luck' when he spotted the convoy. From his periscope mirrors, he registered a large smoke stack steaming from the west. He stalked the liner in parallel for over two hours then fired off a torpedo. It passed under one of the British escorts, but a second, from a distance of over a thousand metres, hit the *Tuscania* midships, the explosion and immediate listing observed by the commander. The rest of the convoy was under orders to remove from the danger of any undetected submarines, but with back up generators and radio, the *Tuscania* managed to send out several SOS messages which were answered by three of the convoy's British escort destroyers, the *Grasshopper*, *Mosquito* and *Pigeon*. Orders were given to abandon ship orderly, but, with the heavy list to starboard, it proved extremely difficult to lower lifeboats properly, resulting in terrible injuries and drownings as men had to jump from the decks. The escorts, however, managed to save over two thousand in the dark, but 166 were listed as missing, presumed dead, and 126 bodies were washed ashore. After an hour, the large vessel slowly sank, and still lies at a depth of some eighty metres, about five miles west of Giol in the Oa. Some survivors managed to reach the island in lifeboats and by swimming in the cold Atlantic waters. On the rocky shore of the Rinns, after struggling ashore and walking some distance, the bedraggled men were well looked after by surprised families in Port Charlotte, Easter Ellister and Craigfad, while local men used to rescuing animals from the Oa cliffs rescued other survivors; some lifeboats came ashore at Port nan Gallan near the Mull of Oa. Families at Killeyan, Kinnabus, Stremnish and Port Ellen took them in, while the menfolk recovered bodies. The last survivor died in 2001; a radio broadcast in 2007 recorded memories from both America and Islay of island women and children distraught as the sad carts and corteges passed, and of American relatives desperate to help in identification.

The island did not yet have the telephone, but the lairds of Islay and Kildalton estates, their agents, police, coastguards and others organised the making of coffins, the funerals and interments of the 126 bodies, some in plots of land hastily prepared. Torrents of rain poured down relentlessly on the British and American flags, pipers, firing party, clergy, official dignatories, survivors and other mourners comprising about four hundred people in all, in Port Charlotte on Saturday 9 February, with several other ceremonies around the Oa. Two years later, it was the macabre task of islanders to exhume most of the bodies which were then reinterred by the American Red Cross either in the American Military Cemetery at Brookwood in Surrey, or in the United States. In 1980 the salvage rights to the *Tuscania* wreck were bought by an islander for £500, and divers later recovered the ship's bell and some other artefacts, now in the Museum of Islay Life. However, diving conditions in the fierce tidal race and reefs of the North Channel have resulted in further loss of life.

In the last weeks before armistice another convoy, HX50, assembled and set off from New York on route for the Clyde and the Mersey on 24 September 1918; there were thirteen liners, carrying some 20,000 men and escorted by two US naval cruisers and one destroyer. Bad weather forced the convoy to take the northern route into the North Channel approaches and was the fundamental cause of the catastrophe ahead. The commodore ship was HMS *Otranto* under the command of Captain Ernest Davidson. Over 12,000 gross tons, the *Otranto* had been built in Belfast in 1909 for the Orient Steam Navigation Company, lavishly fitted out for 300 first class, 140 second and 850 third class passengers. Summer voyages in the Nordic seas were complemented by voyages between Tilbury and Brisbane during southern summers. Immediately before war was declared on 4 August 1914, the owners had been asked, unsuccessfully, if the Admiralty could charter the *Otranto* and another vessel as proposed hospital ships. Steaming between Gibraltar and Plymouth, however, she was requisitioned on 4 August and subsequently commissioned into the Royal Navy as HMS *Otranto*. She spent most of the following years around the coasts of South America as an armed merchantman, on occasion engaging with the enemy, and being refitted in ports such as Esquimault, Prince Rupert, Sydney and Devonport. After refit as a troop ship, the *Otranto* was deployed between New York and Europe.

The American escorts left the convoy on Saturday 5 October, to be replaced by British escorts. October. By Sunday 6 October the convoy was approaching the North Channel, unlit as per orders, in force 11 mountainous seas. In the darkness it had unwittingly sailed through a French fishing fleet, also without lights, and *Otranto* had collided with one French vessel, stopping to rescue her crew and scuttle their boat. Poor visibility had meant that for several days the convoy was forced to navigate using dead reckoning and in the murky conditions had begun to spread out; unknowingly, some vessels had gone off course by some twenty miles to the north. When land was sighted through the murk at about 8 am the officer on the bridge of the *Otranto* decided it was the Irish coast, and turned to port, while the master of another liner in the convoy, HMS *Kashmir*, commandeered from the Peninsular and Oriental Steam Navigation Company and over 8,000 gross tons, correctly identified the coast as that of Islay, not Kintyre, and steered to starboard. Despite taking evasive action, and with helmsmen having difficulty steering in the huge seas, the two ships collided; *Kashmir* managed to reach the Clyde, leaving a badly holed *Otranto*.

Captain Davidson deemed the swell, winds and waves too dangerous for an escort ship, HMS *Mounsey*, to come alongside, now listing heavily to port.

Again, lifeboats and men were lost in circumstances searing to read about. Lt F. W. Craven of the *Mounsey*, however, persisted, came alongside four times, and managed to save 27 officers, 239 crew members, the thirty French sailors and some 300 American troops, and then, hugely overloaded, got to Belfast. Drifting without power, Captain Davidson tried to use the anchors to prevent her being blown into the coast, but *Otranto* settled on an undersea ridge about 500 metres from the shore of Machir Bay. Orders were given to abandon ship; most of the remaining four hundred were drowned while trying to swim through the cold waters and flotsam. Davidson was the last to leave, but he too perished. Altogether, 431 had been lost, of whom 351 were American, and many bodies were never recovered. *Otranto* broke in two and remains under between 9 and 18 metres of water, much plundered, still with live ammunition, salvage rights owned by the same person. Islanders helped sixteen survivors to reach shore, and again they were responsible for laying out over 150 bodies in churches and distilleries, making coffins from the wreckage. Every effort was made to identify individuals by recording physical and other details, correspondence continuing between the island and America for months later. Graphic photographs commemorate the mass funeral procession to a hastily prepared new burial ground above Machir Bay. All of the Americans except three were later disinterred and repatriated. Although the cross of sacrifice is that in all of the military war cemeteries, with the inscription 'Their names liveth for Ever', apart from that of Captain Davidson, the remaining graves are of the British lost, mostly with unnamed stones of 'A sailor of the great War', now looked after by the Commonwealth War Graves Commission.

The American Red Cross commissioned Robert J. Walker of Glasgow to design the 25 metre high monument (after a Pictish tower) 130 metres above the ocean at the Mull of Oa, and now maintained by the Glasgow Islay Association. The dedication is to the American soldiers and sailors on both the *Tuscania* and *Otranto* who gave their lives for their country, and a special iron wreath was added at his express wish from President Woodrow Wilson. There is no acknowledgement of the British lives simultaneously lost in the two disasters, amongst the worst of World War I at sea, but for ever in the island's memory and archives. Without television, let alone telephone, it is perhaps difficult to comprehend the sorrowing men, women, children and survivors, even from perusing the formal, often gruesome, reports and accounts in the newspapers and journals of the time, graphic photographs, heartrending letters and recorded memories. Especially poignant perhaps was the fate of those lost from the *Otranto*, just 36 days before armistice. While the ship had been carrying a smaller number of troops, perhaps since it was realised that the war was nearing its end, and while some six hundred had

This memorial headstone to a member of the family of an assistant lightkeeper at the Rinns lighthouse in 1845 uses the emblem of the Northern Lighthouse Board (Royal Commission on the Ancient and Historical Monuments of Scotland).)

The second lighthouse in Islay, after the Rinns, commemorated the premature death in 1832 of Walter Frederick Campbell's first wife, Lady Eleanor, in a pious plaque.

survived, yet almost as many had been lost. At the subsequent Admiralty court of inquiry both ships were deemed at fault, but that was too late for those drowned off Machir Bay.

Lighthouses and buoys
As early as 1785 a plea had been made for more lighthouses in the Kintyre and Islay sea area, since many shipwrecks had occurred on the west side of Kintyre, when seamen, in poor visibility, mistook the Mull of Oa for the Mull of Kintyre.[16] Ships were small, often overloaded, and bad weather and whisky also contributed to the frequency of shipwrecks around these coasts As ship design improved, as marine regulations were developed and as better navigational aids were provided, the number of such incidents decreased rapidly. Under several Acts of Parliament in the late-eighteenth and early-nineteenth centuries, the Commissioners of Northern Lighthouses were empowered to construct lighthouses at dangerous places along the coast of Scotland. In a country with such a long and indented coastline, the question of priorities must have been one of the biggest problems facing the Commissioners. Around the coasts of Scotland in the 1820s there were only a dozen lighthouses; In January 1823 the Commissioners reported that they had under consideration 'nine different applications from the shipping interest for a new light at the Rhinnes of Islay, on the small island of Oversaa'.[17] Construction started in 1824, the stone being quarried on the south side of the island of Orsay, and the light first shone out from the southern tip of the Rinns in 1825. This was a belated response to a long-felt need; by 1844 as many as 4,350 vessels a year were reported to be passing the Rinns lighthouse, although a few strandings and shipwrecks around Islay were still being reported each year. The map in Appendix B indicates the known locations of Islay mishaps, those with unknown location being listed. Port Ellen lighthouse was conceived by Walter Frederick Campbell as a memorial to his first wife who died in 1832. The operation of this light was taken over by the Commissioners in 1924. In 1835 Robert Stevenson endorsed the necessity for help to navigators through the Sound of Islay.[18] Then, as now, this was 'much frequented by shipping as a sheltered channel, by which they avoid coasting along the island of Islay, exposed to the swell of the Atlantic Ocean'. It was not until 1859, however, that the Rhuvaal light first marked the northern entrance to the Sound; two years later McArthur's Head light shone at the southern end.[19] Port Charlotte's lighthouse provided guidance in Loch Indaal after 1869.[20] Despite lights and buoys, west coast storms could still wreak havoc, as on the night of November 1881 when four vessels alone were lost, followed by others in the next few days. The programme of automated lighthouses completed in the 1990s ended the long tradition of

resident keepers, even if latterly their families were shore-based.

Now, protection to shipping around the coasts of Islay is provided in three main ways: the automated lighthouses, the lifeboat and the coastguard services, co-ordinated by the Maritime and Coastal Agency. The Royal National Lifeboat Institution established its Islay station at Port Askaig in 1934 and, apart from a brief transfer to Port Ellen in 1947–48, it has remained there ever since. Two main boats in service were the *Charlotte Elizabeth* and, as a replacement in 1957, the *Francis Wotherspoon of Paisley*. In 1979, with substantial help from the Schroder family trust, a new self-righting lifeboat, capable of 17 knots, arrived on station. Amidst island ceremony she was named the *Helmut Schroder of Dunlossit* in her father's memory, by Mrs George Mallinckrodt. Her 1990s replacement was a 25-knot Severn-Class boat. Since the 1930s, there have been many hundreds of launchings from Islay; and many RNLI awards have been presented to coxswains and crewmen. Two crewmen were lost in January 1953.[21] A coastguard service for Search and Rescue of ships in distress operated in Islay from 1928 and night watch and bad weather constant watch were maintained by regular officers, supplemented by auxiliaries, until the early 1970s.[22] With improved telecommunications, watchkeeping was discontinued and replaced by a mobile coastguard service still relying on volunteer help for manning rescue equipment at Kilchoman, Port Charlotte, Mull of Oa and Port Ellen. In 1980 a VHF radio station for shipping went on air using the mast at Kilchiaran and providing coverage from south of the Mull of Kintyre to north of Tiree, recalling its wartime forebears. Since the 1990s, expansion and technical developments in all of the rescue services were coordinated by the Maritime and Coastal Agency at Gourock on the Firth of Clyde.

The other way to the island

When internal air services in Britain passed the experimental stage in the 1930s, Islay was one of the first places to benefit. The comparative elegance of the Tiger Moth service from Renfrew Airport was described in the 1930s guidebooks. Several grass landing strips were used, including one at Duich, but Glenegedale was the preferred site. With the coming of war, military flying superseded civil services, flying boats of the RAF Coastal Command used Loch Indaal, and Glenegedale acquired surfaced runways.[23] In the difficult weather conditions of the Hebrides, several aircraft were lost. In January 1943 a Sunderland of the Coastal Command crashed at Blackrock, with loss of life,[24] and there are still remains of a training plane which crashed near Castlehill, whose pilot was also buried in Bowmore. After the Second World War the DC-3, or Pionair as British European Airways termed it, became the standard aircraft on a weekday service from Glasgow

In 1936, a Rolls-Royce was provided, free of charge, by Northern and Scottish Airways Ltd. to convey passengers to the airport at Renfrew, 'North Britain'. The Moths and Spartan Cruisers landed on a grass strip at Glenegedale, or sometimes at Duich (Weir, *Guide to Islay*).

to Campbeltown and Islay. Occasional experiments were made with different route patterns, especially in summer, when an evening service was provided on some days. The DC-3 was replaced by the turbo-prop Herald in 1962 and smaller Herons used on the Tiree, Barra and ambulance services occasionally provided additional flights to Islay.

The 1960s were almost as confusing in the air over Islay as they were on the ferry services. The main difference was that the ferry question was essentially a matter of how best to meet the needs of Islay and the nearby islands; in the air the main problem was how to integrate the Islay service economically with other BEA services. In the mid-1960s BEA's primary concern seemed to be the standardisation of its fleet. Expensive runway strengthening and terminal extensions were made at Glenegedale and other Highland airports so that the Herald could be replaced in 1966 by the Viscount. Less than ten years later the reorganised British Airways abandoned this policy in favour of a more frequent service to Islay and similar places with a special fleet of smaller Islanders or Skyliners which, to put it mildly, required less runway than the Viscount. The Skyvans were not popular and in 1976 British Airways handed the Hebridean services over to Loganair. The latter provided a more frequent service, this time using small Islanders, Trislanders and the occasional 30-seater SD330. Loganair subsequently flew under British Midland, British Airways and FlyBe livery, with varied aircraft. Regrettably a pilot was killed and several islanders were injured when the service plane crashed near Kilbride outside Port Ellen in 1986.

It is possible to see in these frequent changes an echo of the ferry debate: did Islay (or other islands) need a large, comparatively infrequent but comfortable aircraft, or should the emphasis be on simplicity, frequency and cheapness? Besides the regular services operated by successive airlines, what has become Islay Airport has other traffic in private charter flights of specialist holidaymakers, distillery company flights and other private users including jet-owning lairds. In 2010 Hebridean Airways started an Oban and Colonsay service. The peak in passenger numbers was in 1966 when almost 20,000 used the airport, but ten years later the figure was just half, perhaps a reflection of the improved ferry services, but also perhaps of rapidly increasing air fares.[25] Despite certain islander concessions, including accompanied NHS patients, the numbers of passengers this century declined to a few thousand, although multi-million pound investment had upgraded the teminal, runways and operational and safety equipment.

The Scottish Air Ambulance Service carried its first passenger from the island in 1934, although air travel had been used in an emergency a year earlier. One of the pioneers of the service, Captain David Barclay, had a close association with Islay and a plaque in the terminal building marks his retirement in 1965. Another plaque marks one of the service's few fatal accidents, when, in September 1957, an incoming air ambulance crashed into the nearby muir, killing the crew and the volunteer nursing sister. In April 1973 responsibility for providing the ambulance service was transferred from the then British Airways to Loganair and Islanders replaced the Herons. This century the yellow Islander and occasionally, helicopter are called out. Patients include maternity cases (some babies being born in the air, the rest in Paisley, although births are registered as belonging to the island), victims of industrial and road accidents and others requiring more specialist or urgent treatment than the local hospital at Bowmore can provide.[26] An annual Air Show became one of the island's summer attractions in the 2000s, attracting up to a couple of thousand observers with displays from World War I canvas-covered craft to NATO bombers and surveillance aircraft.

Internal communications

Until the twentieth century, many an islander probably knew less about a village on the other side of the island than about the world beyond, gleaned from exiled relatives' letters. Despite this, the improvement of communications within Islay became a continuing theme from the seventeenth century onwards. The overwhelming emphasis was on roads and their associated bridges. Like other Hebridean islands, Islay had its belated share of railway mania, though no serious proposals resulted. *The Guide to Islay* published in 1900 is typical:

> There is no island on the west coast better suited for the purpose of a light railway than Islay. Such a line, running from Portnahaven to Port Ellen, would speedily develop and largely benefit the fishing, the agricultural, and the other industries of the island . . . With suitable pier accommodation at Portnahaven and Bowmore, and with an accelerated service of steamers and trains between Islay and Glasgow, the material prosperity of the island could be vastly increased. Improved travelling facilities would attract many tourists to visit the Queen of the Hebrides.[27]

It was, after all, not very far from Islay to Kintyre, where the Campbeltown and Machrihanish railway had begun operating in 1877.[28] Embanking even appears to have been begun, along the line of the A846 between Port Ellen and Bowmore.[29]

Another form of internal link that has been of small significance is the ferry. Loch Indaal may have appeared an obvious place for such a facility and in the past Skiba and then Port Charlotte were linked with Laggan or Gartbreck in this way, but the potential demand was probably always small. Only between Port Wemyss and Orsay Island were connections essential throughout the period when lighthouse families lived there.

Grouped settlements were linked by foot and cart tracks and the vestiges of these can still be found, as along the tracks on the southern side of the Oa, and on the north side of the 'Glen', tracks that once served several hundred people. These tracks were used both by people and by animals, with belongings carried in creels or panniers. Even narrower were the drove 'roads' across Islay and Jura to the mainland. Traces of these can also be found, for example between Proaig and Storakaig.

Towards the end of the seventeenth century, tracks or roads of a kind that would be recognisable today became more important. Partly this was due to a gradual increase in the number of wheeled vehicles on Islay; partly also because the island was required to respond in some manner to Scottish, then British legislation on road building. Acts of the Scottish Parliament

Neil Macgibbon's precursor of today's coaches waits at Bowmore's old post office in Shore Street (Museum of Islay Life).

Western Ferries' overnight transport revolution meant that roads were inadequate and bridges too narrow and low. This bridge linking sylvan parts of Islay Estate over the A846 had to be raised to enable container vehicles to deliver to the distilleries, but was subsequently removed in the 1990s.

in 1669 and 1670 attempted to initiate road building and maintenance programmes, statutorily based on labour for a number of days each year by all the local male population, together with a rudimentary management system to organise the work and to enforce the obligations.[30] However, this Scottish legislation was only partially effective in the country as a whole and in the Hebrides it had even less effect. By 1718 so little progress had been made with highways in Scotland that the new united parliament at Westminster found it necessary to pass an act for 'Amending and making more effectual the Laws for repairing the Highways, Bridges and Ferries in that part of Great Britain called Scotland'. One of the main functions performed by the Stent meeting on Islay was roads supervision. Some records of the way it discharged this duty have been published for the periods 1714 to 1843, but others are still in manuscript form.[31] Entries in the *Stent Book* record the appointment of overseers to ensure that road work was done, the dates when 'roads be wrought', usually three days in summer and three after harvest, and the amount of money that would be 'stented' or levied. As elsewhere, the practice of such work on the roads by the inhabitants tended to decline during the early-nineteenth century, being replaced by a money payment, in effect a local road tax.

By the end of the eighteenth century, the management of the Stent meeting and the enthusiasm of the Shawfield Campbells had produced some good results. The Rev John McLeish of Kilchoman claimed that 'none of the Western Isles can boast of such good roads and bridges as Islay. The inhabitants are every year called out to work on them; and any gentleman may drive for 30 miles through the isle in his carriage. To complete the line, our communication with the main shore is kept up by a packet'.[32] The Killarow minister took much the same line, noting that 'the roads in Islay are carried on to great perfection. Those already finished are excellent, particularly from the Sound of Islay to Bowmore, a distance of about 12 miles, wherein there are seven bridges, built with stone and lime'.[33] But in Kildalton the picture was rather different. Local enthusiasm was less and the Kildalton minister admitted that the situation was better elsewhere.

The road from Port Askaig to Bowmore was the only link of its kind on Islay at the beginning of the nineteenth century: there was no road between Bowmore and Kildalton. The Commissioners, appointed in 1802 for 'Making Roads and Building Bridges in the Highlands and Islands of Scotland, reported in June 1805 that they had received an application from Islay for financial help towards the extension of the road from Port Askaig through to Portnahaven.[34] In fact Walter Campbell of Shawfield was already at work on the project. With a contribution from the Commissioners, the work was finished by autumn 1806. The Commissioners later admitted that the road was 'made on a moderate scale, and in a manner very inferior to our other roads, but it is sufficient for its purpose and situation'.[35] Meanwhile, links from Bowmore to Kildalton were still inadequate. For a long time the Big Strand along Laggan Bay had provided the most obvious route for those who needed to make the journey. After about 1818 this was gradually replaced by a road some distance inland from the shore. The official records, especially the manuscript minute books of the Islay District Road Trustees, contain details of other improvements and the building of farm access and other roads, most of them planned by the laird or his factor.[36]

When the next *Statistical Account* was published in the 1840s, the quantity and quality of the roads and bridges in the different parishes did not preoccupy the ministers in their reports. This is not to say, however, that the islanders were content and tenants in Glenchatadale or 'The Glen' petitioned Walter Frederick Campbell to improve their road connections with the other populous parts of the island.[37] By this time a new set of circumstances had appeared. The bad harvests and potato disease made road-making a means of providing necessary employment rather than a response to economic and social needs. Based on a survey of 1841–2, commissioned by Walter Frederick Campbell, a new road line from Port Ellen to Bridgend was considered at a special meeting of the Road Trustees in 1845.[38] It was as a result of this that the long and straight road now known as the 'High Road' came into existence. Work on it continued despite the Shawfield sequestration; in July 1852 it was reported:

> The Trustee on the Estate of Islay, and the Highland Relief Committee having entered into an arrangement last Autumn for employing the industrious poor – The sum of Three hundred pounds stg. was given them for that purpose . . . this sum has been expended in forwarding the construction of the new line of road from Bridgend to Port Ellen, and nearly three miles have been formed during the season.[39]

The incoming Morrisons then contributed to the road's completion. By the time Argyll County Council assumed responsibility for the main roads in the late-nineteenth century, the present network was largely in place. It remained generally adequate for the needs of the island until the arrival of the *Sound of Islay* brought in the era of increasingly larger and heavier vehicles, necessitating the alterations to the Port Askaig hill and the removal of the estate bridge at Bridgend which were the first of a series of improvements for the increasing volume of traffic.

The mails and telecommunications
One of the main justifications for the establishment of a regular sailing packet in the second half of the eighteenth century was the need for a reliable

mail service between Islay and the mainland. Postal communications for the islands of Jura and Islay appear to have lagged some way behind their development in other islands.[40] At a Stent meeting in July 1744 it was agreed that 'its necessar a post office be Erected in this Country'.[41] For the rest of the eighteenth century the *Stent Book* contains occasional references indicating that a fairly continuous mail service was maintained. The main problem was the same as that experienced elsewhere: the difficulty of collecting the dues on each letter. Before the prepaid postage of the 1840s the recipient paid the cost and if the postmaster was unable to collect, he had already performed the work involved.

The 1798 Stent meeting described the mail service. The Bowmore postmaster was recommended to dispatch a runner (presumably on horseback) to Port Askaig on each Monday from Candlemas (early February) to Lammas (early August) at 4 o'clock in the afternoon, and from Lammas to Candlemas at 2 o'clock in the afternoon, the difference taking into account the shorter winter daylight. There was some unwillingness, especially in Kildalton, to take on postal duties, because of the difficulties of collecting the fees. The Stent records of 1810 described one attempted solution:

> In order to enable the Letter receiver to draw his postages regulary [sic], it is recommended that a List of Letters not taken up be placed upon the Kirk Door of a Sunday, and after this intimation and after holding the letters over eight days, he is . . . to return the Letters in Course to Bowmore, to the Postmaster there.[42]

The publicity was probably intended to be both a reminder to other addressees and a mild blacklist for the information of others.

Not long after this, postal services became wholly the responsibility of the Post Office from its grand headquarters in London. By 1826 there were postmasters at Port Askaig, Bowmore, Lagavulin, Kilchoman and Portnahaven.[43] In the 1830s Islay was getting three posts a week by the Keills – Jura – Port Askaig overland route, with an additional once-weekly steamboat from Glasgow carrying mail and other packages not paying postage.[44] As new villages were built, additional post offices became necessary and changes in the British postal system after the 1840 Act had their effect on the postal services to and within the island.[45] By the middle of the century David Macbrayne Ltd received its first mail-carrying contract for Islay, whose address was to remain 'via Greenock, North Britain' well into the twentieth century. Caledonian MacBrayne is still an official mail carrier, as is the airline. Post was first carried to the island by air in March 1937 when the steamer *Pioneer* had a mishap.[46] Within Islay there are post buses and mail vans as well as a passenger bus service.

Telegraphs reached Islay in the later-nineteenth century. The island was first connected to the mainland by submarine telegraph in 1871; telegraph offices were subsequently established in the main villages.[47] Thus appeared the first of the overhead wires that, a century or so later, became a focus of island outcry on amenity and environmental grounds; they are mostly still evident, and liable to damage during gales and storms. The first telephone link to the mainland was established on 19 September 1935, with a number of local exchanges providing the customary friendly and informative Hebridean service.[48] They were replaced on 22 October 1974 by a centralised facility in Port Ellen, as the island was linked to the national Subscriber Trunk Dialling system, subsequently digitally upgraded.

A close rival to the ferry service in controversy and complaints in the 1960s and 1970s was the vexed question of radio and television reception on the island, especially in regard to the BBC licence fee, paid for what seemed to be inferior reception. Not surprisingly, the island was often a 'fringe' area for both radio and television reception. For many years, and despite considerable ingenuity, much of the island had to make do with television from transmitters in Ulster, although neither the BBC nor the commercial channel acknowledged such eavesdropping in its programme content such as local news. After 1980, transmitters were erected which provided television and VHF programmes on a more dependable basis to most of the population of Islay. The biggest transformation, however, came with satellite and broadband masts.

Apart from the very small needs of telegraph and telephone services, electricity on Islay was generated privately. The North of Scotland Hydro-Electric Board took over the RAF diesel station outside Bowmore in 1949: this has been enlarged several times and still acts as a back-up facility although the island was linked to the mainland grid in 1962 by a modern version of the overland route through Jura. By the last decade of the twentieth century, the ageing system was causing power surges and interruptions, through technical faults, adverse weather conditions for overhead cables or disruptions for upgrading. A small, experimental wave station near Claddich on the southern tip of the Rinns was developed with sponsorship by Queen's University, Belfast, with output linked into the National Grid in 1991; this was demolished and replaced further north by a larger one operated by WaveGen. Wind power was mooted several times on the island in the 1990s without result, but by the second decade of this century offshore wind arrays beyond Tiree, and Islay and Machrihanish (subsequently withdrawn) on Kintyre were promoted by the Scottish and United Kingdom governments as part of their ambitious renewable energy targets, while the tides of the sound of Islay were harnessed for electricity generation.

Notes and references

[1]   See M. H. B. Sanderson, *Scottish Rural Society in the Sixteenth Century*, (Edinburgh, 1982), *passim*; in John Leyden's *Journal of a Tour in the Highlands and Western Islands of Scotland in1800*, (ed.), James Sinton (Edinburgh, 1903) mention is made of competition between the dukes of Argyll and the Campbells of Shawfield as to the best cattle bred and exported from the west.

[2]   E. R. Cregeen, 'Recollections of an Argyleshire Drover', *Scottish Studies* 3 (1959), p. 143.

[3]   The Commissioners for the Highland Roads and Bridges planned this road, the one from Portnahven to Bridgend, and piers on Jurs in the first decade of the nineteenth century (See their *Annual Reports*, BPP).

[4]   For this and next references see *Stent Book*, pp. 68ff.

[5]   Information on shipping was obtained from C. L. D. Duckworth and G. E. Langmuir, *West Highland Steamers*, (Prescot, 1967) and Nick S. Robins and Donald E. Meek, *The Kingdom of Macbrayne*, (Edinburgh, 2006). Other sources include the *OSA* and *NSA*, J. Lumsden and Son's *Steam-Boat Companions* and various Murray timetables.

[6]   *Argyleshire NSA*, pp. 656–8.

[7]   *Coleraine Chronicle*, 18 September, 1875.

[8]   *Oban Times*, 17 February 1900, p. 5.

[9]   *Scottish Field*, June 1971.

[10] A variety of sources has been used in this section on transport changes: reports of the Highland Transport Board and of the Highlands and Islands Development Board; occasional material produced by the Islay Transport Users' Consultative Committee.

[11] A. Wilson, *The Sound of Silence* (Glasgow, n.d. [1975]), and *The Sound of the Clam*, (Glasgow, n.d. [1975]), and news reports in *The Glasgow Herald*, *The Ileach*, *The Oban Times* and *The Scotsman*.

[12] J. Anderson, *An Account of the Present State of the Hebrides and Western Coasts of Scotland*, Edinburgh, 1785), p. 9.

[13] Brian Lambkin, 'The wreck of the *Exmouth* on Islay, 1847; a window on Emigration from north-West Ulster during the Great Famine', in *A Land that Lies Westward*, pp. 123–148; J. Wiggins, *The Exmouth of Newcastle 1981?–1847. The story of an Irish Emigrant Ship wrecked on the Scottish Isle of Islay* (Bowmore, n.d.).

[14] Quoted in (ed.), Rosemary Goring, *Scotland. The Autobiography* (London, 2007), pp. 245–6.

[15] The archives of Islay Estate and the Museum of Islay Life contain official and unofficial correspondence relating to the 1918 disasters and their aftermath, and the museum displays some of later divers' findings. Other sources are the Admiralty and the National Maritime Museum. See Steve Boardman, *Dive Islay*, (Stoke on Trent, 1986), Peter Moir and Ian Crawford, *Argyll Shipwrecks*, (Wemyss Bay, 1994), and (HMSO) *British Vessels Lost at Sea, 1914–1918*, reprint, Stephens, (Cambridge, 1977). BBC Radio Scotland, 'When the Boats Went Down', 29 August 2007.

[16] Anderson, *Account*, p. 9.

[17] Report of the Commissioners of Northern Lighthouses, *BPP*, 1833, XXXIII, 65.

[18] Ibid., *BPP*, 1836, XLV, 308.

[19] Information from Commissioners of Northern Lighthouses, Edinburgh.

[20] Report of the Commissioners of Northern Lighthouses, *BPP*, 1846, XLIV, 400.

[21] Annual Reports of the Royal National Lifeboat Institution provided much of this information.

[22] Communication from HM Coastguard, Islay, 1980.

[23] D. J. Smith, *Scottish Action Stations 7: Military Airfields of Scotland, the North-East and Northern Ireland*, (Wellingborough, 1989), pp. 56–7 and 172–3. See Crown Film Unit, *Coastal Command*, now on video, DD 985.

[24] A memorial plaque with names of those who lost their lives was erected in 2010 at Blackrock. A description of the crash by Alan Deller (subsequently squadron leader), was published in the *Ileach* of 5 June 2010. Sadly, Deller's age of ninety-five prevented his unveiling the plaque. Three airmen, including the captain, Jack Lever, survived; three others are buried in Bowmore.

[25] *Scottish Abstract of Statistics* 8 (1979), p. 170.

[26] I. Hutchison, *Air Ambulance*, (Erskine, 1996).

[27] J. G. MacNeill, *The New Guide to Islay*, (Glasgow, 1900), p. 22.

[28] N. S. C. Macmillan, *The Campbeltown and Machrihanish Light Railway*, (Glasgow, 1970).

[29] Letter from L. Collin, *Oban Times*, 24 August 1978.

[30] D. G. Moir, 'The Roads of Scotland: The Statute Labour Roads', *Scottish Geographical Magazine* 73 (1957), pp. 101–10 and pp. 167–75.

[31] *Stent Book*; Minute Books of the Islay District Road Trustees, Islay Estate Papers.

[32] *Argyleshire NSA*, p. 282.

[33] *Ibid.*, p. 302.

[34] Report of the Commissioners for making Roads and Bridges in the Highlands and Islands of Scotland, *BPP*, 1805, III, 278.

[35] Reports . . . Roads and Bridges, *BPP*, 1805, III, 237–8; 1814–15, III, 432; 1817, IX, 10 and 1821, X, 54.

[36] Islay Estate Paper, Minute Books of the Islay District Road Trustees.

[37] Islay Estate Papers, Petition from tenants of Glenchatadale.

[38] Islay Estate Papers, Road Survey and Minute Books.

[39] Islay Estate Papers, Minute Books.

[40] A. R. B. Haldane, *Three Centuries of Scottish Posts*, (Edinburgh, 1971), p. 191. J. R. Henderson, *Post Offices in Scotland*, (Edinburgh, 1966). The Post Office archives, St Martins-le-Grand, London, provided background information on this section.

[41] *Stent Book*, pp. 28–9 for this and following references.

[42] *Book of Islay*, p. 187.

[43] Post Office archives.

[44] Haldane, *Three Centuries of Scottish Posts*, p. 192.

[45] See J. A. Mackay, *Island Postal History Series No. 10: Islay, Jura and the other Argyll Islands*, (Dumfries, 1979).

[46] *The Glasgow Herald*, 12 March 1937.

[47] Post Office archives, St Martins le Grand, London.

[48] Inaugural pamphlet, Museum of Islay Life.

CHAPTER 14

Prospect

The tenor of much that was written in the last chapter of previous editions of this book has remained little changed. Nevertheless, changes in the economy, landscape and society have taken place, and at an accelerating pace. Agricultural adjustments, related to national, European and global conditions, visibly affected island farming, landscape, farmers and their wives. Recession or expansion continued to characterise the whisky industry. Islay hit the national and international headlines with controversies over conservation and development issues, especially those related to proposed peat extraction at Duich Moss, which became oversimplified as geese and dragonflies versus jobs. Arguments ran for years between the protection of wild geese and farmers' needs for early grass for their stock, or issues between seals and fishermen. Fiscal forestry and various environmental issues extended this debate. Bases were established on the island by the Nature Conservancy Council, later Scottish Natural Heritage, and the Royal Society for the Protection of Birds. A short-lived Islay Land Use Forum was set up with a remit to 'promote the social and economic needs and the reasonable aspirations of the Islay people as regards the use of the land of Islay, and at the same time sustain the outstanding quality of Islay's natural resources, while recognising and accommodating the roles and obligations of the various agencies which affect the land use on the island'. Prototype wave and tidal energy stations were promoted and constructed with little controversy, onshore and offshore wind proposals inevitably moreso. The perennial ferry debates continued while vessels, infrastructure and services gradually improved. After a generation, it once more became possible to spend summer Wednesdays on the neighbouring islands of Colonsay and Oronsay. Jura's frequent service to and from Islay was supplemented from 2008 by a summer passenger service to and from the mainland. A summer ferry link was also renewed briefly between Ballycastle in Northern Ireland and Campbeltown in Kintyre.

If there are lessons to be learned from the last few centuries in Islay, the principal one is surely the importance of chance and the consequent folly of trying to predict the future with confidence. If, for instance, John Campbell of Cawdor had sought financial advice rather earlier than he did, or even if he had followed the advice that he did receive in 1723, it seems probable that the island could have remained longer in the hands of the Cawdor family. It is certainly most unlikely that it would have passed so easily into the possession of Daniel Campbell of Shawfield. Yet if the Shawfield Campbells had not become the principal landlords on Islay for over a century, the economy, landscape, society, and even the size of the present population would probably all be very different. The characteristic villages would almost certainly not be so numerous and they might have a much less attractive appearance. The landholding system would probably have followed a revolution more characteristic of other parts of the Highlands and Islands, with clearances for sheep and deer grazing and the establishment of crofting townships. In other words, Islay would probably be a Hebridean example rather than a Hebridean exception.[1]

Similarly, the difficulties with the potato crop, the rent arrears and the financial troubles that beset Walter Frederick Campbell of Shawfield and Islay in the decades leading to his bankruptcy in the middle of the nineteenth century were probably less those of an absentee landlord, generally believed to have created many of the Highlands and Islands problems, than by the fact that he had few external resources left on which to draw as population and problems mounted. The turn of events that brought the Campbells to Islay and those that removed them were largely unpredictable and both had results of fundamental importance for Islay. It would be foolish to pretend that similar unpredictable events cannot occur again – chaos theory makes allowance for events such as the 1996 BSE cattle crisis or the financial and economic jolts and turmoils from 2007–8. The financial competence or otherwise of a landlord or his agents is still likely to be crucial, but, as in the past, the more Islay's economy and society interact with a wider Scotland, a wider Britain, a wider Europe and the rest of the world, the more the island's future is shaped by external trends and events.

Islay and the Highland Problem
One of the significant characteristics of Islay until the 1980s was a relative lack of concern about the future. The symptoms of collective worry about economic decline, depopulation, diminution of services and facilities and so on, that were evident in many parts of the Highlands and Islands, were not entirely absent from Islay, but were miniscule in comparison to many other islands and remote Highland areas. This was evident in the ferry

controversy; the debate was not tinged with fears that the island's links with the mainland were weakening. Instead, the argument was about the best way to strengthen these links, albeit including some intra-island rivalry. Another sign of the general lack of concern was the fact that the island had not been the subject of one of those semi-official 'surveys' commissioned for, or by, other islands. Elsewhere, a general sense of malaise often led to a request that a university or other source of supposed wisdom or experience investigate in depth the nature of the problem and provide guidance on how it might be approached and solved. The present author had been involved in surveys of this kind, but the point is that that they were not then felt necessary for Islay.[2] Although, human nature being what it is, it is doubtful whether more than a small minority of any population would declare themselves completely content, there appeared to exist a justifiable awareness that Islay's problems were small by comparison with those elsewhere. The present book, evidently, is not an 'investigation of the roots of the present discontent in Islay' so much as an explanation of why there was, and is, so much on the island to admire and be grateful for. Travel features across the media still refer to the island's 'enchantment'.

This satisfaction appeared to be evident as far away as the then virtual seat of Scottish government in St Andrew's House in Edinburgh and in the Highlands and Islands Development Board in Inverness. Naturally it was more muted in these places even than on Islay itself, lest the charge be made that central government was almost ignoring the island. In 1966 the Scottish Development Department in Edinburgh produced a White Paper entitled *The Scottish Economy 1965–1980: A Plan for Expansion*. Although the document has in many ways been superseded, the thinking it represented has still never been taken on board and followed through. The White Paper was a United Kingdom landmark in the long and continuing analysis of disparities in performance and opportunities between one region and another. Instead of taking those disparities as congenital and devising new or enlarged programmes of government assistance as palliatives, the White Paper argued that it was time to recognise that many of the problems had arisen because of attitudes towards the Highlands and Islands that were outdated and unreal:

> The Highlands and Islands are very different from any other region of the United Kingdom. Much earlier work on them takes this difference as a reason for treating the region as something *sui generis*, justifying its own set of standards and insulation from criteria applied elsewhere in Britain. This tendency was fed both by Highland feeling itself and hardly less by outside sentiment which would preserve a distinctive Highland way of

life. Undeniable benefits have been won as a result of special treatment. But it is arguable that in the long run the Highlands have lost more than they have gained.[3]

Implicitly and occasionally explicitly, the White Paper made it clear that government policy towards the Highlands and Islands was henceforth to be based on a much more realistic appraisal of the social and economic potential of different parts of the area. Since governments exist primarily to serve people, the distribution of the population and its age composition, are among the key factors influencing the nature of government policy. The White Paper went on to list thirteen zones in the Highlands and Islands where the social and economic prospects seemed reasonably bright, along with two other areas in adjacent counties. These fifteen areas then comprised nearly four-fifths of the population and nearly three-quarters of the unemployed in the Highlands and Islands and adjacent areas; they also contained higher proportions of younger people than the areas omitted. Of the 125 islands off the Scottish coast that were inhabited in 1971, only five had over 5,000 people (Lewis/Harris, mainland Shetland, mainland Orkney, Bute and Skye) and only a further ten had between 1,000 and 5,000. Of the remainder, 93 had less than 200 inhabitants each, including twenty lighthouse islands.[4]

The point about the White Paper's view of regional development policy was the middle position that Islay occupied in the official mind. It was not one of the fifteen communities listed in the 1966 White Paper as being a potential centre of continued prosperity and growth. It was assumed that the relatively static 'normally resident' population was not in decline; the island was more characteristic of the areas designated as 'holding' or 'stable' areas. In this situation Islay was the target neither for major government action to encourage development, nor for similar action to arrest or manage decline. Although Islay's ferry and other problems no doubt came before the attention of St Andrew's House and the Highlands and Islands Development Board, the problems were tackled individually as they arose, without the need for a comprehensive strategy.

If indeed this was the official view, then some parallels could be drawn with the situation of Islay during the 1840s. At that time, a series of government enquiries and initiatives sought to establish the need for help to avert famine in the Highlands and Islands and to provide some assistance in creating employment. Throughout much of the decade, the official view was that the island was fortunate in having a landlord who 'has the character of being at all times disposed to . . . attending to the people's wants'.[5] This view was shared to some extent by the landlord himself: although he became increasingly anxious to receive government assistance, he was reluctant to see it accompanied by any restrictions on his own freedom of action. Eventually it became evident that the sensibilities of Walter Frederick Campbell were less important than his ability, or inability, to attend to his people's needs. In the 1960s and 1970s, as in the 1840s, there were many parts of the Highlands and Islands with more serious and more urgent problems than those that confronted Islay. Was this sufficient justification for the general feeling of complacency that tended to exist both on Islay and at the official level? Islay was in a rather more fortunate position than many other areas in the Highlands and Islands and, therefore, St Andrew's House and the Highlands and Islands Development Board could afford to treat it, if not with 'benign neglect', at least with only a relatively small input of effort and finance.

The economy of Islay, as anywhere else, consists of a complex relationship involving a number of fairly distinct, but interrelated, elements. Some of these are primary, in that they are at least partly related to the resources of the island, such as agriculture, fishing, distilling, sport and tourism based on the island's environmental and cultural attractions. Others, such as construction or freight carriers, depend on the existence of a particular level of population and on the income and spending capacity of that population. Employment in agriculture is unlikely to represent a significant basis for expansion in the future. The output of Islay's farms is dependent on the policies of the wider world and the income of the farmer is unlikely to be increased by an expansion in the number of those who work for that farmer; quite the reverse. The situation is scarcely more sanguine in relation to fishing. Islay's relatively good transport links enable it to cater for the growth in demand for lobsters, crabs, clams and other shellfish, exported to London markets and others, particularly in southern Europe. It may well be that in a relatively short space of time what may be described as the 'hunting and gathering' phase of such shellfish collection may yield to more organised 'farming', as in the oyster production of Loch Gruinart, or fish farming, though the employment generated is likely to be small, as is that for sport fishing. The world's capacity to absorb ever-increasing amounts of whisky may continue to increase, with more public relations, advertising and sales people employed beyond the island. The production has, on the whole, been achieved with fewer island employees and increased automation although the ancillary tours, retail outlets and cafés have boosted employment, particularly for women. Other manufacturing in Islay tends to be small in terms both of output and of employment. The creamery and fish factory disappeared along with their grants, and other small crafts concerns and ventures trading on the island's name have likewise turned out financially precarious before folding. However, a regenerated Islay House Square supports crafts outlets and a brewery while the Islay Woollen Mill continues and a boatyard has been successfully launched. Demand and quality in the tourism sector improved, coffee shops and restaurants established and accommodation upgraded. A youth hostel and a field centre were opened at Port Charlotte. Another museum opened, this time at Finlaggan, the intensive archaeological investigations there producing exciting finds. Islay High School has been much extended, although some people mistake its quirky pagodas for an extension to the nearby Bowmore distillery. Attractively laid-out social housing and homes for the elderly were provided in the two villages by various agencies. Houses in the villages and the rural areas were reconstructed or rehabilitated, sensitively on the whole in the villages, often less so elsewhere. Islay airport and Port Askaig and Port Ellen piers were expensively upgraded, and various marinas installed for the more frequent ferries, freight carriers and island fishing fleet; likewise roads, parking, pavements, street lighting, water supplies and broadband availability. Combining IT with further education and training, could provide a fillip to employment on the island, given upgraded electricity.

The last decade of the twentieth century and the first of the next, witnessed considerable inputs of effort and national and European finance. National training and employment initiatives complemented the increased involvement of successive developments boards, companies and councils. Perhaps it is easier for islanders to monitor the outputs of such initiatives. These same islanders are not only taxpayers but the island also contributes disproportionately to the national exchequer in excise duties. Grant mentalities, profligate expenditures, short-lived developments and social schemes of unlikely potential often swallowed up to seven figure sums each before inevitably expiring. Many were conceived by 'outsiders' who often decided that an island was the ideal for a study, experiment, work experience or whatever (and more interesting to visit than problem areas in the cities). Alternatively ill-conceived 'bottom up' initiatives with little context were, and are, just as likely to be wasteful and doomed.

The growth of the public sector also produced more 'service' employment, especially for women, as have increasing visitor numbers (especially whisky enthusiasts) and activities. In the 1980s women were prominent in many positions in Islay, including the member of parliament, regional councillors, head teacher, doctors, vets, church ministers, editors and hoteliers Despite this, at the start of the last decade of the twentieth century, between two and three times as many men as women had full-time work and this created a restriction on the size of family income. Then, only about two-fifths of the women over sixteen were 'economically active', two-fifths of these being in part-time employment. More and more women, single and married, wanted paid employment such as was available to their counterparts in mainland towns and cities. The 2001 census already showed further improvement, while both sexes were often characterised by juggling several part-time jobs. Towards the end of the first decade of this century, with national and global financial disarray, however, family income was once more threatened by loss of employment for both men and women. However, if more 'staycations' are taken instead of foreign holidays, tourism being Scotland's premier industry in the second decade of the century, an obvious activity where growth is to be anticipated is in meeting service and leisure demands. Though many would challenge the thesis and its implications, such demands could cause changes to an island of finite size that could be as profound as those achieved by the Shawfield Campbells and others in previous centuries.

Although there are few formal recreational facilities provided for visitors, apart from the golf course and the tennis, bowling, putting and pitch-and-putt facilities at Port Ellen, there is much informal activity. Evening entertainment for visitors and islanders includes dinners, dances, ceilidhs, concerts, and other gigs, often involving fund-raising for some island charity or activity. The principal island events are the Islay Gaelic Mod in May, the Malt and Music Feis Ìle in May, the Sheep-dog Trials in July, the Kildalton Cross Golf Championship and the Agricultural Show in August, jazz and book festivals in September, fêtes, beach rugby and sports-days, ploughing matches, poultry shows, sailing regattas, and sea-angling competitions. The normal activities of the islanders in their many and various clubs, societies, schools, church and secular organisations, carry on throughout much of the year, except foootball, which is played in summer. In poor weather, in common with many less-developed holiday areas there is still a lack of choice of daytime activities for visitors, but the Mactaggart Leisure Centre, opened in 1991, is enjoyed by residents and visitors alike, as is the community garden at Bridgend. In the 1980s, too, the work of *An Commun Gaidhealach* Meur Ìle was supplemented by that of the Islay Gaelic Working Party, set up with the help of *Comunn na Gaidhlig*. Sadly, the highly successful international Rinns Festival, which attracted Breton, Irish, Manx, Welsh and other Celtic artistes, is no longer. The lighthouse keepers on offshore Orsay Island, however, probably enjoyed the gigs of Runrig and Wolfstone at Portnahaven Hall during Feis Ìle as much as the rest of us did. The Islay Arts Association has brought many different kinds of professional performances to the island since the mid-1980s, playing to enthusiastic audiences for performances ranging from alternative theatre, comedy, dance and Scottish Opera Go Round. Special interest holidays have expanded, based on wildlife, diving and golf. There are still rather few goods handcrafted on the island, despite the creation in 1980 of the Islay Arts and Crafts Guild, but there are some specialist shops, unlike the general Hebridean trend, where shops are usually multi-purpose. Most of the distilleries now have visitor centres, tours and impressive sales points, as does the Islay Woollen Mill.

The island, like mainland Argyll, continued to raise exceptional amounts of charitable monies, from individuals, trusts and grant awarding bodies including six-figure sums to renovate the Round Church in Bowmore and to open a leisure centre, including a swimming pool, in a former whisky bonded warehouse in Bowmore in 1991. Fund-raising for long-established charities such as the Royal National Lifeboat Institution and medical charities has been extended by new activities supplanting the Lions, and the Round Table.

Scenarios for change

What threats to the fabric of Islay economy, landscape and society are conceivable in the future, and what alternative opportunities might arise? Any views expressed are inevitably personal ones and others may well argue that the emphasis is wrong, or that quite different factors will be the key ones in determining Islay's future. So much the better: what is important is that the island's future should be discussed, debated and, ultimately, planned. 'Development' could profoundly change the present character of Islay, though it need not, given careful planning, be disastrous to the economy, society or the environment. Perhaps the biggest change however, has to be in the islanders' awareness of, and increasing knowledge of, their island. In storms, 'the mainland's been cut off' may still pass from lip to lip, cheerily or otherwise, but while there is a greater understanding and realisation of Islay's role in the United Kingdom, Europe and beyond than there appeared to be in the early 1980s, and while there is also more concern over the social problems and social fabric of the islands, with increased personal mobility and more incomers settling, there is a profound democratic deficit. Debate on the island's future has to be more focused and more vigilant through its fortnightly newspaper, The *Ileach*, begun in 1973, and also in other more structured fora.[6]

At this point one has to ask the classical question *cui bono*? Who benefits? There are many who would argue that the benefits that major developments would bring to Islay would be far outweighed by the disadvantages, that the benefits would be concentrated in a few people on Islay, or financiers outwith the island, and that those who have lived their whole lives on the island would encounter most of the disadvantages. It is not difficult to make a strong case for the argument that the present relative tranquillity and prosperity of Islay are precious attributes that should be protected at all costs. Such a view is not solely a selfish one. It might well be supported by a majority of the fairly silent population and it is difficult to deny that in deciding the future of the island the views of the present Ilich should be paramount.[7] At least three different scenarios can be sketched that need to be analysed and compared with each other.

The first scenario is one that is based on the attempt to maintain the present lifestyle and character of Islay. Residents will be on their guard to challenge revolutionary changes, as distinct from evolutionary ones. Proposals for new developments, whether related to 140 offshore wind turbines each 150 metres high with thousands of helicopter movements, consequent onshore and other housing developments, a golf resort or whatever, will be looked at with a jaundiced eye, until Islay is convinced that the development in question is compatible in scale with those things that are most valued in the present situation. The notion of sustainable development is a valid one.

A second and quite different scenario would recognise the value that Islay would gain from the addition of new elements to its economy in the form of well-planned but highly-capitalised ventures, concentrated into a few areas. To varying degrees, the Islay population would seek to encourage such growth and the main concern would be to ensure that such developments produced a net gain, that certain unique sites and irreplaceable resources were protected and that the employment involved in such developments was shared by Islay residents as well as by those coming from outside.

Although these brief outlines appear to be opposed to each other, they have one important feature in common. They both imply the development of a conscious attitude by the people of Islay towards the possibility of major change and the existence of a strategy or plan to discourage or encourage it. A third scenario is, however, much more likely and might be much more dangerous. This would be based on the assumption that changes are probable and can be dealt with on an *ad hoc* basis. It would take the view that the changes which have happened on Islay in the past few decades have on the whole been painless and desirable and that the future can be similarly left to take care of itself. There are several dangers in such an approach. The most important is that it does not really need to be adopted. If there is no conscious desire on the part of Islay's population to develop a view of what the essential elements of the island's future should be, the third scenario will inevitably unfold. The attitude may be justified: the relative tranquillity and steadily increasing prosperity that Islay has enjoyed for much of the recent decades may continue and as the expectations and aspirations of the population rise, the economy and society will develop to satisfy them. But this is not inevitable; continued stability or even decline in Islay may be accompanied by rising standards elsewhere, leading to emigration of those who wish to share in that prosperity, especially by young adults. Incomers are more likely to be older and/or with few local connections. Breeding pairs of human beings are as important as breeding birds.

Or the opposite may happen. Developments with a momentum of their own may be promoted by those with specific agendas who want to 'grow' everything, such as absentee land developers, back-scratching councillors, justificatory bureaucrats, business entrepreneurs, tourism operators and others hoping for an honour; advantages may appear, or be made to appear, considerable and it is only after the transformation has been accomplished that the problems in economy, environment, landscape and society become evident. Even without such major individual initiatives, the slow spread of small-scale activities may eventually bring on a crisis or blight that is the more difficult to solve because it cannot be traced to a single event and cannot be easily rectified. One has only to look across the North Channel to the coasts of Ireland to see the disaster that can happen in a relatively short time. Already some incongruous public and private carbuncles have appeared on the island landscape and the garden-centre suburbanisation of Islay gathers apace. Signposts proliferate, along with yellow lines, CCTV cameras and dog loos. Island society too has been changing. In several districts of Skye and Mull in 2001, the proportion of those born in England was one in three, and in one part of Islay it was approaching this figure. This is not intended to be judgmental on decibels, habits or aspirations, but to suggest the extent of change.

Some conscious collective view has to be developed for the future of the whole of the island, while there is still time to influence that future, and eliminating as far as possible unhelpful intra-island rivalries. For a population of around 3,500 there are too many overlapping organisations and committees to allow an island voice to impinge where it matters in the world outside. This dispersion of effort encourages short-termism. The natural heritage is important, locally, nationally and internationally. The pace of change in the built environment has accelerated in Islay. Aspects of island society are also changing more rapidly than before. Viewed from a world perspective, the odds during the next decades are probably tipped more in favour of change than of stability, and of accelerating change. The long-term balance between conservation and regeneration must be carefully nurtured by managing sustainable development of the interrelated natural, economic, societal and cultural heritage, including the marine environment.

Those advocating 'development' are often guilty of talking down the island, and ignoring the tenets of the 1966 White Paper. Highlands and Islands Enterprise still characterise the region as 'fragile' (with only a few areas excluded), and this word 'fragile', was emphasised in the scoping study prepared for Islay Energy Trust's approach to the proposed offshore wind array.[8] On the other hand, the same enterprise body in the 2010/2011 Ferries Review included Islay in its top six areas (Arran, Islay, Mull, Skye, Orkney and Shetland mainlands) with the highest potential to contribute to Scotland's economic growth.[9] In a separate survey in 2011 for the Islay Energy Trust on the subject of the proposed offshore wind array, the island response was miniscule at about two per cent of islanders, excluding younger schoolchildren.[10] One of the conclusions of another 'consultation' commissioned by Diageo about the same time highlighted this democratic deficit inherent in 'the lack of leadership'.[11] This remains the greatest threat and points towards the third scenario. Vertical challenges to the landscape in wind and other masts; thousands of helicopter flights annually; burgeoning numbers of visitors, motorhomes, construction workers, and an insatiable demand for housing, have to be carefully pondered: an island is, after all, a finite space.

> When I went back to Islay they all said how much the place had changed . . . what a lot had happened since then. There was the new ferry, and cattle grids instead of gates on the Glen road, and had I seen the new houses outside Ballygrant? I wouldn't know the place. In fact, it was the same old Islay, strikingly untouched. The changes which seemed so obvious to the local people . . . would not have been noticed on the mainland . . . I would not have believed how small the changes would be. Nothing had happened to destroy the important thing, Islay's quality of seeming not so much a corner of Scotland as a country in its own right.[12]

Alastair Borthwick's reaction, recorded in 1969 after he revisited the island on which he had lived for seven years in the 1950s, is clearly very different from the emphasis on change that has been the theme of this book. Perhaps if he were to return today he would be astonished at the thirty-metre high granary now dominates the skyline as the ferry approaches Port Ellen, and by the articulated vehicles that roll on and off the still larger ferries several times a day, let alone what the future might bring. But despite much of Islay life that is more 'mainland' than before, there is clearly an element of truth in Mr Borthwick's reaction. Possibly the really distinctive feature about Islay has been the capacity of the landscape and society to absorb change without destroying 'the important thing'. However, for the for the major changes in lifestyle and landscape that are ahead, indeed already beginning to happen, and with national and global economic, environmental, planning and other challenging goals, the Ilich need to be ever more vigilant to remain a Hebridean exception.[13] Our descendants deserve our stewardship: they must not ask "How could they?"

Notes and References

[1]   M. C. Storrie, 'Islay: A Hebridean Exception', *Geographical Review*, 1961, 51, pp. 87–108.

[2]   M. C. Storrie and C. I. Jackson, *Arran 1980–81: 2,021?* (Edinburgh, 1967).

[3]   *The Scottish Economy 1965–70: A Plan for Expansion*, (1966), Cmnd. 2864, p. 52.

[4]   *Census 1981, Preliminary Report*, 1981, Table 3.

[5]   *Minutes of Evidence, Select Committee on Emigration, BPP*, 1841, VI, p. 30.

[6]   The *Ileach* is available from Bowmore and online,

[7]   Since the mid-1990s the Corrom Trust and several others initiated regeneration studies in various parts of the Highlands and Islands, including Islay and Jura, using 'bottom-up' and 'SWOT' techniques, not only became repetitive, but were approached regressively, in continuing contradistinction to the views of the 1966 White Paper.

[8]   Online at islayenergytrust.org.uk. See also snh.gov.uk

[9]   Online at Scotland.gov.uk

[10]   As footnote 8

[11]   Online at liddellthomson.com

[12]   A. Borthwick, 'Return to Islay ', *Scotland's Magazine*, April 1969, p. 21.

[13]   M. C. Storrie, 'Islay: A Hebridean Exception', *GR*, 1961, 51, pp. 87–108.

Appendix A

Genealogical table for the Campbells of Shawfield and Islay, and the Morrisons of Islay.

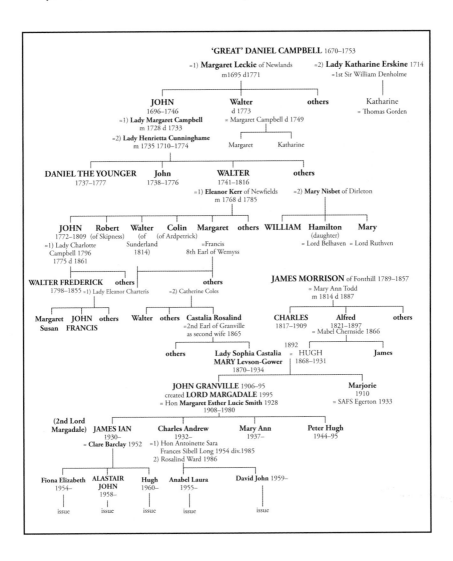

Appendix B

Chronological list of strandings, founderings or wrecks around Islay's coasts, exact location unknown.

1780s	Irish vessel	1881	*Progress*
	American vessel		*Cwmavon*
	American vessel		*Royal Arch*
1817	*Lord Wellington*		*Castle Green*
	Augustus		*Fairy*
1818	*James Hamilton*		*Leonard Hollis*
1820	*Isabella Helen*		*Rob Roy*
1827	*Commerce*		*Susannah*
1833	*Gratitude*		*Isabella Wilson*
	Margaret	1882	*Jane Gwynne*
	Industry		*Mary Stewart*
1834	*Telegraph*		*Texa*
1835	*Kitty and Mary*		*Harold*
	Julia	1883	*Nelson*
	Martin		*Lady of Lake*
1842	*Undine*	1884	*Islay*
1847	*Montcalm*		*Advance*
	Reform		*Hunter*
	Martin		*North Star*
	Ann Falcon		*Hebea*
1865	*Paramount*		*John Evans*
1867	*Falcon*		*Castle Green*
1869	*Isabella Swanson*		*Peter James*
1875	*Ella Glenesdale*		*William Hope*
1877	*Florence Muspratt*		*Louise Ann*
	Providence		*Troubadour*
1880	*Nations*		*James Kenway*
	Challenge	1885	*Islay*
	Waree or Maree	1898	*Plover*
		1934	*St Tudal*

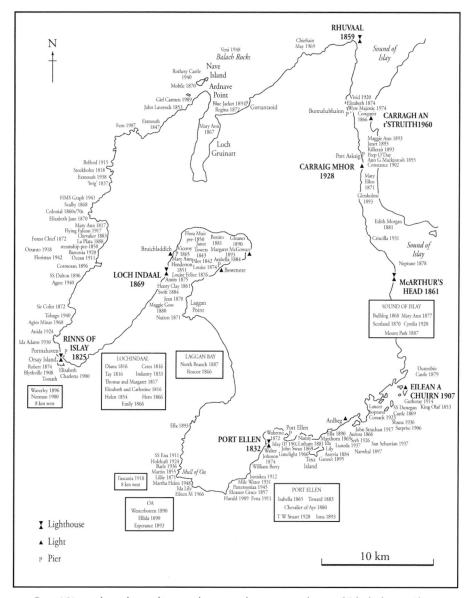

Over 250 wrecks and strandings are known to have occurred around Islay's shores. About two-thirds of these are indicated here, but no exact location is known for the remainder, listed opposite. Lives lost are in three or four figures, but successive Islay lifeboats have saved many lives since the Station was first established at Port Askaig in 1934 (Compiled from information from local sources, particularly the late Gilbert Clark of Port Charlotte and James MacAulay of Port Ellen and from official sources).

Sources

Archives

Annexed Estates Commissioners, Petitions of Daniel Campbell, Younger, of Shawfield, National Records of Scotland, E 727/60 and E 728/47.

James Anderson Papers, National Records of Scotland [NRS], Edinburgh, Advocates Papers 29.1.2.

Campbell of Jura Papers, James Brown, Report to the Creditors and General View of the Funds Realised, NRS, GD64.

Campbell of Melfort Papers, The Library of the University of Edinburgh, Mss. Dk. 73. 151.

Campbell of Shawfield and Islay: Obituaries of Walter Frederick Campbell, Special Collections, University of Glasgow Library, MU43-c.17.

Campbell of Sunderland Papers, NLS, Acc. 6223.

The Cawdor Papers are in Cawdor Castle, Nairn, and are listed in some detail in the National Register of Archives (Scotland) Survey 1400.

Clerk of Penicuik Papers, NRS, GD18.

Copies of each census enumerator's schedules for the censuses in Scotland from 1841 to 1911, NRS; online at http://www.ScotlandsPeople.

Customs and Excise, Official Correspondence, Port Ellen District, Argyll South Collection, NRS, CE81.

Gordon Cumming Papers, NLS, Dep. 175.

Historical Manuscripts Commission, *Report on the Manuscripts of Earl of Bathurst*, (London 1923).

The Islay Estate Papers are in Islay Estate Office, Bridgend, Isle of Islay, and are summarily listed in the National Register of Archives (Scotland) Survey 0123.

Lloyds of London archives.

Museums of Glasgow.

The Museum of Islay Life Archives.

National Galleries of Scotland and Scottish National Portrait Gallery.

Ordnance Survey Ms. name books, maps and plans, RCAHMS/NMRS, Edinburgh.

W. M. Playfair, Drawings, Special Collection, The Library of the University of Edinburgh.

The Post Office Archives, St Martins-le-Grand, London.

The Ramsay of Kildalton Papers are deposited on loan in the City of Glasgow Archives, TD 1284.

The Royal Highland and Agricultural Society of Scotland.

Saltoun Papers, NRS, SB74.

The School of Scottish Studies archives, The University of Edinburgh.

The Shawfield Papers in the Mitchell Library, Glasgow. These mainly relate to the period before Islay was bought by Daniel Campbell of Shawfield.

Threipland Papers, Perth and Kinross Council Archives, MS 169.

University of Cambridge, Committee for Aerial Photography.

Professor John Walker Papers, The Library of the University of Edinburgh.
Wrecks and Casualties, Register of Examinations, NRS, CE60.

Published Books

Adams, I. H. and Somerville, M., *Cargoes of Despair and Hope*, (Edinburgh, 1993).

Adams, J .and Holman, K. (eds.), *Scandinavia and Europe, 800–1350. Contact, Conflict, and Cooexistence*, (Turnhout, 2004).

Adomnàn of Iona. *Life of St Columba*, (trs. Richard Sharpe), (London, 1995).

Anderson, J., *An Account of the Present State of the Hebrides and Western Coasts of Scotland . . . being the Substance of a report to The Lords of the Treasury together with the evidence before the Committee of Fisheries*, (Edinburgh, 1785).

Arrowsmith, A., *Memoir relative to the Construction of the Map of Scotland*. Published by A. Arrowsmith in the year 1807, (London, 1809).

Bailyn, B., *Voyages to the West*, (New York, 1986).

Balfour Paul, Sir J., *The Scots Peerage*, 9 vols. (Edinburgh, 1908).

Bannerman, J. M. W., *Studies in the History of Dalriada*, (Edinburgh, 1974).

Bannerman, J. M. W., *The Beatons*, (Edinburgh, 1986).

Barnard, A., *The Whisky Distilleries of the United Kingdom*, (London, 1887).

Bastin, J., See Hill, J.

Bigwood, F., *Justices of the Peace in Argyll: processes etc. of the JP Courts, 1686–1825*, (North Berwick, 2001); *The Vice Admiral Court of Argyll. Abstracts of processs and other Court Documents, 1685–1825*, (North Berwick, 2001).

Bil, A., *The Sheiling 1600–1840: the case of the Central Highlands*, (Edinburgh, 2003).

Bingham, C. *Beyond the Highland Line*, (London, 1991).

Blackburn, S., *Dive Islay Wrecks*, (Stoke-on-Trent, 1986).

Blake, R., *Disraeli*, (London, 1969).

Boase, F. *Modern English Biography . . . memoirs of persons who have died since 1850*, 6 vols. (Truro, 1892–1921).

Booth, C. G., *Birds in Islay*, (Islay, 1981).

Boyd, J. M. and Bowes, D. R. (eds.), *Natural Environment of the Inner Hebrides*, (Edinburgh, 1983).

Boyd, J. M. and Boyd, I. L., The Hebrides 3 vols. (Edinburgh, 1996).

Brock, W. R., *Scotus Americanus: A Survey of the Sources for links between Scotland and America in the eighteenth century*, (Edinburgh, 1982).

Brogan, C. (ed.), *James Finlay and Company Limited, manufacturers and East India merchants, 1750–1950*, (Glasgow, 1951).

Brown, J. (ed.), *Scottish Society in the Fifteenth Century*, (Edinburgh, 1977).

Bumsted, J. M., *The People's Clearance*, (Edinburgh, 1982).

Burke's *Peerage, Baronetage & Knightage*, (London, 1967).

Burke, J. A., *A Genealogical and Heraldic Dictionary of the Landed Gentry of Great Britain and Ireland*, (London, 1843–9).

Bury (Campbell), Lady C. S. M., *Diary illustrative of the Times of George the Fourth*, 4 vols. (London, 1838–9).

Caldwell, David, Islay. *The Land of the Lordship*, (Edinburgh, 2008).

Callander, R. M. and MacAulay, J., *The Ancient Metal Mines of the Isle of Islay*, (Sheffield, 1984).

Campbell, C., *Vitruvius Britannicus, or the British Architect, containing the plans, elevations, and sections of the regular buildings, both publick and private, in Great Britain . . . in 200 large folio plates*, 2 vols. (London, 1717).

Campbell, J. F., *Popular Tales of the West Highlands*, 4 vols. (Edinburgh, 1860–2),

Campbell, Lady C. S. M. See Bury.

Campbell, W, F., (ed. J. F. Campbell), *Life in Normandy. Sketches of French fishing, farming, cooking, natural history and politics, drawn from nature,* 2 vols. (Edinburgh, 1863).

Cawdor Castle, Guide, (Cawdor, n.d.)

Chapman, J. C. and Mytum, H. C. (eds.), *Settlement in North Britain 1000BC – 1000AD*, (Oxford, 1983).

Clan Donald Lands Trust, *Ceannas nan Gàidheal,* (Skye, 1985).

Clifton, V., *The Book of Clifton*, (London, 1933).

Coleman, T., *Passage to America*, (London, 1972).

Craig, H. C., *The Scotch Whisky Industry Record*, (Dumbarton, 1994).

Crawford, B. E. (ed.), *Scandinavian Settlement in Northern Britain: Thirteen Studies of Place-Names in their Historical Context,* (London, 1995).

Cumming, C. F. G., *In the Hebrides*, (London, 1883).

Darling, F. F., *West Highland Survey*, (Oxford, 1955).

Devine, T. M., *The Tobacco Lords. A study of the tobacco merchants of Glasgow and their trading activities c.1740–1790*, (Edinburgh, 1975); *The Great Highland Famine. Hunger, Emigration and the Scottish Highlands in the Nineteenth Century*, (Edinburgh, 1988*); Clanship to Crofters' War*, (Manchester, 1994); *Exploring the Scottish Past. Themes in the History of Scottish Society*, (East Linton, 1995); *Clearance and Improvement. Land, Power and People in Scotland, 1700–1900*, (Edinburgh, 2006); *The Scottish Nation 1700–2007*, (London, 1999 and 2006); *Scotland's Empire 1600–1815*, (London, 2003).

Dodgshon, R. A., *The Origin of British Field Systems: An Interpretation, (London, 1980); From Chiefs to Landlords: Social and Economic Change in the Western Highlands and Islands c.1493–1820*, (Edinburgh, 1988); *The Age of the Clans: The Highlands from Somerled to the Clearances*, (Edinburgh, 2002).

Donaldson, J., *Agricultural Biography*, (London, 1854).

Dorson, R. M., *The British Folklorists: A History*, (London, 1968).

Driscoll, S., Alba: *The Gaelic Kingdom of Scotland AD 800–1124*, (Edinburgh, 2000).

Duckworth, C. L. D. and Langmuir, G. E., *West Highland Steamers,* (Prescot, 1967).

Dunbar, J. G., *The Historic Architecture of Scotland*, (London, 1966).

Edwards, E. (ed.), *Seanchas Île,* (Glendaruel, 2007); also CD.

Elliott, R. E., *Birds of Islay*, (London, 1989).

Fellows-Jensen, G., *Scandinavian Settlement Names in the North West*, (Copenhagen, 1985).

Fenton, A. and Pálsson, H. (eds.), *The Northern and Western Isles in the Viking World. Survival, Continuity and Change*, (Edinburgh, 1982).

Fleming, R. E., *Eldon Connections*, (Ontario, n.d.).

Forsyth, R., *The Beauties of Scotland*, 5 vols. (Edinburgh, 1808).

Foster, J., *Members of Parliament, Scotland, including the Minor Barons, the Commissioners for the Shires, and the Commissioners for the Burghs, 1357–1882*, (London, 1882).

Fraser, R., *A Letter to the Right Hon. Charles Abbot, Speaker of the House of Commons, containing an inquiry into the most effectual means of the improvement of the Coasts and Western Isles of Scotland, and the extension of the Fisheries, With a letter from Dr. Anderson on the same subject*, (London, 1803).

Fullerton, A. and Baird., C. R., *Remarks on the Evils at present affecting the Highlands and Islands of Scotland; with some suggestions as to their remedies*, (Glasgow, 1838).

Gammeltoft, P., *The Place-Name Element bólstaðr in the North Atlantic Area*, (Copenhagen, 2001).

Gatty, R., *Portait of a Merchant Prince: James Morrison 1789–1857*, (Northallerton, n.d. [1977]).

Giblin, C. (ed.), *Irish Franciscan Mission to Scotland 1619–1646*, (Dublin, 1964).

Gillies, A., *A Hebridean in Goethe's Weimar*, (Oxford, 1969).

Gillies, H. C., *The Place Names of Argyll*, (London, 1906).

Graham, A., *Skipness, Memories of a Highland Estate*, (Edinburgh, 1993).

Graham, R. C., *The Carved Stones of Islay*, (Glasgow, 1895).

Grant, A., and Stringer, K., *Uniting the Kingdom. The Making of Britaish History*, (London, 1995).

Gray, A., *The History of Islay Place Names*, (Glasgow, 1939).

Gray, M., *The Highland Economy 1750–1850*, (London, 1957).

Haldane, A. R. B., *New Ways through the Glens*, (Edinburgh, 1962); *Three Centuries of Scottish Posts*, (Edinburgh, 1971).

Henderson, G., The Norse Influences on Celtic Scotland, (Glasgow, 1910).

Henderson, J. R., *Post Offices in Scotland*, (Edinburgh, 1966).

Hill, J. and Bastin, N., *A Very Canny Scot. 'Great' Daniel Campbell of Shawfield and Islay 1670–1753. His Life and Times*, (Barnham, West Sussex, 2007).

Hobley, L. F., *Customs and Excisemen*, (London, 1974).

Hunter, J., *The Making of the Crofting Community*, (Edinburgh, 1976); *For the People's Cause; from the writings of John Murdoch, Highland and Irish Land Reformer*, (Edinburgh, 1986); *Scottish Highlanders*, (Edinburgh, 1992); *A Dance Called America*, (Edinburgh, 1994).

Hutchison, I., *The Story of Loganair*, (Glasgow, 1987); *Air Ambulance*, (Erskine, 1996).

Innes, C., *The Book of the Thanes of Cawdor, A Series of Papers selected from the Charter Room at Cawdor, 1236–1742*, (Edinburgh, 1859).

Islands Book Trust, *Martin Martin – 300 Years On*, (Lewis, [2004].

Islay Archaeological Survey Group, *The Preliminary Handbook of the Archaeology of Islay*, (Keele, 1960).

Jackson, K. H., *Campbell of Islay*, Celtica Catalogue 6 of the National Library of Scotland (Edinburgh, 1967).

Jackson, M., *Malt Whisky Companion*, (London, 2010).

Jefford, A., *Peat Smoke and Spirit. A Portrait of Islay and its Whiskies*, (London, 2004).

Kyd, J. G., *Scottish Population Statistics*, (Edinburgh, 1952).

Lamont, W. D., *The Early History of Islay*, (Glasgow, 1966); *Ancient and Mediaeval Sculptured Stones of Islay*, (Edinburgh, 1972).

Lenton-Halsall, P. *Nerabus: the story of a small Hebridean settlement since 1850*, (Islay, 1991).

Lewis, S., *A Topographical Dictionary of Scotland*, 2 vols. (London, 1846).

Lindsay, I. G. and Cosh, M., *Inveraray and the Dukes of Argyll*, (Edinburgh, 1973).

Lowry, B. (ed.), *Twentieth Century Defences in Britain,* (York, 1955).

Lumsden, J. and Son, *The Steam-Boat Companion and Stranger's Guide to the Western Islands and Highlands of Scotland*, (Glasgow, 1825).

Lynch, M., *Scotland: A New History*, (London, 1991).

Macairt, S. and MacNiocaill (eds.), *Annals of Ulster to A. D. 1131*, (Dublin, 1983).

MacAlpine, N. *The Argyleshire pronouncing Gaelic Dictionary*, (Edinburgh, 1832); *A Pronouncing Gaelic Dictionary*, (Edinburgh, 1847).

MacBain, A., *Place Names of the Highlands and Islands of Scotland*, (Stirling, 1922).

MacCulloch, J., *The Highlands and Western Isles of Scotland . . . Founded on a series of annual journeys between . . . 1811 and 1821*, 4 vols. (London, 1824).

Macdonald, C. M., *The History of Argyll Up to the Beginning of the Sixteenth Century*, (Glasgow, 1951).

Macdonald, C. (ed)., *The Third Statistical Account of Scotland, The County of Argyll*, (Glasgow, 1961). Parish of Kildalton, Shanks, A. and I. D., (1955), pp. 342–9; Parish of Kilchoman, Torrie, Rev. A., (1955), pp. 350–5; Parish of Kilarrow [*sic*] and Kilmeny, Macrae, Rev. M., (1955), pp. 356–60. [*TSA*]

Macdonald, J., *General View of the Agriculture of the Hebrides or Western Isles of Scotland: with Observations on the Means of their Improvement together with a Separate Account of the Principal Islands*, (Edinburgh, 1811).

MacDonell, M., *The Emigrant Experience*, (Toronto, 1982).

Maceacharna, D., *The Lands of the Lordship*, (Islay, 1976).

Mackay, E. (ed.), *A Description of the Western Islands of Scotland circa 1695*, with *Donald Monroe's Description of the Western Isles, 1774*, (Stirling, 1934).

Mackay, J. A., *Island Postal History Series No. 10: Islay, Jura and the other Argyll Islands*, (Dumfries, 1979); *No. 11: Scottish Islands, Supplement and Catalogue*, (Dumfries, 1980).

Mackay, J. G. (ed.), *More West Highland Tales*, I, (Edinburgh, 1940); II, (Edinburgh, 1960).

Mackechnie, A., *Carragh-chuimhne: Two Islay Monuments and Two Islay People. Hector Maclean and John Francis Campbell*, (Isle of Islay, 2004).

Mackechnie, J. (ed.), *The Dewar Manuscripts*, I, (Glasgow, 1964).

Macleod, F. (ed.), *Togail Tìr. Marking Time. The Map of the Western Isles*, (Stornoway, 1989).

Macmillan, N. S. C., *The Campbeltown and Machrihanish Light Railway*, (Glasgow, 1970).

MacNeill, J. G., *The New Guide to Islay*, (Glasgow, 1900).

Malthus, T. R., *An Essay on The Principle of Population*, (London, 1798).

Maltman, A., Elliott, R., Muir, R. and Finches, B., *A Guide to the Geology of Islay*, (Aberystwyth, 1990).

Martin, M., *A Description of the Western Islands of Scotland*, (London, 1703).

McDonald, R. A., The *Kingdom of the Isles: Scotland's Western Seaboard c.1100 – c.1136*, (East Linton, 1997).

McKay, M. M. (ed.), *The Rev. Dr. John Walker's Report on the Hebrides of 1764 and 1771*, (Edinburgh, 1980).

McLeod, Dr. N., *Extracts of Letters to Dr. [N.] McLeod regarding the famine and destitution in the Highlands and Islands of Scotland, 1847*, (Glasgow, 1847).

McNeill, P. and Nicholson, R. (eds.), *An Historical Atlas of Scotland c.400–c.1600*, (St. Andrews, 1980).

Meek, D. E., *Tuath is Tighearna. Tenants and Landlords*, (Edinburgh, 1995); *Caran an t-Saoghail. The Wiles of the World*, (Edinburgh, 2003); Robins, N. S. and Meek, D. E., *The Kingdom of Macbrayne*, (Edinburgh, 2006).

Meyer, D., *The Highland Scots of Carolina, 1732–1776*, (N. Carolina, 1961).

Middleton, W. E. K., *Invention of the Meteorological Instruments*, (Baltimore, 1969).

Mitchell, Joseph, *Reminiscences of My Life in the Highlands*, 2 vols. (London, 1883).

Mithin, S., *Hunter-gatherer landscape and archaeology. The Southern Hebridean Mesolithic Project, 1988–2008*, (Cambridge, 2000); *To the Islands. An archaeologist's relentless quest to find the prehistoric hunter-gatherers of the Hebrides*, (Lewis, 2010).

Moffat, A., *The Sea-Kingdoms. The History of Celtic Britain and Ireland*, (Edinburgh, 2008).

Moir, D. G. (ed.), *The Early Maps of Scotland to 1850*, (Edinburgh, 1973).

Moir, P. and Crawford, I., *Argyll Shipwrecks*, (Wemyss Bay, 1994).

Morewood, S., *An Essay on the Inventions and Customs of both Ancients and Moderns in the use of Inebriating Liquors*, (Dublin, 1824).

Morrison, C., *An Essay on the Relations between Labour and Capital*, (London, 1854).

Moss. M.S. and Home, J. R., *The Making of the Scotch Whisky Industry*, (Edinburgh, 2000).

Munro, J. and Munro, R.W., *Acts of the Lords of the Isles 1336–1493*, (Edinburgh, 1986).

Munro, R. W., *Monroe's Western Isles of Scotland and Genealogies of the Clans 1549*, (Edinburgh, 1961).

National Library of Scotland, *Lamplighter and Story-Teller, John Francis Campbell of Islay, 1821–1885*, (Edinburgh, 1985).

National Trust, *Basildon Park, Berkshire*, (London, 1980).

Nicolaisen, W. F. H., *Scottish Place Names*, (London, 1976 and Edinburgh, 2001).

Nicolson, A., *Sea Room: an island life*, (London, 2001)

Ogilvie, Malcolm A., *Wild Geese*, (Islay, 1978); *The Birds of Islay*, (Islay, 2003).

Ohlmeyer, J. H., *Civil War and Restoration in the Three Stuart Kingdoms: The career of Randal MacDonnell, marquis of Antrim, 1609–1683*, (Cambridge, 1993).

Osborne, B. D. and Armstrong, R., *Scottish Dates*, (Edinburgh, 1996).

Oxford Dictionary of National Biography, 62 vols. (Oxford, 2004–).

Parry, M. L. and Slater, T. R. (eds)., *The Making of the Scottish Landscape*, (London, 1980).

Patten, J. M., *The Argyle Patent, Excerpted from the History of the Somonauk Presbyterian Church*, (Baltimore, 1979).

Pennant, T., *A Tour in Scotland and Voyage to the Hebrides, 1772*, (Chester, 1774).

Phillipson, N. T., and Mitchison, R., *Scotland in the Age of Improvement*, (Edinburgh, 1970).

Ramsay, F. (ed.), *John Ramsay of Kildalton. Being an Account of his life in Islay and including the Diary of his Trip to Canada in 1870*, (Toronto, 1970); *The Day Book of Daniel Campbell of Shawfield 1767 with relevant papers concerning the Estate of Islay*, (Aberdeen, 1991).

Ramsay, J., *A Letter to . . . the Lord Advocate of Scotland on the State of Education in the Outer Hebrides in 1862*, (Glasgow, 1863).

Ramsay, L. (ed.), *The Stent Book and Acts of the Balliary of Islay 1718–1843*, (Kildalton, 1890).

Ritchie, G., *The Archaeology of Argyll*, (Edinburgh, 1997).

Ritchie, W. G. and Crofts, R., *The Beaches of Islay, Jura and Colonsay*, (Aberdeen, 1974).

Robins, N. S. and Meek, D. E., *The Kingdom of Macbrayne*, (Edinburgh, 2006).

Ronaghan, A., *There'll always be an Islay*, (Islay, Alberta, 1977).

Rosa, M. W., *The Silver Fork School*, (New York, 1936).

Royal Commission on the Ancient and Historical Monuments of Scotland [RCAHMS], *Argyll: An Inventory of the Monuments, 5. Islay, Jura, Colonsay and Oronsay*, (Edinburgh, 1984).

Rubinstein, W. D., *Men of Property*, (London, 1981).

Sadie, S. *The New Grove Dictionary of Opera*, 4 vols. (London, 1992).

Salaman, R. N., *The History and Social Influence of the Potato*, (Cambridge, 1949).

Sanderson, M. H. B., *Scottish Rural Society in the Sixteenth Century*, (Edinburgh, 1982).

Shaw, F. J., *The Northern and Western Islands of Scotland: their Economy and Society in the Seventeenth Century*, (Edinburgh, 1980).

Shore, C. J., Baron Teignmouth, *Sketches of the Coasts and Islands of Scotland, and the Isle of Man*, 2 vols. (London, 1836).

Sillett, S., *Illicit Scotch*, (Aberdeen, 1965); *The Whisky Smugglers*, (Glasgow, 1990).

Sinclair, Sir J. (ed.), *The Statistical Account of Scotland drawn up from the communications of the ministers of the different Parishes*, (Edinburgh, 1794), XI. Kilchoman, Rev J. McLeish, pp. 276–85; Kildalton, Rev. A. Robertson, pp. 286–97; Killarow and Kilmeny, Rev. J. Murdoch, pp. 298–302. [*OSA*].

Smith, B. B. *et al* (eds.), *West Over Sea: Studies in Scandinavian Sea-Borne Expansion and Settlement before 1500*, (Leiden and Boston, 2007).

Smith, D. J., *Action Stations 7: Military airfields of Scotland, the North-East and Northern Ireland*, (Wellingborough, 1989).

Smith, G., *Something to Declare. 1000 years of Customs and Excise*, (London, 1980).

Smith, G. D., *The Secret Still. Scotland's Clandestine Whisky Makers*, (Edinburgh, 2003).

Smith, G. G. (ed.)., *The Book of Islay*, (Edinburgh, 1895).

Smith, J. G., *The Old Country Houses of the Old Glasgow Gentry*, (Glasgow, 1879).

Smout, T. C., *A History of the Scottish People*, 2 vols. (London, 1969).

The Statistical Account of Argyleshire by the Ministers of the Respective Parishes, (Edinburgh, 1845). Kilchoman, Rev. A. Cameron (1844), pp. 644–59; Kildalton, Rev. A. MacTavish (1844), pp. 659–67; Killarow and Kilmeny, Rev. A. Stewart (1843), pp. 668–71. [*NSA*].

Steer, K. A. and Bannerman, J. W. M., *Late Medieval Sculpture in the West Highlands*, (Edinburgh, 1977).

The Stent Book and Acts of the Balliary of Islay: see Ramsay, L.

Stevenson, D., *Highland Warrior, Alasdair MacColla and the Civil Wars*, (Edinburgh, 1994).

Stirk, D., *The Distilleries of Campbeltown. The Rise and Fall of the Whisky Capital of the World*, (Glasgow, 2005).

Stone, J., *Illustrated Maps of Scotland*, (London 1991).

Storrie, M. C. and Jackson, C. I., *Arran 1980–81: 2,021?*, (Edinburgh, 1967).

Storrie, M., *Continuity and Change: The Islay, Jura and Colonsay Agricultural Association, 1838–1988*, (Islay, 1988).

Teignmouth. See Shore.

The Third Statistical Account of Scotland, The County of Argyll: see Macdonald, C. M.

Thomson, D. S., *The Companion to Gaelic Scotland*, (Oxford, 1983).

Townsend, B., *Scotch Missed. The Lost Distilleries of Scotland*, (Glasgow, 1997).

Trevorrow, J. *Celtic Foundations*, (Islay, 1985); *Norse Invasion*, (1987); *Parish Churches*, (1988); *The Days of the Lords* (1991); *Turbulent Times* (1997); *The Campbell Heritage* (2009).

Walker, F. A., *Argyll and Bute*, (London, 2000).

Walker, J., *An Economical History of the Hebrides and Highlands of Scotland*, 2 vols. (Edinburgh, 1808).

Watson, W. J., *The History of Celtic Place Names of Scotland*, (Edinburgh, 1926).

Weir, L. MacN., *Guide to Islay*, (1924 edition, revised under the supervision of A. N. Currie), (Glasgow, 1936).

Weir, R. B., *The History of the Distillers Company 1877 to 1939*, (Oxford, 1995).

Whyte, I. D., *Scotland before the Industrial Revolution*, (London, 1995).

Wiggins, J., *The Exmouth of Newcastle 1811–1847*, (Islay, n.d.).

Williams, C. *Basildon, Berkshire*, (Reading, n.d., [1994]).

Wilkinson, S.B. *The Geology of Islay*, including Oronsay and portion of Colonsay and

Jura, Memoir of the Geological Survey, (Glasgow, 1907).

Wilson, A., *The Sound of Silence*, (Glasgow, n.d.,[1975]); *The Sound of the Clam*, (Glasgow, n.d.,[1975]).

Wilson, N., *Scotch and Water*, (Glasgow, 1998).

Youngson, A. J., *After the Forty Five*, (Edinburgh, 1973).

Youngson, P. J., *Jura. Island of Deer*, (Edinburgh, 2001).

Journals, Book Chapters, Pamphlets and Theses

Abrams, L., 'Conversion and the Church in the Hebrides in the Viking Age: "a very difficult thing indeed"', in Smith *et al* (eds.), *West Over Sea*, pp. 169–93.

Alcock, L. and Alcock, E., 'Scandinavian Settlement in the Inner Hebrides: Recent Research on place-names and in the Field', *Scottish Archaeological Forum* 10 (1980), pp. 61–73.

Anderson, M. L. and Fairbairn, W. A., 'Division of Scotland into Climatic Subregions as an Aid to Silviculture', *Bulletin of the Forestry Department, University of Edinburgh* 1, (1955).

Anon. 'Appendix to report on the Disease of the Potato Crop in Scotland in the year 1845', *Transactions of the Highland and Agricultural Society of Scotland* New Series 15 (1845–7), p. 16.

Bäcklund, J., 'War or Peace? The relations between the Picts and the Norse in Orkney', *Northern Studies* 36 (2001), p. 35.

Bannerman, J. W. M., 'The Lordship of the Isles', in Brown, *Scottish Society in the Fifteenth Century*, pp. 209–40.

Barclay, D., 'Lauchlin Campbell of Campbell Hall and his family', *Historical Papers of Historical Society of Newburgh Bay and the Highlands* 9 (1902), pp. 31–6.

Black, G. F., 'Early Islay Emigration to America', *Oban Times*, 27 March, 2, 23 and 30 April, 1927.

Borthwick, Alastair, ' Return to Islay', *Scots Magazine*, April 1969, pp. 21–3.

Brown, M. M., 'The Norse in Argyll', in Ritchie, *Archaeology of Argyll*, pp. 205–35.

Caldwell, D. H. and Ewart, G., 'Finlaggan and the Lordship of the Isles: an Archaeological Approach', *Scottish Historical Review* 72 (1993), pp. 142–66.

Campbell, W. F., 'Improvement of Wasteland of a District in the Island of Islay', *Trans. of the Royal Highland Society of Scotland* 13 (1841), pp. 232–5.

Cant, R. G., 'Norse Influences in the organization of the medieval church in the Western Isles, *Northern Studies* 21 (1984), pp. 1–14.

Childe, V. G., 'Notes on some duns in Islay'. *Proceedings of the Society of Antiquaries of Scotland* 69, (1934–35), pp. 81–4.

Collin, L., *Oban Times*, 24 August 1978.

Cowan, E. J., 'Clanship, kinship and Campbell acquisition of Islay', *Scottish Historical Review* 58 (1979), pp. 132–57.

Cregeen, E. R., 'Recollections of an Argyleshire Drover', *Scottish Studies* 3 (1959), pp. 143–62.

Cruft, K., 'The Enigma of Woodhall House', *Architectural History* 27 (1984), pp. 210–13.

Dawson, A. G., 'Lateglacial and sea-level changes and Ice-limits in Islay, Jura and Scarba, Scottish Inner Hebrides', *Scottish Journal of Geology* 18 (1982), pp. 253–65.

Dawson, J., 'The Fifth Earl of Argyle, Lordship and Political Power in Sixteenth Century Scotland', *Scottish Historical Review* 67 (1988), pp. 1–27.

Delargy, J. H., 'Three Men of Islay', *Scottish Studies* 4 (1960), pp. 126–33.

Dodgshon, R. A., 'Mediaeval Settlement and Colonisation', in Parry and Slater (eds.), *The*

Making of the Scottish Countryside, (London, 1980), pp. 45–68.

Dodgshon, R. A., 'West Highland and Hebridean Settlement prior to the Clearances. A study in stability of change', *Proceedings of the Society of Antiquaries of Scotland* 125 (1993), pp. 419–33.

Dodgshon, R. A., 'The Little Ice Age in the Scottish Highlands and Islands: Documenting its Human Impact', *Scottish Geographical Magazine* 121 (1995), pp. 321–37.

Donaldson, G., 'Sources for Scottish Agrarian History before the Eighteenth Century', *Agricultural History Review* 8 (1960), pp. 82–90.

Duncan, A., 'Hector MacLean of Islay 1818–1893', *An Gaidheal*, January 1964.

Duncan, J. D., 'Notes on An Inventory of Articles which escaped the hands of the mob on the occasion of the sacking of Shawfield Mansion, 1725', *Trans. of the Glasgow Archaeological Society* 1 (1868,), p. xxiv and pp. 388–97.

Evans, E. E., 'The Atlantic Ends of Europe', *The Advancement of Science* 15 (1958–9), pp. 54–64.

Fairhurst, H., 'The Archaeology of Rural Settlement in Scotland', *Transactions of the Glasgow Archaeological Society*, New Series 15 (1960), pp. 139–58.

Fellows-Jensen, G., 'Common Gaelic àirge, Old Scandinavian ærgi or erg?', *Nomina* 4 (1980), pp. 67–74.

Forman, S., 'Islay House', *Scottish Field*, May 1960, pp. 37–40.

Grant, A., 'Scotland's "Celtic fringe" in the late Middle Ages: the MacDonald lords of the Isles and the kingdom of Scotland', in Davies (ed)., *The British Isles 1100–1500*, (Edinburgh, 1988), pp. 118–41.

Grant, A., 'To the medieval Foundations', *Scottish Historical Review* 73 (1994), pp. 4–24.

Hunter, A. F., *A History of Simcoe County*, (Canada, 1909), Part II, reprint M. Hunter, (Barrie, Ontario, 1948), Chapters 10 and 20.

The *Ileach* is available on subscription and online (Bowmore, Isle of Islay).

Islay Association, *Report* on the Proceedings at the Annual Meeting, (Glasgow, 1878).

Johnston, A. 'Norse Settlement patterns in Coll and Tiree, in Crawford, *Scandinavian Settlement in North Britain*, pp. 108–25.

Jones, G., 'The Gaelic of South Argyll: Jura and Islay Dialects', in McClure, Kirk and Storrie (eds.), *A Land that Lies Westward*, pp. 11–16.

Laing. A. (ed.), 'The Lord of the Isles', *Scott's Poetical Works*, (London, 1898), pp. 653ff.

Lambkin, B., 'The Wreck of the *Exmouth* on Islay, 1847; A Window on Emigration from North-West Ulster during the Great Famine', in McClure, Kirk and Storrie, *A Land that Lies Westward*, pp. 123–48.

Lamont, W. D., 'Old Land Denominations and "Old Extent" in Islay', *Scottish Studies* 1 (1957), pp. 86–106; *ibid.* 2 (1958), pp. 183–203; 'The Islay Charter of 1408', *Proceedings of the Royal Irish Academy*, 1960 C., pp. 163–87; 'Alexander of Islay, son of Angus Mor', *Scottish Historical Review* 60 (1981), pp. 160–8.

Mackinnon, D., 'Education in Argyll and the Isles, 1638–1707', *Scottish Church History Society* 6 (1936), pp. 46–54.

Macniven, A., 'The Norse in Islay: a settlement historical case-study for Medieval Scandinavian activity in western maritime Scotland', unpublished doctoral thesis, University of Edinburgh, 2006.

MacQueen, J., 'Pennyland and Davoch in South-Western Scotland: a Preliminary Note', *Scottish Studies* 23 (1979), pp. 69–74; B. Megaw, 'A Note' on the above, *ibid.*, pp. 75–7.

McCann, S.B., 'The Raised Beaches of North-East Islay and Western Jura', *Transactions of the Intsitute of British Geographers* 35 (1964), pp.1–15.

McDonald, R. A. and McLean, S. A., 'Somerled of Argyll: A new Look at Old Problems', *Scottish Historical Review* 71 (1992), pp. 3–22.

McKerral, A., 'Ancient Denominations of Land in Scotland', *Proceedings of the Society of Antiquaries of Scotland* 78 (1943–4), pp. 39–80; 'Lesser Land and Administrative Divisions in Celtic Scotland', *ibid.*, 85 (1950–1), pp. 52–67.

Meek, D. E., 'The World of William Livingston', in McClure, Kirk and Storrie (eds.), *A Land that Lies Westward*, pp.149–173; 'Making History: William Livingston and the Creation of "Blàr Shunàdail"', *ibid.*, pp. 197–218.

Moir, D. G., 'The Roads of Scotland: The Statute Labour Roads', *Scottish Geographical Magazine* 73 (1957), pp. 101–10 and 167–75.

H. A. Moisley, 'Some Hebridean Field Systems', *Gwerin* 3 (1960), pp. 22–35; 'The Birth of a Crofting Landscape, North Uist in 1799', *Scottish Geographical Magazine* 77 (1961), pp. 89–92.

Morrison, I., 'Climatic Changes and Human Geography: Scotland in a North Atlantic Context, *Northern Studies* 27 (1990), pp. 1–11.

Morton, J. K., 'The Flora of Islay and Jura (V.C. 102)', *Proceedings of the Botanical Society of the British Isles, Supplement,* 1958–60, part 3, pp. 1–59.

Murdoch, A., (ed.), 'A Scottish Document concerning Emigration to North Caroline in 1772', *The North Carolina Historical Review* 67 (1990), pp. 438–49.

Murdoch, J., 'A New and Ready Way of Disposing of that Interesting Island Which would pay the debt, restore the late proprietor, and give the best return to large and small capitalists', in W. MacDonald, *Descriptive and Historical Sketches of Islay*, (Glasgow, 1850).

Nì Gabhlàin, S., 'The origin of Medieval parishes in Gaelic Ireland: the evidence from Kilfearna', *Journal of the Royal Society of Antiquities of Ireland* 126 (1996), pp. 37–61.

Nicolaisen, W. F. H., 'OS Folklore', *The Scots Magazine*, May 1963, p. 115; 'Norse Settlement in the Northern and Western Isles', *Scottish Historical Review* 48 (1969), pp. 6–17; 'Early Scandinavian Naming in the Isles', *Northern Scotland* 3 (1979–80), pp. 105–21; Gaelic *Sliabh* revisited in Arbuthot, S. and Hollo K. (eds*.), Fil súil nglais: a Grey Eye looks Back*, (Ceann Drochais, 2007).

Nieke, M., 'Settlement patterns in the first millennium AD: a case study of the island of Islay', in Chapman and Mytum, *Settlement in North Britain*, pp. 299–326.

Piggott, S. and Piggott, C. M., 'Field work in Colonsay and Islay 1944–45', *Proceedings of the Society of Antiquaries of Scotland* 80 (1945–6), pp. 83–103.

Price, L., 'A note on the use of the world *baile* in Place-Names', *Celtica* 6 (1964), pp. 119–26.

Pryde, G. S., 'Scottish Colonisation in the Province of New York', *Proceedings of the New York Historical Association* 33 (1935), pp. 147–50.

Reid, J. M., 'A New Light on Old Glasgow-1: The Shawfield Papers of Daniel Campbell', *Glasgow Herald*, 1, 2 and 3 June 1959.

Royal National Lifeboat Institution, *Annual Reports*.

Royal Scottish Geographical Society, *The Scottish Geographical Journal* 123 (2006), volume on The Loch Lomond Readvance'.

Russell, Lady C., 'A Canny Scot', *Three Generations of Fascinating Women and other Sketches from Family History*, (London, 1904), pp. 154–82.

Scotus Americanus, *Informations concerning the Province of North Carolina addressed to Emigrants from the Highlands and Western Isles of Scotland. By an Impartial Hand*, (Glasgow, 1773).

Shaw, F. J., 'Landownership in the Western Isles in the Seventeenth Century', *Scottish Historical Review* 56 (1977), pp. 34–48.

Small, A., 'The Historical Geography of the Norse Viking Colonisation of the Scottish Highlands', *Norsk Geografisk Tidsskrift* 22 (1968), pp. 1–16.

Smout, T. C. and Fenton, A., 'Scottish Agriculture before the Improvers: an Exploration', *Agicultural History Review* 13 (1965), pp. 75–93.

Smout, T. C. 'The Landowner and the Planned Village in Scotland, 1730–1830, in N. T. Phillipson and R. Mitchison, *Scotland in the Age of Improvement*, (Edinburgh, 1970), pp. 73–106.

Storrie, M. C., 'Islay: A Hebridean Exception', *Geographical Review* 51 (1961), pp. 87–108; 'The Census of Scotland as a source in the Historical Geography of Islay', *Scottish Geographical Magazine* 78 (1962), pp. 75–93; 'The Scotch Whisky Industry', *Transactions of the Institute of British Geographers* 31 (1962), pp. 97–114; 'Landholdings and Settlement Evolution in West Highland Scotland', *Geografiska Annaler* 47 (1965), pp. 138–61; 'The Isle of Islay', *Scottish Field*, August 1981, pp. 11–14; 'Land Use and Settlement History of the southern Inner Hebrides', *Proceedings of the Royal Society of Edinburgh*, 83B (1983), pp. 549–66; 'Recovering the Historic Designed Landscape of Islay Estate, *Scottish Archives* 7 (2001), pp. 59–77; '"Green Islay" and the "Green Isle"', in *Martin Martin – 300 Years On* (ed.), The Islands Book Trust, (Lewis, [2004]), pp. 25–32; 'Settlement and Naming in the Southern Hebridean Isle of Islay', in McClure, Kirk and Storrie, *A Land that Lies Westward*, pp. 17–47.

Stringer, K. and Grant, A., 'Scottish Foundations', in A. Grant and K. Stringer *Uniting the Kingdom. The Making of British History*, (London, 1995), pp. 85–108.

Sutherland, D. G., 'The Environment of Argyll', in Ritchie, *Archaeology of Argyll*, pp. 10–24.

Synge, F. M. and Stephens, N., 'Late and Post-glacial Shorelines and Ice limits in Argyll and North-East Ulster, *Tranactions. of the Institute of British Geographers* 39 (1966), pp. 101–25.

Taylor, Alexander B., 'Skio and Il', Pridiji Vikingafundur Third Viking Congress, Reykjavik 1956, *Arbok hins islenzka Fornleifafélags Fylgirit*, 1957, pp. 52–60.

Taylor, S. '*SLIABH* in Scottish Place-Names: its meaning and chronology, *The Journal of Scottish Name Studies* 1 (2007), pp. 99–136.

Thomas, F. W. L., 'On Islay Place Names', *Proceedings of the Society of Antiquaries of Scotland* New Series 4 (1881–1882), pp. 241–96.

Whyte, I. D., 'Climatic Change and the North Atlantic Seaways during the Norse expansion, *Northern Studies* 21 (1984), pp. 22–3.

Wilkinson, S. B. *The Geology of Islay, including Oronsay and a portion of Colonsay and Jura*, (Glasgow, 1907).

Wilson, Sir Charles, 'Methods and processes of the Ordnance Survey', *Scottish Geographical Magazine* 7 (1891), pp. 248–59.

British Parliamentary Papers and Official Publications

Abstracts of Education Returns (Scotland) 1834, BPP, 1837, XLVIII, Argyll.

Correspondence . . . relating to the Measures adopted for the Relief of Distress in Scotland, BPP, 1847, LIII.

Census of Great Britain, Abstracts of the Answers and Returns: Enumeration Part III Scotland; Shire of Argyll:

1802(1802); *1811*(1812); *1821*(1822); *1831*(1831–4); *1841*(1843); *1851*(1852–4).

Census of Scotland, Population Tables and Reports; County of Argyll: 1861 (1862–4); 1871 (1872–4); 1881 (1881–3); 1891(1891–3).

Census of Scotland 1951, County of Argyll Report (1953), Table 3.

Census of Scotland 1961, Argyll County Report, (1964), *Supplementary Leaflet 27: Gaelic,* (1966).

Census of Scotland 1971, Argyll County Volume, (1973); *Usual Residence and Birthplace Tables,* (1973); *Gaelic Report,* (1975).

Census of Scotland 1981, Preliminary Report, (1981); *Report for Strathclyde Region,* (1983); *Gaelic Report,* (1983).

Census of Scotland 1991, Small Area Statistics.

Census of Scotland 2001, Standard Area Statistics.

Coastal Command, Crown Film Unit, video DD 985.

Correspondence relating to measures for Relief of Distress, BPP 1847, LIII.

Department of Agriculture and Fisheries for Scotland, *Scottish Peat Surveys: Western Highlands and Islands,* (Edinburgh, 1966), vol. 2.

Historic Scotland: List of Buildings of Architectural or Historic Interest. Killarow or Bowmore Church is category A (of national as well as local interest) and Islay House is category B (of more local than national interest, but also of special interest). The older parts of most of the villages in Islay have been designated 'conservation areas'.

Minutes of Evidence, Poor Law Inquiry Commission for Scotland, BPP, 1844, XXI.

Minutes of Evidence to the Select Committee on the Condition of the Population of the Islands and Highlands of Scotland and into the Practicability of affording the People Relief by means of Emigration, BPP, 1841, VI.

Object or Name Books of the Ordnance Survey. Microfilm copies, Royal Commission on the Ancient and Historical Manuscripts of Scotland.

Report of Her Majesty's Commissioners of Enquiry into the Condition of the Crofters and Cottars in the Highlands and Islands of Scotland, 1884, C.3980.

Reports of the Select Committee appointed to inquire into the Expediency of encouraging Emigration from the United Kingdom, BPP, 1826, IV, 1826–7, V.

Report to Board of Supervision by Sir J. MacNeill on West Highlands and Islands, BPP 1851, XXVI.

Report and Minutes of Evidence, Royal Commission (Highland and Islands 1892), [Deer Forest] (1895), *C.* 7668.

Report of the Parliamentary Commissioners of Inquiry into the Mode of Charging Excise Duties, Fifth Report, BPP, 1823, VII.

Report of the Commissioners of Inquiry into the Excise, Seventh Report, BPP, 1835, XXX, *Appendix.*

Reports of the Fishery Board of Scotland, annual.

Reports of the Highlands and Islands Development Board, annual.

Reports of the Commissioners of Northern Lighthouses, BPP, 1833 XXXIII; 1836 XLV and 1846 XLIV.

Reports of the Tidal Harbours Commissioners, Second Report, BPP, 1848, XXXII, *Appendix C.*

Reports of the Commissioners appointed for building additional Places of Worship in the Highlands and Islands of Scotland, Sixth Report, BPP, 1831, XI.

Reports of the Commissioners for making Roads and Building Bridges in the Highlands and Islands of Scotland, BPP, 1805, III; 1807, III; 1810, IV and 1812–13, V.

Royal Commission on the Ancient and Historical Monuments of Scotland, *Argyll: An Inventory of the Monuments, 5. Islay, Jura, Colonsay and Oronsay,* (Edinburgh, 1984).

Scottish Abstract of Statistics.

The Scottish Economy 1965–70: A Plan for Expansion, (1966), *Cmnd.* 2864.

Maps and Plans

British Geological Survey:

1: 50,000 *South Islay Sheet 19 (Scotland) Solid and Drift Geology Provisional series*, (1996);
North Islay Sheet 27, (1995).

Geological Survey of Scotland:

Quarter Inch Geology 13, (1921); *One Inch Solid and Drift sheet 98*, (1918) and *sheet 27*,
(1900).

Gemmill, William, Ms. plans are in the Islay Estate Papers and relate mainly to the 1820s
and 1830s. Photocopies are in NRS. Others are in Kildalton Papers, Glasgow City
Archives. Gemmill's Ms. Plan of Ardmore is in Gordon Cumming Papers, NLS, Dep.
175.

Laughlan, Andrew, Sketch and sections of proposed road from Bridgend to Port Ellen in
the Isle of Islay 1841–42, Islay Estate Papers.

MacDougall, Stephen, A few extant Ms. plans are in the Islay Estate Papers. The reduced
smaller-scale *Map of Islay*, 1749, lithographed in 1848, is printed in *Book of Islay*, pp.
552–3; *A Map of Taynish . . . in Argyll*, 1747. The British Library Map Room, XLIX
28; *A Map of the Island of Giga*, 1747 loc. cit., XLIX 37 1.

Murdoch Mackenzie, Sen., *The Maritim [sic] Survey of Ireland and the West of Great Britain*,
(London, 1776); chart XX, The South Part of Argyle Shire from the Mule of Cantyre
to Jura and Ila.

de Nicolay, Nicolas, *True and Exact Hydrographic Description of the Maritime Coasts of
Scotland and the Orkney and Hebridean islands*, (Paris, 1583).

Ordnance Survey 1: 10,000 Second Edition (1899 and 1981); 1: 50,000 Second Series,
60 (1987) and *Landranger* 60 (2007) ; 1: 25,000 *Pathfinder* Series (1987–8); Explorer
Islay South 353 and Islay North 352 (2006).

Ortelius, Abraham, *Scotiae Tabula in Theatrum Orbis Terrarum*, (Antwerp, 1573).

Pont, Timothy, *Ila Insula* in J. Blaeu's *Atlas Novus*, (Amsterdam, 1654).

Stone, J., *Illustrated Maps of Scotland*, (London, 1991).

Van Keulen, Johannes, *De nieuwe groote lichtende zee-fakkel*, (Amsterdam, 1682).

Index